The O'Leary Series

Microsoft® Office Access 2007

Brief Edition

The O'Leary Series

Computing Concepts

- *Computing Essentials 2007* Introductory & Complete Editions
- *Computing Essentials 2008* Introductory & Complete Editions

Microsoft® Office Applications

- *Microsoft® Office Word 2007* Brief & Introductory Editions
- *Microsoft® Office Excel 2007* Brief & Introductory Editions
- *Microsoft® Office Access 2007* Brief & Introductory Editions
- *Microsoft® Office PowerPoint 2007* Brief Edition

The O'Leary Series

Microsoft® Office Access 2007

Brief Edition

Timothy J. O'Leary
Arizona State University

Linda I. O'Leary

McGraw-Hill
Higher Education

Boston   Burr Ridge, IL   Dubuque, IA   New York   San Francisco   St. Louis
Bangkok   Bogotá   Caracas   Kuala Lumpur   Lisbon   London   Madrid   Mexico City
Milan   Montreal   New Delhi   Santiago   Seoul   Singapore   Sydney   Taipei   Toronto

McGraw-Hill
Higher Education

THE O'LEARY SERIES MICROSOFT® OFFICE ACCESS 2007 BRIEF
Published by McGraw-Hill, a business unit of The McGraw-Hill Companies, Inc., 1221 Avenue of the Americas, New York, NY, 10020. Copyright © 2008 by The McGraw-Hill Companies, Inc. All rights reserved. No part of this publication may be reproduced or distributed in any form or by any means, or stored in a database or retrieval system, without the prior written consent of The McGraw-Hill Companies, Inc., including, but not limited to, in any network or other electronic storage or transmission, or broadcast for distance learning.

Some ancillaries, including electronic and print components, may not be available to customers outside the United States.

This book is printed on acid-free paper.

1 2 3 4 5 6 7 8 9 0 QPD/QPD 0 9 8 7

ISBN 978-0-07-329454-4
MHID 0-07-329454-3

Vice President/Director of Marketing: *John Biernat*
Vice President/Editor in Chief: *Elizabeth Haefele*
Associate sponsoring editor: *Janna Martin*
Director, Editing/Design/Production: *Jess Ann Kosic*
Developmental editor: *Kelly L. Delso*
Marketing manager: *Sarah Wood*
Media producer: *Benjamin Curless*
Project manager: *Marlena Pechan*
Production supervisor: *Jason I. Huls*
Designer: *Srdjan Savanovic*
Senior photo research coordinator: *Jeremy Cheshareck*
Typeface: *10.5/13 New Aster*
Compositor: *Laserwords Private Limited*
Printer: *Quebecor World Dubuque Inc.*

Library of Congress Cataloging-in-Publication Data

O'Leary, Timothy J., 1947-
     Microsoft Office Access 2007: brief edition / Timothy J. O'Leary, Linda I. O'Leary.—1st ed.
   p. cm.—(The O'Leary series)
     Includes index.
     ISBN-13: 978-0-07-329454-4 (alk. paper)
     ISBN-10: 0-07-329454-3 (alk. paper)
     1. Microsoft Access. 2. Database management. I. O'Leary, Linda I. II. Title.
QA76.9.D3O387 2008
005.75'65—dc22

2007014630

www.mhhe.com

DEDICATION

We dedicate this edition to Nicole and Katie who have brought love and joy to our lives.

Brief Contents

Detailed Contents

Lab 2

Modifying and Filtering a Table and Creating a Form AC2.1

Lab 3

Querying Tables and Creating Reports AC3.1

Acknowledgments

We would like to extend our thanks to the professors who took time out of their busy schedules to provide us with the feedback necessary to develop the 2007 Edition of this text. The following professors offered valuable suggestions on revising the text:

Adida Awan, Savannah State University

Jacqueline Bakal, Felician College

Chet Barney, Southern Utah University

Bruce W. Bryant, University of Arkansas Community College Morrilton

Kelly D. Carter, Mercer University

Cesar Augusto Casas, St. Thomas Aquinas College

Sally Clements, St. Thomas Aquinas College

Donna N. Dunn, Beaufort County Community College

Donna Ehrhart, Genesee Community College

Saiid Ganjalizadeh, The Catholic University of America

Dr. Jayanta Ghosh, Florida Community College

Carol Grazette, Medgar Evers College/CUNY

Susan Gundy, University of Illinois at Springfield

Greg R. Hodge, Northwestern Michigan College

Christopher M. J. Hopper, Bellevue Community College

Ginny Kansas, Southwestern College

Robert Kemmerer, Los Angeles Mission College

Diana I. Kline, University of Louisville

Linda Klisto, Broward Community College North Campus

Nanette Lareau, University of Arkansas Community College Morrilton

Deborah Layton, Eastern Oklahoma State College

Keming Liu, Medgar Evers College/CUNY

J. Gay Mills, Amarillo College

Kim Moorning, Medgar Evers College/CUNY

Dr. Belinda J. Moses, University of Phoenix/Baker College/Wayne County Community College

Lois Ann O'Neal, Rogers State University

Andrew Perry, Springfield College

Michael Philipp, Greenville Technical College

Julie Piper, Bucks County Community College

Brenda Price, Bucks County Community College

Thali N. Rajashekhara, Camden County College

Dr. Marcel Marie Robles, Eastern Kentucky University

Jose (Joe) Sainz, Naugatuck Valley Community College

Pamela J. Silvers, Asheville-Buncombe Technical Community College

Glenna Stites, Johnson County Community College

Joyce Thompson, Lehigh Carbon Community College

Michelle G. Vlaich-Lee, Greenville Technical College

Mary A. Walthall, St. Petersburg College

We would like to thank those who took the time to help us develop the manuscript and ensure accuracy through pain-staking edits: Brenda Nielsen of Mesa Community College–Red Mountain, Rajiv Narayana of SunTech Info-Labs, and Craig Leonard.

Our thanks also go to Linda Mehlinger of Morgan State University for all her work on creating the PowerPoint presentations to accompany the text. We are grateful to Harry Knight of Franklin University, the author of the Instructor's Manual and Testbank, for his careful revision of these valuable resources and creation of online quizzing materials.

Finally, we would like to thank team members from McGraw-Hill, whose renewed commitment, direction, and support have infused the team with the excitement of a new project. Leading the team from McGraw-Hill are Janna Martin, Associate Editor; Sarah Wood, Marketing Manager; and Developmental Editors Kelly Delso and Alaina Grayson.

The production staff is headed by Marlena Pechan, Project Manager, whose planning and attention to detail have made it possible for us to successfully meet a very challenging schedule; Srdjan Savanovic, Designer; Jason Huls, Production Supervisor; Ben Curless, Media Producer; Jeremy Cheshareck, Photo Researcher; and Betsy Blumenthal, copyeditor—team members whom we can depend on to do a great job.

Preface

The 20th century brought us the dawn of the digital information age and unprecedented changes in information technology. There is no indication that this rapid rate of change will be slowing—it may even be increasing. As we begin the 21st century, computer literacy is undoubtedly becoming a prerequisite in whatever career you choose.

The goal of the O'Leary Series is to provide you with the necessary skills to efficiently use these applications. Equally important is the goal to provide a foundation for students to readily and easily learn to use future versions of this software. This series does this by providing detailed step-by-step instructions combined with careful selection and presentation of essential concepts.

Times are changing, technology is changing, and this text is changing too. As students of today, you are different from those of yesterday. You put much effort toward the things that interest you and the things that are relevant to you. Your efforts directed at learning application programs and exploring the Web seem, at times, limitless.

On the other hand, students often can be shortsighted, thinking that learning the skills to use the application is the only objective. The mission of the series is to build upon and extend this interest by not only teaching the specific application skills but by introducing the concepts that are common to all applications, providing students with the confidence, knowledge, and ability to easily learn the next generation of applications.

Instructor's Resource CD-ROM

The **Instructor's Resource CD-ROM** contains a computerized Test Bank, an Instructor's Manual, and PowerPoint Presentation Slides. Features of the Instructor's Resource are described below.

- **Instructor's Manual CD-ROM**   The Instructor's Manual, authored by Harry Knight of Franklin University, contains lab objectives, concepts, outlines, lecture notes, and command summaries. Also included are answers to all end-of-chapter material, tips for covering difficult materials, additional exercises, and a schedule showing how much time is required to cover text material.

- **Computerized Test Bank**   The test bank, authored by Harry Knight, contains over 1,300 multiple choice, true/false, and discussion questions. Each question will be accompanied by the correct answer, the level of learning difficulty, and corresponding page references. Our flexible Diploma software allows you to easily generate custom exams.

- **PowerPoint Presentation Slides** The presentation slides, authored by Linda Mehlinger of Morgan State University, include lab objectives, concepts, outlines, text figures, and speaker's notes. Also included are bullets to illustrate key terms and FAQs.

Online Learning Center/Web Site

Found at **www.mhhe.com/oleary,** this site provides additional learning and instructional tools to enhance the comprehension of the text. The OLC/Web Site is divided into these three areas:

- **Information Center** Contains core information about the text, supplements, and the authors.

- **Instructor Center** Offers instructional materials, downloads, and other relevant links for professors.

- **Student Center** Contains data files, chapter competencies, chapter concepts, self-quizzes, flashcards, additional Web links, and more.

Simnet Assessment for Office Applications

Simnet Assessment for Office Applications provides a way for you to test students' software skills in a simulated environment. Simnet is available for Microsoft Office 2007 and provides flexibility for you in your applications course by offering:

Pre-testing options

Post-testing options

Course placement testing

Diagnostic capabilities to reinforce skills

Web delivery of test

MCAS preparation exams

Learning verification reports

For more information on skills assessment software, please contact your local sales representative, or visit us at **www.mhhe.com**.

O'Leary Series

The O'Leary Application Series for Microsoft Office is available separately or packaged with *Computing Essentials*. The O'Leary Application Series offers a step-by-step approach to learning computer applications and is available in both brief and introductory versions. The introductory books are MCAS Certified and prepare students for the Microsoft Certified Applications Specialist exam.

Computing Concepts

Computing Essentials 2008 offers a unique, visual orientation that gives students a basic understanding of computing concepts. *Computing Essentials* encourages "active" learning with exercises, explorations, visual illustrations, and inclusion of screen shots and numbered steps. While combining the "active" learning style with current topics and technology, this text provides an accurate snapshot of computing trends. When bundled with software application lab manuals, students are given a complete representation of the fundamental issues surrounding the personal computing environment.

GUIDE TO THE O'LEARY SERIES

The O'Leary Series is full of features designed to make learning productive and hassle free. On the following pages you will see the kind of engaging, helpful pedagogical features that have helped countless students master Microsoft Office Applications.

EASY-TO-FOLLOW INTRODUCTORY MATERIALS

INTRODUCTION TO MICROSOFT OFFICE 2007

Each text in the O'Leary Series opens with an Introduction to Office 2007, providing a complete overview of this version of the Microsoft Office Suite.

What Is the 2007 Microsoft Office System?

Microsoft's 2007 Microsoft Office System is a comprehensive, integrated system of programs, servers, and services designed to solve a wide array of business needs. Although the programs can be used individually, they are designed to work together seamlessly, making it easy to connect people and organizations to information, business processes, and each other. The applications include tools used to create, discuss, communicate, and manage projects. If you share a lot of documents with other people, these features facilitate access to common documents. This version has an entirely new user interface that is designed to make it easier to perform tasks and help users more quickly take advantage of all the features in the applications. In addition, the communication and collaboration features and integration with the World Wide Web have been expanded and refined.

The 2007 Microsoft Office System is packaged in several different combinations of programs or suites. The major programs and a brief description are provided in the following table.

Program	Description
Word 2007	Word Processor program used to create text-based documents
Excel 2007	Spreadsheet program used to analyze numerical data
Access 2007	Database manager used to organize, manage, and display a database
PowerPoint 2007	Graphics presentation program used to create presentation materials
Outlook 2007	Desktop information manager and messaging client
InfoPath 2007	Used to create XML forms and documents
OneNote 2007	Note-taking and information organization tools
Publisher 2007	Tools to create and distribute publications for print, Web, and e-mail
Visio 2007	Diagramming and data visualization tools
SharePoint Designer 2007	Web site development and management for SharePoint servers
Project 2007	Project management tools
Groove 2007	Collaboration program that enables teams to work together

The four main components of Microsoft Office 2007—Word, Excel, Access, and PowerPoint—are the applications you will learn about in this series of labs. They are described in more detail in the following sections.

Overview of Microsoft Office Word 20

What Is Word Processing?

Office Word 2007 is a word processing software application whose p is to help you create any type of written communication. A word pro can be used to manipulate text data to produce a letter, a report, a an e-mail message, or any other type of correspondence. Text data letter, number, or symbol that you can type on a keyboard. The grou the text data to form words, sentences, paragraphs, and pages results in the creation of a document. Through a word processor, y create, modify, store, retrieve, and print part or all of a document.

Word processors are one of the most widely used application software programs. Putting your thoughts in writing, from the simplest note to the most complex book, is a time-consuming process. Even more time-consuming is the task of editing and retyping the document to make it better. Word processors make errors nearly nonexistent—not because they are not made, but because they are easy to correct. Word processors let you throw away the correction fluid, scissors, paste, and erasers. Now, with a few keystrokes, you can easily correct errors, move paragraphs, and reprint your document.

Word 2007 Features

Word 2007 excels in its ability to change or edit a document. Editing involves correcting spelling, grammar, and sentence-structure errors. In addition, you can easily revise or update existing text by inserting or deleting text. For example, a document that lists prices can easily be updated to reflect new prices. A document that details procedures can be revised by deleting old procedures and inserting new ones. This is especially helpful when a document is used repeatedly. Rather than recreating the whole document, you change only the parts that need to be revised.

Revision also includes the rearrangement of selected areas of text. For example, while writing a report, you may decide to change the location of a single word or several paragraphs or pages of text. You can do it easily by cutting or removing selected text from one location, then pasting or placing the selected text in another location. The selection also can be copied from one document to another.

To help you produce a perfect document, Word 2007 includes many additional support features. The AutoCorrect feature checks the spelling and grammar in a document as text is entered. Many common errors are corrected automatically for you. Others are identified and a correction suggested. A thesaurus can be used to display alternative words that have a meaning similar or opposite to a word you entered. A Find and Replace feature can be used to quickly locate specified text and replace it with other text throughout a document. In addition, Word 2007 includes a

WDO.1

INTRODUCTION TO WORD 2007

Each text in the O'Leary Series also provides an overview of the specific application features.

ENGAGING LAB INTRODUCTIONS

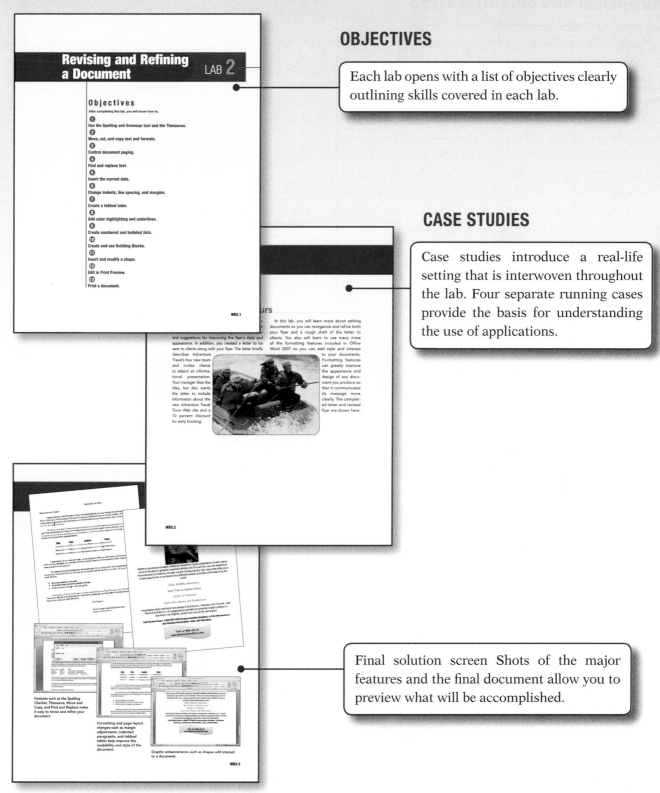

OBJECTIVES

Each lab opens with a list of objectives clearly outlining skills covered in each lab.

CASE STUDIES

Case studies introduce a real-life setting that is interwoven throughout the lab. Four separate running cases provide the basis for understanding the use of applications.

Final solution screen Shots of the major features and the final document allow you to preview what will be accomplished.

STEP-BY-STEP INSTRUCTION

NUMBERED AND BULLETED STEPS

Numbered and bulleted steps provide clear step-by-step instructions on how to complete a task, or series of tasks.

All steps and bullets appear in the left-hand margin, making it easy not to miss a step.

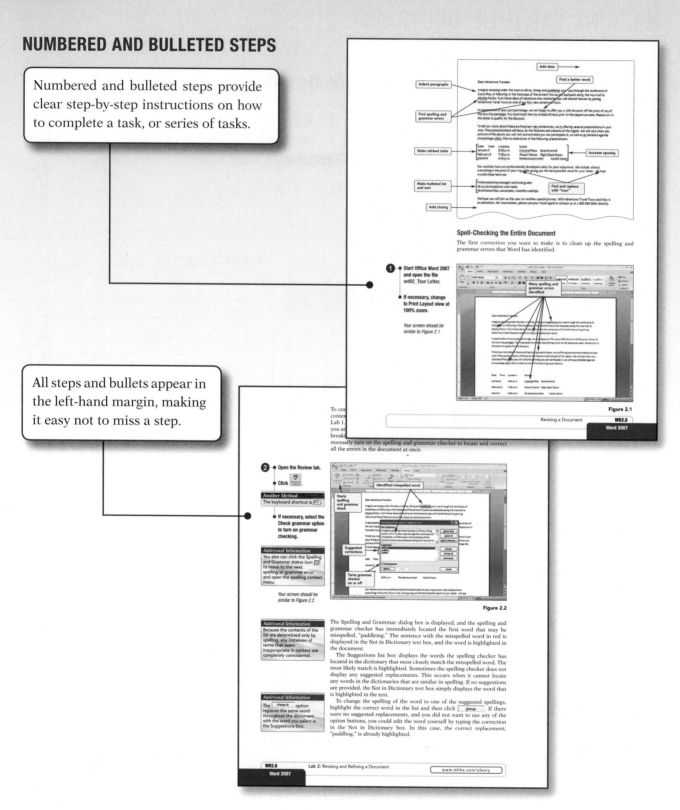

AND EASY-TO-FOLLOW DESIGN

TABLES

Tables provide quick summaries of concepts and procedures for specific tasks.

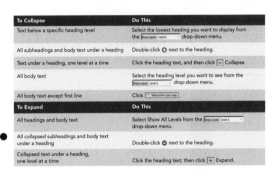

To Collapse	Do This
Text below a specific heading level	Select the lowest heading you want to display from the Show Level1 drop-down menu.
All subheadings and body text under a heading	Double-click ⊖ next to the heading.
Text under a heading, one level at a time	Click the heading text, and then click [–] Collapse.
All body text	Select the heading level you want to see from the Show Level1 drop-down menu.
All body text except first line	Click Show First Line Only.

To Expand	Do This
All headings and body text	Select Show All Levels from the Show Level1 drop-down menu.
All collapsed subheadings and body text under a heading	Double-click ⊕ next to the heading.
Collapsed text under a heading, one level at a time	Click the heading text; then click [+] Expand.

To change the amount of information displayed, you will collapse the display of the text under the Geography and Climate heading first. Then you will collapse everything below a level 3 heading so you can quickly check the report organization.

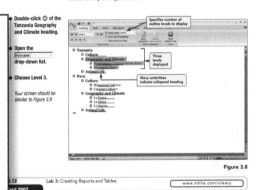

- **Double-click ⊖ of the Tanzania Geography and Climate heading.**

- **Open the** Show Levels **drop-down list.**

- **Choose Level 3.**

Your screen should be similar to Figure 3.8

Figure 3.8

3.12 Lab 3: Creating Reports and Tables
Word 2007 www.mhhe.com/oleary

To correct the misspelled words and grammatical errors, you can use the context menu to correct each individual word or error, as you learned in Lab 1. However, in many cases, you may find it more efficient to wait until you are finished writing before you correct errors. Rather than continually breaking your train of thought to correct errors as you type, you can manually turn on the spelling and grammar checker to locate and correct all the errors in the document at once.

2 **Open the Review tab.**

- **Click** Spelling.

Another Method
The keyboard shortcut is F7.

- **If necessary, select the Check grammar option to turn on grammar checking.**

Additional Information
You also can click the Spelling and Grammar status icon to move to the next spelling or grammar error and open the spelling context menu.

Your screen should be similar to Figure 2.2

Additional Information
Because the contents of the list are determined only by spelling, any instances of terms that seem inappropriate in context are completely coincidental.

Additional Information
The Change All option replaces the same word throughout the document with the word you select in the Suggestions box.

Figure 2.2

The Spelling and Grammar dialog box is displayed, and the spelling and grammar checker has immediately located the first word that may be misspelled, "paddling." The sentence with the misspelled word in red is displayed in the Not in Dictionary text box, and the word is highlighted in the document.

The Suggestions list box displays the words the spelling checker has located in the dictionary that most closely match the misspelled word. The most likely match is highlighted. Sometimes the spelling checker does not display any suggested replacements. This occurs when it cannot locate any words in the dictionaries that are similar in spelling. If no suggestions are provided, the Not in Dictionary text box simply displays the word that is highlighted in the text.

To change the spelling of the word to one of the suggested spellings, highlight the correct word in the list and then click Change. If there were no suggested replacements, and you did not want to use any of the option buttons, you could edit the word yourself by typing the correction in the Not in Dictionary box. In this case, the correct replacement, "paddling," is already highlighted.

WD2.6 Lab 2: Revising and Refining a Document
Word 2007 www.mhhe.com/oleary

FIGURES

Large screen figures make it easy to identify elements and read screen content.

SCREEN CALLOUTS

Meaningful screen callouts identify the results of the steps as well as reinforce the associated concept.

SUPPORTIVE MARGIN NOTES

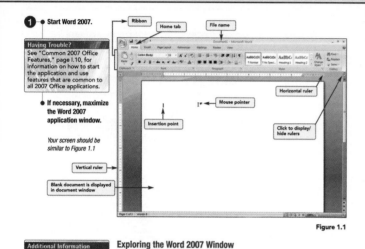

1 ● Start Word 2007.

Having Trouble?
See "Common 2007 Office Features," page 1.10, for information on how to start the application and use features that are common to all 2007 Office applications.

● If necessary, maximize the Word 2007 application window.

Your screen should be similar to Figure 1.1

Ribbon
Home tab
File name
Horizontal ruler
Mouse pointer
Insertion point
Click to display/hide rulers
Vertical ruler
Blank document is displayed in document window

Figure 1.1

ADDITIONAL INFORMATION

Additional Information offers brief asides with expanded coverage of content.

Additional Information
The Ribbon may display additional tabs if other application add-ins associated with Office are on.

Additional Information
If the ruler is not displayed, click View Ruler above the vertical scroll bar to turn it on. You also can temporarily display the horizontal or vertical ruler by pointing to the top or left edge of the document window.

Additional Information
The mouse pointer also may appear in other shapes, depending upon the task being performed.

Exploring the Word 2007 Window

The Word 2007 Ribbon below the title bar consists of seven command tabs that provide access to the commands and features you will use to create and modify a document.

The large area below the toolbars currently displays a blank Word document. called the **cursor**, is the blinking vertical the document. A vertical and horizontal both edges of the document window. The document window shows the line length margins, tab stops, and indents. The v shows the page length in inches and show

The mouse pointer may appear as an I or right-facing arrow, depending on its l appears as an I-beam, it is used to move appears as an arrow, it is used to select ite

1 ● Press ←Enter 3 times.

Your screen should be similar to Figure 1.8

Blank lines inserted by pressing ←Enter

Adventure Travel Tours four new adventures

Figure 1.8

Pressing the first ←Enter ended the first line of text and inserted a blank line. The next two inserted blank lines.

Revealing Formatting Marks

While you are creating your document, Word automatically inserts formatting marks that control the appearance of your document. These marks are not displayed automatically so that the document is not cluttered. Sometimes, however, it is helpful to view the underlying formatting marks. Displaying these marks makes it easy to see, for example, if you have added an extra space between words or at the end of a sentence.

ANOTHER METHOD

Another Method offers additional ways to perform a procedure.

1 ● Open the Home tab and click ¶ Show/Hide in the Paragraph group.

Another Method
You also can use the keyboard shortcut Ctrl + * to display formatting marks.

Your screen should be similar to Figure 1.9

Displays formatting marks

Adventure·Travel·Tours·four·new·adventures¶

Entered space by pressing Spacebar
End line by pressing ←Enter
Inserted blank lines by pressing ←Enter

Figure 1.9

The document now displays the formatting marks. The ¶ character on the line above the insertion point represents the pressing of ←Enter that created the blank line. The ¶ character at the end of the text represents the pressing of ←Enter that ended the line and moved the insertion point to the beginning of the next line. Between each word, a dot shows where the Spacebar was pressed. Formatting marks do not appear when the document is printed. You can continue to work on the document while the formatting marks are displayed, just as you did when they were hidden.

You have decided you want the flyer heading to be on two lines, with the words "four new adventures" on the second line. To do this, you will insert a blank line after the word Tours. You will move the insertion point to the location in the text where you want to insert the blank line.

2 ● Click on the right side of the "s" in "Tours" before the dot for a space.

● Press ←Enter 2 times.

● Press Delete to remove the space at the beginning of the line.

● Press ↓.

Your screen should be similar to Figure 1.10

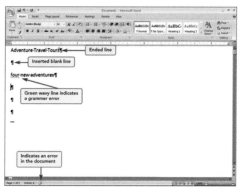

Figure 1.10

As you continue to create a document, the formatting marks are automatically adjusted.

Identifying and Correcting Errors Automatically

Having Trouble?
If the green underline is not displayed, click Office Button, click Word Options, Proofing, and select the "Check spelling as you type", "Mark grammar errors as you type", and "Check grammar with spelling" options.

Notice that a green wavy underline appears under the word "four." This indicates an error has been detected.

As you enter text, Word is constantly checking the document for spelling and grammar errors. The Spelling and Grammar Status icon in the status bar displays an animated pencil icon while you are typing, indicating Word is checking for errors as you type. When you stop typing, it displays either a blue checkmark, indicating the program does not detect any errors, or a red X, indicating the document contains an error.

Identifying and Correcting Errors Automatically **WD1.15**
Word 2007

HAVING TROUBLE

Having Trouble helps resolve potential problems as students work through each lab.

2 ● Click OK.

● Delete the closing in the letter.

● Click Quick Parts ▾

● Click on the Best Regards building block.

● Save the document again.

Your screen should be similar to Figure 2.57

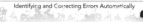

MORE ABOUT
▶ See 4.1 Structure Content by Using Quick Parts in the More About Appendix to learn how to use the Building Block Organizer to sort and edit properties of building blocks.

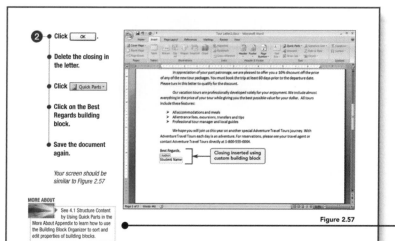

Figure 2.57

Additional Information
You will learn more about Quick Parts and use several of the other supplied building blocks in later labs.

The custom building block you created appeared as a gallery item at the top of the Quick Parts menu, making it easy for you to access and use. The selected block was inserted into the document at the location of the insertion point. As you can see, using Quick Parts was much quicker than the closing.

MORE ABOUT

New to this edition, the More About icon directs students to the More About appendix found at the end of the book. Without interrupting the flow of the text, this appendix provides additional coverage required to meet MCAS certification.

The default range setting, All, is the correct setting. In the Copies section, the default setting of one copy of the document is acceptable. You will print using the default print settings.

2 • If you need to change the selected printer to another printer, open the Name drop-down list box and select the appropriate printer (your instructor will tell you which printer to select).

• Click [OK].

Your printer should be printing the document. The printed copy of the flyer should be similar to the document shown in the Case Study at the beginning of the lab.

Exiting Word

You are finished working on the flyer for now and want to save the last few changes you have made to the document and close the Word application. The [X Exit Word] command in the File menu is used to quit the Word program. Alternatively, you can click the [X] Close button in the application window title bar. If you attempt to close the application without first saving your document, Word displays a warning asking if you want to save your work. If you do not save your work and you exit the application, any changes you made since last saving it are lost.

Another Method
The keyboard shortcut for the Exit command is [Alt] + [F4]

1 • Click [X] Close.

• Click [Yes] to save the changes you made to the file.

The Windows desktop is visible again.
If multiple Word documents are open, clicking [X] closes the application window containing the document you are viewing only.

Focus on Careers

EXPLORE YOUR CAREER OPTIONS

Food Service Manager
Have you noticed flyers around your campus advertising job positions? Many of these jobs are in the food service industry. Food service managers are traditionally responsible for overseeing the kitchen and dining room. However, these positions increasingly involve administrative tasks, including recruiting new employees. As a food service manager, your position would likely include creating newspaper notices and flyers to attract new staff. These flyers should be eye-catching and error-free. The typical salary range of a food service manager is $34,000 to $41,700. Demand for skilled food service managers is expected to increase through 2010.

Exiting Word **WD1.71**
Word 2007

FOCUS ON CAREERS

Focus on Careers provides an example of how the material covered may be applied in the "real world."

Each lab highlights a specific career, ranging from forensic science technician to food services manager, and presents job responsibilities and salary ranges for each.

Case Study

Adventure Travel Tours

Adventure Travel Tours provides information on their tours in a variety of forms. Travel brochures, for instance, contain basic tour information in a promotional format and are designed to entice potential clients to sign up for a tour. More detailed regional information packets are given to people who have already signed up for a tour, so they can prepare for their vacation. These packets include facts about each region's climate, geography, and culture. Additional informational formats include pages on Adventure Travel's Web site and scheduled group presentations.

Part of your responsibility as advertising coordinator is to gather the information that Adventure Travel will publicize about each regional tour. Specifically, you have been asked to provide background information for two of the new tours: the Tanzania Safari and the Machu Picchu trail. Because this information is used in a variety of formats, your research needs to be easily adapted. You will therefore present your facts in the form of a general report on Tanzania and Peru.

In this lab, you will learn to use many of the features of Office Word 2007 that make it easy to create an attractive and well-organized report. A portion of the completed report is shown here.

WD3.2

CONTINUING CASE STUDIES

Within each series application, the same Case Study is used to illustrate concepts and procedures.

AND INTEGRATION

WORKING TOGETHER LABS

At the completion of the brief and introductory texts, a final lab demonstrates the integration of Microsoft Office applications. Each Working Together lab also includes end-of-chapter materials.

Working Together 1: Word 2007 and Your Web Browser
Case Study

Adventure Travel Tours

The Adventure Travel Tours Web site is used to promote its products and broaden its audience of customers. In addition to the obvious marketing and sales potential, it provides an avenue for interaction between the company and the customer to improve customer service. The company also uses the Web site to provide articles of interest to customers. The articles, which include topics such as travel background information and descriptions, changes on a monthly basis as an added incentive for readers to return to the site.

You want to use the flyer you developed to promote the new tours and presentations on the Web

site. To do this, you will use Word 2007's Web-editing features that help you create a Web page quickly and easily. While using the Web-editing features, you will be working with Word and with a Web browser application. This capability of all 2007 Microsoft Office applications to work together and with other applications makes it easy to share and exchange information between applications. Your completed Web pages are shown here.

Note: The Working Together tutorial is designed to show how two applications work together and to present a basic introduction to creating Web pages.

WDWT1.1

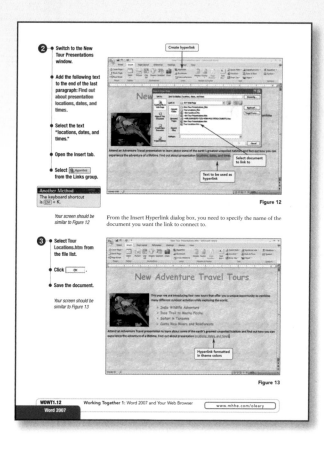

2 ● Switch to the New Tour Presentations window.

● Add the following text to the end of the last paragraph: **Find out about presentation locations, dates, and times.**

● Select the text "**locations, dates, and times.**"

● Open the Insert tab.

● Select Hyperlink from the Links group.

Another Method
The keyboard shortcut is Ctrl + K.

Your screen should be similar to Figure 12

Figure 12

From the Insert Hyperlink dialog box, you need to specify the name of the document you want the link to connect to.

3 ● Select Tour Locations.htm from the file list.

● Click OK.

● Save the document.

Your screen should be similar to Figure 13

Figure 13

Lab Exercises

rating system
★ Easy
★★ Moderate
★★★ Difficult

step-by-step

Adding a New Web Page ★

1. You want to continue working on the Web pages about the new tour presentations for the Adventure Travel Web site. Your next step is to create links from each location on the Presentation Locations Web page to information about each location's presentation date and times. Your completed Web page for the Los Angeles area should be similar to the one shown here.

   a. In Word, open the Web page file Tour Locations you created in this lab.

   b. Open the document wdwt_LosAngeles. Save the document as a Web page to the ATT Web Page folder with the file name LosAngeles and a page title of **Los Angeles Presentation Information.**

   c. Change the page color to a gradient fill effect of your choice. Change the first title line to the Title style and the second title line to a Heading 1 style. Change the title lines to a color of your choice.

   d. Increase the font size of the table to 12 points. Add color to the table headings. Enhance the Web page with any features you feel are appropriate.

   e. Two lines below the table, add the text **Contact [your name] at (909) 555-1212 for more information.** Apply the Emphasis style to this line and increase the font size to 14 points.

   f. On the Tour Locations page, create a link from the Los Angeles text to the Los Angeles page. Test the link.

   g. Resave both Web pages and preview them in your browser. Print the Los Angeles Web page.

   h. Exit the browser and Word.

REINFORCED CONCEPTS

CONCEPT PREVIEW

Concept Previews provide an overview to the concepts that will be presented throughout the lab.

Concept Preview

The following concepts will be introduced in this lab:

1. **Grammar Checker** The grammar checker advises you of incorrect grammar as you create and edit a document, and proposes possible corrections.
2. **Spelling Checker** The spelling checker advises you of misspelled words as you create and edit a document, and proposes possible corrections.
3. **AutoCorrect** The AutoCorrect feature makes some basic assumptions about the text you are typing and, based on these assumptions, automatically corrects the entry.
4. **Word Wrap** The word wrap feature automatically decides where to end a line and wrap text to the next line based on the margin settings.
5. **Font and Font Size** Font, also commonly referred to as a typeface, is a set of characters with a specific design that has one or more font sizes.
6. **Alignment** Alignment is the positioning of text on a line between the margins or indents. There are four types of paragraph alignment: left, centered, right, and justified.
7. **Graphics** A graphic is a nontext element or object such as a drawing or picture that can be added to a document.

Introducing Office Word 2007

Adventure Travel Tours has recently upgraded their computer systems at all locations across the country. As part of the upgrade, they have installed the latest version of the Microsoft Office 2007 suite of applications. You are very excited to see how this new and powerful application can help you create professional letters and reports as well as eye-catching flyers and newsletters.

Starting Office Word 2007

...tion Microsoft Office Word 2007
...and presentations.

CONCEPT BOXES

Concept boxes appear throughout the lab providing clear, concise explanations and serving as a valuable study aid.

3 • Click outside the menu to close it.

• Open the spelling context menu for "lern" and choose "learn".

The spelling is corrected, and the spelling indicator in the status bar indicates that the document is free of errors.

Using Word Wrap

Now you will continue entering more of the paragraph. As you type, when the text gets close to the right margin, do not press ←Enter to move to the next line. Word will automatically wrap words to the next line as needed.

Concept 4

Word Wrap

4 The word wrap feature automatically decides where to end a line and wrap text to the next line based on the margin settings. This feature saves time when entering text because you do not need to press ←Enter at the end of a full line to begin a new line. The only time you need to press ←Enter is to end a paragraph, to insert blank lines, or to create a short line such as a salutation. In addition, if you change the margins or insert or delete text on a line, the program automatically readjusts the text on the line to fit within the new margin settings. Word wrap is common to all word processors.

Enter the following text to complete the sentence.

1 • Press End to move to the end of the line.

www.mhhe.com/oleary

CONCEPT SUMMARIES

The Concept Summary offers a visual summary of the concepts presented throughout the lab.

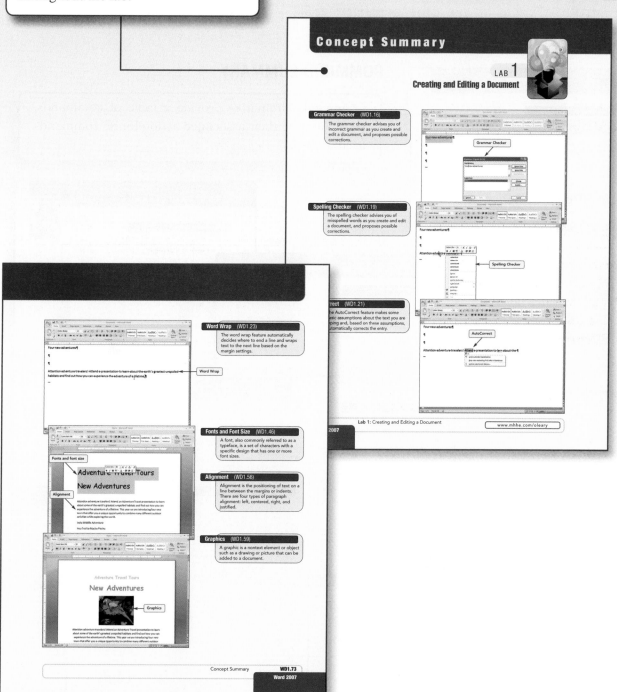

LAB REVIEW

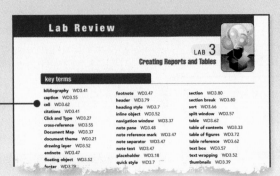

KEY TERMS

Includes a list of all bolded terms with page references.

COMMAND SUMMARY

Command Summaries provide a table of commands, shortcuts, and their associated action for all commands used in the lab.

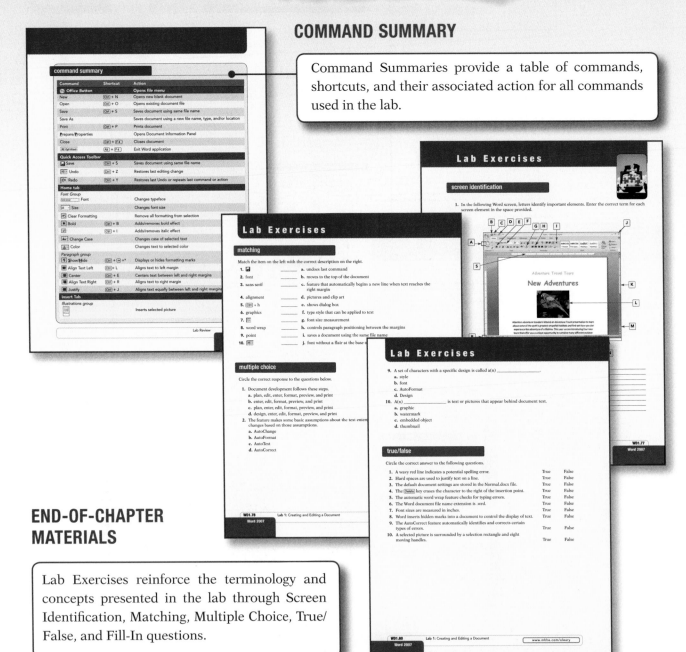

END-OF-CHAPTER MATERIALS

Lab Exercises reinforce the terminology and concepts presented in the lab through Screen Identification, Matching, Multiple Choice, True/False, and Fill-In questions.

AND SKILL DEVELOPMENT

LAB EXERCISES

Lab Exercises provide hands-on practice and develop critical-thinking skills through step-by-step and on-your-own practice exercises. Many cases in the practice exercises tie to a running case used in another application lab. This helps demonstrate the use of the four applications across a common case setting. For example, the Adventure Tours case used in Word is continued in practice exercises in Excel, Access, and PowerPoint.

ON YOUR OWN

STEP-BY-STEP

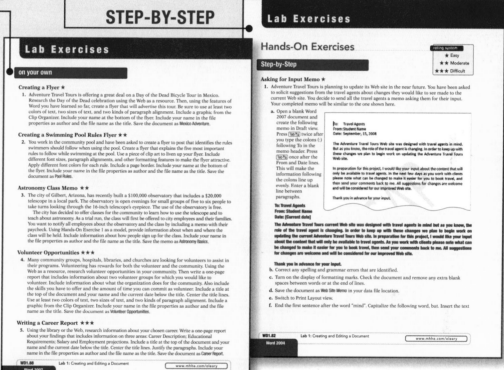

RATING SYSTEM

These exercises have a rating system from easy to difficult and test your ability to apply the knowledge you have gained in each lab. Exercises that build off of previous exercises are noted with a Continuing Exercises icon.

rating system

★ Easy

★★ Moderate

★★★ Difficult

END-OF-BOOK RESOURCES

COMPREHENSIVE COMMAND SUMMARY

Provides a table of commands, shortcuts, and their associated action for all commands used throughout each text in the O'Leary Series.

2007 Word Brief Command Summary

Command	Shortcut	Action
Office Button		Opens File menu
New	Ctrl + N	Opens new document
Open	Ctrl + O	Opens existing document file
Save	Ctrl + S, 🖫	Saves document using same file name
Save As	F12	Saves document using a new file name, type, and/or location
Save as/Save As type/ Web Page		Saves file as a Web page document
Print	Ctrl + P	Specify print settings before printing document
Print/Print Preview		Displays document as it will appear when printed
Print/Quick Print		Prints document using default printer settings
Prepare/Properties		Opens Document Information Panel
Close	Ctrl + F4	Closes document
Word Options /Proofing		Changes settings associated with Spelling and Grammar checking
Word Options /Advanced/ Mark formatting inconsistencies		Checks for formatting inconsistencies
Exit Word	Alt + F4, ✕	Closes the Word application
Quick Access Toolbar		
Save		Saves document using same file name
Undo	Ctrl + Z	Restores last editing change
Redo	Ctrl + Y	Restores last Undo or repeats last command or action
Home tab		
Clipboard Group		
Cut	Ctrl + X	Cuts selection to Clipboard
Copy	Ctrl + C	Copies selection to Clipboard
Paste	Ctrl + V	Pastes item from Clipboard
Format Painter		Copies format to selection

2007 Word Brief Command Summary   **WDCS.1**
Word 2007

Command	Shortcut	Action
Font Group		
Calibri (Body) ▾ Font		Changes typeface
11 ▾ Size		Changes font size
A Grow Font		Increases font size
Clear Formatting		Clears all formatting from selected text, leaving plain text
B Bold	Ctrl + B	Makes selected text bold
I Italic	Ctrl + I	Applies italic effect to selected text
U Underline	Ctrl + U	Adds underline below selected text
Aa Change Case		Changes case of selected text
Text Highlight Color		Applies highlight color to selection
A Font Color		Changes selected text to selected color
Paragraph group		
Bullets		Creates a bulleted list
Numbering		Creates a numbered list
Indents and Spacing		Indents paragraph from left margin
Sort		Rearranges items in a selection into ascending alphabetical/numerical order
Show/Hide	Ctrl + ⇧ + *	Displays or hides formatting marks
Align Text Left	Ctrl + L	Aligns text to left margin
Center	Ctrl + E	Centers text between left and right margins
Align Text Right	Ctrl + R	Aligns text to right margin
Justify	Ctrl + J	Aligns text equally between left and right margins
Line Spacing	Ctrl + #	Changes amount of white space between lines
Styles Group		
More		Opens Quick Styles gallery
Editing Group		
Find ▾	Ctrl + F	Locates specified text
Replace	Ctrl + H	Locates and replaces specified text
Insert tab		
Pages group		
Cover Page ▾		Inserts a preformatted cover page
Blank Page		Inserts a blank page
Page Break	Ctrl + ⏎Enter	Inserts a hard page break
Tables group		
Table		Inserts a table

WDCS.2   2007 Word Brief Command Summary   www.mhhe.com/oleary
Word 2007

Glossary of Key Terms

GLOSSARY

Bolded terms found throughout each text in the O'Leary Series are defined in the glossary.

active window The window containing the insertion point and that will be affected by any changes you make.

alignment How text is positioned on a line between the margins or indents. There are four types of paragraph alignment: left, centered, right, and justified.

antonym A word with the opposite meaning.

author The process of creating a Web page.

AutoCorrect A feature that makes basic assumptions about the text you are typing and automatically corrects the entry.

bibliography A listing of source references that appears at the end of the document.

browser A program that connects you to remote computers and displays the Web pages you request.

building blocks Document fragments that include text and formatting and that can be easily inserted into a document.

bulleted list Displays items that logically fall out from a paragraph into a list, with items preceded by bullets.

caption A title or explanation for a table, picture, or graph.

case sensitive The capability to distinguish between uppercase and lowercase characters.

cell The intersection of a column and row where data are entered in a table.

character formatting Formatting features such as bold and color that affect the selected characters only.

citations Parenthetical source references that give credit for specific information included in a document.

Click and Type A feature available in Print Layout and Web Layout views that is used to quickly insert text, graphics, and other items in

a blank area of a document, avoiding the need to enter blank lines.

clip art Professionally drawn graphics.

control A graphic element that is a container for information or objects.

cross-reference A reference in one part of a document related to information in another part.

cursor The blinking vertical bar that shows you where the next character you type will appear. Also called the insertion point.

custom dictionary A dictionary of terms you have entered that are not in the main dictionary of the spelling checker.

default The initial Word document settings that can be changed to customize documents.

destination The location to which text is moved or copied.

Document Map A feature that displays the headings in the document in the navigation window.

document properties Details about a document that describe or identify it and are saved with the document content.

document theme A predefined set of formatting choices that can be applied to an entire document in one simple step.

document window The area of the application window that displays the contents of the open document.

drag and drop A mouse procedure that moves or copies a selection to a new location.

drawing layer The layer above or below the text layer where floating objects are inserted.

drawing object A simple object consisting of shapes such as lines and boxes.

edit The process of changing and correcting existing text in a document.

Glossary of Key Terms   **WDG.1**
Word 2007

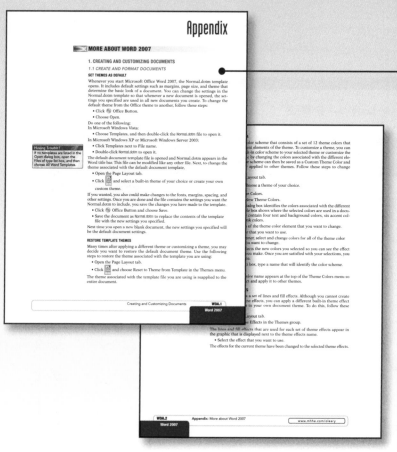

MORE ABOUT APPENDICES

A More About appendix appears at the end of the brief and introductory texts. This appendix offers students additional coverage needed to meet MCAS requirements. Skills pertaining to additional MCAS coverage are denoted by a More About icon in the margins of the text.

REFERENCE 1 - DATA FILE LIST

The Data File List is a reference guide that helps organize data and solution files. It identifies the names of the original and saved files.

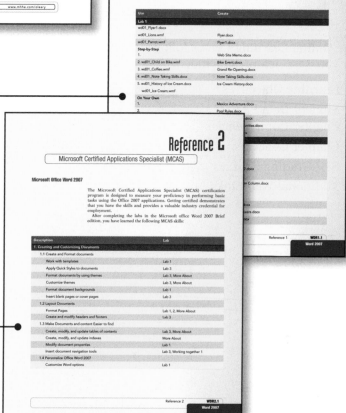

REFERENCE 2 - MCAS CERTIFICATION GUIDE

Links all MCAS objectives to text content and end-of-lab exercises. You will always know which MCAS objectives are being covered. Introductory texts are MCAS certified.

ONLINE LEARNING CENTER (OLC)

www.mhhe.com/oleary

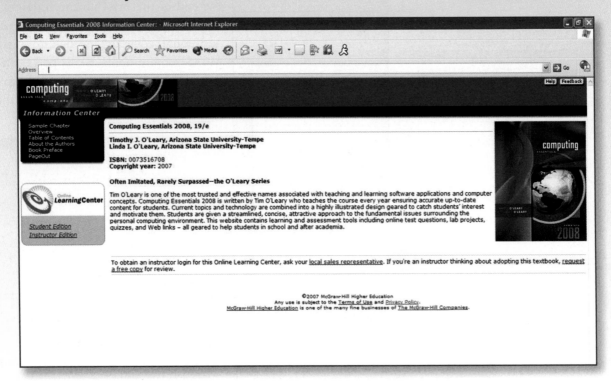

The Online Learning Center follows The O'Leary Series lab by lab, offering all kinds of supplementary help for you. OLC features include:

- Learning Objectives
- Student Data Files
- Chapter Competencies
- Chapter Concepts
- Self-Grading Quizzes
- Additional Web Links

ABOUT THE AUTHORS

Tim and Linda O'Leary live in the American Southwest and spend much of their time engaging instructors and students in conversation about learning. In fact, they have been talking about learning for over 25 years. Something in those early conversations convinced them to write a book, to bring their interest in the learning process to the printed page. Today, they are as concerned as ever about learning, about technology, and about the challenges of presenting material in new ways, in terms of both content and method of delivery.

A powerful and creative team, Tim combines his 25 years of classroom teaching experience with Linda's background as a consultant and corporate trainer. Tim has taught courses at Stark Technical College in Canton, Ohio, and at Rochester Institute of Technology in upstate New York, and is currently a professor at Arizona State University in Tempe, Arizona. Linda offered her expertise at ASU for several years as an academic advisor. She also presented and developed materials for major corporations such as Motorola, Intel, Honeywell, and AT&T, as well as various community colleges in the Phoenix area.

Tim and Linda have talked to and taught numerous students, all of them with a desire to learn something about computers and applications that make their lives easier, more interesting, and more productive.

Each new edition of an O'Leary text, supplement, or learning aid has benefited from these students and their instructors who daily stand in front of them (or over their shoulders). The O'Leary Series is no exception.

Introduction to Microsoft Office 2007

Objectives

After completing the Introduction to Microsoft Office 2007, you should be able to:

1 Describe the 2007 Microsoft Office System.

2 Describe the Office 2007 applications.

3 Start an Office 2007 application.

4 Recognize the basic application features.

5 Use menus, context menus, and shortcut keys.

6 Use the Ribbon, dialog boxes, and task panes.

7 Use Office Help.

8 Exit an Office 2007 application.

What Is the 2007 Microsoft Office System?

Microsoft's 2007 Microsoft Office System is a comprehensive, integrated system of programs, servers, and services designed to solve a wide array of business needs. Although the programs can be used individually, they are designed to work together seamlessly, making it easy to connect people and organizations to information, business processes, and each other. The applications include tools used to create, discuss, communicate, and manage projects. If you share a lot of documents with other people, these features facilitate access to common documents. This version has an entirely new user interface that is designed to make it easier to perform tasks and help users more quickly take advantage of all the features in the applications. In addition, the communication and collaboration features and integration with the World Wide Web have been expanded and refined.

The 2007 Microsoft Office System is packaged in several different combinations of programs or suites. The major programs and a brief description are provided in the following table.

Program	Description
Word 2007	Word Processor program used to create text-based documents
Excel 2007	Spreadsheet program used to analyze numerical data
Access 2007	Database manager used to organize, manage, and display a database
PowerPoint 2007	Graphics presentation program used to create presentation materials
Outlook 2007	Desktop information manager and messaging client
InfoPath 2007	Used to create XML forms and documents
OneNote 2007	Note-taking and information organization tools
Publisher 2007	Tools to create and distribute publications for print, Web, and e-mail
Visio 2007	Diagramming and data visualization tools
SharePoint Designer 2007	Web site development and management for SharePoint servers
Project 2007	Project management tools
Groove 2007	Collaboration program that enables teams to work together

The four main components of Microsoft Office 2007—Word, Excel, Access, and PowerPoint—are the applications you will learn about in this series of labs. They are described in more detail in the following sections.

Word 2007

Word 2007 is a word processing software application whose purpose is to help you create text-based documents. Word processors are one of the most flexible and widely used application software programs. A word processor can be used to manipulate text data to produce a letter, a report, a memo, an e-mail message, or any other type of correspondence.

Two documents you will produce in the first two Word 2007 labs, a letter and flyer, are shown here.

A letter containing a tabbed table, indented paragraphs, and text enhancements is quickly created using basic Word features.

September 15, 2008

Dear Adventure Traveler:

Imagine camping under the stars in Africa, hiking and paddling your way through the rainforests of Costa Rica, or following in the footsteps of the ancient Inca as you backpack along the Inca trail to Machu Picchu. Turn these dreams of adventure into memories you will cherish forever by joining Adventure Travel Tours on one of our four new adventure tours.

To tell you more about these exciting new adventures, we are offering several presentations in your area. These presentations will focus on the features and cultures of the region. We will also show you pictures of the places you will visit and activities you can partici... to attend one of the following presentations:

Date	Time
January 5	8:00 p.m. Cro
February 3	7:30 p.m. Air
March 8	8:00 p.m. Re

In appreciation of your past patronage, we ... of the new tour packages. You must book the trip at ... letter to qualify for the discount.

Our vacation tours are professionally devel... everything in the price of your tour while giving you ... these features:

➢ All accommodations and meals
➢ All entrance fees, excursions, transfers and ...
➢ Professional tour manager and local guides

We hope you will join us this year on anothe... Travel Tours each day is an adventure. For reservati... Travel Tours directly at 1-800-555-0004.

Adventure Travel Tours
New Adventures

Attention adventure travelers! Attend an Adventure Travel presentation to learn about some of the earth's greatest unspoiled habitats and find out how you can experience the adventure of a lifetime. This year we are introducing four new tours that offer you a unique opportunity to combine many different outdoor activities while exploring the world.

India Wildlife Adventure

Inca Trail to Machu Picchu

Safari in Tanzania

Costa Rica Rivers and Rainforests

Presentation dates and times are January 5 at 8:00 p.m., February 3 at 7:30 p.m., and March 8 at 8:00 p.m. All presentations are held at convenient hotel locations in downtown Los Angeles, Santa Clara, and at the LAX airport.

Call Student Name 1-800-555-0004 for presentation locations, a full color brochure, and itinerary information, costs, and trip dates.

Visit our Web site at
www.adventuretraveltours.com

A flyer incorporating many visual enhancements such as colored text, varied text styles, and graphic elements is both eye-catching and informative.

What Is the 2007 Microsoft Office System?   I.3

Access 2007

The beauty of a word processor is that you can make changes or corrections as you are typing. Want to change a report from single spacing to double spacing? Alter the width of the margins? Delete some paragraphs and add others from yet another document? A word processor allows you to do all these things with ease.

Word 2007 includes many group collaboration features to help streamline how documents are developed and changed by group members. You also can create and send e-mail messages directly from within Word using all its features to create and edit the message. In addition, you can send an entire document as your e-mail message, allowing the recipient to edit the document directly without having to open or save an attachment.

Word 2007 is closely integrated with the World Wide Web, detecting when you type a Web address and automatically converting it to a hyperlink. You also can create your own hyperlinks to locations within documents, or to other documents, including those at external locations such as a Web site or file server. It also includes features that help you quickly create Web pages and blog entries.

Excel 2007

Excel 2007 is an electronic worksheet that is used to organize, manipulate, and graph numeric data. Once used almost exclusively by accountants, worksheets are now widely used by nearly every profession. Marketing professionals record and evaluate sales trends. Teachers record grades and calculate final grades. Personal trainers record the progress of their clients.

Excel 2007 includes many features that not only help you create a well-designed worksheet, but one that produces accurate results. Formatting features include visual enhancements such as varied text styles, colors, and graphics. Other features help you enter complex formulas and identify and correct formula errors. You also can produce a visual display of data in the form of graphs or charts. As the values in the worksheet change, charts referencing those values automatically adjust to reflect the changes.

Excel 2007 also includes many advanced features and tools that help you perform what-if analysis and create different scenarios. And like all Office 2007 applications, it is easy to incorporate data created in one application into another. Two worksheets you will produce in Labs 2 and 3 of Excel 2007 are shown on the next page.

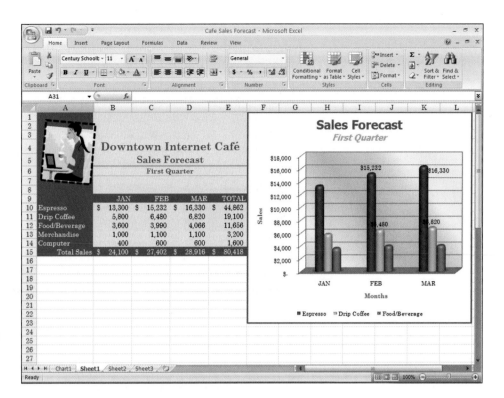

A worksheet showing the quarterly sales forecast containing a graphic, text enhancements, and a chart of the data is quickly created using basic Excel 2007 features.

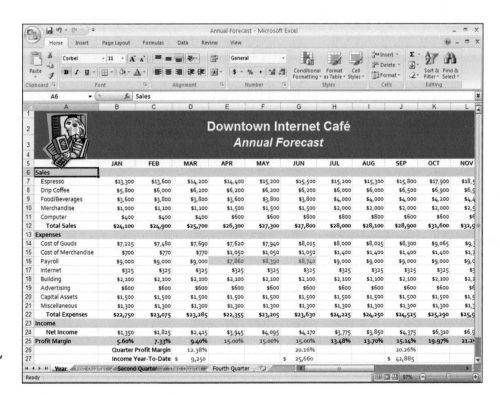

A large worksheet incorporating more complex formulas, visual enhancements such as colored text, varied text styles, and graphic elements is both informative and attractive.

What Is the 2007 Microsoft Office System?   I.5

Access 2007

You will see how easy it is to analyze data and make projections using what-if analysis and what-if graphing in Lab 3 and to incorporate Excel data in a Word document as shown in the following figures.

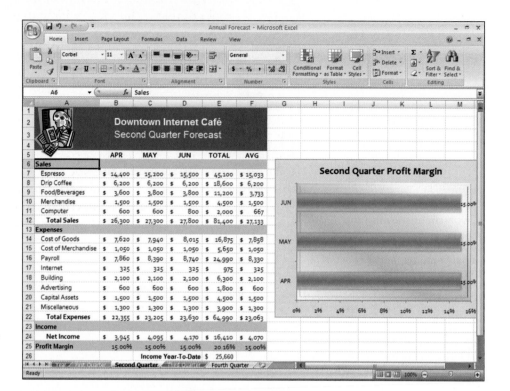

Changes you make in worksheet data while performing what-if analysis are automatically reflected in charts that reference that data.

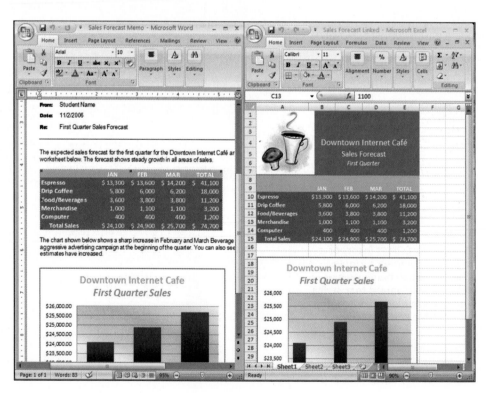

Worksheet data and charts can be copied and linked to other Office documents such as a Word document.

Access 2007

Access 2007 is a relational database management application that is used to create and analyze a database. A database is a collection of related data. In a relational database, the most widely used database structure, data is organized in linked tables. Tables consist of columns (called *fields*) and rows (called *records*). The tables are related or linked to one another by a common field. Relational databases allow you to create smaller and more manageable database tables, since you can combine and extract data between tables.

The program provides tools to enter, edit, and retrieve data from the database as well as to analyze the database and produce reports of the output. One of the main advantages of a computerized database is the ability to quickly add, delete, and locate specific records. Records also can be easily rearranged or sorted according to different fields of data, resulting in multiple table arrangements that provide more meaningful information for different purposes. Creation of forms makes it easier to enter and edit data as well. In the Access labs, you will create and organize the database table shown below.

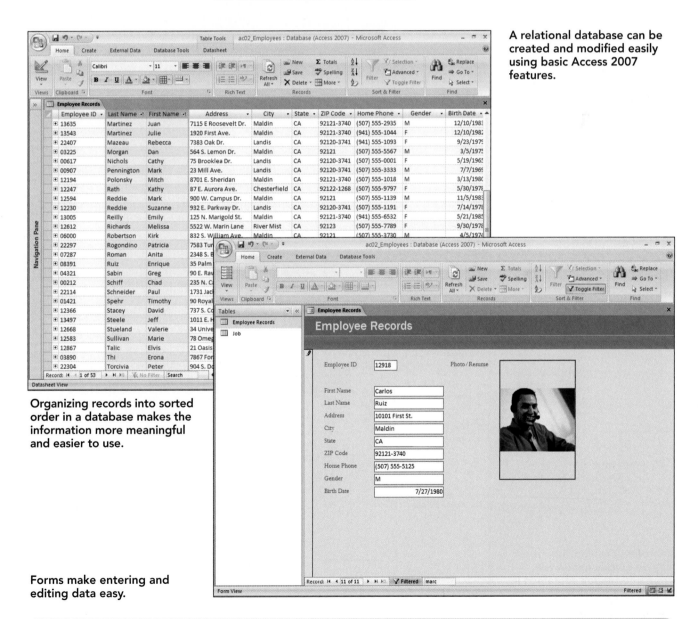

A relational database can be created and modified easily using basic Access 2007 features.

Organizing records into sorted order in a database makes the information more meaningful and easier to use.

Forms make entering and editing data easy.

Another feature is the ability to analyze the data in a table and perform calculations on different fields of data. Additionally, you can ask questions or query the table to find only certain records that meet specific conditions to be used in the analysis. Information that was once costly and time-consuming to get is now quickly and readily available. This information can then be quickly printed out in the form of reports ranging from simple listings to complex, professional-looking reports in different layout styles, or with titles, headings, subtotals, or totals.

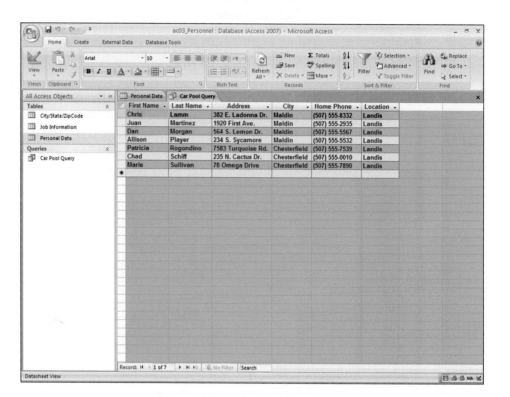

A database can be queried to locate and display only specified information.

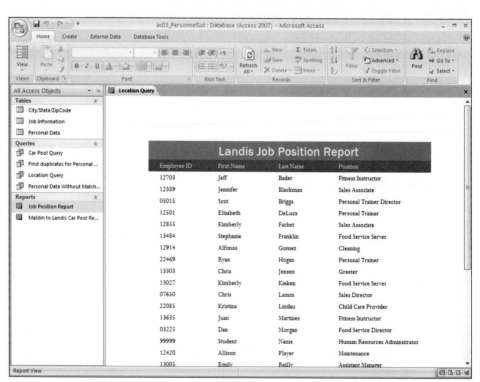

A professional-looking report can be quickly generated from information contained in a database.

PowerPoint 2007

PowerPoint 2007 is a graphics presentation program designed to help you produce a high-quality presentation that is both interesting to the audience and effective in its ability to convey your message. A presentation can be as simple as overhead transparencies or as sophisticated as an on-screen electronic display. In the first two PowerPoint labs, you will create and organize the presentation shown below.

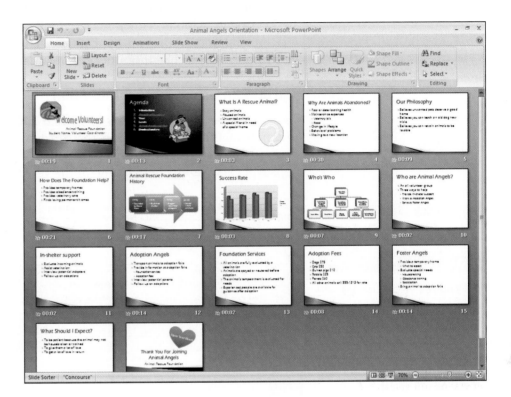

A presentation consists of a series of pages or "slides" presenting the information you want to convey in an organized and attractive manner.

When running an on-screen presentation, each slide of the presentation is displayed full-screen on your computer monitor or projected onto a screen.

What Is the 2007 Microsoft Office System?   I.9

Access 2007

Common Office 2007 Interface Features

Additional Information

Please read the Before You Begin and Instructional Conventions sections in the Overview of Microsoft Office Access 2007 (ACO.4) before starting this section.

Now that you know a little about each of the applications in Microsoft Office 2007, we will take a look at some of the interface features that are common to all Office 2007 applications. This is a hands-on section that will introduce you to the features and allow you to get a feel for how Office 2007 works. Although Word 2007 will be used to demonstrate how the features work, only common **user interface** features, a set of graphical images that represent various features, will be addressed. These features include using the File menu, Ribbon, Quick Access Toolbar, task panes, and Office Help, and starting and exiting an application. The features that are specific to each application will be introduced individually in each application text.

Starting an Office 2007 Application

There are several ways to start an Office 2007 application. The two most common methods are by using the Start menu or by clicking a desktop shortcut for the program if it is available. If you use the Start menu, the steps will vary slightly depending on the version of Windows you are using.

1 ● Click **start** to display the Start menu.

Having Trouble?
In Windows Vista, click 🟢

● **Choose Microsoft Office Word 2007.**

Having Trouble?
If you do not see the program name on the Start menu, select All Programs, select Microsoft Office, and then choose Microsoft Office Word 2007.

OR

1 ● Double-click the shortcut on the desktop.

2 ● If necessary, click ▢ Maximize in the title bar to maximize the window.

Your screen should be similar to Figure 1

Having Trouble?
Your screen may look slightly different based on your Windows operating system settings.

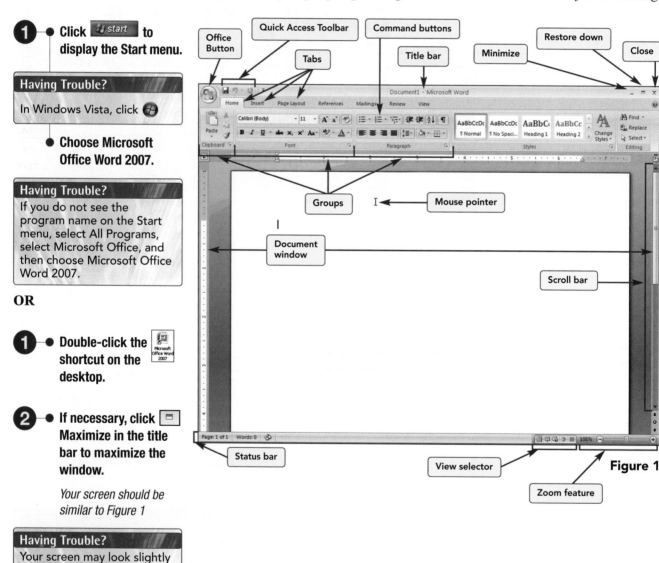

Figure 1

The Word 2007 program is started and displayed in a window on the desktop. The application window title bar displays the file name followed by the program name, Microsoft Word. The right end of the title bar displays the ⊟ Minimize, ▱ Restore Down, and ⊠ Close buttons. They perform the same functions and operate in the same way as all Windows versions.

Below the title bar is the **Ribbon**, which provides a centralized area that makes it easy to find ways to work in your document. The Ribbon has three basic parts: tabs, groups, and commands. **Tabs** are used to divide the Ribbon into major activity areas. Each tab is then organized into **groups** that contain related items. The related items are commands that consist of command buttons, a box to enter information, or a menu. As you use the Office applications, you will see that the Ribbon contains many of the same groups and commands across the applications. You also will see that many of the groups and commands are specific to an application.

The upper left area of the window's title bar displays the 🔵 Office Button and the Quick Access Toolbar. Clicking 🔵 Office Button opens the File menu of commands that allows you to work *with* your document, unlike the Ribbon that allows you to work *in* your document. For example, it includes commands to open, save, and print files. The **Quick Access Toolbar** (QAT) provides quick access to frequently used commands. By default, it includes the 🔲 Save, 🔄 Undo, and 🔁 Redo buttons, commands that Microsoft considers to be crucial. It is always available and is a customizable toolbar to which you can add your own favorite buttons.

The large center area of the program window is the **document window** where open application files are displayed. Currently, there is a blank Word document open. In Word, the mouse pointer appears as I when positioned in the document window and as a ⍖ when it can be used to select items.

On the right of the document window is a vertical scroll bar. A **scroll bar** is used with a mouse to bring additional lines of information into view in a window. The vertical scroll bar is used to move up or down. A horizontal scroll bar is also displayed when needed and moves side to side in the window. At the bottom of the window is the **status bar**, a view selector, and a document zoom feature. Similar information and features are displayed in this area for different Office applications. You will learn how these features work in each individual application.

Using the File Menu

Clicking the 🔵 Office Button opens the File menu of commands that are used to work with files.

Click 🔘 **Office Button to open the File menu.**

Click to open File menu

Your screen should be similar to Figure 2

File menu of nine commands

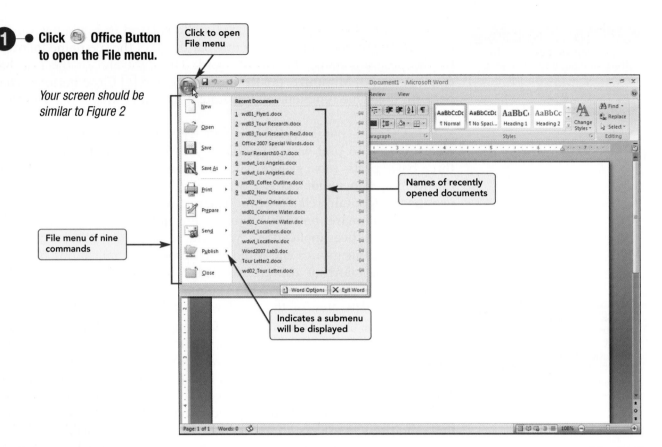

Names of recently opened documents

Indicates a submenu will be displayed

Figure 2

Additional Information

Clicking the 📌 next to a file name pins the file and permanently keeps the file name in the recently used list until it is unpinned.

The menu lists nine commands that are used to perform tasks associated with files. Notice that each command displays an underlined letter. This identifies the letter you can type to choose the command. Five commands display a ▶, which indicates the command includes a submenu of options. The right side of the command list currently displays the names of recently opened files (your list will display different file names). The default program setting displays a maximum of 17 file names. Once the maximum number of files is listed, when a new file is opened, the oldest is dropped from the list.

Once the File menu is open, you can select a command from the menu by pointing to it. A colored highlight bar, called the **selection cursor**, appears over the selected command.

2 ● **Point to the Open command.**

Your screen should be similar to Figure 3

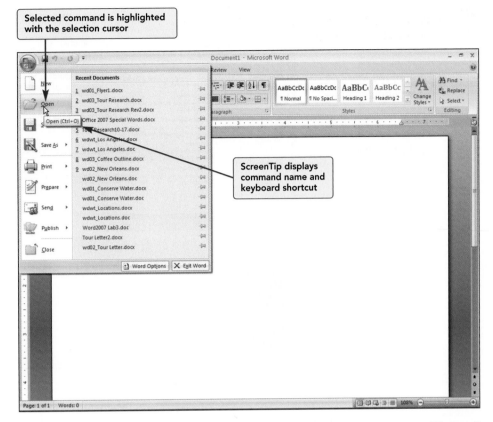

Selected command is highlighted with the selection cursor

ScreenTip displays command name and keyboard shortcut

Figure 3

A **ScreenTip**, also called a **tooltip**, briefly appears displaying the command name and the keyboard shortcut, Ctrl + O. The keyboard shortcut can be used to execute this command without opening the menu. In this case, if you hold down the Ctrl key while typing the letter O, you will access the Open command without having to open the File menu first. ScreenTips also often include a brief description of the action a command performs.

Next you will select a command that will display a submenu of options.

3 ● Point to the Prepare
command.

● Point to the Mark as
Final submenu option.

*Your screen should be
similar to Figure 4*

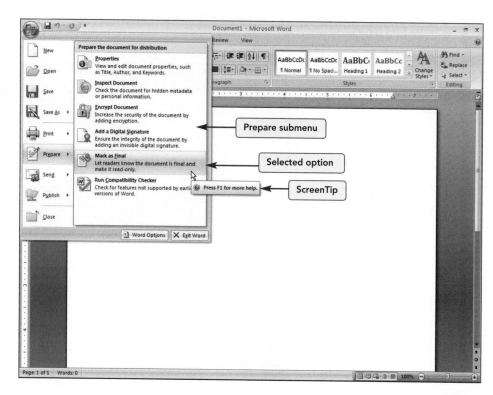

Figure 4

The submenu lists the six Prepare command submenu options and the
Mark as Final option is selected. A ScreenTip provides information about
how to get help on this feature. You will learn about using Help shortly.

4 ● Point to the Print
command.

● Point to the ▸ of the
Print command.

*Your screen should be
similar to Figure 5*

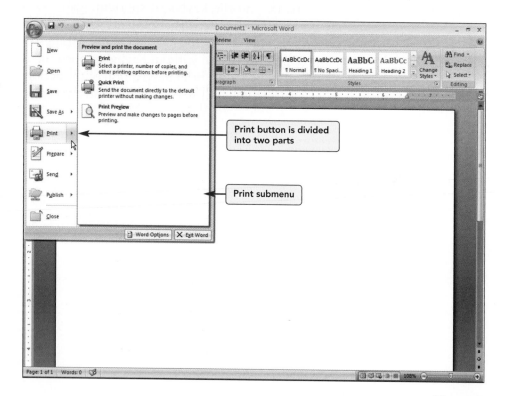

Figure 5

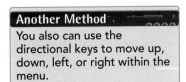
So far you have only selected commands; you have not chosen them. To choose a command, you click on it. When the command is chosen, the associated action is performed. Notice the Print command is divided into two parts. Clicking the Print section on the left will choose the command and open the Print dialog box. Clicking ⋅ in the right section has no effect and only the submenu is displayed.

5 ● **Click the Print command.**

Your screen should be similar to Figure 6

Print dialog box is used to specify print settings

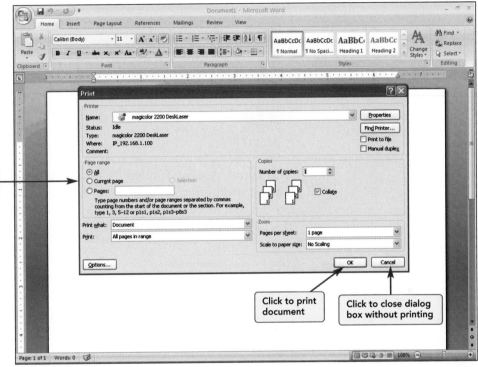

Click to print document

Click to close dialog box without printing

Figure 6

In the Print dialog box, you would specify the print settings and click ⟨ OK ⟩ to actually print a document. In this case, you will cancel the action and continue to explore other features of the Office 2007 application.

6 ● **Click** ⟨ Cancel ⟩.

Using Context Menus

Another way to access some commands is to use a context menu. A **context menu** is opened by right-clicking on an item on the screen. This menu is context sensitive, meaning it displays only those commands relevant to the item. For example, right-clicking on the Quick Access Toolbar will display the commands associated with using the Quick Access Toolbar only. You will use this method to move the Quick Access Toolbar.

① • **Point to the Quick Access Toolbar and right-click.**

Another Method

You also can click ⏷ at the end of the Quick Access toolbar to open the menu.

• **Click the Show Quick Access Toolbar below the Ribbon option.**

Your screen should be similar to Figure 7

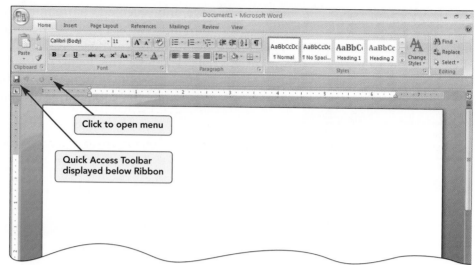

Click to open menu

Quick Access Toolbar displayed below Ribbon

Figure 7

The Quick Access Toolbar is now displayed full size below the Ribbon. This is useful if you have many buttons on the toolbar; however, it takes up document viewing space. You will return it to its compact size using the toolbar's drop-down menu.

② • **Click ⏷ on the right end of the Quick Access Toolbar.**

• **Choose Show Above the Ribbon.**

Your screen should be similar to Figure 8

Quick Access Toolbar displayed above Ribbon again

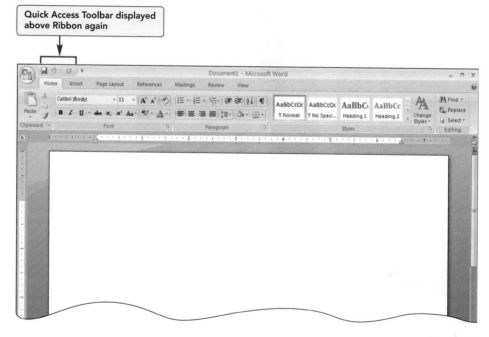

Figure 8

MORE ABOUT

▶ See the More About appendix to learn how to customize the Quick Access Toolbar.

The Quick Access Toolbar is displayed above the Ribbon again. The toolbar's drop-down menu contains a list of commands that are often added to the toolbar. Clicking on the command selects it and adds it to the toolbar.

Using the Ribbon

The Ribbon displays tabs that organize similar features into groups. In Word, there are seven tabs displayed. To save space, some tabs, called **contextual** or **on-demand tabs**, are displayed only as needed. For example, when you are working with a picture, the Picture Tools tab appears. The contextual nature of this feature keeps the work area uncluttered when the feature is not needed and provides ready access to it when it is needed.

Opening Tabs

The Home tab is open when you first start the application or open a file. It consists of five groups: Clipboard, Font, Paragraph, Styles, and Editing. Each group contains command buttons that when clicked on perform their associated action or display a list of additional commands. The commands in the Home tab help you perform actions related to creating the content of your document.

1 ● **Click on the Insert tab.**

Additional Information
The open tab appears highlighted.

Your screen should be similar to Figure 9

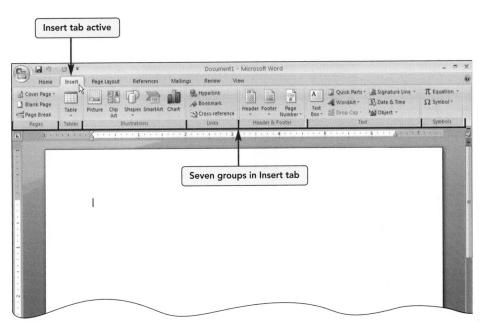

Figure 9

This Insert tab is now the active tab. It contains seven groups whose commands have to do with inserting items into a document.

2 ● **Click on each of the other tabs, ending with the View tab, to see their groups and commands.**

Your screen should be similar to Figure 10

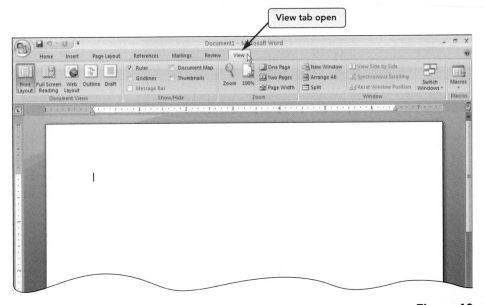

Figure 10

Each tab relates to a type of activity; for example, the View tab commands perform activities related to viewing the document. Within each tab, similar commands are grouped together to make finding the commands you want to use much easier.

Displaying Super Tooltips

Many command buttons immediately perform the associated action when you click on them. The buttons are graphic representations of the action they perform. To help you find out what a button does, you can display the button's ScreenTip.

1 ● Open the Home tab.

● Point to the upper part of the ⬚ button in the Clipboard group.

● Point to the lower part of the ⬚ button in the Clipboard group.

● Point to ⬚ Format Painter in the Clipboard group.

Your screen should be similar to Figure 11

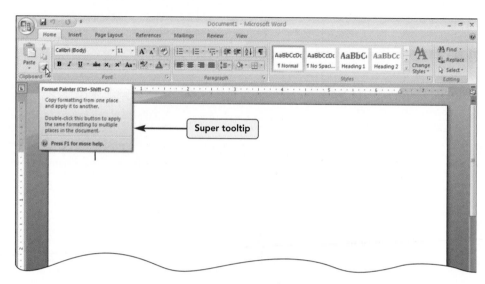

Super tooltip

Figure 11

> **Additional Information**
> Not all commands have shortcut keys.

> **Additional Information**
> You will learn about using Help shortly.

The ⬚ button is a **split button.** Both parts of the button display tooltips containing the button name, the shortcut key combination, Ctrl + V, and a brief description of what clicking the button does. Pointing to ⬚ Format Painter displays a **super tooltip** that provides more detailed information about the command. Super tooltips may even display information such as procedures or illustrations. You can find out what the feature does without having to look it up in Help. If a feature has a Help article, you can automatically access it by pressing F1 while the super tooltip is displayed.

Using Galleries and Lists

Many commands in the groups appear as a **gallery** that displays small graphics that represent the result of applying a command. For example, in the Styles group, the command buttons to apply different formatting styles to text display examples of how the text would look if formatted using that command. These are called **in-Ribbon galleries** because they appear directly in the Ribbon. Other commands include multiple options that appear in **drop-down galleries** or drop-down lists that are accessed by clicking the ⬚ in the split button. To see an example of a drop-down gallery, you will open the ⬚ Bullets drop-down gallery.

1 • Click ⬝ in the ⬝ Bullets button.

Your screen should be similar to Figure 12

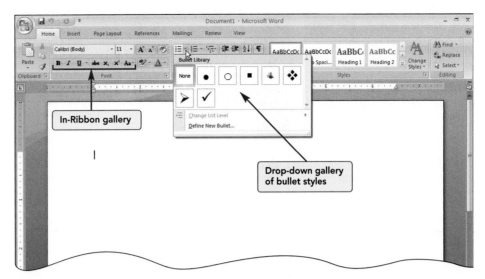

In-Ribbon gallery

Drop-down gallery of bullet styles

Figure 12

A drop-down gallery of different bullets is displayed. The drop-down gallery will disappear when you make a selection or click on any other area of the window. To see an example of a drop-down list, you will open the ⬝11 ⬝⬝ Font Size drop-down list.

2 • Click outside the Bullet gallery to clear it.

• Click ⬝ in the ⬝11 ⬝⬝ Font Size button.

Your screen should be similar to Figure 13

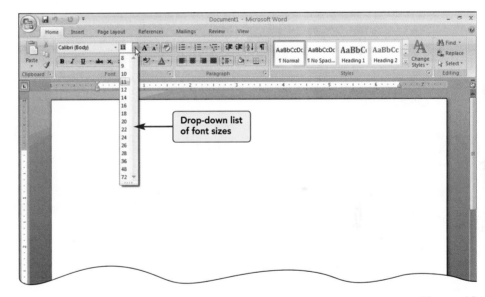

Drop-down list of font sizes

Figure 13

If you click on the button itself, not the ⬝ section of the button, the associated command is performed.

Using the Dialog Box Launcher

Because there is not enough space, only the most used commands are displayed in the Ribbon. If there are more commands available, a ⬝ button, called the **dialog box launcher**, is displayed in the lower-right corner of the group. Clicking ⬝ opens a dialog box or **task pane** of additional options.

1 • **Click outside the Font size list to clear it.**

• **Point to the ⬜ of the Paragraph group to see the tooltip.**

• **Click ⬜ of the Paragraph group.**

Your screen should be similar to Figure 14

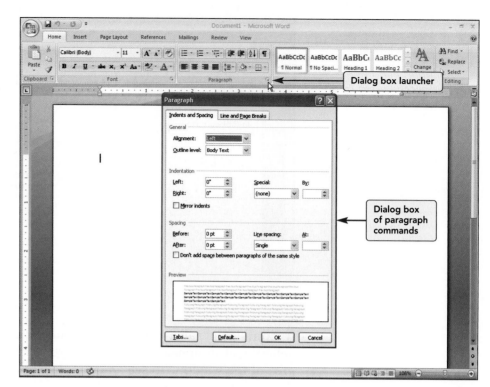

Figure 14

The Paragraph dialog box appears. It provides access to the more advanced paragraph settings features. Selecting options from the dialog box and clicking ⬚ OK ⬚ will close the dialog box and apply the settings as specified. To cancel the dialog box, you can click ⬚ Cancel ⬚ or ⬚✕⬚ in the dialog box title bar.

2 • **Click ⬚ Cancel ⬚ to close the dialog box.**

• **Click ⬜ in the Clipboard group.**

Your screen should be similar to Figure 15

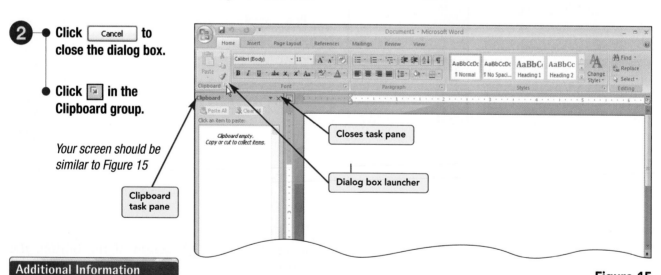

Figure 15

Additional Information
You will learn about using dialog boxes, task panes, and the Clipboard as they are used in the labs.

A task pane is open that contains features associated with the Clipboard. Unlike dialog boxes, task panes remain open until you close them. This allows you to make multiple selections from the task pane while continuing to work on other areas of your document.

3 • **Click ⬚✕⬚ in the upper-right corner of the task pane to close it.**

Using Access Key Shortcuts

Another way to use commands on the Ribbon is to display the access key shortcuts by pressing the [Alt] key and then typing the letter for the feature you want to use. Every Ribbon tab, group, and command has an access key.

1 ● Press [Alt].

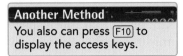
Your screen should be similar to Figure 16

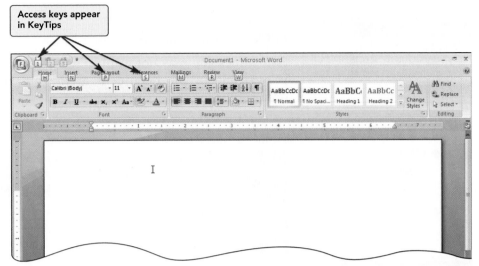

Access keys appear in KeyTips

Figure 16

The letters are displayed in **KeyTips** over each available feature. Now typing a letter will access that feature. Then, depending on which letter you pressed, additional KeyTips may appear. To use a Ribbon command, press the key of the tab first, then the group, and then continue pressing letters until you press the letter of the specific command you want to use. You will use KeyTips to display the Paragraph dialog box again.

2 ● Type the letter **H** to access the Home tab.

● Type the letters **PG** to access the Paragraph group and open the dialog box.

Your screen should be similar to Figure 17

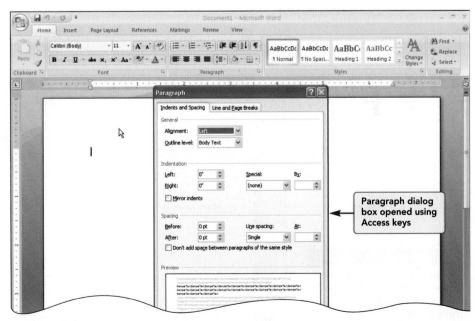

Paragraph dialog box opened using Access keys

Figure 17

Three keystrokes opened the Paragraph dialog box.

Once the Access key feature is on, you can also use the ← or → directional key to move from one tab to another, and the ↓ key to move from a tab to a group and the ↑ key to move from a group to a tab. You can use all four directional keys to move among the commands in a Ribbon. Tab↹ and ⇧Shift + Tab↹ also can be used to move right or left. Once a command is selected, you can press Spacebar or ←Enter to activate it.

Minimizing the Ribbon

Sometimes you may not want to see the entire Ribbon so that more space is available in the document area. You can minimize the Ribbon by double-clicking the active tab.

1 ● Click  to close the Paragraph dialog box.

● Double-click the Home tab.

Your screen should be similar to Figure 18

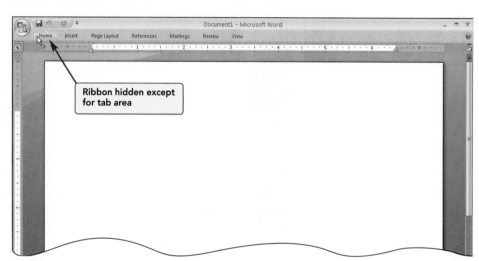

Ribbon hidden except for tab area

Figure 18

Now, the only part of the Ribbon that is visible is the tab area. This allows you to quickly reopen the Ribbon and, at the same time, open the selected tab.

2 ● Double-click the Insert tab.

Your screen should be similar to Figure 19

Ribbon redisplayed

Insert tab open

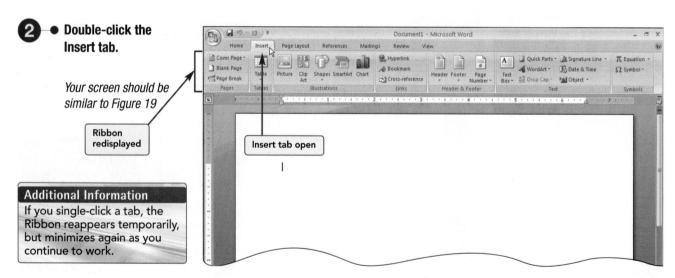

Figure 19

The full Ribbon reappears and the Insert tab is open and ready for use.

Using the Mini Toolbar

Another method of accessing commands is through the Mini toolbar. The **Mini toolbar** appears automatically when you select text in a document and provides commands that are used to format (enhance) text. It also appears along with the context menu when you right-click an item in a document. Both the Mini toolbar and context menus are designed to make it more efficient to execute commands.

You can see what these features look like by right-clicking in a blank area of the document window.

1 ● **Right-click the blank document window space.**

Your screen should be similar to Figure 20

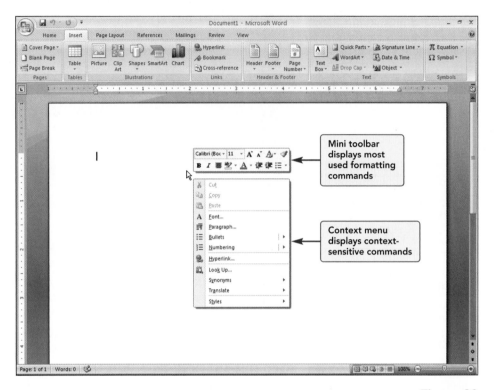

Figure 20

The Mini toolbar displays the most frequently used formatting commands. For example, when the Home tab is closed, you can use the commands in the Mini toolbar to quickly change selected text without having to reopen the Home tab to access the command. When the Mini toolbar appears automatically, it is faded so that it does not interfere with what you are doing, but changes to solid (as it is here) when you point at it.

The context menu below the Mini toolbar displays a variety of commands that are quicker to access than locating the command on the Ribbon. The commands that appear on this menu change depending on what you are doing at the time.

Using Office Help

Another Method

You also can press F1 to access Help.

Notice the ⓘ in the upper-right corner of the Ribbon. This button is used to access the Microsoft Help system. The Help button is always visible even when the Ribbon is hidden. Because you are using the Office Word 2007 application, Office Word Help will be accessed.

1 ● Click 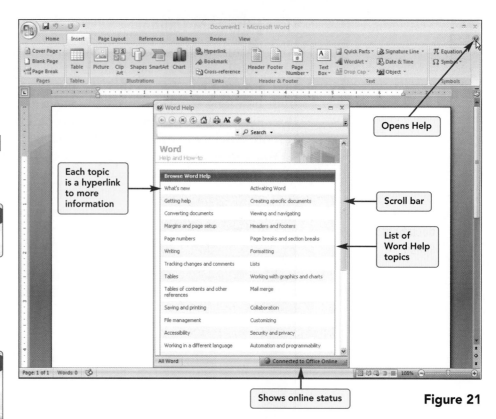 **Microsoft Office Word Help.**

● If a Table of Contents list is displayed along the left side of the Help window, click [📖] in the Help window toolbar to close it.

Additional Information

You will learn about using the Table of Contents shortly.

Your screen should be similar to Figure 21

Additional Information

Clicking the scroll arrows scrolls the text in the window line by line, and dragging the scroll bar up or down moves to a general location within the window area.

Additional Information

Because Help is an online feature, the information is frequently updated. Your screens may display slightly different information than those shown in the figures in this lab.

Having Trouble?

In addition to being connected to the Internet, the feature to show content from the Internet must be selected. If necessary, click the [🔘 Offline] button at the bottom of the Help window and choose Show content from Office Online.

Figure 21

The Microsoft Word Help feature is opened and displayed in a separate window. The Help window on your screen will probably be a different size and arrangement than in Figure 21. Depending on the size of your Help window, you may need to scroll the window to see all the Help information provided.

It displays a listing of Help topics. If you are connected to the Internet, the Microsoft Office Online Web site is accessed and help information from this site is displayed in the window. If you are not connected, the offline help information that is provided with the application and stored on your computer is located and displayed. Generally, the listing of topics is similar but fewer in number.

Selecting Help Topics

There are several ways you can get help. The first is to select a topic from the listing displayed in the Help window. Each topic is a **hyperlink** or connection to the information located on the Online site or in Help on your computer. When you point to the hyperlink, it appears underlined and the mouse pointer appears as 🖑. Clicking the hyperlink accesses and displays the information associated with the hyperlink.

1 • **Click "Getting help."**

Your screen should be similar to Figure 22

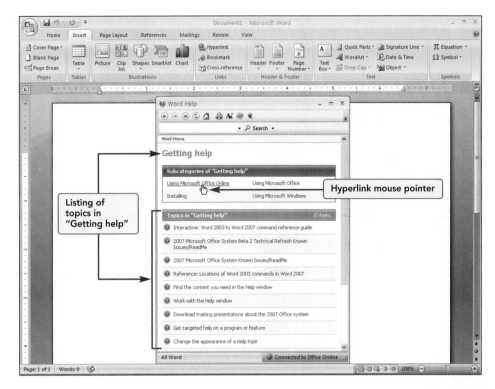

Figure 22

A listing of topics about getting help is displayed. You will get help on using Microsoft Office and the Ribbon.

2 • **Click "Using Microsoft Office."**

• **Click "Use the Ribbon."**

Your screen should be similar to Figure 23

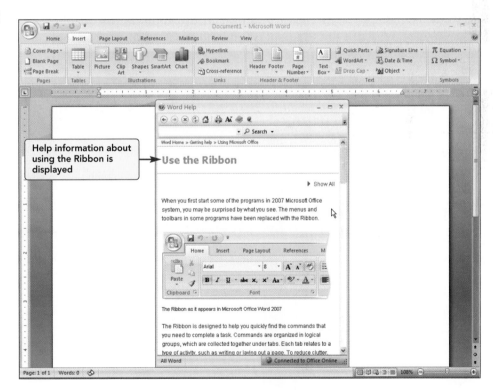

Figure 23

The information on the selected topic is displayed in the window.

3 ● Use the scroll bar to scroll the Help window to read the information about the Ribbon.

● Display the "In this article" section of the window.

Your screen should be similar to Figure 24

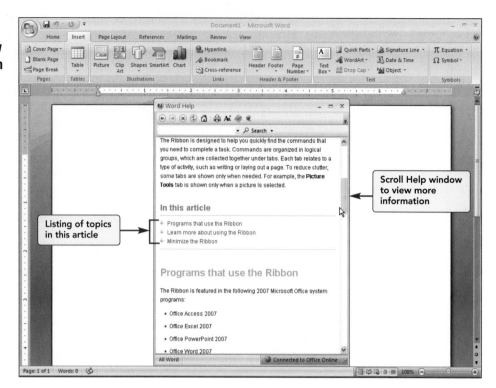

Figure 24

This area of the Help window provides a table of contents listing of the information in this window. Clicking on a link will take you directly to that location in the Help window. As you are reading the information in the window, you will see many topics preceded with ▶. This indicates the information in the topic is not displayed. Clicking on the topic heading displays the information about the topic.

4 ● Click "Learn more about using the Ribbon."

● Click "Microsoft Office Word 2007."

● If necessary, scroll the window to see all the information on this topic.

Your screen should be similar to Figure 25

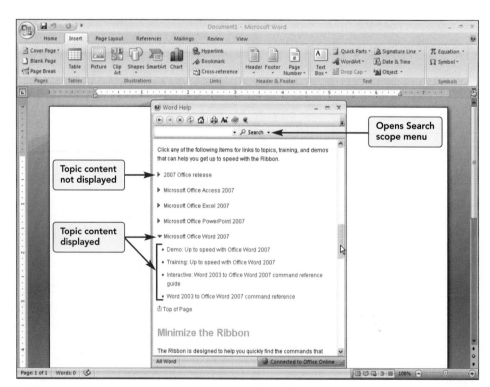

Figure 25

The information on the selected subtopic is displayed. Clicking the table of contents link jumped directly to this section of the window, saving you time by not having to scroll. The ▶ preceding the subtopic has changed to ▼, indicating the subtopic content is displayed.

You can continue to click on the subtopic headings to display the information about each topic individually. Likewise, clicking on an expanded topic hides the information. Additionally you can click ▶ Show All located at the top of the window to display all the available topic information and ▼ Hide All to hide all expanded information.

Additional Information

In Windows Vista, these buttons are ⊞ Show All and ⊟ Hide All .

Searching Help Topics

Another method to find Help information is to conduct a search by entering a sentence or question you want help on in the Search text box of the Help window. Although you also can simply enter a word in the Search box, the best results occur when you type a phrase, complete sentence, or question. A very specific search with 2–7 words will return the most accurate results.

When searching, you can specify the scope of the search by selecting from the Search scope drop-down menu. The broadest scope for a search, All Word, is preselected. You will narrow the scope to search Word Help only.

1 ● Open the 🔍 Search ▾ drop-down list.

● Click "Word Help."

● Click in the Search text box to display the insertion point.

● Type What is the Ribbon.

● Click 🔍 Search ▾ .

Additional Information

You also could press ←Enter to start the search.

Your screen should be similar to Figure 26

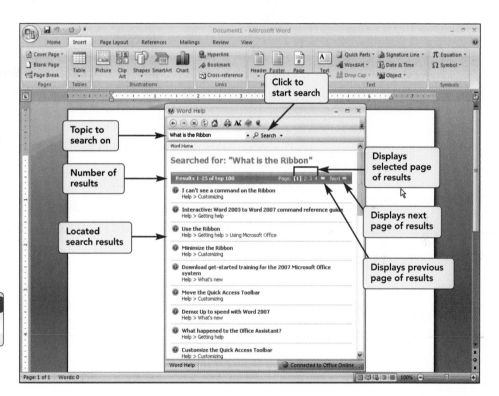

Figure 26

The first 25 located results of the top 100 are displayed in a window. There are four pages of results. The results are shown in order of relevance, with the most likely matches at the top of the list. Now you can continue to locate the information you need by selecting from the topic links provided. To see the next page of results, you can click ▐Next▌ or ▐■▌ or click the specific page number you want to see from the Page count area. To see the previous page of results, click ▐■▌ .

Topics preceded with 🔘 indicate the window will display the related Help topic. Those preceded with a 🔲 indicate a tutorial about the topic is available from the Microsoft Training Web site.

② ● Click "Use the Ribbon."

Your screen should be similar to Figure 27

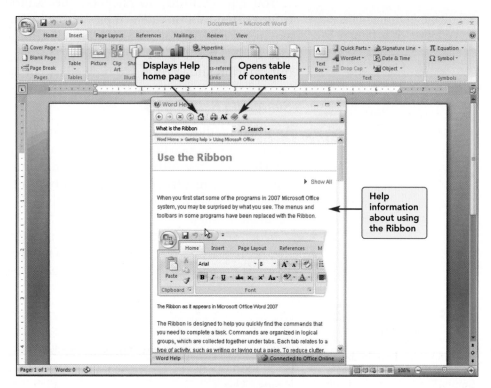

Figure 27

The same Help information you saw previously is displayed.

Using the Help Table of Contents

A third source of help is to use the Help table of contents. Using this method allows you to browse the entire list of Help topics to locate topics of interest to you.

1 ● **Click** 🏠 **Home in the Help window toolbar to return to the opening Help window.**

● **Click** 📖 **Show Table of Contents from the Help window toolbar.**

Additional Information

You also could click ⬅ Back in the Help window toolbar to return to the previous page, page by page.

Your screen should be similar to Figure 28

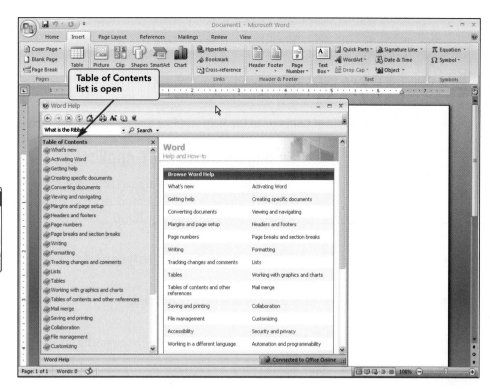

Figure 28

Additional Information

Pointing to an item in the Table of Contents displays a ScreenTip of the entire topic heading.

The entire Word Help Table of Contents is displayed in a pane on the left side of the Help window. Clicking on an item preceded with a 📖 Closed Book icon opens a chapter, which expands to display additional chapters or topics. The 📖 Open Book icon identifies those chapters that are open.

Clicking on an item preceded with 🔘 displays the specific Help information.

2 ● **Click "Getting help" to open this chapter.**

● **Click "Using Microsoft Office."**

● **Scroll the table of contents list and click "Use the Ribbon."**

Your screen should be similar to Figure 29

Opens chapter

Help topics

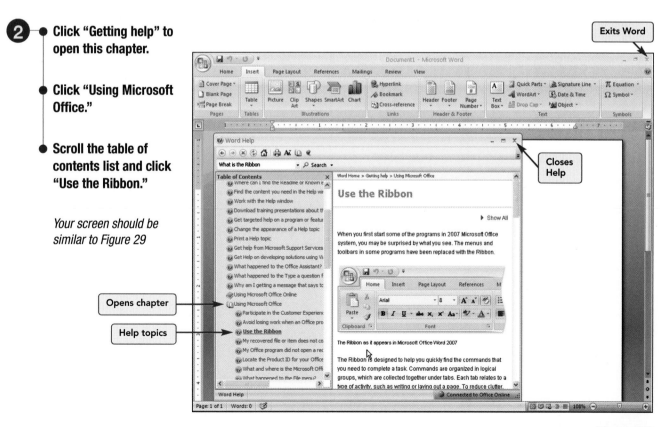

Exits Word

Closes Help

Figure 29

Common Office 2007 Interface Features

I.29

The right side of the Help window displays the same Help information about the Ribbon. To close a chapter, click the 🔲 icon.

3 • Click 🔲 to close the Using Microsoft Office chapter.

• Click 🔲 Hide Table of Contents in the Help window toolbar to hide the table of contents list again.

Exiting an Office 2007 Application

Now you are ready to close the Help window and exit the Word program. The ☒ Close button located on the right end of the window title bar can be used to exit most application windows.

1 • Click ☒ Close in the Help window title bar to close the Help window.

• Click ☒ Close in the Word window title bar to exit Word.

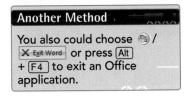

Another Method
You also could choose 🔘 / ☒ Exit Word or press Alt + F4 to exit an Office application.

The program window is closed and the desktop is visible again.

Lab Review

Introduction to Microsoft Office 2007

key terms

context menu I.15	in-Ribbon gallery I.18	selection cursor I.12
contextual tabs I.16	KeyTips I.21	split button I.18
dialog box launcher I.19	Mini toolbar I.23	status bar I.11
document window I.11	on-demand tab I.16	super tooltip I.18
drop-down gallery I.18	Quick Access Toolbar I.11	tab I.11
gallery I.18	Ribbon I.11	task pane I.19
group I.11	ScreenTip I.13	tooltip I.13
hyperlink I.24	scroll bar I.11	user interface I.10

command summary

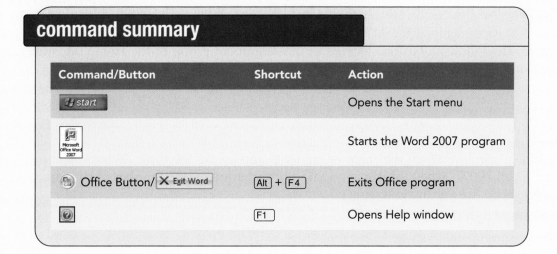

Command/Button	Shortcut	Action
start		Opens the Start menu
Microsoft Office Word 2007		Starts the Word 2007 program
Office Button/ ✕ E_xit Word	Alt + F4	Exits Office program
❔	F1	Opens Help window

Lab Exercises

rating system

★ Easy

★★ Moderate

★★★ Difficult

step-by-step

Using an Office Application ★

1. All Office 2007 applications have a common user interface. You will explore the Excel 2007 application and use many of the same features you learned about while using Word 2007 in this lab.

   a. Use the Start menu or a shortcut icon on your desktop to start Office Excel 2007.

   b. What shape is the mouse pointer when positioned in the document window area? _____

   c. Excel has _____ tabs. Which tabs are not the same as in Word?
   _____

   d. Open the Formulas tab. How many groups are in the Formulas tab? _____

   e. Which tab contains the group to work with charts? _____

   f. From the Home tab, click the Number group dialog box launcher. What is the name of the dialog box that opens? How many number categories are there? _____ Close the dialog box.

   g. Display tooltips for the following buttons located in the Alignment group of the Home tab and identify what action they perform.

   ⊟ _____

   ⊟ _____

   ⊟ _____

   h. Open the Excel Help window. Open the table of contents and locate the topic "What's new in Microsoft Office Excel 2007?" Open this topic and find information on the number of rows and columns in a worksheet. Answer the following questions:

   How many rows are in a worksheet? _____

   How many columns are in a worksheet? _____

   What are the letters of the last column? _____

   i. Close the table of contents. Close the Help window. Exit Excel.

on your own

Exploring Microsoft Help ★

1. In addition to the Help information you used in this lab, Office 2007 Online Help also includes many interactive tutorials. Selecting a Help topic that starts a tutorial will open the browser program on your computer. Both audio and written instructions are provided. You will use one of these tutorials to learn more about using Word 2007.

   Start Word 2007. Open Help and open the topic "What's New?" Click on the topic "Up to speed with Word 2007." Follow the directions in your browser to run the tutorial. When you are done, close the browser window, close Help, and exit Word 2007.

Add, Delete, and Modify Records

Using Access, it is also easy to add and delete records from the table. Once you locate a record, you can edit the contents of the fields to update the record or delete the record entirely from the table. You also can add new records to a table. When you enter a new record, it is automatically placed in the correct organizational location within the table.

Sort and Filter Records

The capability to arrange or sort records in the table according to different fields can provide more meaningful information. You can organize records by name, department, pay, class, or any other category you need at a particular time. Sorting the records in different ways can provide information to different departments for different purposes.

Additionally, you can isolate and display a subset of records by specifying filter criteria. The criteria specify which records to display based on data in selected fields.

Analyze Data

Using Access, you can analyze the data in a table and perform calculations on different fields of data. Instead of pulling each record from a filing cabinet, recording the piece of data you want to use, and then performing the calculation on the recorded data, you can simply have the database program perform the calculation on all the values in the specified field. Additionally, you can ask questions or query the table to find only certain records that meet specific conditions to be used in the analysis. Information that was once costly and time-consuming to get is now quickly and readily available.

Generate Reports

Access includes many features that help you quickly produce reports ranging from simple listings to complex, professional-looking reports. You can create a simple report by asking for a listing of specified fields of data and restricting the listing to records meeting designated conditions. You can create a more complex professional report using the same restrictions or conditions as the simple report, but you can display the data in different layout styles, or with titles, headings, subtotals, or totals.

Case Study for Office Access 2007 Labs

You have recently accepted a job as employment administrator for Lifestyle Fitness Club. The club has recently purchased Microsoft Access 2007, and you are using it to update their manual system for recording employee information.

Lab 1: You will learn how to design and create the structure for a computerized database and how to enter and edit records in the database. You also will print a simple report of the records you enter in the database file.

Lab 2: You will continue to build, modify, and use the employee database of records. You will learn how to sort the records in a database file to make it easier to locate records. You also will learn about filtering a table to display only the information you need. Additionally, you will create a form to make it easier to enter and edit data in the database file.

Lab 3: You will learn how to query the database to locate specific information. You also will learn how to create a report and link multiple tables.

Working Together: You will learn how to share information between applications by incorporating database information from Access into a Word memo.

Before You Begin

To the Student

The following assumptions have been made:

- Microsoft Access 2007 has been properly installed on your computer system.

- The data files needed to complete the series of labs and practice exercises are supplied by your instructor. These may be supplied by your instructor and are also available at the online learning center Web site found at www.mhhe.com/oleary.

- You are already familiar with how to use Microsoft Windows XP or Vista and a mouse.

To the Instructor

A complete installation of Microsoft Office 2007 is required in which all components are available to students while completing the labs. In several labs, an online connection to the Web is needed to fully access a feature.

Please be aware that the following settings are assumed to be in effect for the Office Access 2007 program. These assumptions are necessary so that the screens and directions in the labs are accurate. These settings are made using ⊞ Office Button/ 🔲 Access Options in the categories shown below.

Popular

- Always use ClearType is on.
- Show feature descriptions in ScreenTips is on.
- Show shortcut keys in ScreenTips is on.
- The Default file format is Access 2007.
- Default database folder is My Documents.
- New database sort order is General.

Current Database/Application Options

- Display Status Bar is on.
- Tabbed Documents is on.

- Display Document Tabs is on.
- Use Access Special Keys is on.
- Use Windows-themed Controls on Forms is on.
- Enable Layout View for this database is on.
- Enable design changes for tables in Datasheet view is on.
- Check for truncated number fields is on.
- Preserve source image format is on.

Current Database/Navigation

- Display Navigation Pane is on.
- Open objects with double-click is on.

Current Database/Ribbon and Toolbar Options

- Allow Full Menus is on.
- Allow Default Shortcut Menus is on.

Current Database/Name AutoCorrect Options

- Track name AutoCorrect info is on.
- Perform name AutoCorrect is on.

Datasheet/Default Colors

- All default colors are set to Automatic.

Datasheet/Gridlines and cell effects

- Default gridlines showing Horizontal and Vertical are on.
- Default cell effect is flat.
- Default column width is 1 inch.

Datasheet/Default font

- Font is Calibri.
- Font size is 11.
- Weight is Normal.

Object Designers/Table design

- Default field type is Text.
- Default text field size is 255.
- Default number field size is Long Integer.
- Show Property Update Options is on.

Object Designers/Query design

- Show table names is on.
- Enable AutoJoin is on.
- Query design font is Segoe UI with a point size of 8.

Object Designers/Forms/Reports

- Selection behavior is partially enclosed.
- Form and Report templates are Normal.

Object Designers/Error Checking

- All error checking options are on.
- Error indicator color is green.

Proofing

- All AutoCorrect options are on.
- Ignore words in Uppercase is on.
- Ignore words that contain numbers is on.
- Ignore Internet and file addresses is on.
- Flag repeated words is on.

Advanced/Editing

- Move after enter: Next field.
- Behavior entering field: Select entire field.
- Arrow key behavior: Next field.
- Default find/replace behavior: Fast search.
- All Confrim options are on.
- Default direction: Left-to-right.
- General Alignment: Interface mode.
- Cursor Movement: Logical.

Advanced/Display

- Show 9 recent documents.
- Display Status bar.
- Show animations is on.
- Show SmartTags on datasheets is on.
- Show SmartTags on forms and reports is on.

Advanced/Printing

- All margins are set to 0.25 inch.

Advanced/General

- No options are on.

Advanced/Advanced

- Default open mode is Shared.
- Default record locking is No locks.
- Open databases by using record-level locking is on.

Customize

- The Quick Access Toolbar displays the Save, Undo, and Redo buttons.
- Finally, the feature to access Online Help is on. (From the Help window, open the Connection Status menu and choose Show Content from Office Online.)

All figures in the text reflect the use of a display screen set at 1024 by 768 and the Windows XP operating system. If other monitor display settings are used, there may be more or fewer lines of information displayed in the windows than in the figures. If the Windows Vista operating system is used, some features may look slightly different.

Instructional Conventions

Hands-on instructions you are to perform appear as a sequence of numbered steps. Within each step, a series of bullets identifies the specific actions that must be performed. Step numbering begins over within each topic heading throughout the lab. Four types of marginal notes appear throughout the labs. Another Method notes provide alternate ways of performing the same command. Having Trouble? notes provide advice or cautions for steps that may cause problems. Additional Information notes provide more information about a topic. More About notes refer you to the More About appendix for additional information about related features.

Commands

Commands that are initiated using a command button and the mouse appear following the word "Click." The icon (and the icon name if the icon does not include text) is displayed following "Click." If there is another way to perform the same action, it appears in an Another Method margin note when the action is first introduced as shown in Example A.

When a feature has already been covered and you are more familiar with using the application, commands will appear as shown in Example B.

Example A

1 ● Open the Home tab.

● Open the View drop-down list in the Views group.

● Choose Datasheet view.

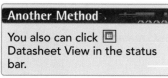

Another Method

You also can click 📧 Datasheet View in the status bar.

Example B

1─● Click 🖾 **Datasheet View.**

OR

1─● **Change the view to Datasheet View.**

File Names and Information to Type

Plain blue text identifies file names you need to select or enter. Information you are asked to type appears in blue and bold. (See Example C.)

Example C

1─● **Open the database file** ac02_Employees.

   ● **Type 9/23/01 in the Hire Date field.**

 Office Button Menu

Clicking 🖾 Office Button opens the File menu of commands. File menu commands that you are to perform appear following the word "Choose." Items that need to be selected will follow the word "Select" and will appear in black text. You can select items with the mouse or directional keys. Initially these commands will appears as in Example A. As you become more familiar with the application, commands will appear as shown in Example B.

Example A

1─● Click 🖾 **Office Button.**

   ● **Choose Open.**

   ● **Select My Documents from the Look In drop-down menu.**

   ● **Select** ac02_Employees.

   ● **Click** [Open].

Example B

1 ● **Choose** 🔘 **Office Button/Open.**

● **Choose** ac02_Employees.

OR

1 ● **Open the file** ac02_Employees.

Creating a Database

LAB 1

Objectives

After completing this lab, you will know how to:

1 Plan, create, and modify a database.

2 Create and save a table structure.

3 Define field names, data types, field properties, and primary key fields.

4 Enter and edit data.

5 Add attachments.

6 Change views.

7 Adjust column widths.

8 Use the Best Fit feature.

9 Create a second table.

10 Create a Lookup field.

11 Delete records.

12 Preview and print a table.

13 Change page orientation.

14 Close and open a table and database.

Case Study

Lifestyle Fitness Club

You have recently accepted a job as a human resources administrator with Lifestyle Fitness Club. Like many fitness centers, Lifestyle Fitness Club includes exercise equipment, free weights, aerobics classes, tanning and massage facilities, swimming pool, steam room and sauna, and child-care facilities. In addition, it promotes a healthy lifestyle by including educational seminars on good nutrition and proper exercise. It also has a small snack bar that serves healthy drinks, sandwiches, and snacks.

The Lifestyle Fitness Clubs are a franchised chain of clubs that are individually owned. You work at a club owned by Felicity and Ryan Albright, who also own two others in California. Accounting and employment functions for all three clubs are handled centrally at the Landis location.

You are responsible for maintaining the employment records for all employees, as well as records for traditional employment activities such as hiring and benefits. Currently the club employment records are maintained on paper forms and are stored in file cabinets organized alphabetically by last name. Although the information is well organized, it still takes time to manually look through the folders to locate the information you need and to compile reports from this data.

The Club has recently purchased new computers, and the owners want to update the employee record-keeping system to an electronic database management system. The software tool you will use to create the database is the database application Office Access 2007. In this lab, you will learn about entering, editing, previewing, and printing information in the database you create for the Club.

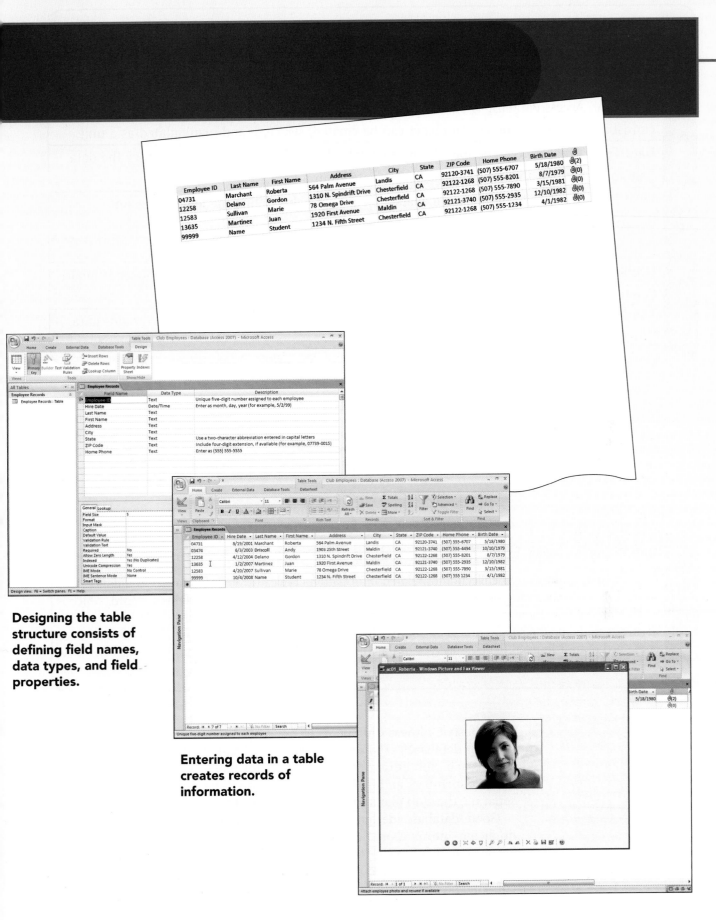

Designing the table structure consists of defining field names, data types, and field properties.

Entering data in a table creates records of information.

Fields can contain attachments, such as pictures or files.

Concept Preview

The following concepts will be introduced in this lab:

1 **Database** A database is an organized collection of related information.

2 **Object** An Access database is made up of several types of objects, such as a table or report, consisting of many elements. An object can be created, selected, and manipulated as a unit.

3 **Data Type** The data type defines the type of data the field will contain. Access uses the data type to ensure that the right kind of data is entered in a field.

4 **Field Property** A field property is a characteristic that helps define the appearance and behavior of a field.

5 **Primary Key** A primary key is a field that uniquely identifies each record.

6 **LookUp Field** A lookup field provides a list of values from which the user can choose to make entering data into that field simpler and more accurate.

7 **Subdatasheet** A subdatasheet is a data table nested in another data table that contains data related or joined to the table where it resides.

Designing a New Database

The Lifestyle Fitness Club recently purchased the 2007 Microsoft Office System software suite. You are very excited about learning to use the Access 2007 database management system to store and maintain the club's records.

Concept 1

Database

1 A **database** is an organized collection of related information. Typically, the information in a database is stored in a **table** consisting of vertical columns and horizontal rows. Each row contains a **record**, which is all the information about one person, thing, or place. Each column is a **field**, which is the smallest unit of information about a record. Access databases can contain multiple tables that can be linked to produce combined output from all tables. This type of database is called a **relational database**. See the "Overview of Microsoft Office Access 2007" for more information about relational databases.

The Lifestyle Fitness Club plans to use Access to maintain several different types of databases. The database you will create will contain information about each club employee. Other plans for using Access include keeping track of members and inventory. To keep the different types of information separate, the club plans to create a database for each group.

Good database design follows two basic principles: do not include duplicate information (also called redundant data) in tables and enter accurate and complete information. Redundant data wastes space, wastes the time that is required to enter the same information multiple times, and consequently increases the possibility of errors and inconsistencies between tables. The information that is stored in a database may be used to make business decisions and if the information is inaccurate, any decisions that are based on the information would be misinformed.

To attain these principles, the database design process is very important and consists of the following steps: plan, design, develop, implement, and refine and review. You will find that you will generally follow these steps in order as you create your database. However, you will probably retrace steps as the final database is developed.

Step	Description
Plan	The first step in the development of a database is to define the purpose of the database in writing. This includes establishing the scope of the database, determining its feasibility, and deciding how you expect to use it and who will use it.
Design	Using the information gathered during the planning step, you can create an implementation plan and document the functional requirements. This includes finding and organizing the information required for the database and deciding how this information should be divided into subject groups. You also need to think about the types of questions you might want the database to answer and determine the types of output you need such as reports and mailings.
Develop	Using the design you created, you are ready to create tables to hold the necessary data. Create separate tables for each of the major subjects to make it easier to locate and modify information. Define fields for each item that you want to store in each table. Determine how each table is related to another and include fields to clarify the relationships as needed. Try not to duplicate information in the different tables.
Implement	After setting up the tables, populate the tables by entering sample data to complete each record. Then work with the data to make sure it is providing the information you need.
Refine and Review	Refine the design by adding or removing fields and tables and continue to test the data and design. Apply the data normalization rules to see if the tables are structured correctly. Periodically review the database to ensure that the initial objectives have been met and to identify required enhancements.

As you develop the employee database for the Lifestyle Fitness Club, you will learn more about the details of the design steps and how to use Access 2007 to create a well-designed and accurate database.

Planning the Club Database

Your first step is to plan the design of your database tables: the number of tables, the data they will contain, and the relationship of the tables. You need to decide what information each table in the employee database should contain and how it should be structured or laid out.

You can obtain this information by analyzing the current record-keeping procedures used in the company. You need to understand the existing procedures so that your database tables will reflect the information that is maintained by different departments. You should be aware of the forms that are the basis for the data entered into the department records and of the information that is taken from the records to produce periodic reports. You also need to determine the information that the department heads would like to be able to obtain from the database that may be too difficult to generate with current procedures.

After looking over the existing record-keeping procedures and the reports that are created from the information, you decide to create several separate tables of data in the database file. Each table should only contain information about the subject of the table. Additionally, try not to duplicate information in different tables. If this occurs, create a separate table for this information. Creating several smaller tables of related data rather than one large table makes it easier to use the tables and faster to process data. This is because you can join several tables together as needed.

The main table will include the employee's basic information, such as employee number, name, birth date, and address. Another will contain the employee's job title and work location only. A third will contain data on pay rate and hours worked each week. To clarify the organization of the database, you sketched the structure for the employee database as shown below.

Club Records Database

Employee Records Table

Emp #	Last Name	First Name	Street	City	State	Zipcode	Phone	Birth Date
7721	Brown	Linda	——	——	——	——	——	——
7823	Duggan	Michael	——	——	——	——	——	——

link on common field

link on common field

Clubs Table

Emp #	Location	Position
7721	Iona	Greeter
7823	Fort Myers	Server

Pay Table

Emp #	Pay	Hours
7721	8.25	30
7823	7.50	20

Creating and Naming the Database File

Now that you have decided on the information you want to include in the tables, you are ready to create a new database for the employee information using the Microsoft Office Access 2007 database management program.

Having Trouble?

See "Introduction to 2007 Microsoft Office System" for information about starting the application and for a discussion of features that are common to all Office 2007 applications.

Your screen should be similar to Figure 1.1

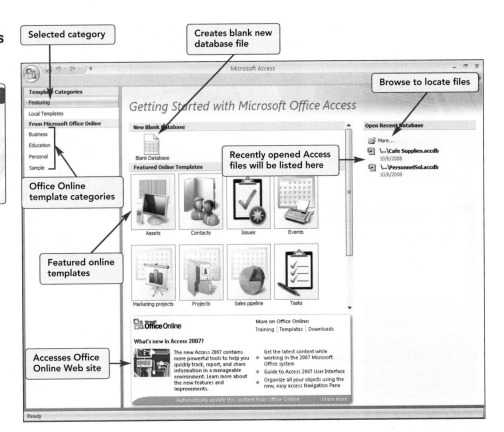

Figure 1.1

The Getting Started with Microsoft Office Access page is displayed. It is divided into several areas that provide a starting point for working with Access. It can be used to create a new database, open an existing database file, or access the Microsoft Office Online Web site. You want to create a new database.

Several methods can be used to create a new database. One method is to use one of the many templates that are provided by Microsoft as the basis for your new database. A **template** is a ready-to-use database that includes the data structure for the selected type of database. Another method is to start with a blank database that contains the basic database objects and then add your own content. A third is to copy or import data from another source into an Access database file. Finally, you can use a custom template that you created and saved as the basis for your new database.

Using the Getting Started with Microsoft Office Access page, you can create a new database by selecting a template design. The left side of the page displays the template categories. Currently, the Featuring category is selected and displays graphics of the featured templates in the middle of the page. Clicking on a different category in the list displays templates associated with that category. Although using a template is sometimes the fastest way to create a database, it often requires a lot of work to adapt the template to suit the needs of the existing data.

The Featuring category also provides access to the Blank Database template that includes the basic structure for a database file, but does not include a data structure that is specific to a type of database. You decide to create the club database from a blank database file.

2 ● Click in the New Blank Database section of the Getting Started window.

Your screen should be similar to Figure 1.2

Additional Information

Depending on your Windows settings, your screens may not display file extensions.

Additional Information

Windows files can have up to 255 characters in the file name. Names can contain letters, numbers, and spaces; the symbols \, /, ?, :, *, ", <, and > cannot be used. The file name can be entered in either uppercase or lowercase letters and will appear exactly as you type it.

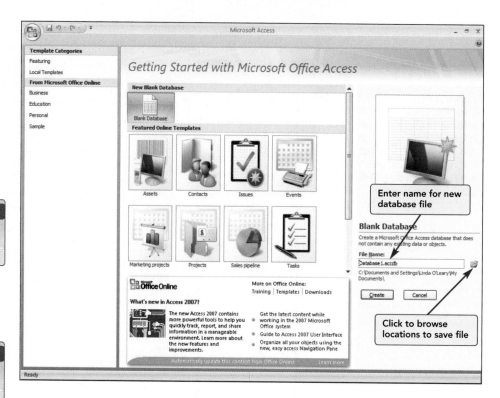

Figure 1.2

In the Blank Database section of the page, you need to enter a file name and specify the location on your computer where you want it saved. The File Name box displays Database1.accdb, the default database file name. The file extension .accdb identifies the file as an Access 2007 database.

3 ● Replace the text in the File Name text box with **Club Employees**.

Having Trouble?

If the default file name is not highlighted, triple-click on it to select the entire file name.

Additional Information

You do not need to type the file extension as Access will add it automatically for you.

● Click to browse locations.

Your screen should be similar to Figure 1.3

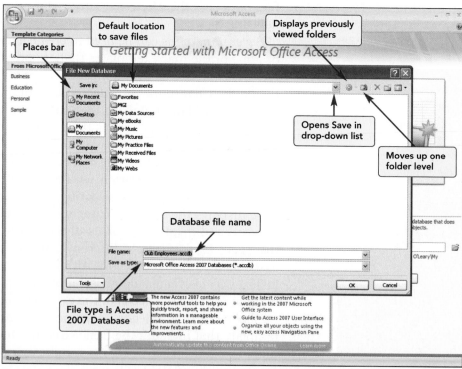

Figure 1.3

Having Trouble?
The default location, folders, and files displayed on your screen may be different from those shown here.

Having Trouble?
If you are using Windows Vista, the buttons in your dialog box will be different than those shown here.

More About

▶ To learn how to save an Access database in another format, see "6 Managing and Maintaining Databases" in the More About appendix.

In the File New Database dialog box, you need to select the location where you want the database file saved. The Save in drop-down list box displays the default folder, My Documents, as the location where the file will be saved. You can use this drop-down list to specify another location. You also can select the location to save from the Places bar along the left side of the dialog box. The icons bring up a list of recently accessed files and folders (History), the contents of the My Documents and Favorites folders, items on the Windows desktop, and the locations on a network. You also can click the 🔘 Back button in the toolbar to return to folders that were previously opened and 🔳 Up One Level to move up a level in the folder hierarchy.

The file list section of the dialog box displays the names of folders and database files in the default location. Only Access 2007 database (.accdb) file names are displayed because this is the selected file type in the Save As Type text box. In addition to the .accdb file type, Access database files also can be saved in several different file formats that have different file extensions. The file type you select determines the file extension that will be automatically added to the file name when the file is saved. The new file name you specified appears in the File Name text box.

4 ● Open the Save in drop-down list.

● Select the appropriate drive and folder where you will save your database files (check with your instructor if you are not sure).

● Click [OK].

● Click [Create].

Your screen should be similar to Figure 1.4

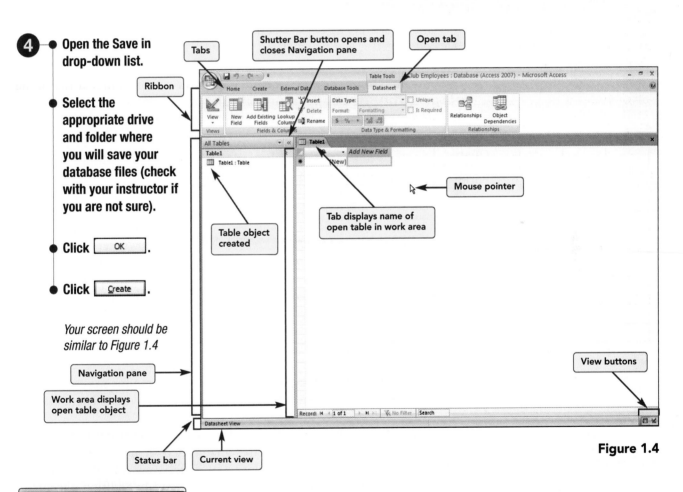

Figure 1.4

Having Trouble?
If your screen looks slightly different, this is because Access remembers settings that were on when the program was last used.

The blank database file is opened in the Access application window. The name of the database, Club Employees, followed by the application name appears in the window title bar.

Exploring the Access Window

The Access 2007 Ribbon, located below the title bar, currently consists of five tabs. These tabs contain the commands and features you will use to create and modify a database. Most tabs appear automatically as you perform different tasks and open different windows. The Table Tools Datasheet tab is open and contains buttons that are used to access basic database features.

The mouse pointer appears as $\mathbb{\hat{k}}$ on your screen. The mouse pointer changes shape depending upon the task you are performing or where the pointer is located in the window.

The large area below the Ribbon is the work area where different Access components are displayed as you are using the program. When the new database file is created, it includes one empty table named Table1. A table is one of several different database components or objects that can be included in the database file.

Concept 2

Object

2   An Access database is made up of several types of objects, such as a table or report, consisting of many elements. An **object** can be created, selected, and manipulated as a unit. The basic database objects are described below.

Object	Use
Table	Store data
Query	Find and display selected data
Form	View, add, and update data in tables
Report	Analyze and print data in a specific layout

The table object is the basic unit of a database and must be created first, before any other types of objects are created. Access displays each different type of object in its own window. You can open multiple objects from the same database file in the work area; however, you cannot open more than one database file at a time in a single instance of Access. To open a second database file, you need to start another instance of Access and open the database file in it.

The work area displays a tab containing the table name for the open table. It is used to switch between open objects in the work area. There is only one tab because only one object is open.

Just below the work area, the status bar provides information about the task you are working on and about the current Access operation. Currently, the left end of the status bar displays Datasheet view and the right end displays two buttons that are used to change the view. In addition, the status bar displays messages such as instructions to help you use the program more efficiently.

Using the Navigation Pane

The **Navigation pane** along the left edge of the work area displays all the objects in the database and is used to open and manage the objects. Because your database only contains one object, Table1, it is the only object listed in the pane. When there are many different objects, the pane organizes the objects into categories and groups within each category. It is used to quickly access the different objects.

The Navigation pane is always displayed, but can be collapsed to a bar to provide more space in the work area. The Shutter Bar close button « , located in the upper-right corner of the pane, is used to show or hide the pane.

---

1 ● Click « to close the Navigation pane.

Your screen should be similar to Figure 1.5

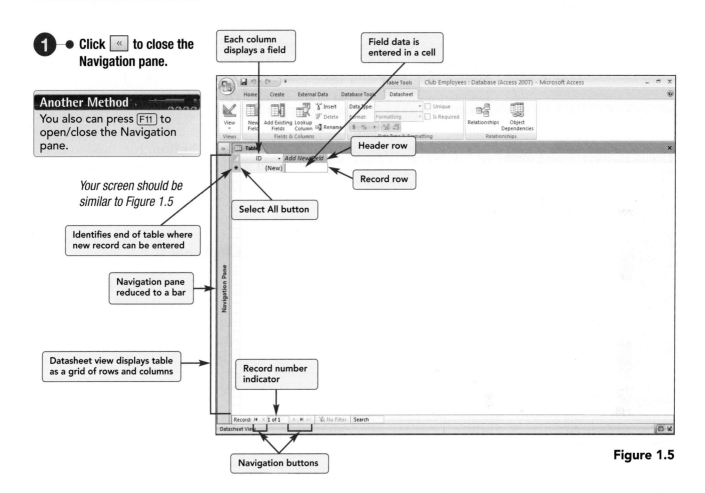

Figure 1.5

The Navigation pane is reduced to a bar along the left side of the window and the work area expands to fill the space. The pane can be easily displayed again by clicking » . You will learn more about using the Navigation pane throughout the labs.

Using Datasheet View

In anticipation of your entering information in the table, Access displays the blank table in Datasheet view, one of several different window formats, called **views,** that are used to display and work with the objects in a database. Each view includes its own Ribbon tab that includes commands that are designed to work with the object in that view. The available views change according to the type of object you are using. The basic views are described in the following table.

View	Purpose
Datasheet view	Provides a row-and-column view of the data in tables or query results.
Form view	Displays the records in a form.
Report view	Displays the table data in a report layout.
Design view	Used to create a table, form, query, or report. Displays the underlying design structure, not the data.
Layout view	Displays the object's data while in the process of designing the object.
Print Preview	Displays a form, report, table, or query as it will appear when printed.

Datasheet view is a visual representation of the data that is contained in a database table. It consists of a grid of rows and columns that is used to display each field of a table in a column and each record in a row. The field names are displayed in the **header row** at the top of the datasheet.

Below the header row is a blank row. The intersection of the row and column creates a **cell** where you will enter the data for the record. The square to the left of each row is the **Select All button.** It is used to select an entire record and appears colored to identify the **current record,** the record containing the insertion point and that will be affected by your next action. The * in the Select All button identifies the end of the table or where a new record can be entered.

The bottom of the work area displays a record number indicator and navigation buttons. The **record number indicator** shows the number of the current record as well as the total number of records in the table. Because the table does not yet contain records, the indicator displays "Record: 1 of 1" in anticipation of your first entry. On both sides of the record number are the **navigation buttons,** which are used to move through records with a mouse. In addition, two buttons that are used to filter and search for data in a table are displayed. You will learn about using all these features throughout the text.

Defining Fields

Now you are ready to begin defining the fields for the table. You have already decided that the main table in this database will include the employee's basic information such as employee number, name, birth date, and address. Next, you need to determine what information you want to appear in each column (field) about the subject recorded in the table. For example, you know you want to include the employee's name. However, should the entire name be in a single column or should it appear as two separate columns: first name and last name? Because you may want to sort or search for information based on the employee's name, it is better to store the information in separate columns. Similarly, the address actually consists of four separate parts—address, city, state, and zip code—and it also makes sense to store them in separate columns.

Generally when deciding how to store the information about a subject in a table, break down the information into its smallest logical parts. If you combine more than one kind of information in a field, it is difficult to retrieve individual facts later.

A second factor that should be considered when adding fields to a table is to store only raw data, not the result of calculations, in the table. This is because you can have Access quickly perform the calculations when you want to see the result. This saves both time and space.

After looking at the information currently maintained in the personnel folder on each employee, you have decided to include the following fields in the table: Employee #, Hire Date, Last Name, First Name, Address, City, State, Zip, Home Phone, Birth Date, and Photo. The data for the first employee record you will enter is shown below.

Field Name	Data
Employee #	04731
Hire Date	August 19, 2001
Last Name	Marchant
First Name	Roberta
Address	564 Palm Avenue
City	Landis
State	CA
Zip	92120–3741
Home Phone	(507) 555–6707
Birth Date	May 18, 1980
Photo	Roberta.jpg

Entering Data

Notice that the first field in the table, ID, is already defined. This field is automatically included in each table when it is created. It automatically assigns a number to each record as it is added to a table and is useful for maintaining record order. The second column header displays Add New Field and is used to define a new field in the table.

In Datasheet view, you can enter data for a record and create a new field at the same time. The first field of data you will enter is the employee number, which is assigned to each employee when hired. Each new employee is given the next consecutive number, so that no two employees can have the same number. It is a maximum of five digits.

When you enter data in a record, it should be entered accurately and consistently. The data you enter in a field should be typed exactly as you want it to appear. This is important because any printouts of the data will display the information exactly as entered. It is also important to enter data in a consistent form. For example, if you decide to abbreviate the word "Avenue" as "Ave." in the Address field, then it should be abbreviated the same way in every record where it appears. Also be careful not to enter a blank space before or after a field entry. This can cause problems when using the table to locate information.

As you type, the insertion point shows your location in the entry. If you make a typing error, use the (Backspace) key to delete the characters back to the error and retype the entry.

1 • **Click in the blank cell below the Add New Field column header.**

• **Type 04731.**

• **Press ⏎Enter.**

Your screen should be similar to Figure 1.6

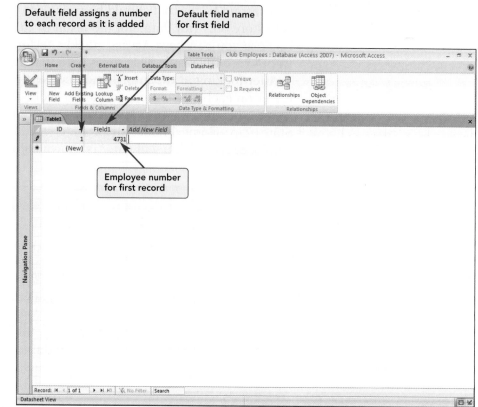

Default field assigns a number to each record as it is added

Default field name for first field

Employee number for first record

Figure 1.6

The employee number for the first record is entered in the table and Access is ready for you to enter the data for the next field. However, the number does not display the leading zero. You will learn the reason for this and how to correct it shortly.

The new field has been assigned the default field name of Field1. Also notice that the ID field displays the number 1 for the first record entered in the table.

Changing Field Names

Before entering more data, you want to replace the default field name with a more descriptive field name. A **field name** is used to identify the data stored in the field. A field name should describe the contents of the data to be entered in the field. It can be up to 64 characters long and can consist of letters, numbers, spaces, and special characters, except a period, an exclamation point, an accent grave (`), and brackets ([]). You also cannot start a field name with a space. It is best to use short field names to make the tables easier to manage.

1 ● Double-click on the Field1 column header.

● Type **Employee #** (be sure to include a space before the #).

Another Method
You also can choose Rename Column from the column header's shortcut menu.

Additional Information
The field name can be typed in uppercase or lowercase letters. It will be displayed in your database table exactly as you enter it.

Your screen should be similar to Figure 1.7

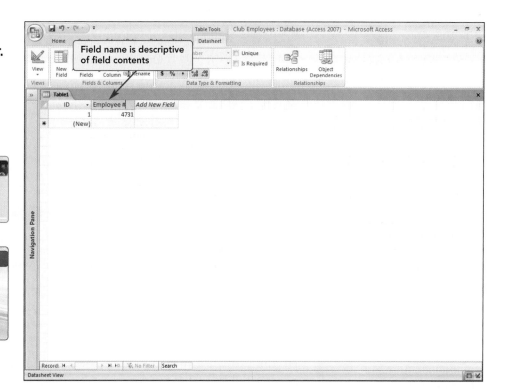

Figure 1.7

The highlighted text is deleted and replaced by the new field name you typed. You realize that "Employee ID" is the more common term used on company forms, so you decide to use this as the field name instead.

Editing Entries

As you enter text, you are bound to make typing errors that need to be corrected. Other types of changes you may want to make are to edit or update information. In this case, you want to edit the field name entry you are currently working on. When editing, you need to position the insertion point in the entry at the location where you want to make the change. To position the insertion point using the mouse, simply click at the location where you want it to appear.

Additionally, the keyboard keys shown in the table below also can be used to move the insertion point in an entry.

Key	Movement
→	One character to right
←	One character to left
↑	Up to current field in previous record
↓	Down to next line
Ctrl + →	One word to right
Ctrl + ←	One word to left
Home	Beginning of field in single-line field
End	End of field in single-line field
Ctrl + Home	Beginning of field in multiple-line field
Ctrl + End	End of field in multiple-line field

Additional Information

You can use the directional keys on the numeric keypad or on the dedicated directional keypad area. If using the numeric keypad, make sure the Num Lock feature is off; otherwise, numbers will be entered in the document. The Num Lock indicator light above the keypad is lit when on. Press Num Lock to turn it off.

Additional Information

These same key and mouse movement procedures can be used in all Access views.

Holding down a directional key or key combination moves the insertion point quickly in the direction indicated, saving multiple presses of the key. Many of the insertion point movement keys can be held down to execute multiple moves.

Depending on what you are doing, one method may be more efficient than another. For example, if your hands are already on the keyboard as you are typing, it may be quicker to use the keyboard rather than take your hands off to use the mouse.

Once the insertion point is in the correct position, you can use the Backspace or Delete key to remove text. The Backspace key removes a character or space to the left of the insertion point. The Delete key removes the character or space to the right of the insertion point.

In this case, the insertion point is already in the correct position and you just need to delete the character to the left of it.

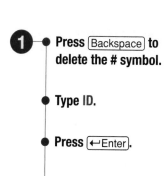

1 ● **Press** Backspace **to delete the # symbol.**

● **Type** ID.

● **Press** ←Enter.

● **Click in the cell containing the Employee ID number.**

Your screen should be similar to Figure 1.8

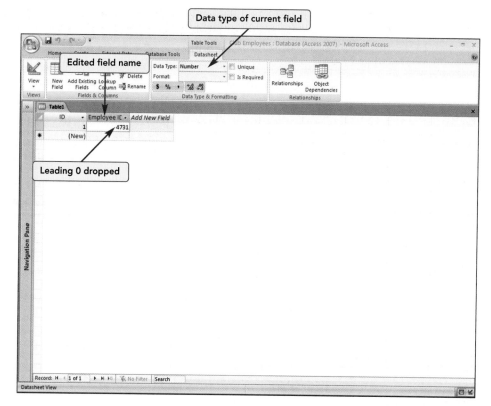

Figure 1.8

The field name has been completed and it is now easy to know what the data in that column represents.

Defining Data Type

Notice the leading 0 of the Employee ID number has been dropped. This is because Access automatically detects and assigns a data type to each field based upon the data that is entered. In this case, the field entry consisted of numbers only, and Access assigned the field a Number data type. This data type drops any leading zeros.

Concept 3

Data Type

3 The **data type** defines the type of data the field will contain. Access uses the data type to ensure that the right kind of data is entered in a field. It is important to choose the right data type for a field before you start entering data in the table. You can change a data type after the field contains data, but if the data types are not compatible, such as a text entry in a field whose data type accepts numbers only, you may lose data. The data types are described in the following table.

Data Type	Purpose
Text	Use in fields that contain alphanumeric data (words, combinations of words and numbers, and numbers that are not used in calculations). Text field entries can be up to 255 characters in length. Names and phone numbers are examples of Text field entries. Text is the default data type.
Memo	Use in fields where you want to store more than 255 characters of alphanumeric data. A memo field holds up to 1GB of characters or 2GB of storage, of which 65,535 characters can be displayed. Text in this field can be formatted.
Number	Use in fields that contain numeric data only and that will be used to perform calculations on the values in the field. Number of units ordered is an example of a Number field entry. Leading zeros are dropped. Do not use in fields involving money or that require a high degree of accuracy because number fields round to the next highest value. Fields that contain numbers only but will not be used in calculations are usually assigned a Text data type.
Date/Time	Use in fields that will contain dates and times. Access allows dates from AD January 1, 100, to December 31, 9999. Access correctly handles leap years and checks all dates for validity. Even though dates and times are formatted to appear as a date or time, they are stored as **serial values** so that they can be used in calculations. The date serial values are consecutively assigned beginning with 1, which corresponds to the date January 1, 1900, and ending with 2958465, which is December 31, 9999.
Currency	Use in number fields that are monetary values or that you do not want rounded. Numbers are formatted to display decimal places and a currency symbol.
AutoNumber	Use when you need a unique, sequential number that is automatically incremented by one whenever a new record is added to a table. After a number is assigned to a record, it can never be used again, even if the record is deleted.
Yes/No	Use when the field contents can only be a Yes/No, True/False, or On/Off value. Yes values are stored as a 1 and No values as 0 so that they can be used in expressions.
OLE Object	Use in fields to store an object such as a graphic (picture), sound, document, or graph. The object is converted to a bitmap image and displayed in the table field, form, or report. An OLE server program must be on the computer that runs the database in order to render the object. Generally, use the Attachment field type rather than OLE Object because the objects are stored more efficiently and it does not require the supporting program.
Hyperlink	Use when you want the field to store a link to an object, document, Web page, or other destinations.
Attachment	Use to add multiple files of different types to a field. For example, you could add a photograph and set of resumes for each employee. Unlike OLE object fields, the files are not converted to bitmap images and additional software is not needed to view the object, thereby saving space. Attachments also can be opened and edited from within Access in their parent programs.

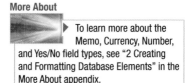
Notice the Data Type box in the Data Type & Formatting group shows the current data type for the field is Number. Access accurately specified this data type because the Employee ID field contains numbers. However, unless the numbers are used in calculations, the field should be assigned the Text data type. This designation allows other characters, such as the parentheses or hyphens in a telephone number, to be included in the entry. Also, by specifying the type as Text, leading zeros will be preserved.

You need to override the data type decision and change the data type for this field to Text.

1 ● **Open the**

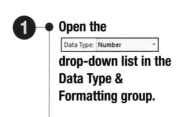

drop-down list in the Data Type & Formatting group.

● **Choose Text.**

● **Click at the beginning of the Employee ID entry to place the insertion point and type 0.**

● **Press** End **to move to the end of the entry.**

● **Press** → **to move to the next column.**

Your screen should be similar to Figure 1.9

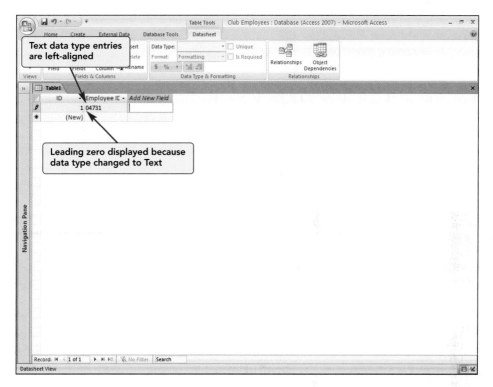

Figure 1.9

The leading zero is now correctly displayed. Also notice that the entry is now left-aligned in the cell space whereas it was right-aligned when the data type was set to Number. Many data types also include formatting settings that control the appearance of the data in the field. In this case, the Text field format is to align the text with the left edge of the cell space. You will learn more about formatting later in the lab.

Now you are ready to enter the data for the next field, Hire Date.

2 ● Type **Aug 19, 2001.**

● Click in the Fields & Columns group.

● Type **Hire Date.**

● Press ←Enter.

● Click on the hire date.

Your screen should be similar to Figure 1.10

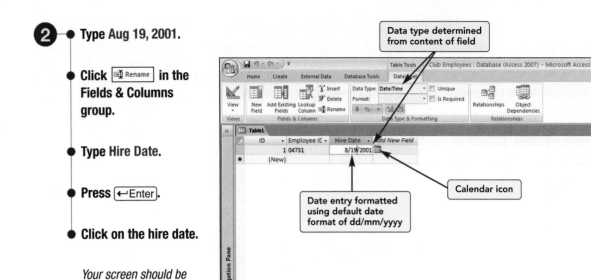

Figure 1.10

Access correctly determined that the entry is a Date type and displays the date using the default date format of mm/dd/yyyy.

Using Field Templates

The next few fields you need to enter are for the employee name and address information. Another way you can specify field names is to select them from a list of predefined fields called **field templates.** Each field template definition includes a field name, a data type, and other settings that control the appearance and behavior of the field.

First you will add a field for the employee's last name.

① ● Click [New Field] in the Fields & Columns group.

Your screen should be similar to Figure 1.11

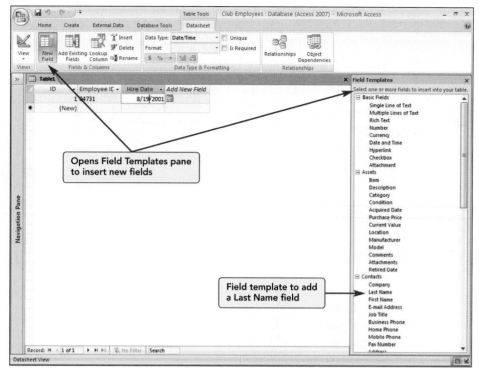

Opens Field Templates pane to insert new fields

Field template to add a Last Name field

Figure 1.11

From the Field Templates pane, you can select and drag the field name to the table. When the insertion bar appears where you want the new field inserted, drop the field in position. You can also double-click on the field name and it will be inserted in the next empty field column in the datasheet.

② ● Double-click Last Name in the Contacts section of the Field Templates list.

Your screen should be similar to Figure 1.12

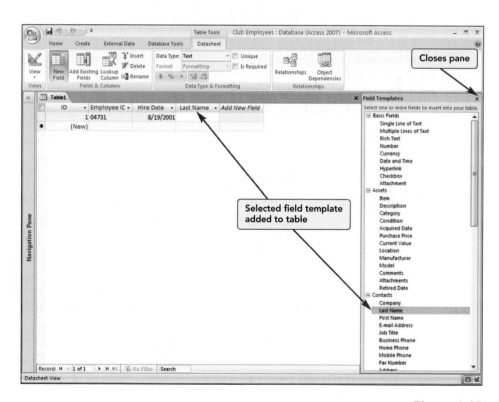

Closes pane

Selected field template added to table

Figure 1.12

The Last Name field was inserted in the datasheet following the last defined field in the datasheet. It has a data type of Text. Next you will add the remaining address fields. Multiple field templates can be selected and inserted into the datasheet at the same time.

3 ● Select the First Name, Address, City, State/Province, and Zip/Postal Code field names.

Having Trouble?
Hold down Ctrl while selecting multiple field templates.

● Drag them into the datasheet and release the mouse pointer when the insertion bar appears after the Last Name column.

● Move to the Add New Field column and double-click the Home Phone field to add it at that location.

● Click ☒ in the title bar of the Field Templates pane to close it.

● Move the horizontal scroll bar to the left.

Your screen should be similar to Figure 1.13

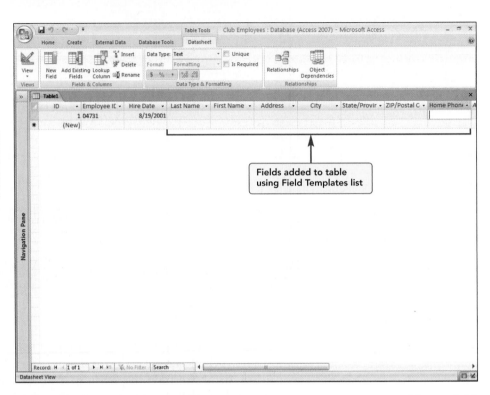

Fields added to table using Field Templates list

Figure 1.13

Using a field template saves time and provides the basis from which you can start. Once inserted, it can be modified like any other field name.

Switching Views

Next, you will switch to Design view. This view makes it easier to focus on the structure of the table because it displays information about the fields only, not the data in the table.

You can easily switch between views using the ◪ button in the Ribbon. The graphic in the button changes to indicate the view that will be displayed when selected. Currently the button displays the graphic for Design view. If the view you want to change to is displayed in the button, you can simply click on the button to change to that view. Otherwise, you can open the View button's drop-down list and select the view you want to use. Before you can change views, you will be asked to save the table.

1 ● Click ⟫ to open the Navigation pane.

● Click 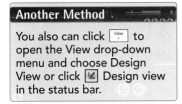 Design View in the Views group.

Another Method

You also can click [View] to open the View drop-down menu and choose Design View or click ✎ Design view in the status bar.

Your screen should be similar to Figure 1.14

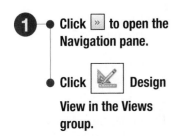
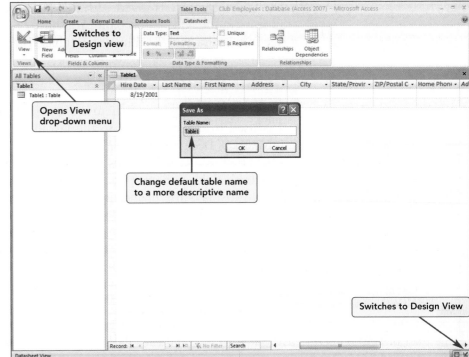

Figure 1.14

Additional Information

You also could click 🖫 Save in the Records group of the Home tab, or use the keyboard shortcut ⟨⇧Shift⟩ + ⟨←Enter⟩, or click 🖫 Save in the Quick Access Toolbar to save the changes to the table at any time.

The first time you switch views, you are asked to save the table design by naming it. In the Save As dialog box, you want to replace the default name, Table1, with a more descriptive name. A table name follows the same set of standard naming conventions or rules that you use when naming fields. It is acceptable to use the same name for both a table and the database, although each table in a database must have a unique name. You will save the table using the table name Employee Records.

2 ● Type Employee Records.

● Click ⟨ OK ⟩.

Your screen should be similar to Figure 1.15

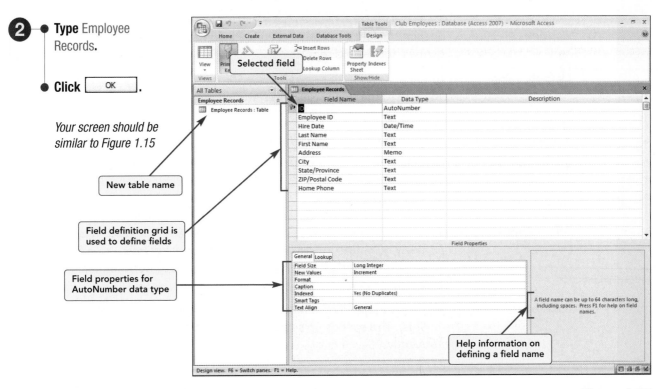

Figure 1.15

The table structure is saved with the database file and the new table name appears in the Navigation pane. You have created a table named Employee Records in the Club Employees database file.

Using Design View

Additional Information

You can get more Help information about the current selection by pressing F1 to open Access Help.

Design view displays the structure of the table, not the table data. Therefore, it is used to make changes to the layout and fields in the table only. The Table Tools Design tab is displayed and open. The upper section consists of a field definition grid that displays the field names, the data type associated with each field, and an area to enter a description of the field. The lower section displays the properties associated with each field and a Help box that provides information about the current task.

Concept 4

Field Property

4 A **field property** is a characteristic that helps define the appearance and behavior of a field. Each field has a set of field properties associated with it, and each data type has a different set of field properties. Setting field properties enhances the way your table works. Some of the more commonly used properties and their functions are described in the following table.

Field Property	Description
Field Size	Sets the maximum number of characters that can be entered in the field.
Format	Specifies the way data displays in a table and prints.
Input Mask	Simplifies data entry by controlling the data that is required in a field and the way the data is to be displayed.
Caption	Specifies a field label other than the field name that is used in queries, forms, and reports.
Default Value	Automatically fills in a certain value for this field in new records as you add to the table. You can override a default value by typing a new value into the field.
Validation Rule	Limits data entered in a field to values that meet certain requirements.
Validation Text	Specifies the message to be displayed when the associated Validation Rule is not satisfied.
Required	Specifies whether a value must be entered in a field.
Allow Zero Length	Specifies whether an entry containing no characters is valid. This property is used to indicate that you know no value exists for a field. A zero-length string is entered as "" with no space between the quotation marks.
Indexed	Sets a field as an index field (a field that controls the order of records). This speeds up searches on fields that are searched frequently.

The first field in the field definition grid, ID, is the selected field or **current field** and will be affected by any changes you make. It has a data type of AutoNumber. The properties associated with the current field are displayed in the Field Properties section.

You will look at the properties associated with the first field you added to the table. Positioning the insertion point in any column of the field definition grid will select that field and display the associated field properties.

1 ● **Select Employee ID.**

Your screen should be similar to Figure 1.16

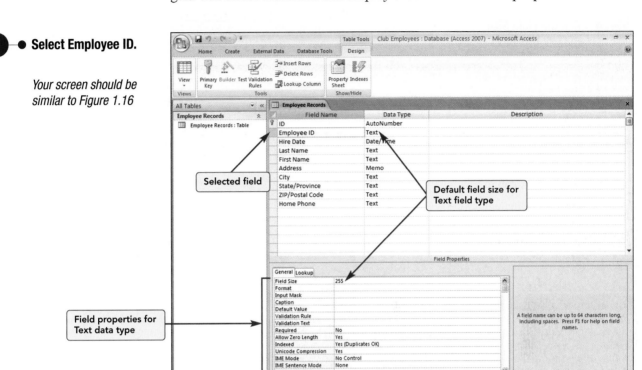

Figure 1.16

The data type of this field is Text and the default properties associated with a Text data type are displayed in the Field Properties area. Although some of the properties are the same as those for the AutoNumber data type, most are different. Access sets the field size for a Text field to 255 characters. It also sets the Required property to no, which allows the field to be blank. The Allow Zero Length property is set to yes, which allows entries with no characters. The Indexed property is also set to yes, meaning indexing is on, and duplicate entries are allowed in the field, as, for example, the same name could be entered in the Name field of multiple records. All these settings seem appropriate, except for the field size, which is much too large.

Modifying Field Properties

Although Access uses only the amount of storage space necessary for the text you actually store in a Text field, setting the field size to the smallest possible size can decrease the processing time required by the program. Additionally, if the field data to be entered is a specific size, setting the field size to that number restricts the entry to the maximum number.

Because the employee number will never be more than five digits long, you will change the field size from the default of 255 to 5. Another way to edit text is to select (highlight by dragging or double-clicking) a character or characters (including complete words and sentences) and press the (Delete) key to erase the selection.

1 ● **Click the Field Size property text box.**

Another Method

You also can press the (F6) key to switch between the upper and lower areas of the Design window.

● **Double-click 255 to select it.**

● **Type 5 to replace the default entry.**

Additional Information

You can cancel changes you are making in the current field at any time before you move on to the next field. Just press (Esc), and the original entry is restored.

Your screen should be similar to Figure 1.17

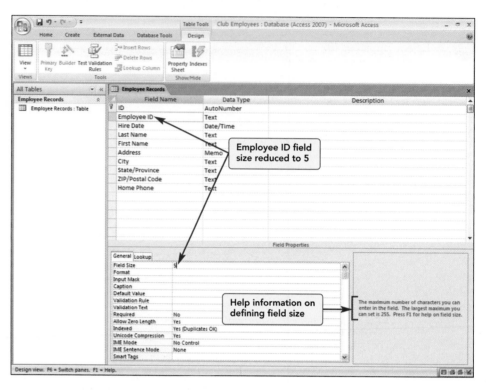

Employee ID field size reduced to 5

Help information on defining field size

The maximum number of characters you can enter in the field. The largest maximum you can set is 255. Press F1 for help on field size.

Figure 1.17

The maximum number of characters that can be entered in this field is now restricted to 5. Notice the Help box displays a brief description of the selected property.

Likewise, you will adjust the field sizes of several other fields.

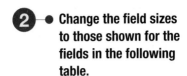

2 ● Change the field sizes to those shown for the fields in the following table.

Field	Size
Last Name	25
First Name	25
City	25
ZIP/Postal Code	10
Home Phone	15

Your screen should be similar to Figure 1.18

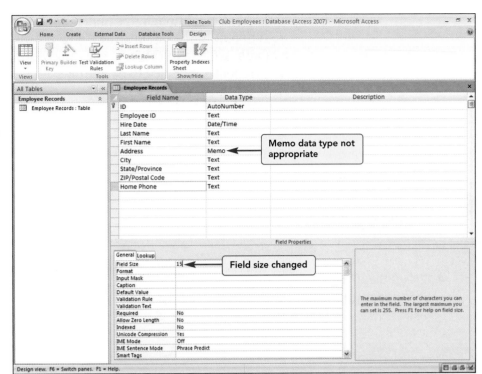

Figure 1.18

Changing Data Type

As you look at the field definitions, you see that the Address field type was set to Memo by the field template. This setting allows text entries longer than 255 characters and lets you add formatting to the text, such as bold or italics. You do not feel this data type is appropriate for the field and will change it to Text with a field size of 50.

1 ● Click in the Data Type column for the Address field.

● Click ▼ to open the drop-down list and choose Text.

● Change the field size to 50.

Your screen should be similar to Figure 1.19

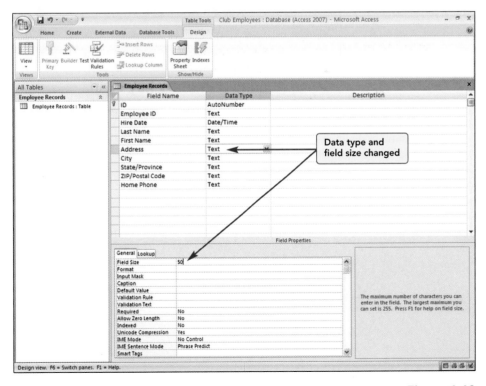

Figure 1.19

Notice that even though this field has a text data type, the property settings are different. For example, the Allow Zero Length and Indexed properties are both set to No. This is because the fields were defined using field templates that included these settings.

Editing Field Names

As you continue to look over the fields, you decide to change several of the field names that were assigned when you selected the field templates.

1 • Change the State/Province field name to State.

• Change the ZIP/Postal Code field name to ZIP Code.

Having Trouble?
Double-click on the field name to select it.

Your screen should be similar to Figure 1.20

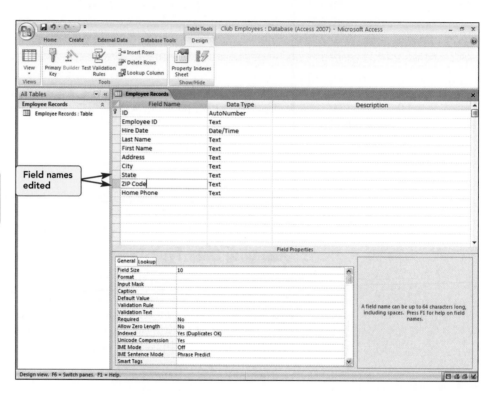

Figure 1.20

Defining a Primary Key Field

The next change you want to make is to define the Employee ID field as a primary key field.

Primary Key

5 A **primary key** is a field that uniquely identifies each record and is used to associate data from multiple tables. To qualify as a primary key field, the data in the field must be unique for each record. For example, a Social Security Number field could be selected as the primary key because the data in that field is unique for each employee. Other examples of a primary key field are parts numbers or catalog numbers. (One example of a field that should not be used as the primary key is a name field, because more than one person can have the same last or first name.) A second requirement is that the field can never be empty or null. A third is that the data in the field never, or rarely, changes.

A primary key prevents duplicate records from being entered in the table and is used to control the order in which records display in the table. This makes it faster for databases to locate records in the table and to process other operations.

Most tables have at least one field that is selected as the primary key. Some tables may use two or more fields that, together, provide the primary key of a table. When a primary key uses more than one field, it is called a **composite key**.

More About

For information about defining multifield primary keys, see "1.3 Add, Set, Change, or Remove Primary Keys" in the More About appendix.

Notice the ⧉ icon that is displayed to the left of the ID field. This indicates that this field is a primary key field. You want to define the Employee ID field as the primary key field so that duplicate employee ID numbers will not be allowed.

1 ● Click on the Employee ID field name.

● Click [Primary Key] in the Tools group.

Your screen should be similar to Figure 1.21

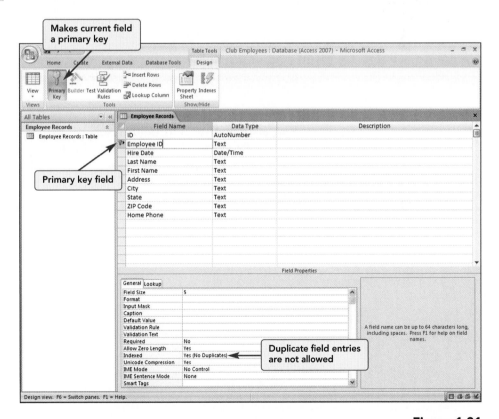

Figure 1.21

Notice the Indexed property setting for this field has changed to Yes (No Duplicates) because the field is defined as the primary key field. This setting prohibits duplicate values in a field. Also, the primary key status has been removed from the default ID field.

Entering a Field Description

To continue defining the Employee ID field, you will enter a brief description of the field. Although it is optional, a field description makes the table easier to understand and update because the description is displayed in the status bar when you enter data into the table.

1
- Click the Description text box for the Employee ID field.

- Type **Unique five-digit number assigned to each employee.**

Additional Information
The Description box scrolls horizontally as necessary to accommodate the length of the text entry. The maximum length is 255 characters.

Your screen should be similar to Figure 1.22

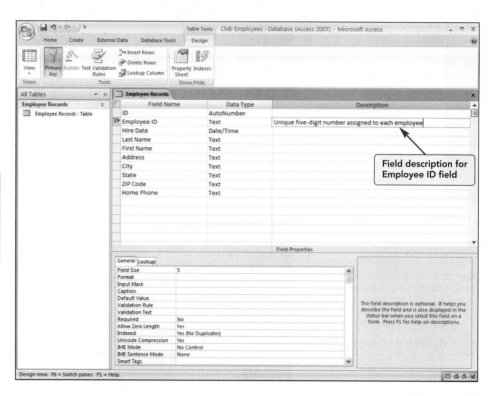

Figure 1.22

You also want to add field descriptions to several other fields. As you do, the ⓩ Property Update Options button appears. Clicking on this button opens a menu whose option will update the description in the status bar everywhere it is used.

2 • Add descriptions to the fields shown in the table below.

Your screen should be similar to Figure 1.23

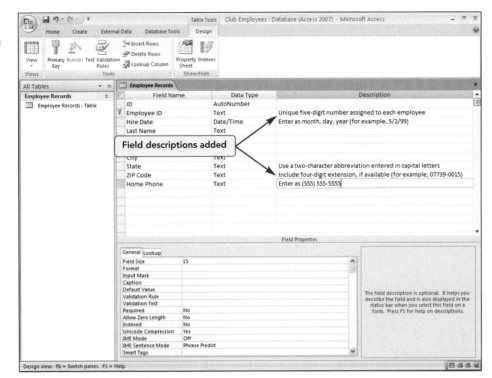

Figure 1.23

Field	Description
Hire Date	Enter as month, day, year (for example, 5/2/99)
State	Use a two-character abbreviation entered in capital letters
ZIP Code	Include four-digit extension, if available (for example, 07739-0015)
Home Phone	Enter as (555) 555-5555

Additional Information

In a table that contains a lot of data, it is a good idea to create a backup copy of the table before you delete a field in case you need to recover the deleted data.

Deleting a Field

Because the ID field essentially duplicates the purpose of the Employee ID field, you will delete the ID field. Deleting a field permanently removes the field column and all the data in the field from the table.

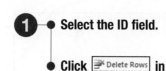

1 ● Select the ID field.

● Click [Delete Rows] in the Tools group.

● Click [Yes] in response to the advisory messages.

Your screen should be similar to Figure 1.24

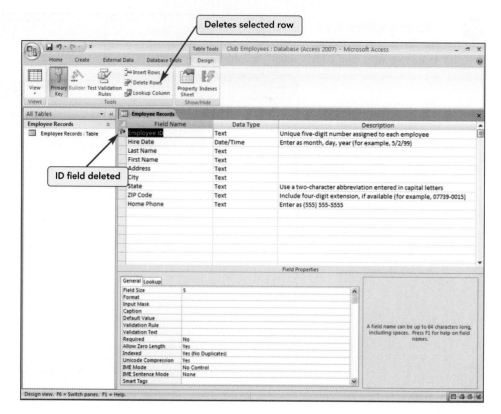

Figure 1.24

Another Method

You also can delete a field in Datasheet view by choosing Delete Column from the shortcut menu or [Delete] in the Fields & Columns group of the Table Tools Datasheet tab for the column you want to delete.

The field is permanently removed from the table.

Defining Additional Fields

You still need to add two fields to the table: one for the employee's date of birth and the other to display the employee photo. You will add the new fields and define their properties in Design view.

1
- **Click** in the blank Field Name row below the Home Phone field name.

- **Type** Birth Date.

- **Press** ⬅Enter, Tab⇥, or → to move to the Data Type column.

- **Open** the Data Type drop-down list and choose Date/Time.

- **Enter** the field description Enter as month, day, year (for example, 5/2/74).

Your screen should be similar to Figure 1.25

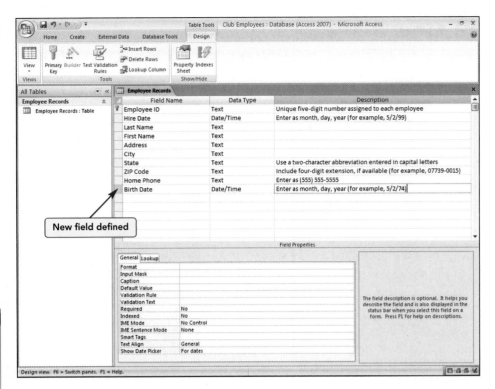

New field defined

Figure 1.25

The default field properties for the selected data type are displayed. Because the format line is blank, you decide to check the format to make sure that the date will display as you want.

2 ● Click in the Format property box.

● Click ☑ to open the drop-down list of Format options.

Your screen should be similar to Figure 1.26

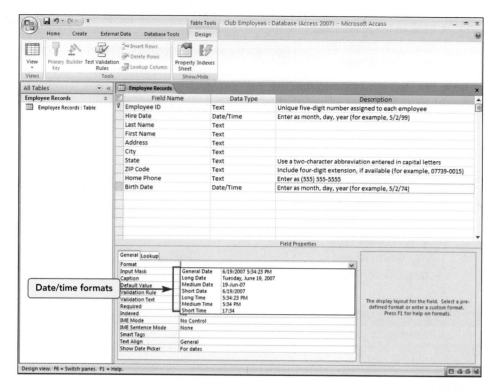

Figure 1.26

The names of the seven predefined layouts for the Date/Time field type are displayed in the list. An example of each layout appears to the right of the name. The General Date format is the default format. It displays dates using the Short Date format. If a time value is entered, it also will display the time in the Long Time format.

3 ● Choose General Date.

Your screen should be similar to Figure 1.27

Additional Information
Access automatically assumes the first two digits of a year entry. If you enter a year that is between /30 and /99, Access reads this as a 20th century date (1930 to 1999). A year entry between /00 and /29 is assumed to be a 21st century date (2000 to 2029).

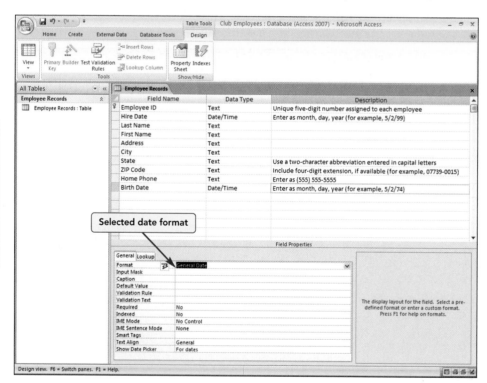

Figure 1.27

The Date property setting is now displayed in the Format text box.

The last field you will enter will display a photo and resume if available of each employee. The data type for this type of input is Attachment. Once a field has been assigned, this data type cannot be changed. You can, however, delete the field and then redefine it if you think you made an error.

4 • **In the next blank field name row, enter the field name Photo/ Resume with a data type of Attachment.**

• **Include the description Attach employee photo and resume if available.**

Your screen should be similar to Figure 1.28

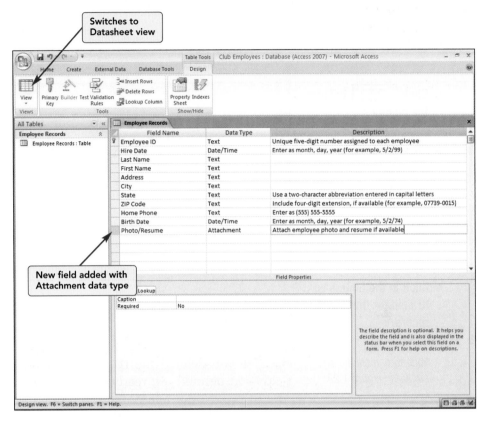

Figure 1.28

Specifying the Attachment data type allows you to store multiple files of different file types in a single field.

Entering and Editing Data

Now that the table structure is complete, you want to continue entering the employee data into the table. To do this, you need to switch back to Datasheet view.

Because you have made many changes to the table design, you will be asked to save the changes before you switch views. You also will be advised that data may be lost because you decreased field sizes in several fields. Since there is very little data in the table, this is not a concern.

1 ● Click 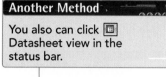 in the View group to switch to the Datasheet View.

Another Method
You also can click Datasheet view in the status bar.

● Click [Yes] to save the changes.

● Click [Yes] in response to the data may be lost warning.

● Hide the Navigation pane.

● Click in the Employee ID field for the first record.

Your screen should be similar to Figure 1.29

Additional Information
You will learn how to change the column width shortly.

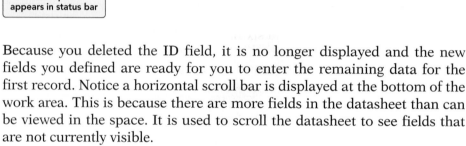

Figure 1.29

Because you deleted the ID field, it is no longer displayed and the new fields you defined are ready for you to enter the remaining data for the first record. Notice a horizontal scroll bar is displayed at the bottom of the work area. This is because there are more fields in the datasheet than can be viewed in the space. It is used to scroll the datasheet to see fields that are not currently visible.

The first field, Employee ID, of the first record is outlined in orange, indicating that the program is ready to accept data in this field. The field name and Select All button also are highlighted in orange to identify the current field and current record. The status bar displays the description you entered for the field.

Notice also in this view that the column widths are all the same, even though you set different field sizes in the Table Design window. This is because the Table Datasheet view has its own default column width setting.

Verifying Data Accuracy and Validity

To see how field properties help ensure data accuracy, you will reenter the employee number for the first record and try to enter a number that is larger than the field size of five that you defined in Table Design view.

1 • If necessary, double-click on the number to select it.

• Type 047310.

Your screen should be similar to Figure 1.30

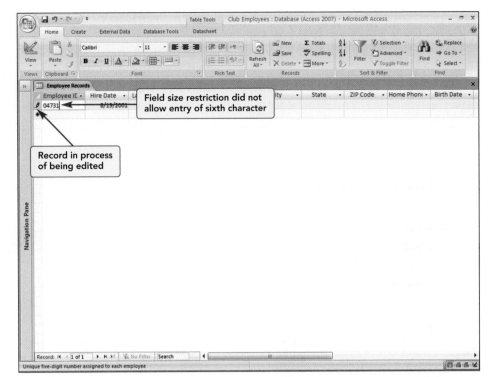

Figure 1.30

The program accepted only the first five digits and would not let you type a sixth. The field size restriction helps control the accuracy of data by not allowing an entry larger than specified. Notice also that the current record symbol has changed to 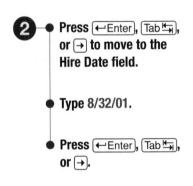. The pencil symbol means the record is in the process of being entered or edited and has not yet been saved.

Next, you will intentionally enter an invalid date to see what happens.

2 • Press ⏎Enter, Tab⇥, or → to move to the Hire Date field.

• Type 8/32/01.

• Press ⏎Enter, Tab⇥, or →.

Your screen should be similar to Figure 1.31

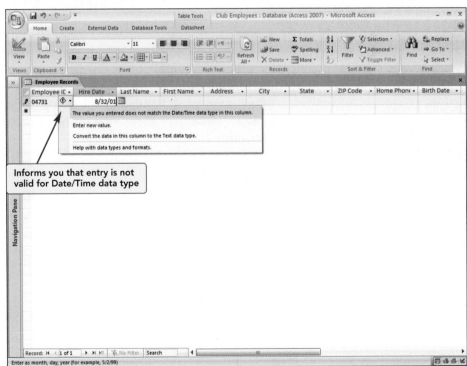

Figure 1.31

An informational message box is displayed advising you that the entry is not valid. In this case, the date entered (8/32/01) could not be correct because a month cannot have 32 days. Access automatically performs some basic checks on the data as it is entered based upon the field type specified in the table design. This is another way that Access helps you control data entry to ensure the accuracy of the data.

You will need to edit the date entry to correct it.

3 ● **Select Enter new value from the message box.**

● **Double-click on 32 to select it.**

● **Type 19.**

● **Press** [Tab ⇥].

Your screen should be similar to Figure 1.32

Status bar displays name of view when field does not contain a description

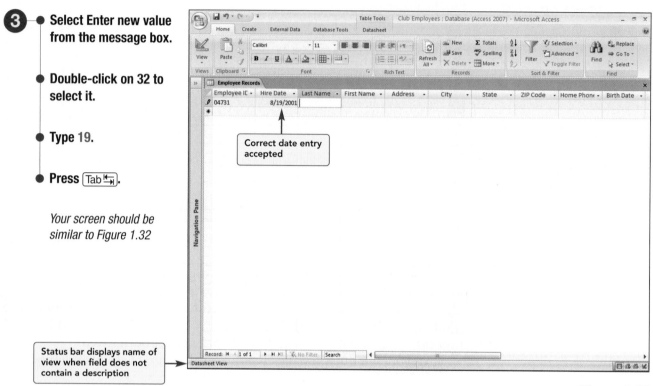

Figure 1.32

The corrected date is accepted, and the insertion point moves to the Last Name field. The year in the date changed to four digits, which reflects the date format you specified in the field's property.

Because you did not enter a description for this field, the status bar displays "Datasheet View," the name of the current view, instead of a field description.

Using AutoCorrect

Now you are ready to continue entering the data for the first record. As you are typing, you may make errors and they may be corrected automatically for you. This is because the AutoCorrect feature automatically corrects obvious errors such as capitalizing names of days, the first letter of sentences, and other common typing errors and misspellings such as words starting with two initial capital letters. The AutoCorrect Options button ⧉ will appear next to any text that was corrected. You have the option of undoing the correction or leaving it as is. Most times the typing error is not corrected, and you will need to fix it manually.

To see how this works, you will enter the last name incorrectly by typing the first two letters using capital letters.

1 ● **Type MArchant.**

● **Press** Tab↹.

Your screen should be similar to Figure 1.33

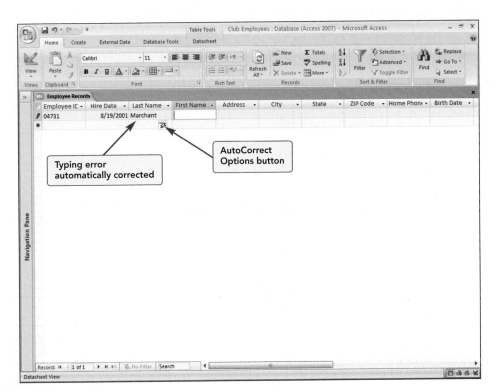

Figure 1.33

The name was automatically corrected and the AutoCorrect Options button ⧉ appears. You will leave the correction as is and continue to enter data for this record.

2 ● Enter the data shown in the table below for the remaining fields, typing the information exactly as it appears.

Additional Information
The fields will scroll on the screen as you move to the right in the record.

Your screen should be similar to Figure 1.34

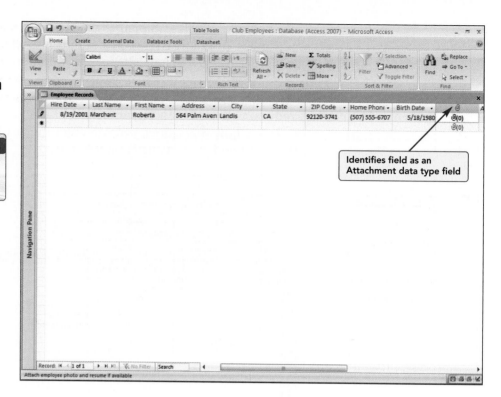

Identifies field as an Attachment data type field

Figure 1.34

Field Name	Data
First Name	**Roberta**
Address	**564 Palm Avenue**
City	**Landis**
State	**CA**
ZIP Code	**92120–3741**
Home Phone	**(507) 555–6707**
Birth Date	**May 18, 1980** (press [Tab ⇥] to complete the entry)

All the information for the first record is now complete, except for the last field for the employee photo and resume.

Attaching a File

Notice the field name in the header for this field is not Photo/Resume, as you defined in Design view. This is because Access does not allow field names for Attachment data types. Instead it displays a paperclip icon in the field header to show that the field has an Attachment data type. The field description that appears in the status bar is particularly important because there is no descriptive field name.

To complete the information for this field, you plan to attach the employee photo and a copy of the employee's resume if it is available. A photo is one of several different types of graphic objects that can be added to a database table. A **graphic** is a nontext element or object. A graphic can be a simple **drawing object** consisting of shapes such as lines and boxes that can be created using a drawing program such as Paint or it can be a picture. A **picture** is an illustration such as a scanned photograph. A resume is a text document that is typically created using a word processor application.

Because you have not organized all the employees' badge photographs yet, you will only insert the photo for Roberta Marchant to demonstrate this feature to the club owners. You also will attach a sample resume that was created using Word 2007.

1 ● Double-click on the Attachment field cell for this record.

Another Method
You also can choose Manage Attachments from the field's shortcut menu.

Your screen should be similar to Figure 1.35

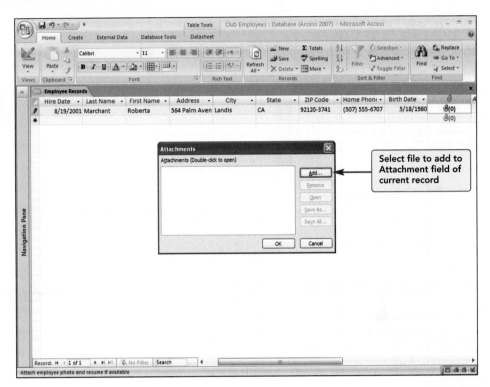

Figure 1.35

The Attachments box is used to manage the items that are in an attachment field. Because there are currently no attachments associated with this field, it is empty. You will select the photo and resume files you want to add to the field.

② ● **Click** 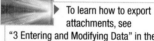.

● **If necessary, open the Look in drop-down list box and specify the location of your data files.**

● **Select** ac01_Roberta **and** ac01_Resume **from the file list box.**

Having Trouble?
Hold down Ctrl while clicking on the file names to select multiple files.

● **Click** Open .

Your screen should be similar to Figure 1.36

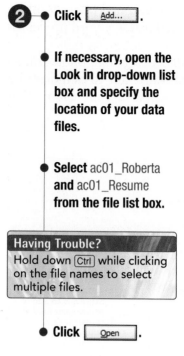

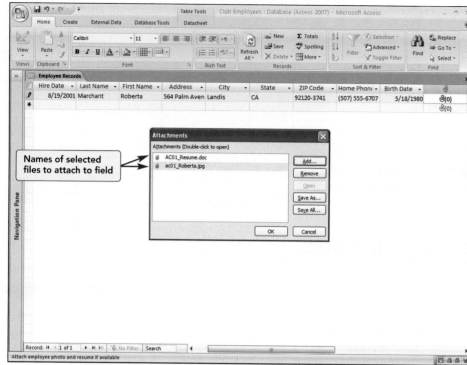

Figure 1.36

Additional Information
To remove a file from the attachment field, select the file name from the list and click Remove .

More About
To learn how to export attachments, see "3 Entering and Modifying Data" in the More About appendix.

The Attachments dialog box is displayed again and now displays the names of the selected files.

3 • Click [OK].

Your screen should be similar to Figure 1.37

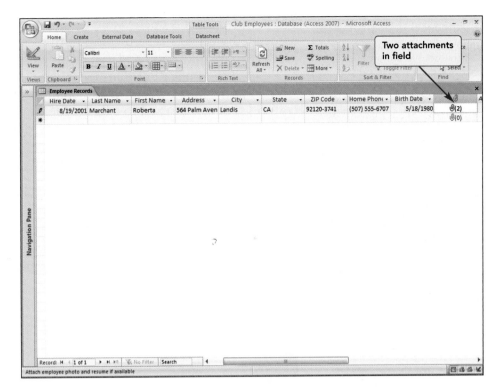

Figure 1.37

The selected files are inserted as attachments and identified with the number 2 in the cell. The number indicates how many attachments have been added to the field. You will now display the photograph from the Attachment field to check that it has been inserted properly.

4 • Double-click the cell.

• Select the ac01_Roberta **file from the Attachments dialog box.**

• Click [Open].

Another Method
You also can double-click the file to both select and open it.

Your screen should be similar to Figure 1.38

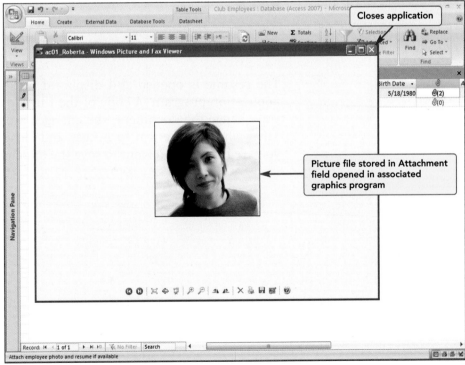

Figure 1.38

The picture object is opened and displayed in the graphics program that is associated with this type of file—in this case, Windows Picture and Fax Viewer. Yours may open and display in a different graphics program such as Paint. The application that opens is not necessarily the application in which the file was created. If the application in which it opens includes features that can be used to edit the file, you will be prompted to save any changes before closing the Attachments dialog box. If you do not save them, the changes will be lost.

5 ● Click ☒ Close in the graphics application window title bar to close the application.

● Select and open the ac01_Resume attachment.

Your screen should be similar to Figure 1.39

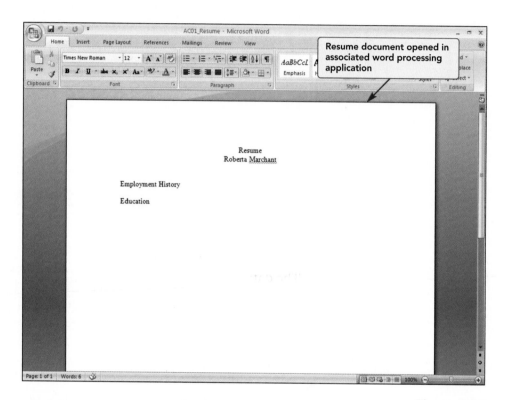

Figure 1.39

The resume is opened and displayed in the associated word processing application program. A copy of the file is placed in a temporary folder. If you change the document, the changes are saved to the temporary copy. Then when you return to Access and close the Attachments dialog box, you are asked if you want to save the attached file again.

6 • Click ⊠ Close in the application window title bar to close the application.

• Click ⊠ Close to close the Attachments dialog box.

• Press ⏎Enter to move to the beginning of the next record.

Your screen should be similar to Figure 1.40

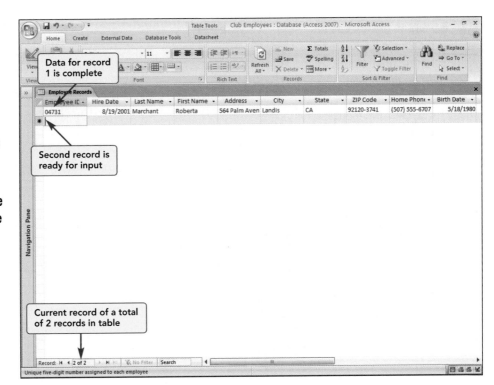

Figure 1.40

The data for the first record is now complete. The insertion point moves to the first field in the next row and waits for input of the employee number for the next record. As soon as the insertion point moves to another record, the data is saved to the table file and the number of the new record appears in the status bar. The second record was automatically assigned the record number 2.

Moving between Fields

Next, you will check the first record for accuracy. To quickly move from one field to another in a record, you can first select (highlight) the entire field contents and then you can use the keyboard keys shown in the following table to move quickly between field columns.

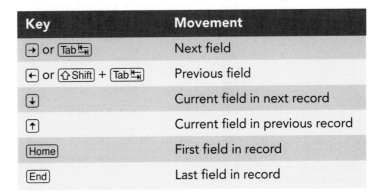

Key	Movement
→ or Tab⇥	Next field
← or ⇧Shift + Tab⇥	Previous field
↓	Current field in next record
↑	Current field in previous record
Home	First field in record
End	Last field in record

You will select the Employee ID field for the first record and then move to the Address field to check its contents.

1 ● **Point to the left end of the Employee ID field for the first record. When the mouse pointer appears as ✛, click the mouse button.**

● **Press → four times.**

Your screen should be similar to Figure 1.41

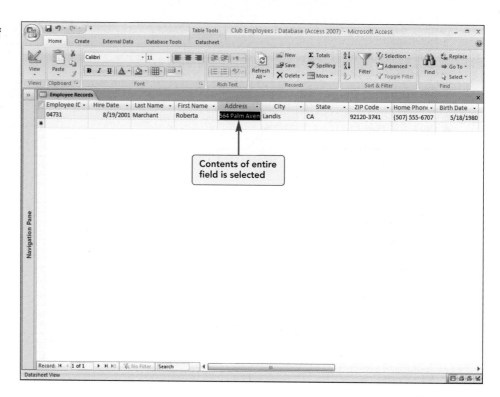

Figure 1.41

Additional Information

If you press [Delete] or [Backspace] while the entire field is selected, the entire field contents will be deleted.

Because the entire field contents are selected, you need to be careful that you do not type a character as that will delete the selection and replace it with the new text. To switch back to editing, you need to display the insertion point in the field and then edit the entry.

---

2 ● **Click the Address field with the mouse pointer shape as an I-beam.**

Your screen should be similar to Figure 1.42

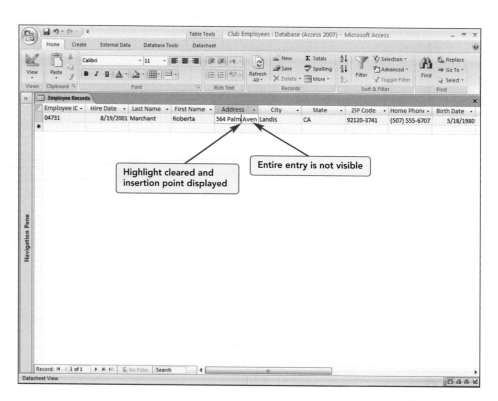

Figure 1.42

The highlight is cleared and the insertion point is visible in the field. Now, using the directional keys moves the insertion point within the field and you can edit the field contents if necessary.

Zooming a Field

The beginning of the field looks fine, but because the column width is too narrow, you cannot see the entire entry. You will move the insertion point to the end of the address so you can check the rest of the entry.

1 ● **Press** End.

Your screen should be similar to Figure 1.43

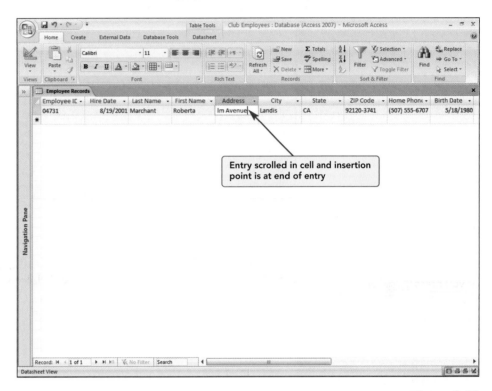

Entry scrolled in cell and insertion point is at end of entry

Figure 1.43

The text scrolled in the field, and the insertion point is positioned at the end of the entry. However, now you cannot see the beginning of the entry, which makes it difficult to edit. Another way to view the field's contents is to expand the field.

2 ● **Press** ⇧Shift + F2 .

*Your screen should be
similar to Figure 1.44*

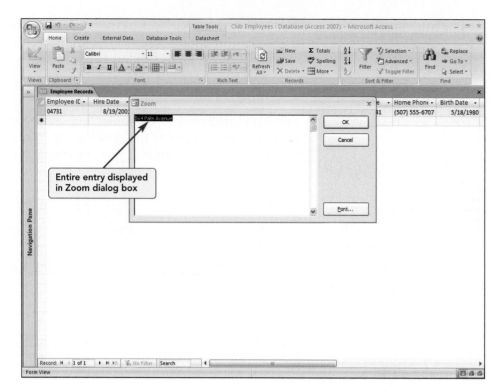

Entire entry displayed
in Zoom dialog box

Figure 1.44

The entry is fully displayed in the Zoom dialog box. You can edit in the
dialog box just as you can in the field.

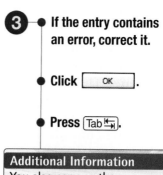

3 ● If the entry contains an error, correct it.

● Click [OK].

● Press [Tab ⇥].

Additional Information
You also can use the horizontal scroll bar to scroll the window and check fields that are not currently visible.

● Continue to check the first record for accuracy and edit as needed.

● Enter the data shown in the table for the second record (you will leave the attachment field empty).

● Check the second record for accuracy and edit it if necessary.

● Move to the first field of the blank record row.

Your screen should be similar to Figure 1.45

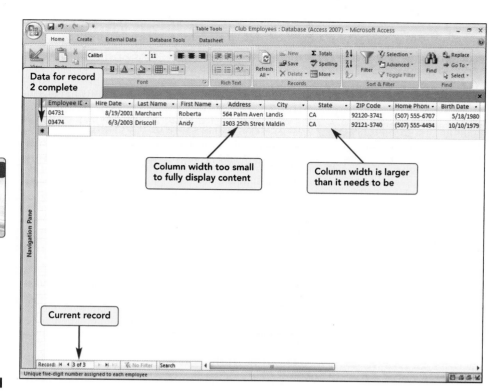

Figure 1.45

Field Name	Data
Employee ID	03474
Hire Date	June 3, 2003
Last Name	Driscoll
First Name	Andy
Address	1903 25th Street
City	Maldin
State	CA
ZIP Code	92121-3740
Home Phone	(507) 555-4494
Birth Date	October 10, 1979

The record indicator in the status bar tells you that record 3 is the current record of a total of three records.

Changing Column Width

As you have noticed, some of the fields (such as the Address field) do not display the entire entry, while other fields (such as the State field) are much larger than the field's column heading or contents. This is because the default width of a column in the datasheet is not the same size as the field sizes you specified in Design view. **Column width** refers to the size of a field column in a datasheet. The column width does not affect the amount of data you can enter into a field, but it does affect the data that you can see.

Additional Information

The default datasheet column width is set to display 15.6667 characters.

You can adjust the column width to change the appearance of the datasheet. Usually you should adjust the column width so that the column is slightly larger than the column heading or longest field contents, whichever is longer. Do not confuse column width with field size. Field size is a property associated with each field; it controls the maximum number of characters that you can enter in the field. If you shorten the field size, you can lose data already entered in the field.

Resizing a Column

The first thing you want to do is make the Address column wider so that you can see each complete field entry without having to move to the field and scroll or expand the field box. There are several ways that you can manipulate the rows and columns of a datasheet so that it is easier to view and work with the table data.

To quickly resize a column, simply drag the right column border line in the field selector in either direction to increase or decrease the column width. The mouse pointer shape is ↔ when you can drag to size the column. As you drag, a column line appears to show you the new column border. When you release the mouse button, the column width will be set. First you will increase the width of the Address field so that the entire address will be visible.

1 ● Point to the right column border line in the field selector for the Address field.

● When the mouse pointer is ↔, click and drag to the right until you think the column width will be wide enough to display the field contents.

● Adjust the column width again if it is too wide or not wide enough.

Another Method

You also can adjust the column width to a specific number of characters using [More ▾] in the Records group of the Home tab and choosing Column Width. This command is also on the shortcut menu when an entire column is selected.

Your screen should be similar to Figure 1.46

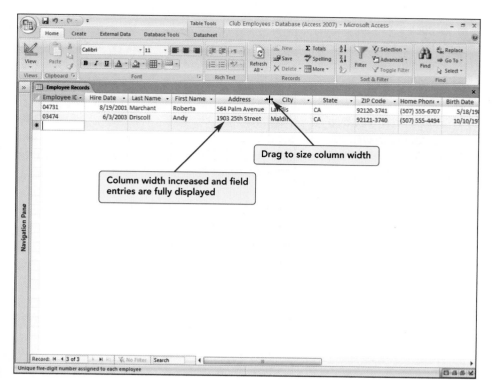

Drag to size column width

Column width increased and field entries are fully displayed

Figure 1.46

Using Best Fit

Rather than change the widths of all the other columns individually, you can select all columns and change their widths at the same time using the **Best Fit** feature. To select multiple columns, point to the column heading in the header row of the first or last column you want to select. Then, when the mouse pointer changes to ↓, click, and without releasing the mouse button, drag in either direction across the column headings.

1 ● Click [ ] to the left of
the first field name to
quickly select the
entire table.

*Your screen should be
similar to Figure 1.47*

Click to select entire table

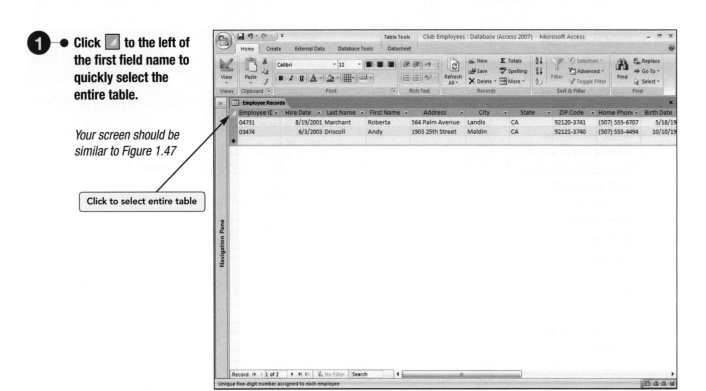

Figure 1.47

All the table columns are highlighted. Now, if you were to drag the column border of any selected column, all the selected columns would change to the same size. However, you want the column widths to be adjusted appropriately to fit the data in each column. To do this, you can double-click the column border to activate the Best Fit feature. The Best Fit feature automatically adjusts the column widths of all selected columns to accommodate the longest entry or column heading in each of the selected columns.

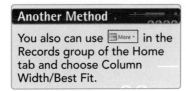 **2** ● **Double-click any column border line (in the field selector row) when the mouse pointer is ✛.**

● **Click anywhere on the table to deselect the datasheet.**

Another Method

You also can use ⊞More▾ in the Records group of the Home tab and choose Column Width/Best Fit.

Your screen should be similar to Figure 1.48

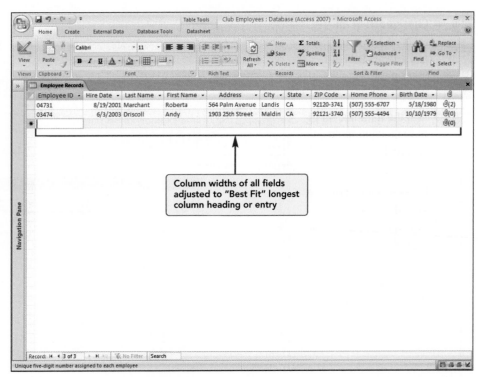

Column widths of all fields adjusted to "Best Fit" longest column heading or entry

Figure 1.48

The column widths for each field have been sized to accommodate the longest entry or column heading. As you add more records to the table that contain longer field entries, you will need to use Best Fit again to readjust the column widths.

3 ● Check each of the records again and edit any entries that are incorrect.

● Add the data shown in the following table as record 3.

● Press ←Enter twice to skip the Attachment field and complete the record.

Your screen should be similar to Figure 1.49

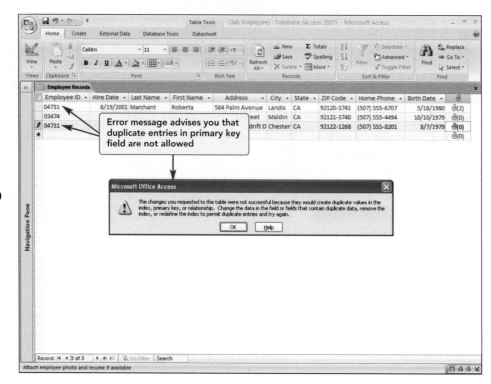

Error message advises you that duplicate entries in primary key field are not allowed

Figure 1.49

Field Name	Data
Employee ID	04731
Hire Date	April 12, 2004
Last Name	Delano
First Name	Gordon
Address	1310 N. Spindrift Drive
City	Chesterfield
State	CA
ZIP Code	92122-1268
Phone	(507) 555-8201
Birth Date	August 7, 1979

As soon as you complete the record, an error message dialog box appears indicating that Access has located a duplicate value in a key field. The key field is Employee ID. You realize you were looking at the employee number from Roberta Marchant's record when you entered the employee number for this record. You need to clear the message and enter the correct number.

4 • Click [OK].

• Press (Home) to move to the first field.

• Change the Employee ID for record 3 to **12258**.

• Press (↓).

Your screen should be similar to Figure 1.50

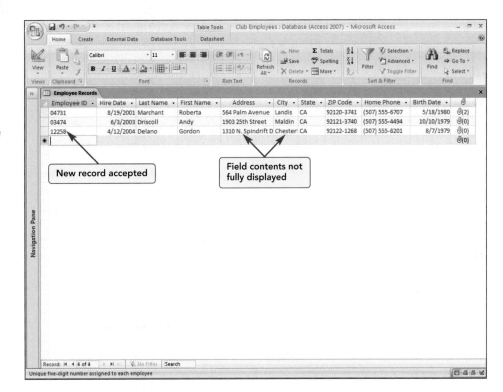

Figure 1.50

The record is accepted with the new employee number. However, you notice that the address and city for this record are not fully displayed in the fields.

5 • Best fit the Address and City fields.

Your screen should be similar to Figure 1.51

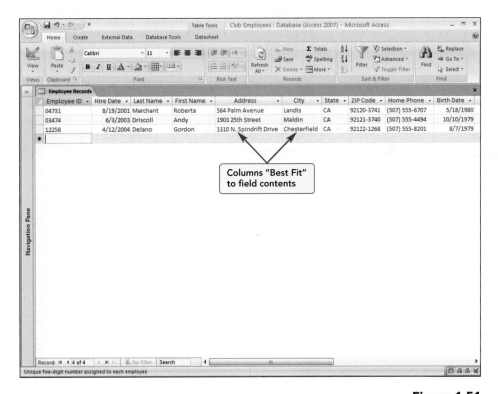

Figure 1.51

When you add new records in a datasheet, the records are displayed in the order you enter them. However, they are stored on disk in order by the primary key field.

You will add three more records to the table. If data for some fields, such as the City, State, or ZIP Code, is the same from record to record, you can save yourself some typing by copying the data from one of the other records. Just select the field contents and click [icon] Copy in the Clipboard group. Then move to the field where you want the copy to appear and click [Paste icon] in the Clipboard group.

6 ● Enter the data for the two records shown in the following table.

Field	Record 4	Record 5
Employee ID	13635	12583
Hire Date	January 2, 2007	April 20, 2007
Last Name	Martinez	Sullivan
First Name	Juan	Marie
Address	1920 First Avenue	78 Omega Drive
City	Maldin	Chesterfield
State	CA	CA
ZIP Code	92121-3740	92122-1268
Phone	(507) 555-2935	(507) 555-7890
Birth Date	December 10, 1982	March 15, 1981

7 ● Enter a final record using your first and last names. Enter 99999 as your employee number and the current date as your date hired. The information you enter in all other fields can be fictitious.

● Check each of the records and correct any entry errors.

Your screen should be similar to Figure 1.52

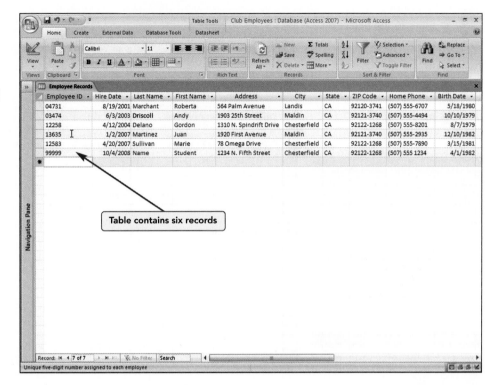

Table contains six records

Figure 1.52

There are now a total of six records in the table

Deleting Records

Another Method

You also can move to the record and choose Select from the [Select ▾] drop-down list in the Find group of the Home tab.

While you are entering the employee records, you find a memo from one of your managers stating that Andy Driscoll is no longer working at the club and asking you to remove his record from the employee files.

You can remove records from a table by selecting the entire record and pressing the [Delete] key. After pressing [Delete], you will be asked to confirm that you really want to delete the selected record. This is because this action cannot be reversed.

Additional Information

You can select multiple noncontiguous records by holding down [Ctrl] while clicking the Select All button of each record. To select contiguous records, click and drag along the Select All buttons.

1 ● Point to the Select All button for record 2 and click when the mouse shape is ➡.

● Press [Delete].

Another Method

You also can use ⟨ Cut in the Clipboard group to delete a selected record.

● Click [Yes] to confirm that you want to delete the record.

Additional Information

Clicking [No] restores the record.

Your screen should be similar to Figure 1.53

Another Method

You also can choose Delete Record from the [X Delete ▾] drop-down list in the Records group of the Home tab. The current record is both selected and deleted at the same time.

Additional Information

A SharePoint list is a list of data that is stored on a SharePoint server and is available to others in an organization.

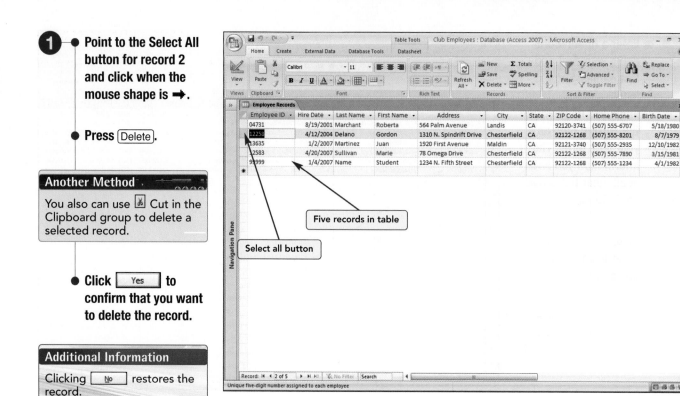

Figure 1.53

The table now consists of five employee records.

Creating a Second Table

Following your plan for the employee database, you will add another table to the existing database file. This table will hold information about the employee's work location and job title.

There are several ways to create a new table in an existing database. You can insert a blank table and define the fields in datasheet view as you already did or you can create a table based on a table template. You also can import from or link to data from another source, such as another database, an Excel worksheet, or a SharePoint list. Finally, you can create a new table starting in Design view. You will use this last method to define the two fields in the table, club location and job title.

1 ● Open the Create tab and click 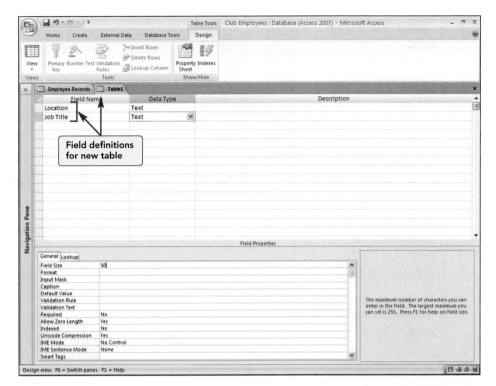 in the Tables group.

● Define the fields in the following table.

Your screen should be similar to Figure 1.54

Field definitions for new table

Figure 1.54

Field Name	Data Type	Field Size
Location	Text	20
Job Title	Text	50

The new table has a default table name of Table1 displayed in the table tab.

Adding an Existing Field

As you look at the design, you realize you need to include a field that will be used to refer back to the primary key field of the Employee Records table in order to create an association between the two tables. A field that refers to the primary key field in another table is called a **foreign key** field. The new table will use the same field as the Employee Records table, employee number, as the foreign key field. The field names of these two fields do not have to match, although their data types must be the same. Instead of recreating the field, you will copy it from the Employee Records table into the new table.

1 ● Switch to Datasheet view.

● Click [Yes] to save the table.

● Enter **Job** as the table name and click [OK].

● Click [No] in response to the prompt to create a primary key.

● Display the Navigation pane.

● Open the Table Tools Datasheet tab and click [Add Existing Fields] from the Fields & Columns group.

Your screen should be similar to Figure 1.55

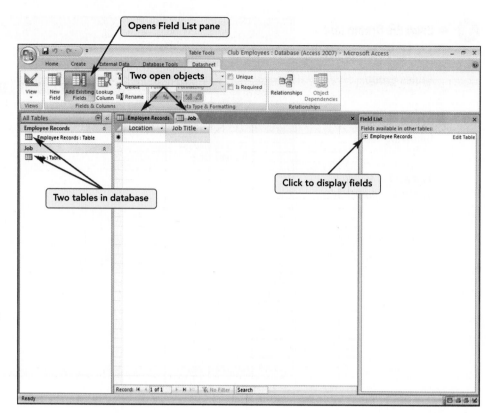

Figure 1.55

The Navigation pane displays the names of both tables in the database and a tab for both open objects appears above the work area. A Field List pane appears on the right side of the work area. It displays the name of the only other table in the database, Employee Records. Clicking the ⊞ next to the table name will display a list of the fields in the table. Then you can select and drag the field name to the new table, much as you did when using the Field Templates pane. When the insertion bar appears where you want the new field inserted, drop the field in position. You also can double-click on the field name and it will be inserted in the next empty field column in the datasheet.

2
- Click ⊞ to display the field names.

- Select the Employee ID field.

- Drag the field from the pane and drop it to the left of the Location field.

Your screen should be similar to Figure 1.56

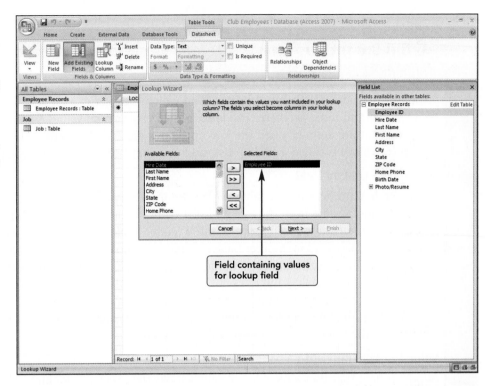

Field containing values for lookup field

Figure 1.56

Using the Lookup Wizard

The **Lookup Wizard** automatically starts and is used to create a lookup field that will allow you to select from a list of values when entering the employee number into the new table. A **wizard** is a feature that guides you step by step through the process to perform a task.

Concept 6

Lookup Field

6 A **lookup field** provides a list of values from which the user can choose to make entering data into that field simpler and more accurate. The lookup field can get the values from an existing table or a fixed set of values that are defined when the lookup field is created. A lookup field that uses another table as the **source** for values is called a **lookup list**, and one that uses fixed values is called a **value list**.

Lookup List Lookup Field

When the lookup field uses a table for the values it displays, an association is created between the two tables. Picking a value from the lookup list sets the foreign key value in the current record to the primary key value of the corresponding record in the related table. A foreign key is a field in one table that refers to the primary key field in another table and indicates how the tables are related. The field names of these two fields do not have to match, although their data types must be the same.

The related table displays but does not store the data in the record. The foreign key is stored but does not display. For this reason, any updates made to the data in the related table will be reflected in both the list and records in the table containing the lookup field. You must define a lookup list field from the table that will contain the foreign key and display the lookup list.

Value List Lookup Field

A lookup field that uses a fixed list of values looks the same as a lookup field that uses a table, except the fixed set of values is entered when the lookup field is created. A value list should be used only for values that will not change very often and do not need to be stored in a table. For example, a list for a Salutation field containing the abbreviations Mr., Mrs., or Ms. would be a good candidate for a value list. Choosing a value from a value list will store that value in the record—it does not create an association to a related table. For this reason, if you change any of the original values in the value list later, they will not be reflected in records added before this change was made.

Additional Information

You will create a value list lookup field in Lab 2.

In the first Lookup Wizard dialog box, you specify the source for the values for the lookup field. The Employee ID field is already correctly selected.

Click `Next >`.

Your screen should be similar to Figure 1.57

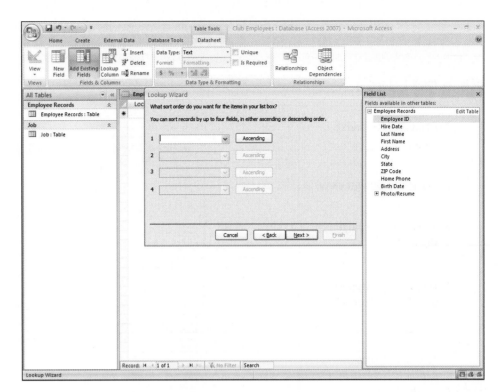

Figure 1.57

The next step is to specify a sort order. Since the items will automatically appear in the same order as in the Employee Records table, you can skip this step and move to the next step to specify the column width. Again, you want to use the same width setting you established in the Employee Records table so you will skip this step as well.

Click `Next >` **twice.**

Your screen should be similar to Figure 1.58

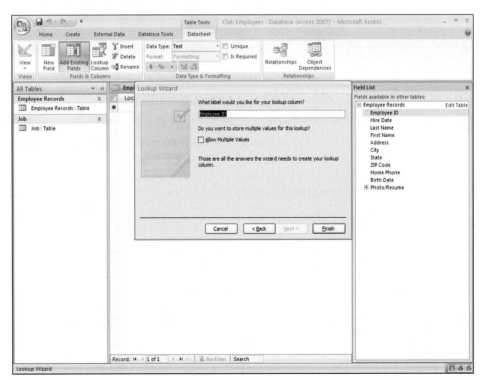

Figure 1.58

Finally, you are asked to specify a field name. You will accept the default name, which is the same as the name used in the Employee Records table.

3 ● Click [Finish].

● Close the Field List pane.

● Switch to Design view.

● Select the Employee ID field.

● Open the Lookup tab in the Field Properties area.

Your screen should be similar to Figure 1.59

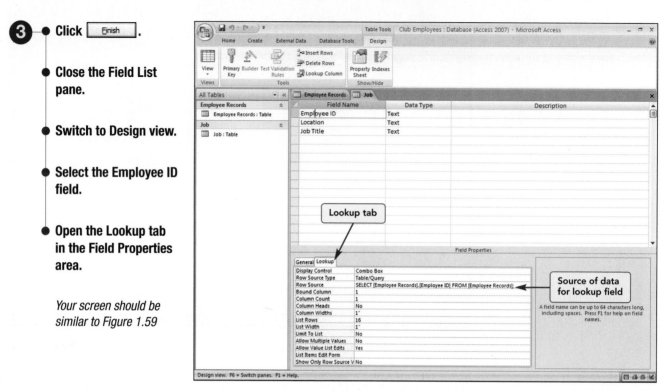

Figure 1.59

The new field has been added to the table and includes the same properties as the Employee ID field in the Employee Records table. It is a primary key field with a field size of 5. In addition, an association between the two tables has been established, as can be seen in the Row Source row of the Lookup properties, which identifies the source of the data for this row as the Employee Records table.

Additional Information
You will learn about table relationships in later labs.

Using a Lookup Field

Next, you will use the Employee ID lookup field to enter the employee numbers for each record. Then you will complete the information for each record.

1 ● **Switch to Datasheet view.**

● **If necessary, click in the Employee ID field to make it active.**

● **Click ⊻ at the end of the box to open the drop-down list of options.**

Your screen should be similar to Figure 1.60

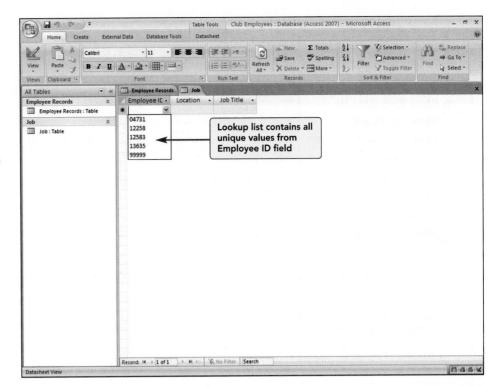

Lookup list contains all unique values from Employee ID field

Figure 1.60

The lookup list displays a drop-down list of all the values in the Employee ID field of the Employee Records table. Clicking on an entry in the list inserts it into the field.

2 • Choose 04731 and press ←Enter to move to the Location field.

• Enter **River Mist** for the location and **Fitness Coordinator** for the job title.

• In a similar manner, add the remaining records to the table.

• Best fit the columns.

Your screen should be similar to Figure 1.61

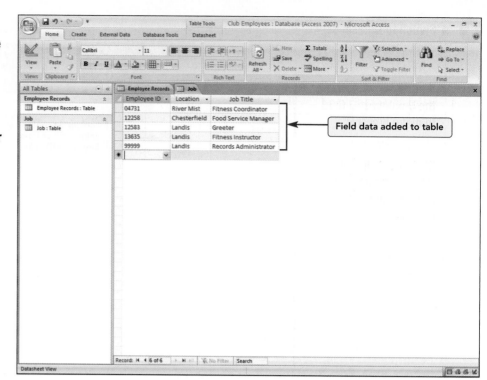

Figure 1.61

ID	Location	Position
12258	Chesterfield	Food Service Manager
12583	Landis	Greeter
13635	Landis	Fitness Instructor
99999	Landis	Records Administrator

The table now includes information on the location and job titles for the same five records as in the Employee Records table.

Inserting a Field

As you consider the contents of the two tables, you realize that the Hire Date information also should be in the Job table because the subject matter is related to the employee's job, not to his or her personal information.

- Move to any row in the Location field.

- Click ⚏ Insert in the Fields & Columns group of the Table Tools Datasheet tab to insert a blank field column to the left of the current column.

- Name the field Hire Date.

- Change the data type to Date/Time.

- Click Format: [▼] in the Data Type & Formatting group and choose Short Date.

Your screen should be similar to Figure 1.62

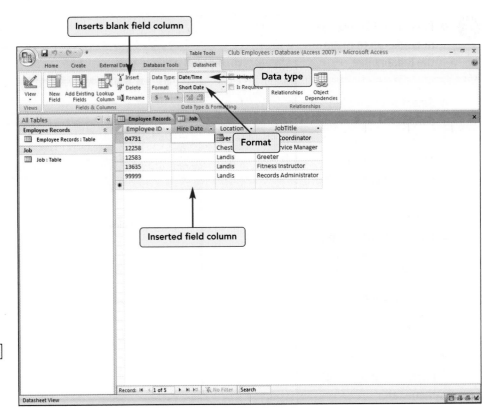

Figure 1.62

The new field has been inserted and defined.

Copying Field Content

Next, you will copy the data from the Hire Date field in the Employee Records table to the new field in the Job table. A selection that is copied creates a duplicate of the original, called the *source,* and stores it in the **Clipboard,** a temporary storage area in memory. Then, to insert the copied data from the Clipboard, you paste it in a new location, called the **destination.**

1
- Click on the Employee Records tab to make the table active.

- Select the Hire Date column.

- Click 📋 Copy in the Clipboard group of the Home tab.

- Click on the Job tab to make the table active.

- Select the Hire Date column.

- Click 📋 in the Clipboard group of the Home tab.

- Click Yes to confirm the paste operation.

Your screen should be similar to Figure 1.63

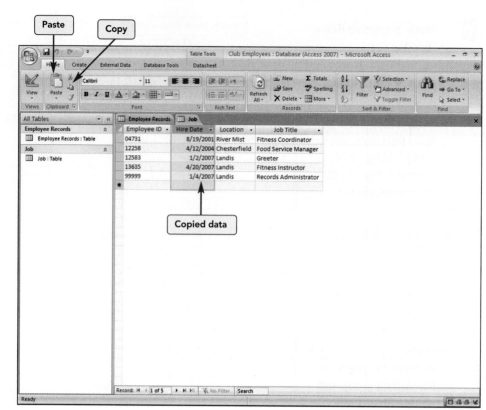

Figure 1.63

The hire date data for each record has been copied into the Hire Date field of the Job table. All you need to do now is delete the Hire Date field in the Employee Records table.

2
- Make the Employee Records table active.

- Delete the Hire Date field from the table.

Now, the Employee Records table only contains the employee's personal information and the Job table contains information about the employee's job.

Previewing and Printing a Table

Now that you have completed designing and entering some sample data in the two tables, you want to print a copy of the tables to get your managers' approval before you begin entering more employee records. Before printing the tables, you will preview them onscreen to see how they will look when printed.

Previewing the Table

Previewing a table displays each page in a reduced size so you can see the layout. Then, if necessary, you can make changes to the layout before printing, to both save time and avoid wasting paper.

1
- Make the Job table active.

- Click 🔘 Office Button.

- Select Print and choose Print Preview.

- Hide the Navigation pane.

Your screen should be similar to Figure 1.64

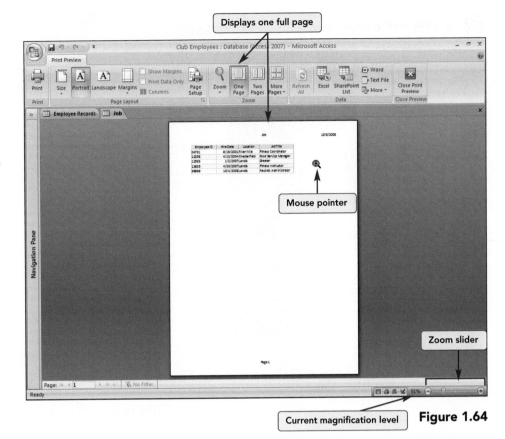

Figure 1.64

Displays one full page

Mouse pointer

Zoom slider

Current magnification level

Additional Information
The current magnification level is displayed in the status bar.

The Print Preview window displays how the table will appear when printed. The Print Preview tab is open and includes commands that are used to modify the print settings.

To see the information in the table more clearly, you can change the magnification level of the preview window. The current setting, One Page, adjusts the magnification to display an entire page in the preview window. You can drag the zoom slider in the status bar to increase the onscreen character size up to 10 times the normal display (1000 percent) or reduce the character size to 10 percent. Clicking ⊖ or ⊕ on the zoom slider increases or decreases the magnification by 10 percent increments.

Notice that the mouse pointer is a 🔍 magnifying glass when it is positioned on the page. This indicates that you can click on the page to switch between the One Page setting and the last-used magnification level (initially 100%).

Additional Information

The location where you click will determine the area that is displayed initially.

Your screen should be similar to Figure 1.65

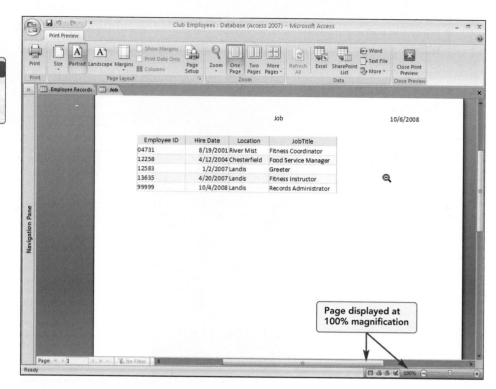

Figure 1.65

The table appears in 100 percent magnification. This is the size it will appear when printed.

Printing a Table

The 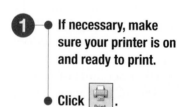 button in the Print group is used to define the printer settings and print the document.

1 • If necessary, make sure your printer is on and ready to print.

• Click .

Your screen should be similar to Figure 1.66

Having Trouble?

Please consult your instructor for printing procedures that may differ from the directions given here.

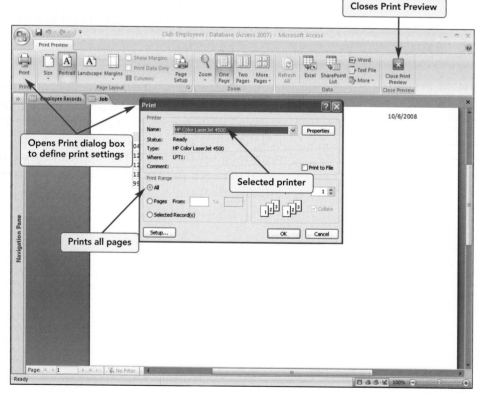

Figure 1.66

From the Print dialog box, you specify the printer you will be using and the document settings. The printer that is currently selected is displayed in the Name drop-down list box in the Printer section of the dialog box.

The Print Range area of the Print dialog box lets you specify the amount of the document you want printed. The range options are described in the following table.

Option	Action
All	Prints the entire document.
Pages	Prints pages you specify by typing page numbers in the text box.
Selected Records	Prints selected records only.

You will print the entire document.

2 • **If you need to change the selected printer to another printer, open the Name drop-down list box and select the appropriate printer (your instructor will tell you which printer to select).**

• **Click OK.**

A status message box is displayed briefly, informing you that the table is being printed. Your printed copy should be similar to the printout shown in the Case Study at the beginning of the lab.

Changing the Page Orientation and Margins

Next, you will preview and print the Employee Records table.

1 • **Click Close Print Preview in the Close Preview group.**

• **Make the Employee Records table active.**

• **Click Office Button.**

• **Select Print and choose Print Preview.**

• **Click on the table to zoom the preview.**

Your screen should look similar to Figure 1.67

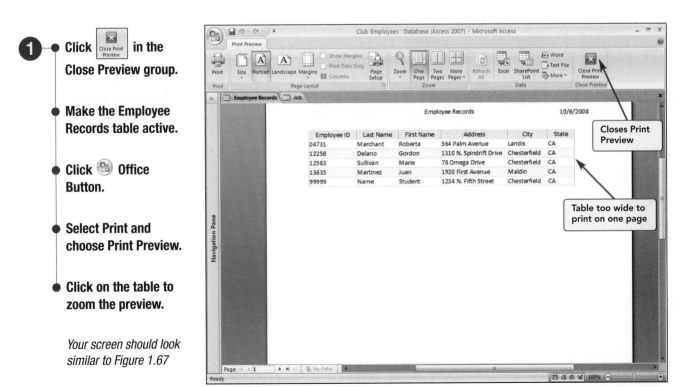

Figure 1.67

Notice that because the table is too wide to fit across the width of a page, only the first six fields are displayed on the page. Tables with multiple columns are typically too wide to fit on an $8^1/_2$ by 11 piece of paper. You would like to see both pages displayed onscreen.

2 ● Click ⊞ **Two Pages** in the Zoom group.

Your screen should be similar to Figure 1.68

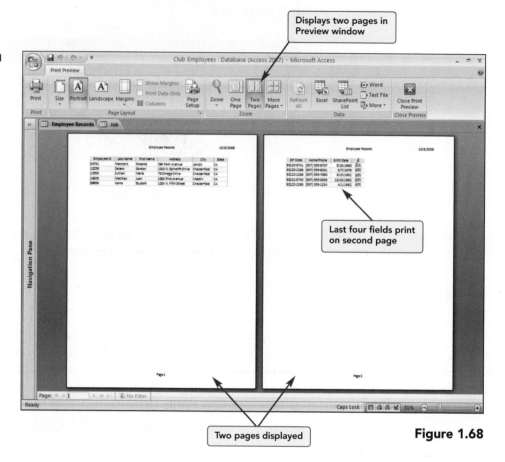

Displays two pages in Preview window

Last four fields print on second page

Two pages displayed

Figure 1.68

Rather than print the table on two pages, you decide to see whether changing the orientation of the table will allow you to print it on one page. **Orientation** refers to the direction that text prints on a page. Normal orientation is to print across the width of an $8^1/_2$-inch page. This is called **portrait orientation.** You can change the orientation to print across the length of the paper. This is called **landscape orientation.**

3 • Click 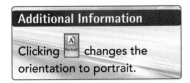 in the
Page Layout group.

Additional Information

Clicking 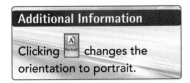 changes the
orientation to portrait.

*Your screen should be
similar to Figure 1.69*

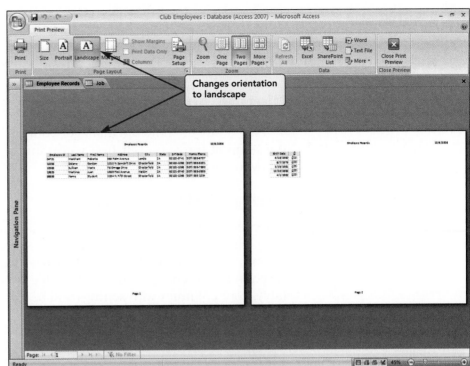

Figure 1.69

Although this helps, there are still two fields that do not fit on the page. To
fix this, you will try reducing the size of the page margins. The **margin** is
the blank space around the edge of a page. You will decrease the right and
left margin settings to 0.25 inch to see if this helps all fields fit on the page.

4 • Click 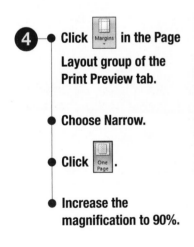 in the Page
Layout group of the
Print Preview tab.

• Choose Narrow.

• Click One Page.

• Increase the
magnification to 90%.

*Your screen should be
similar to Figure 1.70*

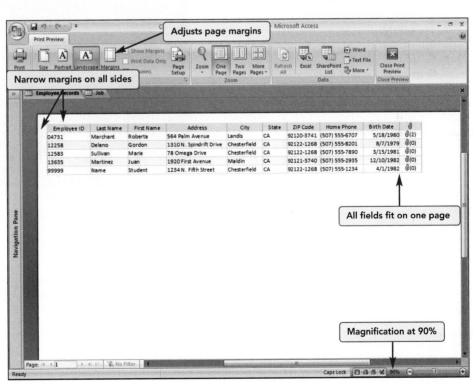

Figure 1.70

You can now see that all the fields will print on one page.

Previewing and Printing a Table   **AC1.73**

Access 2007

5 ● Print the table.

● Close the Print Preview window.

Closing and Opening a Table and Database

You are ready to show the manager your printed table to get approval on the setup of the data. But first you want to close the table and database that you created.

Closing a Table and Database

You close a table by closing its window and saving any layout changes you have made since your last Access session. Because you changed the column widths of the table in Datasheet view, you will be prompted to save the layout changes before the table is closed. If you do not save the table, your column width settings will be lost.

1 ● Display the Navigation pane.

● Click ⊠ Close 'Employee Records' in the datasheet window.

● If necessary, click ⎡ Yes ⎤ in response to the prompt to save the table.

● In a similar manner, close the Job table.

Your screen should be similar to Figure 1.71

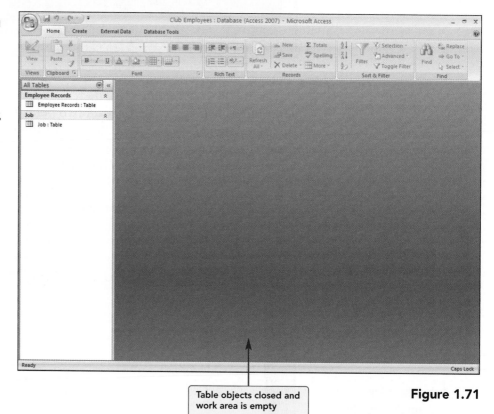

Table objects closed and work area is empty

Figure 1.71

The work area is empty because there are no open objects. The Navigation pane still displays the names of the table objects. Next, you will close the database.

2 ● Click  Office Button
and choose Close
Database.

Another Method

Do not click ☒ Close in the
Access window title bar as
this will exit the application.

*Your screen should be
similar to Figure 1.72*

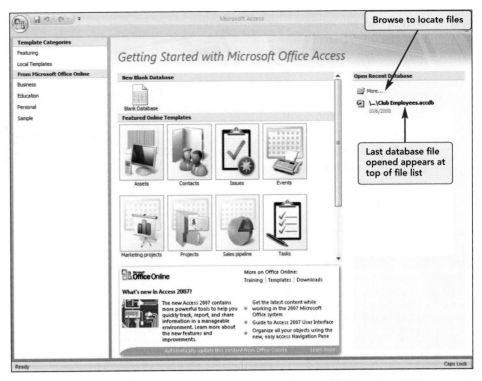

Figure 1.72

The Getting Started window is displayed again so you can open another
existing database file or create a new one.

More About

 See "6 Managing and
Maintaining Databases" in
the More About appendix to learn how to
save databases as a previous version.

Opening a Table and Database

You want to make sure that you know how to access your table of
employee records, so you will reopen it and then close it again. Because
opening a file is a very common task, there are many ways to do it. You can
select the file name from the Open Recent Database list, which displays the
names of the last nine recently used files. If the file name is not listed, you
can click  to browse your computer to locate the file.

You also can open database files that were created in previous versions of
Access that used the .mdb file extension. It must be converted to Access
2007 file format, however, if you want to take advantage of the new features
in Access 2007. If you plan to share a file with someone using Access 2003
or earlier, you can save the file using the .mdb file type; however, some
features may be lost. Otherwise, if you save it as an .accdb file type, the
recipient will not be able to open the file.

Another Method

You also can click 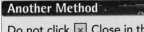 Office
Button and select the file
name from the Recent
Document list or choose
Open to browse your
computer to locate the file.
You also can use the
keyboard shortcut Ctrl + O
to browse for files.

Additional Information

The default setting is to
display the last nine recently
used files. This setting can be
changed using 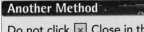 Office

Button/ ⊡ Access Options
/Advanced/Display.

1 ● **Choose** Club Employees from the Open Recent Database list.

● **Click** [Options...] in the Security Warning bar, select Enable this content, and click [OK] from the Microsoft Office Security Options dialog box.

Having Trouble?

Depending upon the security settings on your system, a Security Warning may not be displayed below the Ribbon.

● **Double-click on the Employee Records table.**

Another Method

You also can drag the object from the Navigation pane to the work area to open it.

Your screen should be similar to Figure 1.73

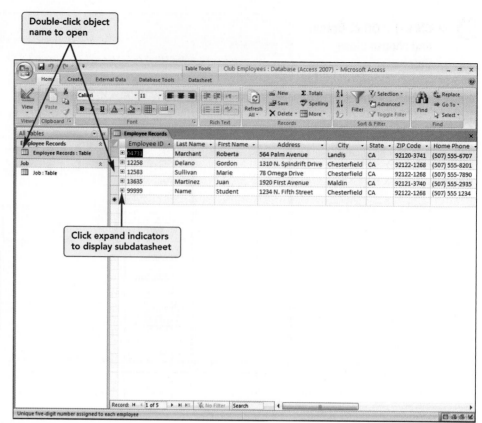

Figure 1.73

The database file is open and the Navigation pane displays the table name. The Employee Records table is open in the work area. Notice the expand indicators ⊞ at the beginning of each row. This indicates there is a subdatasheet linked to the records in this table.

Concept 7

Subdatasheet

7 A **subdatasheet** is a data table nested in another data table that contains data related or joined to the table where it resides. A subdatasheet allows you to easily view and edit related data. Subdatasheets are created automatically whenever relationships are established between tables.

In this case, the subdatasheet is to the Job table. Clicking ⊞ will expand the table to show the information in the subdatasheet table, Job.

2 ● Click ⊞ next to the first record.

Your screen should be similar to Figure 1.74

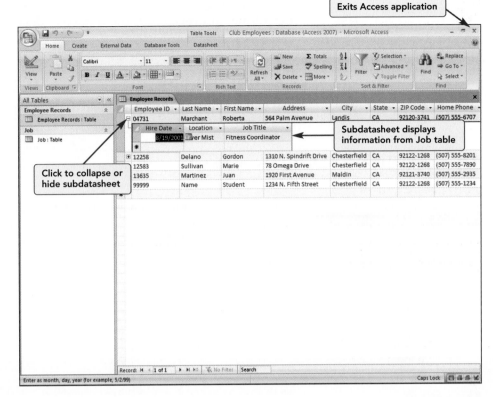

Exits Access application

Subdatasheet displays information from Job table

Click to collapse or hide subdatasheet

Figure 1.74

A subdatasheet appears and displays the location and job title information contained in the Job table for Roberta Marchant. Then, to hide or collapse the subdatasheet again, you click the collapse indicator ⊟.

3 ● Click ⊟ next to the first record.

Additional Information
You will learn more about relationships and subdatasheets in later labs.

You have created a database file that contains two tables and that follows the two basic principles of database design: do not include redundant information in tables and enter accurate and complete information. Although you may think the employee number is redundant data, it is the only way the information in the two tables can be associated. The database attains the goals of **normalization,** a design technique that identifies and eliminates redundancy by applying a set of rules to your tables to confirm that they are structured properly. These rules ensure that your design meets the **normal form** standards, a set of constraints that must be satisfied. There are five sequential normal form levels; however, meeting the third level, commonly called 3NF, is the level that is required for most database designs. This level requires that every nonkey column be dependent on the primary key and that nonkey columns are independent of each other.

You also have followed the five steps (plan, design, develop, implement, and refine and review) of the database design process while creating the database.

Exiting Access

You will continue to build and use the database of employee records in the next lab. Until then, you can exit Access.

1 ● **Click** ☒ **Close in the Access window title bar.**

Notice that this time you were not prompted to save the table because you did not make any changes to it since last opening it. If you had made changes, you would be prompted to save the file before exiting Access.

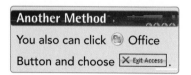

Focus on Careers

EXPLORE YOUR CAREER OPTIONS

Admitting Nurse

Can you imagine trying to organize the information of hundreds of patients in a busy emergency room? This is the job of an admitting nurse. They have to be able to enter, edit, and format data; add and delete records; and so on. This information is used by all departments of the hospital, from the doctors, to the pharmacy, and to the billing department. Without a proper understanding of database software, a hospital cannot run efficiently. The average salary of an admitting nurse is in the $40,000 to $50,000 range. The demand for nurses is expected to remain high.

Concept Summary

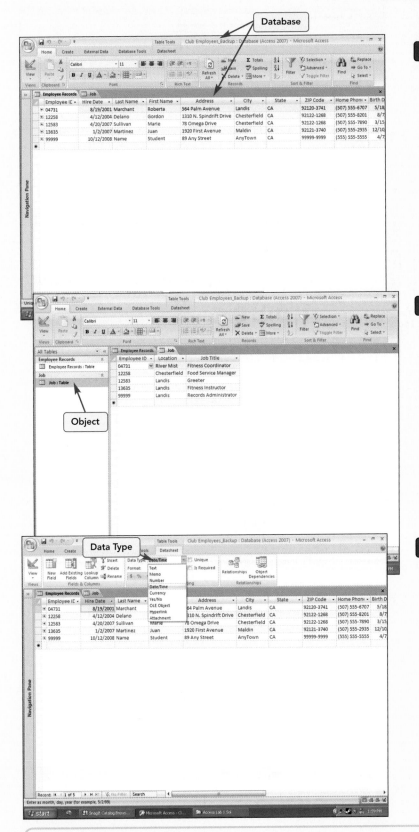

Database (AC1.4)

A database is an organized collection of related information.

Object (AC1.10)

An Access database is made up of several types of objects, such as a table or report, consisting of many elements. An object can be created, selected, and manipulated as a unit.

Data Type (AC1.17)

The data type defines the type of data the field will contain. Access uses the data type to ensure that the right kind of data is entered in a field.

Concept Summary

Field Property (AC1.24)

A field property is a characteristic that helps define a field. A set of field properties is associated with each field.

Primary Key (AC1.29)

A primary key is a field that uniquely identifies each record.

Lookup Field (AC1.62)

A lookup field provides a list of values from which the user can choose to make entering data into that field simpler and more accurate.

Subdatasheet (AC1.76)

A subdatasheet is a data table nested in another data table that contains data related or joined to the table where it resides.

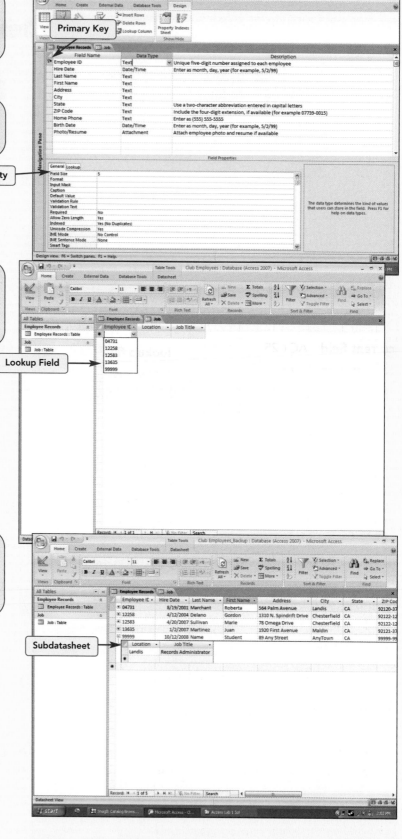

Lab Review

key terms

Allow Zero Length property AC1.24

Attachment data type AC1.18

AutoNumber data type AC1.18

Best Fit feature AC1.51

Caption property AC1.24

cell AC1.12

Clipboard AC1.67

column width AC1.50

composite key AC1.29

Currency data type AC1.18

current field AC1.25

current record AC1.12

data type AC1.17

database AC1.4

Datasheet view AC1.12

Date/Time data type AC1.18

Default Value property AC1.24

Design view AC1.12

destination AC1.67

drawing object AC1.40

field AC1.4

field name AC1.14

field property AC1.24

Field Size property AC1.24

field template AC1.20

foreign key AC1.59

form AC1.10

Form view AC1.12

Format property AC1.24

graphic AC1.40

header row AC1.12

Hyperlink data type AC1.18

Indexed property AC1.24

Input Mask property AC1.24

landscape orientation AC1.72

Layout view AC1.12

lookup field AC1.62

lookup list AC1.62

Lookup Wizard AC1.61

margin AC1.73

Memo data type AC1.18

navigation buttons AC1.12

Navigation pane AC1.11

normal form AC1.77

normalization AC1.77

Number data type AC1.18

object AC1.10

OLE Object data type AC1.18

orientation AC1.72

picture AC1.41

portrait orientation AC1.72

primary key AC1.29

Print Preview AC1.12

query AC1.10

record AC1.4

record number indicator AC1.12

relational database AC1.4

report AC1.10

Report view AC1.12

Required property AC1.24

Select All button AC1.12

serial value AC1.18

source AC1.62

subdatasheet AC1.76

table AC1.4

template AC1.7

Text data type AC1.18

Validation Rule property AC1.24

Validation Text property AC1.24

value list AC1.62

view AC1.11

wizard AC1.61

Yes/No data type AC1.18

MCAS Skills

The Microsoft Certified Applications Specialist (MCAS) certification program is designed to measure your proficiency in performing basic tasks using the Office 2007 applications. Getting certified demonstrates that you have the skills and provides a valuable industry credential for employment. See Reference 2: Microsoft Certified Applications Specialist (MCAS) for a complete list of the skills that were covered in Lab 1.

Lab Review

command summary

Command	Shortcut	Action
🗔 Office Button		
New		Opens a new blank database
Open	Ctrl + O	Opens an existing database
Save	Ctrl + S	Saves database object
Print/Print	Ctrl + P	Specifies print settings and prints current database object
Print/Print Preview		Displays file as it will appear when printed
Close Database		Closes open window
✕ Exit Access		Closes Access
Home tab		
Views group		
☑ Design View	☑	Displays object in Design view
▦ Datasheet View	▤	Displays object in Datasheet view
Clipboard group		
✂ Cut	Ctrl + X	Removes selected item and copies it to the Clipboard
▦ Copy	Ctrl + C	Duplicates selected item and copies to the Clipboard
📋 Paste	Ctrl + V	Inserts copy of item from Clipboard
Records group		
✕ Delete ▾	Delete	Deletes current record
▦ More ▾ /Column Width		Adjusts width of selected column
Find group		
⬚ Select ▾ /Select		Selects current record
Table Tools Datasheet tab		
Views group		
☑ Design View		Displays table in Design view
▦ Datasheet View		Displays table in Datasheet view
Fields & Columns group		
▦ New Field		Inserts a new field
▦ Delete		Removes selected field column

command summary

Command	Shortcut	Action
Rename		Renames selected field
Data Type & Formatting group		
Data Type: Text		Changes the data type for current field
Format: Formatting		Sets the display format of the selected field

Table Tools Design Tab

Command	Shortcut	Action
Views group		
Design View		Displays table in Design view
Datasheet View		Displays table in Datasheet view
Tools group		
Primary Key		Makes current field a primary key field
Delete Rows		Deletes selected field row

Print Preview Tab

Command	Shortcut	Action
Print group		
Print		Prints displayed object
Page Layout group		
Portrait		Changes print orientation to portrait
Landscape		Changes print orientation to landscape
Zoom group		
One Page		Displays one entire page in Print Preview
Two Pages		Displays two entire pages in Print Preview
Close Preview group		
Close Print Preview		Closes Print Preview window

screen identification

1. In the following Access screen, several items are identified by letters. Enter the correct term for each item in the spaces provided.

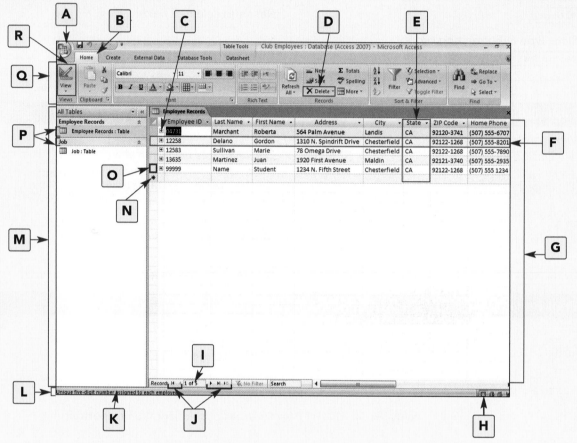

Possible answers for the screen identification are:

Design view	Select All button	**A.** _____	**J.** _____
Cell	Primary key indicator	**B.** _____	**K.** _____
Record number	Navigation buttons	**C.** _____	**L.** _____
indicator	Datasheet View button	**D.** _____	**M.** _____
Field name	Status bar	**E.** _____	**N.** _____
Work area	Tabs	**F.** _____	**O.** _____
Ribbon	Delete record	**G.** _____	**P.** _____
Object	Field	**H.** _____	**Q.** _____
Field description	Navigation pane	**I.** _____	**R.** _____
End of table indicator	Record		
Open tab	File menu		

matching

Match the numbered item with the correct lettered description.

1. primary key   _____   **a.** collection of related fields

2. Navigation pane   _____   **b.** a unit of a database

3. Datasheet view   _____   **c.** contains multiple tables linked by a common field

4. Attachment   _____   **d.** used to define the table structure

5. Design view   _____   **e.** used to open and manage database objects

6. field size   _____   **f.** a data type that stores multiple files of different file types in a single field

7. data type   _____   **g.** field that uniquely identifies each record

8. object   _____   **h.** displays table in row and column format

9. record   _____   **i.** defines the type of data the field will contain

10. relational database   _____   **j.** controls the maximum number of characters that can be entered in a field

fill-in

Complete the following statements by filling in the blanks with the correct terms.

1. You use the _____ located at the left of the work area to select the type of object you want to work with.

2. The _____ field property specifies how data displays in a table.

3. A field name is used to identify the _____ stored in a field.

4. The _____ data type restricts data to digits only.

5. Using _____ orientation prints across the length of the paper.

6. The field property that limits a text data type to a certain size is called a(n) _____.

7. A _____ is a data table nested in another data table that contains data related or joined to the table where it resides.

8. An Access database is made up of several types of _____.

9. The _____ is a field that uniquely identifies each record.

10. The _____ data type can be used to store a graphic file in a field.

Lab Exercises

Circle the correct answer to the following statements.

1.	A field description is a required part of the field definition.	True	False
2.	Interactive databases define relationships between tables by having common data in the tables.	True	False
3.	A field contains information about one person, thing, or place.	True	False
4.	The data type defines the information that can be entered in a field.	True	False
5.	You can format the text in a Memo field.	True	False
6.	A foreign key is a field in one table that refers to the primary key field in another table and indicates how the tables are related.	True	False
7.	Tables and queries are two types of database objects.	True	False
8.	A lookup field that uses another table as the source for values is called a value list.	True	False
9.	A table is a required object in a database.	True	False
10.	Changing the column width in the datasheet changes the field size.	True	False

multiple choice

Circle the letter of the correct response.

1. The last step of database development is _____.
   a. design
   b. develop
   c. review
   d. plan

2. _____ is a design technique that identifies and eliminates redundancy by applying a set of rules to your tables.
   a. Database development
   b. Normalization
   c. Validation
   d. Orientation

3. A _____ is often used as the primary key.
   a. phone number
   b. catalog number
   c. last name
   d. first name

4. You may lose data if your data and _____ are incompatible.
   a. field name
   b. data type
   c. default value
   d. field size

5. _____ affects the amount of data that you can enter into a field.
   a. Column width
   b. Field size
   c. Format
   d. Description size

6. A _____ is a field in one table that refers to the primary key field in another table and indicates how the tables are related.
   a. foreign key
   b. common key
   c. related key
   d. data key

7. A(n) _____ provides a list of values from which the user can choose.
   a. value field
   b. lookup field
   c. related field
   d. attachment field

8. Graphics can be inserted into a field that has a(n) _____ data type.
   a. graphic
   b. text
   c. attachment
   d. memo

9. The basic database objects are _____.
   a. panes, tables, queries, and reports
   b. tables, queries, forms, and reports
   c. forms, reports, data, and files
   d. portraits, keys, tables, and views

10. _____ view is only used to modify the table structure.
    a. Design
    b. Report
    c. Datasheet
    d. Query

Hands-On Exercises

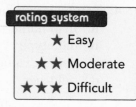

rating system

★ Easy

★★ Moderate

★★★ Difficult

step-by-step

Oak Ridge School Parent Contact Database ★

1. Oak Ridge Elementary School has decided to set up a database with the contact information for all students. As a parent, you have volunteered to do the initial database creation and teach the secretary at the school to maintain it. The database table you create will have the following information: student's last name, student's first name, guardian's name, home address, and home phone number. When you have finished, a printout of your completed database table should look similar to the one shown here.

ID	Student Last Name	Student First Name	Guardian	Street Address	City	State	ZIP Code	Home Phone	Alternate Phone
1	Roderick	Smithy	Shannon Roderick	1293 Hillview Rd.	Oak Ridge	UT	22301	(802) 555-0914	
3	Salazar	Gloria	Betha Salazar	103 Oak Ave.	Oak Ridge	UT	22301	(802) 555-8411	
4	Name	Student	Ricardo Ramirez	107 Oak Ave.	Oak Ridge	UT	22301	(802) 555-8632	(802) 555-9711

a. Create a blank database named **Oak Ridge School.** Design a table using the following field information:

Field Data	Type	Description	Field Size
ID	AutoNumber		Long Integer
Student Last Name	Text	Student's legal last name	25
Student First Name	Text	Include student's nickname in parentheses	25
Guardian	Text	First and last name of primary guardian.	55
Street Address	Text		75
City	Text		20
State	Text	Two-letter abbreviation.	2
ZIP Code	Text		5
Home Phone	Text		15

b. Switch to Datasheet view. Save the table as **Students**.
c. Enter the following records into the table, using Copy and Paste for fields that have the same data (such as the city):

Record 1	Record 2	Record 3
Roderick	Avery	Salazar
Smithy	Wilson	Gloria
Shannon Roderick	Rita Avery-Montoya	Betha Salazar
1293 Hillview Rd.	102 4th Street	103 Oak Ave.
Oak Ridge	Oak Ridge	Oak Ridge
UT	UT	UT
22301	22301	22301
(802) 555-0914	(802) 555-3375	(802) 555-8411

d. Adjust the column widths appropriately.

e. Delete record 2. Add another record with the following data:

> **[Your last name]**
>
> **[Your first name]**
>
> **Ricardo Ramirez**
>
> **107 Oak Ave.**
>
> **Oak Ridge**
>
> **UT**
>
> **22301**
>
> **(802) 555-8632**

f. Make the following changes to the table design:

g. Add a new field after the Home Phone field with the following definitions:

> **Field Name:**   **Alternate Phone**
>
> **Data Type:**   Text
>
> **Field Size:**   **15**

Change the ZIP code field size to **10**.

h. Enter the Alternate Phone number of **(802) 555-9711** and the ZIP Code of **22301-4459** for record 4.

i. Best fit all columns.

j. View the table in Print Preview; change the page orientation to landscape and margins to Narrow.

k. Print, save, and close the table.

EchoPlex Records Database ★★

2. Your record collection has expanded beyond a hobby into an online business. In order to meet the needs of your expanding client base, you need to get your inventory cataloged. When you are finished, your printed database table should be similar to the one shown here.

Records   10/6/2008

Catalog Number	Item	Title	Acquired Date	📎
1	LP	Up	8/13/2002	📎(1)
3	12"	Forever Blue	7/8/2005	📎(0)
4	LP	Definitive Collection	3/3/2003	📎(0)
5		Student Name	9/4/2006	📎(0)

a. Create a blank database named EchoPlex.

b. From the Assets Field Templates list, add the following fields to the table:

Item

Description

Acquired Date

Attachments

c. Switch to Design view. Save the table as **Records**.

d. Change the ID Field Name to **Catalog Number**. Change the Description Field Name to **Title**.

e. Change the Field Size of the Item field to **4**.

f. Return to Datasheet view. Add the following records to the table:

Item	LP	12"	12"	LP
Title	Up	Rank	Forever Blue	Definitive Collection
Acquired Date	8/13/2002	4/1/2006	7/8/2005	3/3/2003

g. Insert the image file ac01_Guitar in the Attachment field of the first record.

h. Adjust the column widths using the Best Fit feature.

i. Delete the record for the title Rank. Add a new record and enter your name in the Title field and the current date in the Acquired Date field.

j. Preview and print the table in portrait orientation with wide margins.

k. Save and close the table. Exit Access.

Library Catalog Database ★★

3. You are a volunteer at a small county library. The library recently received a large collection of young adult books and would like to keep better track of the titles. The library is still using an antiquated method for cataloging most its books. Because of your computer skills, you have been asked to create a database containing the catalog number, title, author, and copyright date of each

of the new books. The young adult titles database will serve as a model for the library's entire collection; after it is done, the database will make search, tracking, and inventory functions much easier. Your printed database table should be similar to the one shown here.

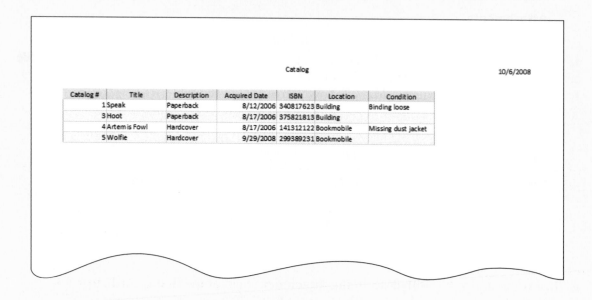

Catalog						10/6/2008
Catalog #	Title	Description	Acquired Date	ISBN	Location	Condition
1	Speak	Paperback	8/12/2006	340817623	Building	Binding loose
3	Hoot	Paperback	8/17/2006	375821813	Building	
4	Artemis Fowl	Hardcover	8/17/2006	141312122	Bookmobile	Missing dust jacket
5	Wolfie	Hardcover	9/29/2008	299389231	Bookmobile	

a. Create a blank database named County Library.

b. Add fields using the following field templates from the Assets list:

   Item

   Description

   Acquired Date

   Manufacturer

c. Switch to Design view. Save the table as **Catalog**.

d. Edit the Field Properties using the following information:

Field Data	Type	Description	Field Size
Catalog #	AutoNumber		
Title	Text	Include complete title	150
Description	Text	Hardcover or paperback	
Acquired Date	Date/Time		15
ISBN	Number	Unique 10-digit number	

e. Add the following new fields:

Field Name	Data Type	Description	Field Size
Location	Text	Building or Bookmobile	30
Condition	Memo	Describe condition of book if needed	

f. Switch to Datasheet view and enter the following records into the table:

	Record 1	Record 2	Record 3	Record 4
Title	Speak	Freak the Mighty	Hoot	Artemis Fowl
Description	Paperback	Paperback	Paperback	Hardcover
Acquired Date	8/12/2006	8/12/2006	8/17/2006	8/17/2006
Location	Building	Bookmobile	Building	Bookmobile
ISBN	0340817623	0439286069	0375821813	0141312122
Condition	Binding loose			Missing dust jacket

g. Best Fit all column widths.
h. Delete record 2. Add another record with the following data:

Wolfie

9/29/08

Hardcover

Bookmobile

0299389231

i. Check the table in Print Preview. Change the page layout to landscape with wide margins. Print, save, and close the table. Exit Access.

DownTown Internet Café Inventory Database ★★★

4. The Downtown Internet Café, which you helped get off the ground, is an overwhelming success. The clientele is growing every day, as is the demand for the beverages the café serves. Up until now, the information about the vendors has been kept in an alphabetical card file. This has become quite unwieldy, however, and Evan, the owner, would like a more sophisticated tracking system. He would like you to create a database containing each supply item and the contact information for the vendor that sells that item. When you are finished, your database tables should be similar to those shown here.

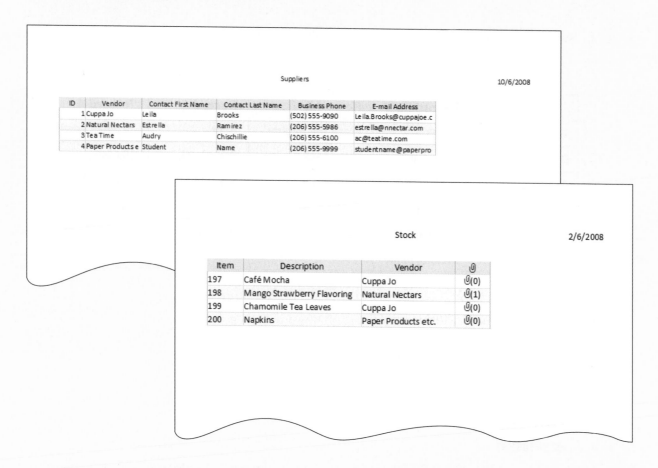

Suppliers 10/6/2008

ID	Vendor	Contact First Name	Contact Last Name	Business Phone	E-mail Address
1	Cuppa Jo	Leila	Brooks	(502) 555-9090	Leila.Brooks@cuppajoe.c
2	Natural Nectars	Estrella	Ramirez	(206) 555-5986	estrella@nnectar.com
3	Tea Time	Audry	Chischillie	(206) 555-6100	ac@teatime.com
4	Paper Products e	Student	Name	(206) 555-9999	studentname@paperpro

Stock 2/6/2008

Item	Description	Vendor	🔗
197	Café Mocha	Cuppa Jo	🔗(0)
198	Mango Strawberry Flavoring	Natural Nectars	🔗(1)
199	Chamomile Tea Leaves	Cuppa Jo	🔗(0)
200	Napkins	Paper Products etc.	🔗(0)

a. Create a blank database named Cafe Inventory.

b. Design a table using the following field templates:

  From Assets:

  Item

  Description

c. Switch to Design view. Save the table as **Stock**.

d. Delete the ID field. Make Item the primary key field.

e. Add the following information to the field properties:

Field Data	Type	Description	Field Size
Item	Text	Unique three-digit product number	3
Description	Text	Name of product	50

f. Create a second table using the following field templates:

  From Contacts:

  Company

  First Name

  Last Name

  Business Phone

  E-mail Address

g. Switch to Design view. Save the table as **Suppliers**.

h. Edit the field properties as shown here:

Vendor	Text	Company name of supplier	50
Contact First Name	Text		50
Contact Last Name	Text		50
Business Phone	Text	Include the area code in parentheses: (800) 555-5555	15
E-mail	Text	E-mail address of contact person	50

i. Enter the following records into the Stock and Suppliers tables:

Stock table			
Record 1	**Record 2**	**Record 3**	
197	198	199	
Café Mocha	Mango Strawberry Flavoring	Chamomile Tea Leaves	
Suppliers table			
Record 1	**Record 2**	**Record 3**	**Record 4**
Cuppa Jo	Natural Nectars	Tea Time	Paper Products etc.
Leila	Estrella	Audry	Enter your first name
Brooks	Ramirez	Chischillie	Enter your last name
(502) 555-9090	(206) 555-5986	(206) 555-6001	(206) 555-9999
lbrooks@cuppajo.com	estrella@nnectar.com	ac@teatime.com	Yourname@paperproducts.com

j. Add the existing field, Vendor, from the Suppliers table as the last field in the Stock table.

k. In the Stock table, select Cuppa Jo as the vendor for the first record, Natural Nectars for the second record, and Tea Time for the third record.

l. In the Suppliers table, edit the record for ID 1 by changing the E-mail address to **Leila.Brooks@cuppajo.com**.

m. Add a new field to the Stock table named **Picture.** Make the data type Attachment. For item number 198 insert the file ac01_Flavoring.

n. Add the following new item to the Stock file.

Item:	**200**
Description:	**Napkins**
Vendor:	**Paper Products etc.**

o. Adjust the column widths in both tables using Best Fit.

p. Preview the Suppliers table. Change to landscape orientation. Change the margins to wide and print the table.

q. Close the database. Exit Access.

Kodiak Construction Database ★ ★ ★

5. You have just been hired by Kodiak Paint and Construction to create and maintain a database containing information about their clients and jobs. The company has grown rapidly and they need ready access to information about jobs spread across the city. When you are finished, your tables should be similar to those shown here.

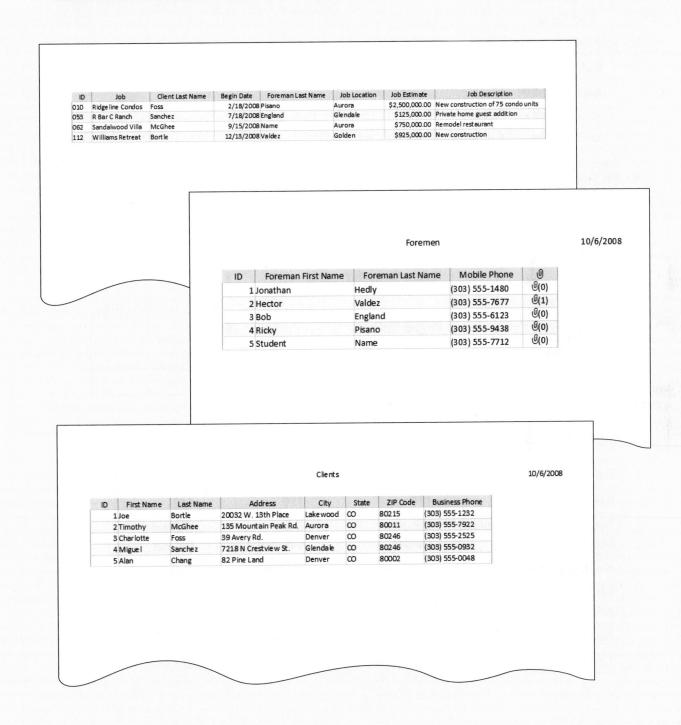

ID	Job	Client Last Name	Begin Date	Foreman Last Name	Job Location	Job Estimate	Job Description
010	Ridgeline Condos	Foss	2/18/2008	Pisano	Aurora	$2,500,000.00	New construction of 75 condo units
053	R Bar C Ranch	Sanchez	7/18/2008	England	Glendale	$125,000.00	Private home guest addition
062	Sandalwood Villa	McGhee	9/15/2008	Name	Aurora	$750,000.00	Remodel restaurant
112	Williams Retreat	Bortle	12/13/2008	Valdez	Golden	$925,000.00	New construction

Foremen   10/6/2008

ID	Foreman First Name	Foreman Last Name	Mobile Phone	🔗
1	Jonathan	Hedly	(303) 555-1480	🔗(0)
2	Hector	Valdez	(303) 555-7677	🔗(1)
3	Bob	England	(303) 555-6123	🔗(0)
4	Ricky	Pisano	(303) 555-9438	🔗(0)
5	Student	Name	(303) 555-7712	🔗(0)

Clients   10/6/2008

ID	First Name	Last Name	Address	City	State	ZIP Code	Business Phone
1	Joe	Bortle	20032 W. 13th Place	Lakewood	CO	80215	(303) 555-1232
2	Timothy	McGhee	135 Mountain Peak Rd.	Aurora	CO	80011	(303) 555-7922
3	Charlotte	Foss	39 Avery Rd.	Denver	CO	80246	(303) 555-2525
4	Miguel	Sanchez	7218 N Crestview St.	Glendale	CO	80246	(303) 555-0932
5	Alan	Chang	82 Pine Land	Denver	CO	80002	(303) 555-0048

Lab Exercises

a. Create a blank database named Kodiak Construction. Design a table using the following field templates:

   From Projects:

   Project Name

   Begin Date

   End Date

b. Add the following additional fields to the table.

Field Name	Type
Job Description	Memo
Job Location	Text
Job Estimate	Currency

c. Save the table as **Jobs**. Switch to Design view.

d. Change the Project Name field name to **Job**. Delete the End Date field. Add field descriptions and make the changes to the field properties shown in the following table:

Field Data	Type	Description	Field Size	Format
ID	Number	Unique three-digit job ID	3	
Begin Date				General date
Job		Project Name	75	
Description		Brief description of project		
Job Location	Text	Enter city only	25	

e. Enter the following records into the table:

Record 1	Record 2	Record 3	Record 4	Record 5
034	131	110	120	142
Summit Lakes	Sandalwood Villa	Ridgeline Condos	R Bar C Ranch	Williams Retreat
4/13/2008	9/15/2008	2/18/2008	7/18/2008	12/13/2008
Remodel golf club	Remodel restaurant	New construction of 75 condo units	Private home guest addition	New construction
Denver	Aurora	Aurora	Glendale	Golden
1,200,000	750,000	2,500,000	125,000	925,000

f. Adjust the column widths using Best Fit.

g. Delete the record for the Summit Lakes job.

h. Create a second table for the client information using the following field templates:

> **From Contacts:**
>> **First Name**
>>
>> **Last Name**
>>
>> **Address**
>>
>> **City**
>>
>> **State/Province**
>>
>> **ZIP/Postal Code**
>>
>> **Business Phone**

i. Save the table as **Clients**.

j. Add field descriptions and make the changes to the field properties shown in the following table:

First Name		First name of client	25
Last Name		Last name of client	25
Address	Text		50
State		Use two character abbreviation	2
ZIP Code		Enter 10 digit code, if available	10
Business Phone		Enter phone as (###) ###-####	14

k. Add the following client information:

Joe	Timothy	Charlotte	Miguel	Alan
Bortle	McGhee	Foss	Sanchez	Chang
20032 W. 13th Place	135 Mountain Peak Rd.	39 Avery Rd.	7218 N. Crestview St.	82 Pine Lane
Lakewood	Aurora	Denver	Glendale	Denver
CO	CO	CO	CO	CO
80215	80011	80012	80246	80002
(303) 555-1232	(303) 555-7922	(303) 555-2525	(303) 555-0932	(303) 555-0048

l. Create a third table for the foreman information with the following fields:

Field Data	Type	Description	Field Size
Foreman First Name	Text		25
Foreman Last Name	Text		25
Mobile Phone	Text	Enter phone as (###) ###-####	14
Picture	Attachment	Photo of foreman	

m. Save the table as **Foremen.**

n. Enter the following information for the five foremen.

Jonathan Hedly	Hector Valdez	Bob England	Ricky Pisano	Your Name
(303) 555-1480	(303) 555-7677	(303) 555-6123	(303) 555-9438	(303) 555-7712

o. Add the file ac01_Valdez to the attachment field for Hector Valdez.

p. Add the existing field Foreman Last Name from the Foremen table to the Jobs table after the Begin Date field.

q. Enter the following foremen for each job:

Job	Foreman
010	Pisano
053	England
062	Your Name
112	Valdez

r. Add the existing field Last Name from the Clients table to after the Job field in the Jobs table. Rename the field **Client Last Name.**

s. Enter the following clients for each job:

Job	Client
010	Foss
053	Sanchez
062	McGhee
112	Bortle

t. Best fit all fields in all tables.

u. Preview and print the Jobs table in landscape orientation with narrow margins. Print the Foremen table in portrait orientation with wide margins.

v. Save and close all tables and exit Access.

on your own

Valley View Newsletter Advertising Database ★

1. Your homeowner's association distributes a monthly newsletter, *Valley View News,* to keep residents up to date with neighborhood news. In the past year, there has been rapid growth in building, including more houses and small office complexes. There are also plans to build an elementary school, fire station, and shopping center in the community. Consequently, the newsletter is now the size of a small newspaper, and the homeowners' dues are not covering the expense of publishing it.

The editorial staff has already begun selling ad space in the newsletter to local businesses, and, based on your background in database management, they have asked you to set up a database to keep track of the advertiser contact information. You agree to design such a database, called Valley View News, and tell them you will have something to show them at the next meeting. Your finished database should include each advertiser's billing number, business name and address, and contact name and phone number in a table named **Advertisers**. Include a record that has your name as the contact name. Preview and print the table when you are finished.

Lab Exercises

Music Collection Database ★

2. You have just purchased a 200-disk CD carousel and now you would like to organize and catalog your CDs. You realize that without an updatable list, it will be difficult to maintain an accurate list of what is in the changer. To get the most out of your new purchase, you decide a database is in order. Create a new database called Music Collection and a table called **CD Catalogue**. The table you create should include the Artist's Name, Album Title, Genre, and Position Number. Make the Position field the primary key (because you may have multiple CDs by a given artist). Enter at least 15 records. Include an entry that has your name as the artist. Preview and print the table when you are finished.

Patient Database ★

3. You are the manager of a newly opened dental office. As one of your first projects, you need to create a patient database. Create a database called Dental Patients and a table named **Personal Information**. The database table you set up should contain patient identification numbers, last and first names, addresses, and phone numbers. Also include a field named "Referred by" and another field named "Patient since". Use appropriate field sizes and make the ID number field the primary key. Enter at least ten records, adjusting the column widths as necessary. Include a record that contains your name as the patient. Preview and print the table.

Old Watch Database Using the Web ★★

4. You have a small online business, Timeless Treasures, that locates and sells vintage wrist and pocket watches. Your business and inventory has grown large enough now that you have decided to use a database to track your inventory. Create a simple database named Timeless Treasures with a table named **Watches** that contains identification numbers, manufacturer (Waltham, Hamilton, Melrose), category (pocket watch, wrist watch), description, price, and quantity on hand. Size the fields appropriately and assign a primary key to one of them. Enter at least 10 records in the table. To obtain data about watches to include in your table, search the Web on "old watches". Use the information you locate to complete the data for the records in your table. Adjust column widths as necessary. Include your name as the manufacturer in one of the records. Preview and print the table.

Expense Tracking Database ★★★

5. You work in the accounting department at a start-up company called EMP Enterprises. One of your duties is to process, which up until now was a simple task of having the employees fill out a form and submit it to you for payment. You would then cut a check for them and charge it to the general expense fund of the company. However, the company has grown tremendously in the last year, adding employees and departments at a rapid rate, and the executive team has decided that it is time to start managing the income and expenses on a much more detailed level. To this end, you need to create a database that includes the employee ID, employee name, submission date, expense type, and expense amount for each expense report that is turned in. Name the database EMP Enterprises. Create two tables, one for the employee information named Employee Info and the other for employee expenses named Employee Expenses. Include the Employee ID, First Name and Last Name fields in the Employee Data table. Include the Employee ID, Submission Date, Expense Type and Expense Amount fields in the Employee Expenses table. Use the Currency data type for the Expense Amount field, and appropriate data types for all other fields. Size the fields appropriately. Delete the ID field from the Employee Data table and make the Employee ID field the primary key. Enter at least 15 records. Adjust the column widths as necessary. Delete one of the records you just entered, and then edit one of the remaining records so it contains your name as the employee. Preview and print both tables.

Modifying and Filtering a Table and Creating a Form

LAB 2

Objectives

After completing this lab, you will know how to:

1 Navigate a large table.

2 Change field format properties.

3 Set default field values.

4 Insert a field.

5 Define validation rules.

6 Hide and redisplay fields.

7 Create a lookup field.

8 Find and replace data.

9 Sort records.

10 Format a datasheet.

11 Filter a table.

12 Create, modify, and use a form.

13 Preview, print, close, and save a form.

14 Identify object dependencies.

15 Add file and object documentation.

Case Study

Lifestyle Fitness Club

The Lifestyle Fitness Club owners, Ryan and Felicity, are very pleased with your plans for the organization of the database and with your progress in creating the first table of basic employee data. As you have seen, creating a database takes planning and a great deal of time to set up the structure and enter the data. As you have continued to add more employee records to the table, you have noticed several errors. You also realize that you forgot to include a field for the employee's gender. Even with the best of planning and care, errors occur and the information may change. You will see how easy it is to modify the database

structure and to customize field properties to provide more control over the data that is entered in a field.

Even more impressive, as you will see in this lab, is the program's ability to locate information in the database. This is where all the hard work of entering data pays off. With a click of a button, you can find data that might otherwise take hours to locate. The result saves time and improves the accuracy of the output.

You also will see how you can make the data you are looking at onscreen more pleasing and easier to read by creating and using a form.

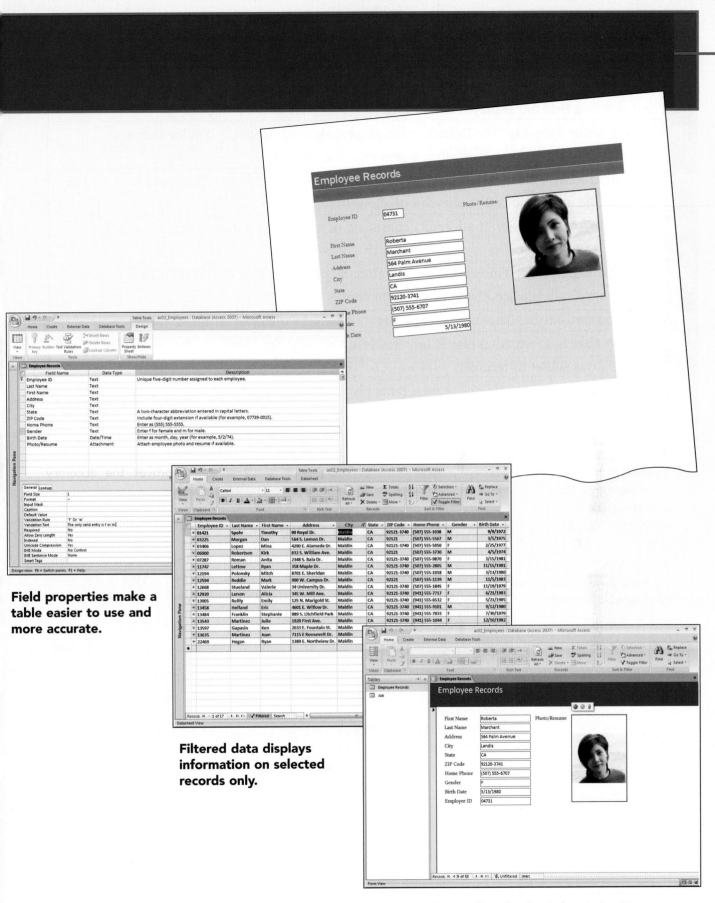

Field properties make a table easier to use and more accurate.

Filtered data displays information on selected records only.

Forms can be used to display information in an easy-to-read manner and make data entry easier.

Concept Preview

The following concepts will be introduced in this lab:

1 **Format Property** The Format property is used to specify the way that numbers, dates, times, and text in a field are displayed and printed.

2 **Default Value Property** The Default Value property is used to specify a value that is automatically entered in a field when a new record is created.

3 **Validation Rule** Validation rules are used to control the data that can be entered in a field by defining the input values that are valid or allowed.

4 **Expression** An expression is a formula consisting of a combination of symbols that will produce a single value.

5 **Find and Replace** The Find and Replace feature helps you quickly find specific information and automatically replace it with new information.

6 **Sort** You can sort the data in a table to quickly rearrange the order of the records.

7 **Filter** A filter is a restriction placed on records in the open datasheet or form to quickly isolate and display a subset of records.

8 **Form** A form is a database object used primarily to display records onscreen to make it easier to enter new records and to make changes to existing records.

9 **Controls** Controls are objects that display information, perform actions, or enhance the design of a form or report.

Navigating a Large Table

You have continued to add more records to the Lifestyle Fitness Club employee database. As you entered the data, you know you made data entry errors that still need to be corrected. Additionally, you have found that with the addition of records, it takes much longer to move around in the datasheet. Typical database tables are very large and consequently can be very inefficient to navigate. Learning how to move around in a large table will save time and help you get the job done faster. You want to open the expanded database that you saved using a new file name, and to continue working on and refining the Records table.

Note: Before you begin, you may want to create a backup copy of the ac02_Employees file by copying and renaming it.

1
- Start Office Access 2007.

- In the Open Recent Database list, click [📂 More...].

- Change the location to the location containing your data files.

- Double-click ac02_Employees.

- Click [Options...] in the Security Warning bar just below the ribbon.

- Choose Enable this content and click [OK].

- Open the Employee Records table.

Your screen should be similar to Figure 2.1

Having Trouble?
Your screen may display a different number of records depending on your monitor settings.

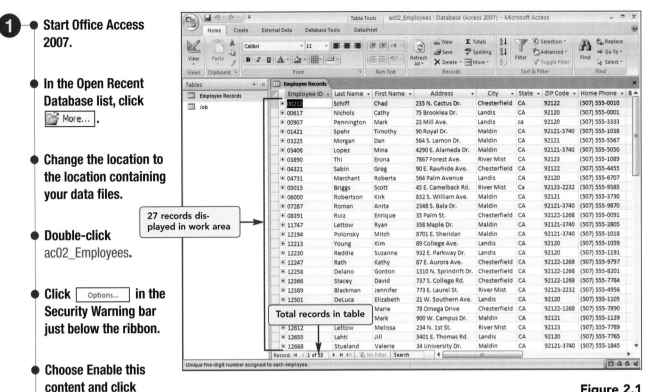

27 records displayed in work area

Total records in table

Figure 2.1

By default, the table is displayed in Datasheet view. As you can see from the record number indicator, the updated table now contains 53 records.

Moving Using the Keyboard

In a large table, there are many methods you can use to quickly navigate through records in Datasheet view. You can always use the mouse to move from one field or record to another. However, if the information is not visible in the window, you must scroll the window using the scroll bar first. The following table presents several keyboard methods that will help you move around in the datasheet.

Keys	Effect
Page Down	Down one window
Page Up	Up one window
Ctrl + Page Up	Left one window
Ctrl + Page Down	Right one window
Ctrl + End	Last field of last record
Ctrl + Home	First field of first record
Ctrl + ↑	Current field of first record
Ctrl + ↓	Current field of last record

Currently, records 1 through 27 are displayed in the work area. You can easily move from one window of records to the next.

1 ● Press Page Down.

Having Trouble?
If your screen displays a different number of records, this is because your monitor and system setup may be different than those used to create the figures in the text.

Your screen should be similar to Figure 2.2

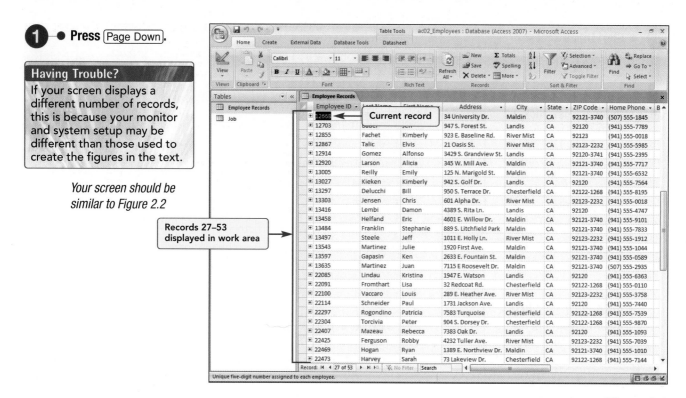

Figure 2.2

Now records 27 through 53 are displayed in the window. The first record in the window is now the current record.

Because of the number and width of the fields, all of the fields cannot be displayed in the window at the same time. Rather than scrolling the window horizontally to see the additional fields, you can quickly move to the right a window at a time.

2 ● Press Ctrl + Page Down.

Your screen should be similar to Figure 2.3

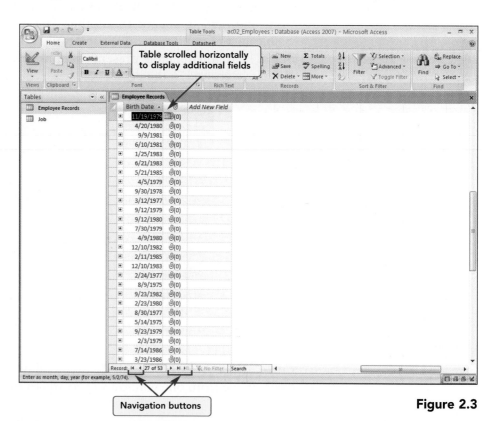

Figure 2.3

The table scrolled horizontally one window to the right and the last two fields in the table are now visible.

Moving Using the Navigation Buttons

The navigation buttons in the status bar also provide navigation shortcuts. These buttons are described in the following table.

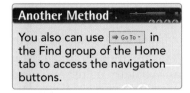

Another Method

You also can use ⇒ Go To ▾ in the Find group of the Home tab to access the navigation buttons.

Button	Effect
◄	First record, same field
◄	Previous record, same field
►	Next record, same field
►►	Last record, same field
►*	New (blank) record

Additional Information

You can move to a specific record by typing the record number in the Record Number Indicator box.

You will use the navigation buttons to move to the same field that is currently selected in the last record, and then back to the same field of the first record. Then you will move to the first field of the first record.

1 ● Click ►► **Last Record.**

● Click ◄ **First Record.**

● Press [Home].

Your screen should be similar to Figure 2.4

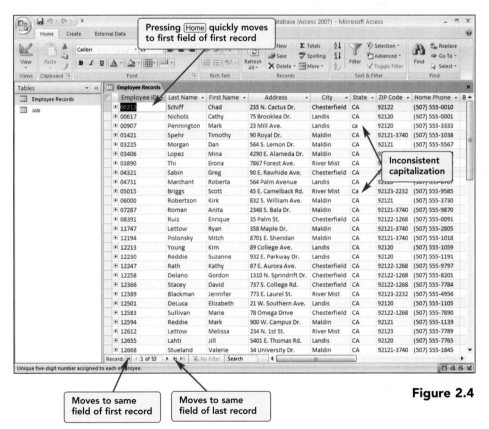

Figure 2.4

The first field of the first record is selected.

Customizing and Inserting Fields

As you looked through the records, you noticed that record 3 has a lowercase entry in the State field and that record 10 has a mixed-case entry. You want all the State field entries to be consistently entered in all uppercase letters. Also, because all the club locations are in California, it is unlikely that any club employees live in another state. Rather than repeatedly entering the same state for each record, you want the State field to automatically display CA. You will make these changes to the State field by modifying its properties.

Additionally, you realize that you forgot to include a field for each employee's gender. While developing a table, you can modify and refine how the table operates. You can easily add and delete fields and add restrictions on the data that can be entered in a field as well as define the way that the data entered in a field will be displayed.

Setting Display Formats

You will begin by fixing the display of the entries in the State field. Instead of manually editing each field, you will fix the entries by defining a display format for the field to customize the way the entry is displayed.

Concept 1

Format Property

1   The **Format property** is used to specify the way that numbers, dates, times, and text in a field are displayed and printed. Format properties do not change the way Access stores data, only the way the data is displayed. To change the format of a field, you can select from predefined formats or create a custom format by entering different symbols in the Format text box. Text and Memo data types can use any of the four symbols shown in the following table.

Symbol	Meaning	Example
@	Requires a text character or space	@@@-@@-@@@ would display 123456789 as 123-45-6789. Nine characters or spaces are required.
>	Forces all characters to uppercase	> would display SMITH whether you entered SMITH, smith, or Smith.
<	Forces all characters to lowercase	< would display smith whether you entered SMITH, smith, or Smith.
&	Allows an optional text character	@@-@@& would display 12345 as 12-345 and 12.34 as 12-34. Four out of five characters are required, and a fifth is optional.

You want to change the format of the State field to display the entries in all uppercase characters.

1 • Click  Design View.

• Click the State field to make it the current field.

• Move to the Format field property text box.

• Type >.

Your screen should be similar to Figure 2.5

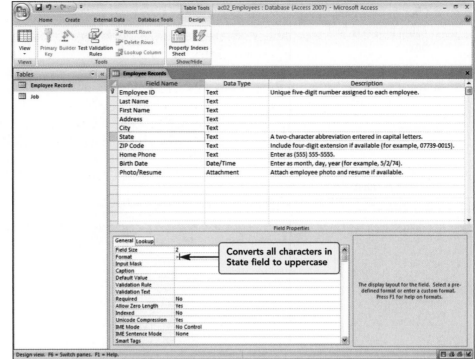

Converts all characters in State field to uppercase

Figure 2.5

Setting Default Values

Next, you want to change the State field for new records to automatically display CA. To do this, you specify a default value property.

Concept 2

Default Value Property

2 The **Default Value property** is used to specify a **value** that is automatically entered in a field when a new record is created. This property is commonly used when most of the entries in a field will be the same for the entire table. That default value is then displayed automatically in the field. When users add a record to the table, they can either accept this value or enter another value. This saves time while entering data.

You will set the State field's default value to display CA.

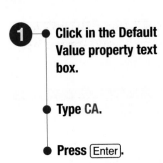

1 ● Click in the Default Value property text box.

● Type **CA**.

● Press (Enter).

Your screen should be similar to Figure 2.6

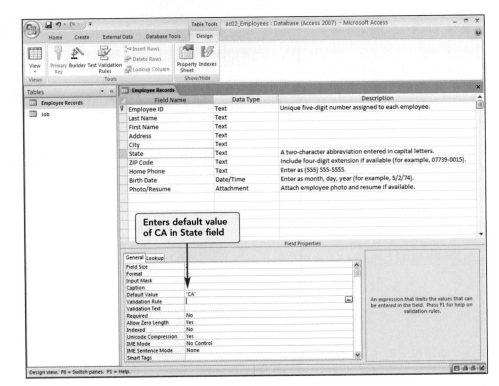

Enters default value of CA in State field

Figure 2.6

The default value is automatically enclosed in quotation marks to identify the entry as a group of characters called a **character string.** To see the effect on the table of setting a default value, you will return to Datasheet view and look at a new blank record.

Next, you want to see the effect of the modifications to the State field's properties on the table.

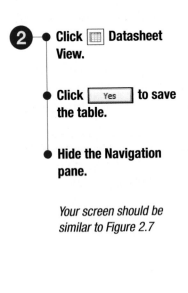

2 ● Click ▦ Datasheet View.

● Click [Yes] to save the table.

● Hide the Navigation pane.

Your screen should be similar to Figure 2.7

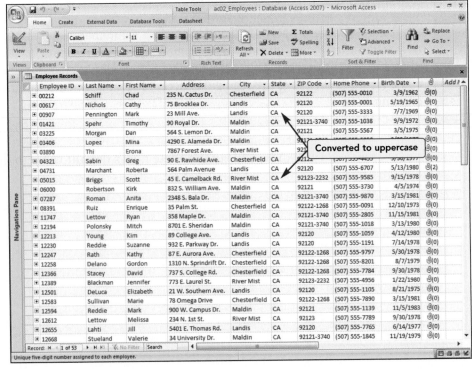

Converted to uppercase

Figure 2.7

You can see that records 3 (Mark Pennington) and 10 (Scot Briggs) now correctly display the state in capital letters. Setting the format for the field will prevent this type of error from occurring again.

3 ● **Click** 🔲 **New (blank) Record on the status bar to move to a new record.**

Your screen should be similar to Figure 2.8

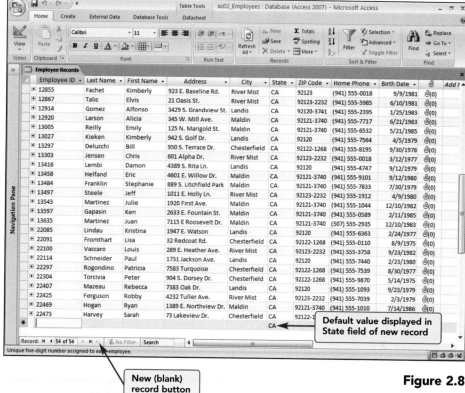

New (blank) record button

Figure 2.8

The new blank record at the end of the table displays CA as the default value for the State field. If you did need to enter a different state, it would display in all capital letters because of the format property setting associated with the field.

Inserting a Field

Now you want to add the new field to hold each employee's gender. Although it is better to include all the necessary fields when creating the table structure, it is possible to add fields to a table at a later time. After looking at the order of the fields, you decide to add the Gender field between the Home Phone and Birth Date fields. To do so, you will switch to Design view to insert the new field in the table.

Another Method

You also can insert a field in Datasheet view by moving to the location where you want to insert the new field and using ⬚ Insert on the Datasheet tab. However, you still need to switch to Design view to set the new field's properties.

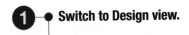

1 ● Switch to Design view.

● Make the Birth Date
field current.

● Click `Insert Rows` in the
Tools group of the
Design tab.

Another Method
You also can use Insert Rows
on the shortcut menu.

*Your screen should be
similar to Figure 2.9*

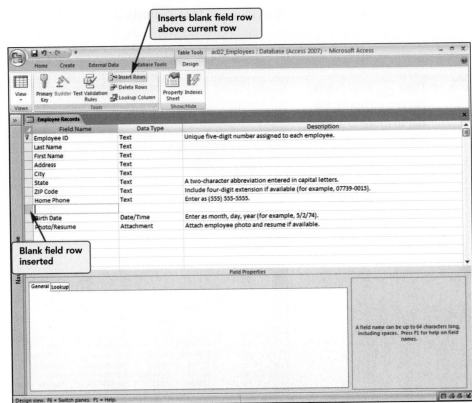

Figure 2.9

A new blank row is inserted into the table. Next, you will name the field
and set its properties.

2 ● Enter the new field
definitions from the
table shown here:

Field Name	Gender
Data Type	Text
Description	Ener f for female and m for male.
Field Size	1
Format	>

*Your screen should be
similar to Figure 2.10*

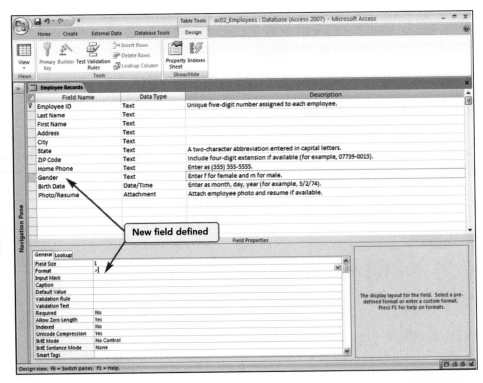

Figure 2.10

Defining Validation Rules

The only two characters you want the Gender field to accept are F for female and M for male. To specify that these two characters are the only entries acceptable in the Gender field, you will add a validation rule to the field's properties.

Concept 3
Validation Rule

3 **Validation rules** are used to control the data that can be entered in a field by defining the input values that are valid or allowed. Certain checks on the validity of the data that is entered in a field are performed automatically based on the field's data type and size. For example, in a field whose data type is Number and size is five, the type of data that can be entered in the field is restricted to a maximum of five numeric entries. You can further refine these basic restrictions by adding a validation rule to the field's properties that defines specific restrictions for the type of data that can be entered in the field.

You also can include a validation text message. **Validation text** is an explanatory message that appears if a user attempts to enter invalid information in a text field for which there is a validity check. If you do not specify a message, Access will display a default error message, which may not clearly describe the reason for the error.

You will create a validation rule for the Gender field to restrict the data entry to the two valid characters. A validation rule is specified by entering an expression in the validation rule property that limits the values that can be entered in the field.

Concept 4

4   An **expression** is a formula consisting of a combination of symbols that will produce a single value. You create an expression by combining identifiers, operators, and values to produce the desired results. An **identifier** is an element that refers to the value of a field, a graphical object, or a property. In the expression [Sales Amount] + [Sales Tax], [Sales Amount] and [Sales Tax] are identifiers that refer to the values in the Sales Amount and Sales Tax fields.

An **operator** is a symbol or word that indicates that an operation is to be performed. Common mathematical operators are + for addition, - for subtraction, * for multiplication, and / for division. A **comparison operator** is a symbol that allows you to make comparisons between two items. The following table describes the comparison operators:

Operator	Meaning
=	Equal to
<>	Not equal to
<	Less than
>	Greater than
<=	Less than or equal to
>=	Greater than or equal to

In addition, the OR and AND operators allow you to enter additional criteria in the same field or different fields.

Values are numbers, dates, or character strings. Character strings such as "F", "M", or "Workout Gear" are enclosed in quotation marks. Dates are enclosed in pound signs (#), as in #1/1/99#.

The following table shows some examples of possible expressions.

Expression	Result
[Sales Amount] + [Sales Tax]	Sums values in two fields.
"F" OR "M"	Restricts entry to the letters F or M only.
>= #1/1/99# AND <= #12/31/99#	Restricts entries to dates greater than or equal to 1/1/99 and less than or equal to 12/31/99.
"Workout Gear"	Allows the entry Workout Gear only.

You will enter the expression to restrict the data entry in the Gender field to the letters "f" or "m."

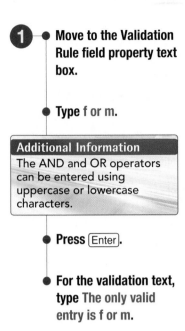

1 • **Move to the Validation Rule field property text box.**

• **Type f or m.**

Additional Information
The AND and OR operators can be entered using uppercase or lowercase characters.

• **Press Enter.**

• **For the validation text, type The only valid entry is f or m.**

Your screen should be similar to Figure 2.11

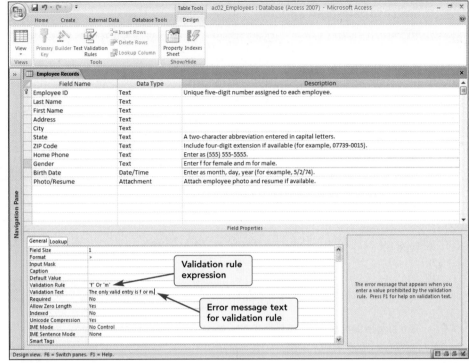

Figure 2.11

The expression states that the acceptable values can only be equal to an F or an M. Notice that Access automatically added quotation marks around the two character strings and changed the "o" in "or" to uppercase. Because the Format property has been set to convert all entries to uppercase, this means that an entry of f or m is as acceptable as F or M.

Next, you will switch back to Datasheet view to test the validation rule by entering data for the Gender field. In addition to a message box asking whether you want to save the design changes, another message box will appear to advise you that the data integrity rules have been changed. When you restructure a table, you often make changes that could result in a loss of data. Changes such as shortening field sizes, creating validity rules, or changing field types can cause existing data to become invalid. Because the field is new, it has no data values to verify, and a validation check is unnecessary at this time.

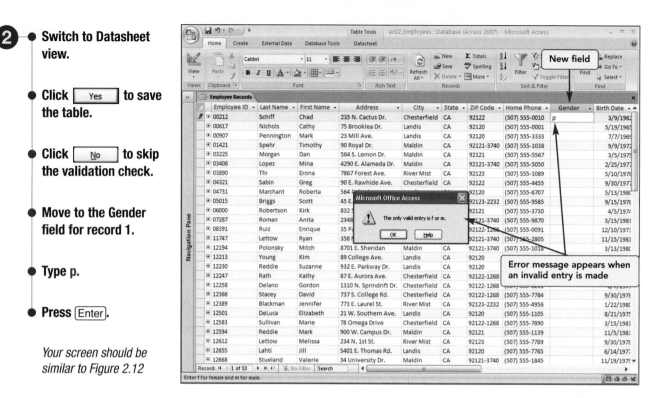

2
- Switch to Datasheet view.

- Click [Yes] to save the table.

- Click [No] to skip the validation check.

- Move to the Gender field for record 1.

- Type p.

- Press [Enter].

Your screen should be similar to Figure 2.12

Figure 2.12

The new field was added to the table between the Home Phone and Birth Date fields. Because the letter p is not a valid entry, Access displays the error message you entered as the Validation Text for the field. You will clear the error message and correct the entry.

3
- Click [OK].

- Press [←Backspace].

- Type m.

- Press [↓].

Your screen should be similar to Figure 2.13

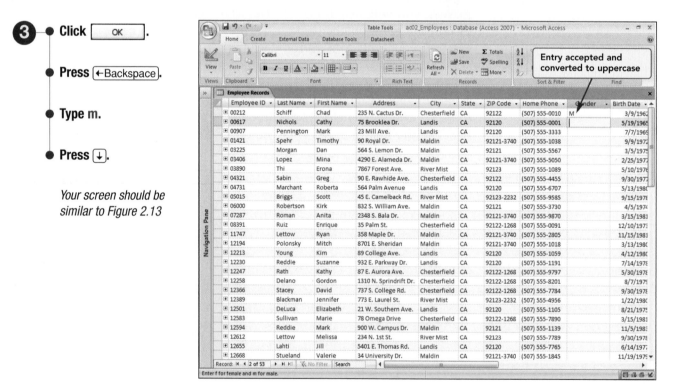

Figure 2.13

The entry for the first record is accepted and displayed as an uppercase M.

Hiding and Redisplaying Fields

To enter the gender data for the rest of the fields, you will use the First Name field as a guide. Unfortunately, the First Name and Gender fields are currently on opposite sides of the screen and will require you to look back and forth across each record. You can eliminate this problem by hiding the fields you do not need to see, and then redisplaying them when you have finished entering the gender data.

Hiding Fields

A quick way to view two fields side by side (in this case, the First Name and Gender fields) is to hide the fields that are in between (the Address through Home Phone fields).

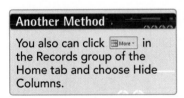

1 ● **Select the Address field through the Home Phone field.**

Additional Information

Drag along the column heads when the mouse pointer is ↓ to select the fields.

● **Right-click on the selection.**

● **Choose Hide Columns from the shortcut menu.**

Another Method

You also can click 🔲More ▾ in the Records group of the Home tab and choose Hide Columns.

Your screen should be similar to Figure 2.14

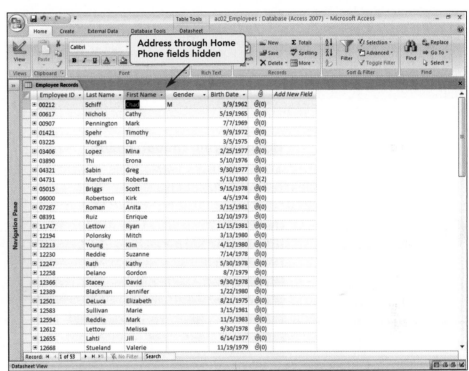

Figure 2.14

Now that the First Name and Gender columns are next to each other, you can refer to the first name in each record to enter the correct gender data.

2 • Enter the Gender field values for the remaining records by looking at the First Name field to determine whether the employee is male or female.

• Reduce the size of the Gender column using the Best Fit command.

Having Trouble?

Remember, to best fit data in a column, you double-click its right border.

Your screen should be similar to Figure 2.15

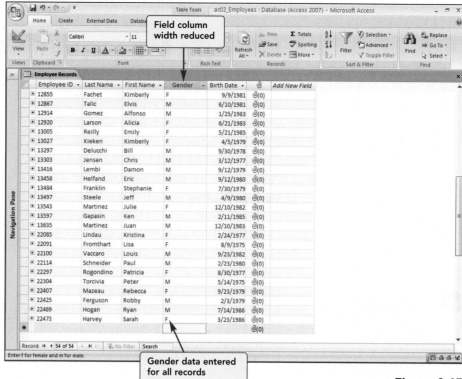

Gender data entered for all records

Figure 2.15

Redisplaying Hidden Fields

After you have entered the gender data for all of the records, you can redisplay the hidden fields.

1 • Right-click on any column header.

• Choose Unhide columns from the shortcut menu.

Another Method

You also can click [More ▾] in the Records group of the Home tab and choose Unhide Columns.

Your screen should be similar to Figure 2.16

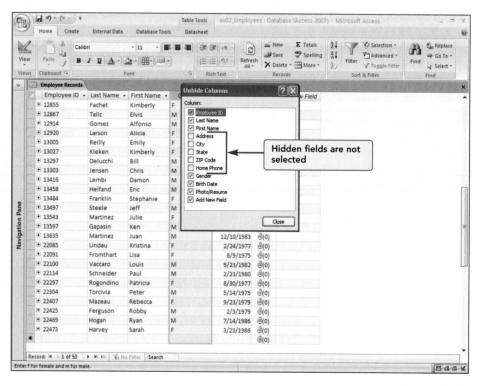

Hidden fields are not selected

Figure 2.16

You use the Unhide Columns dialog box to select the currently hidden columns you want to redisplay. A checkmark in the box next to a column name indicates that the column is currently displayed; column names with no checkmarks indicate that they are currently hidden. You want to unhide all hidden columns in your table.

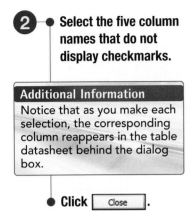

2 ● **Select the five column names that do not display checkmarks.**

Additional Information
Notice that as you make each selection, the corresponding column reappears in the table datasheet behind the dialog box.

● **Click** [Close].

Your screen should be similar to Figure 2.17

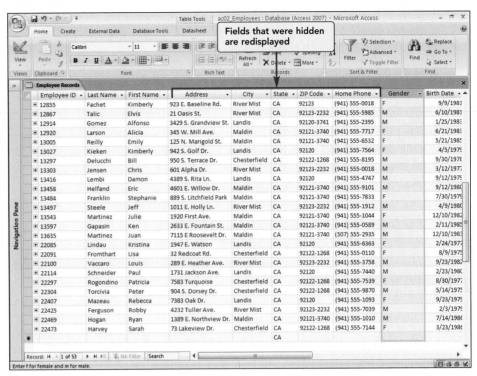

Figure 2.17

All of the fields are displayed again.

Creating a Lookup Field

Next you decide to change the Location field in the Job table to a lookup field that will make entering the location information easier, faster, and less prone to errors. There are three club locations: Landis, Chesterfield, and River Mist. You want the club locations to be listed so that anyone entering a new employee record will merely have to choose from this list to enter the club location for that employee.

Having Trouble?
Refer to Concept 6 in Lab 1 to review Lookup fields.

You will use the Lookup Wizard to change the existing Location field to a lookup field that uses fixed values.

1 ● Display the Navigation pane and open the Job table.

● Hide the Navigation pane and switch to Design view.

● Make the Location field active.

● Open the Data Type drop-down list and choose Lookup Wizard.

Your screen should be similar to Figure 2.18

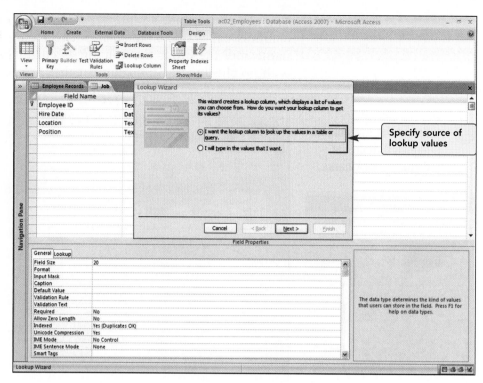

Using 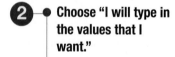 in the Fields & Columns group of the Datasheet tab inserts a new field column and starts the Lookup Wizard.

Figure 2.18

In the first Lookup Wizard dialog box, you specify the source for the values for the lookup field. You will enter your own values, the club locations, for this field.

2 ● Choose "I will type in the values that I want."

● Click [Next >].

Your screen should be similar to Figure 2.19

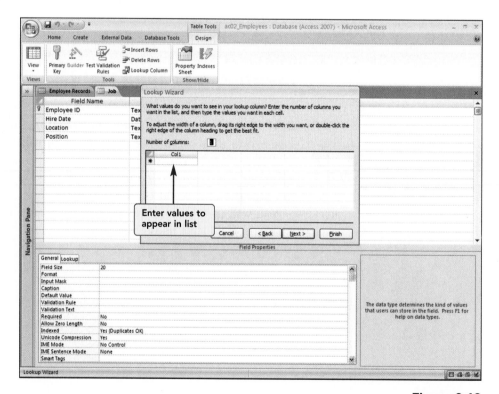

Figure 2.19

The next step is to enter the values you want listed in the lookup field. You also can add columns and adjust their widths to fit the values you enter, if necessary. You only need one column, and the current width is sufficient for the values you will enter.

3 ● **Click the entry box under Col1.**

● **Type Landis.**

● **Press** Tab.

● **Enter Chesterfield and River Mist locations next, pressing** Tab **to go from one cell to the next.**

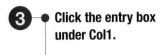

Having Trouble?
You can correct these entries the same way you do when entering data into any other field.

Your screen should be similar to Figure 2.20

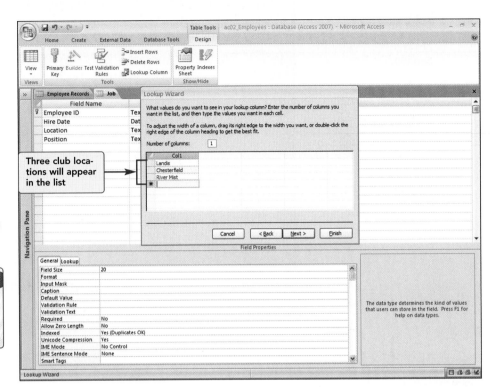

Figure 2.20

After entering the field values, you will move to the next step to enter a field name and finish the wizard. You will leave the field name as Location. Then you will check the field property settings established for this field to see whether any changes are necessary.

4 ● Click [Next >].

● Click [Finish].

● **Open the Lookup tab
in the Field Properties
section.**

*Your screen should be
similar to Figure 2.21*

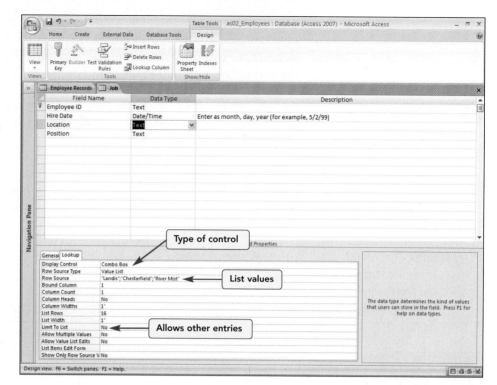

Figure 2.21

The lookup list will display in a combo box (drop-down list) control on
forms. It gets its list values from the value list containing the values you
specified as the source. The other properties are set to the defaults for
lookup fields. The only change you want to make is to restrict the data
entry in that field to values in the lookup list. Then you will test that the
Location field is performing correctly.

⑤ **Change the Limit to List property to Yes.**

Having Trouble?
Select the property and click ☑ at the end of the box to open the drop-down list of options.

● **Save the table design and switch to Datasheet view.**

Additional Information:
If you do not save the table design before switching views, Access will prompt you to save it. Click [Yes] to continue.

● **Click in the Location field of the first record.**

● **Replace the current location with Maldin and press** [Enter].

Your screen should be similar to Figure 2.22

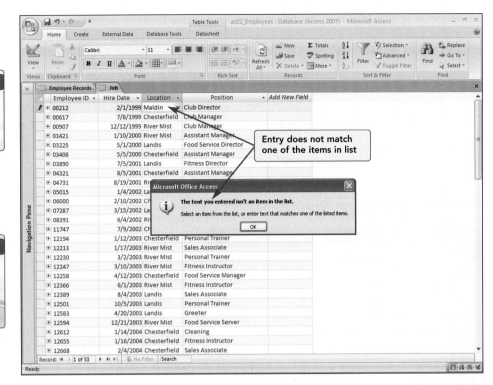

Figure 2.22

A warning box advises you that the entry is not one of the listed items because you restricted the field entries in the Location field to the lookup values you specified.

⑥ **Click** [OK].

● **Select Landis from the list of values.**

● **Press** [Enter].

Your screen should be similar to Figure 2.23

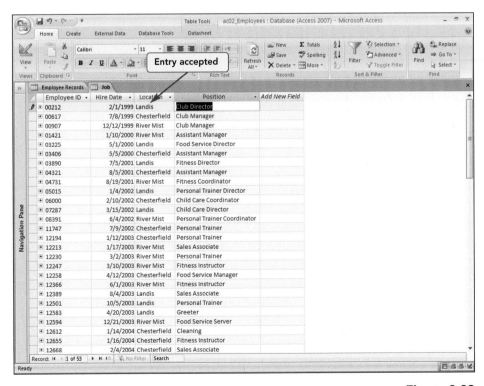

Figure 2.23

The Location lookup field is working correctly. Using a lookup field makes entering repetitive information faster and more accurate.

Finding and Replacing Data

Over the past few days, you have received several change-request forms to update the employee records. Rather than have to scroll through all the records to locate the ones that need to be modified, you can use the Find and Replace feature.

Concept 5

Find and Replace

5 The **Find and Replace** feature helps you quickly find specific information and automatically replace it with new information. The Find command will locate all specified values in a field, and the Replace command will both find a value and automatically replace it with another. For example, in a table containing supplier and item prices, you may need to increase the price of all items supplied by one manufacturer. To quickly locate these items, you would use the Find command to locate all records with the name of the manufacturer and then update the price appropriately. Alternatively, you could use the Replace command if you knew that all items priced at $11.95 were increasing to $15.99. This command would locate all values matching the original price and replace them with the new price.

Finding and replacing data is fast and accurate, but you need to be careful when replacing not to replace unintended matches.

Finding Data

The first change request is for Melissa Lettow, who recently married and has both a name and address change. To quickly locate this record, you will use the Find command.

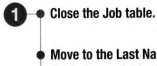

1 ● **Close the Job table.**

● **Move to the Last Name field of record 1 in the Employee Records table.**

● **Click 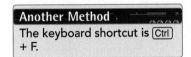 in the Find group of the Home tab.**

Another Method

The keyboard shortcut is Ctrl + F.

Your screen should be similar to Figure 2.24

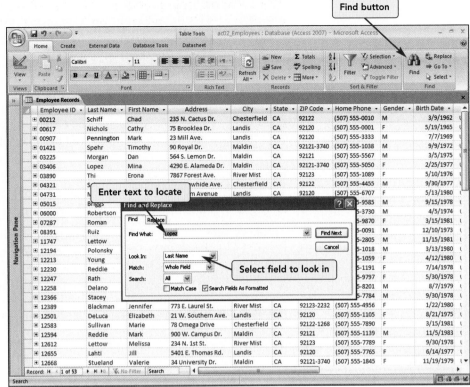

Figure 2.24

You use the Find and Replace dialog box to specify the information you are looking for and the way that you want Access to search the table. In the Find What text box, you specify the **criteria** or a set of limiting conditions records must meet by entering the text you want to locate. You can enter a specific character string or use wildcards to specify the criteria. **Wildcards** are symbols that are used to represent characters. The * symbol represents any collection of characters and the ? symbol represents any individual character. For example, ?ar will locate any three-letter text such as bar, far, and car. In contrast, *ar will locate the same text, but in addition will expand the criteria to locate any text ending with ar, such as star, popular, and modular.

You can further refine your search by using the options described in the following table.

Option	Effect
Look In	Searches the current field or the entire table for the specified text.
Match	Locates matches to the whole field, any part of the field, or the start of the field.
Search	Specifies the direction in which the table will be searched: All (search all records), Down (search down from the current insertion point location in the field), or Up (search up from the current insertion point location in the field).
Match Case	Finds words that have the same pattern of uppercase letters as entered in the Find What text box. Using this option makes the search case sensitive.
Search Fields as Formatted	Finds data based on its display format.

Because the insertion point is already in the field you want to search, the Look In location is correctly specified. If you wanted to search on a different field, you could click on the field you want in the datasheet without closing the dialog box. You also can select the table name from the Look In list if you want to search the entire table.

The other default options, to match the whole field and to search all records, are also appropriately set.

First, you will use the * wildcard to find all records whose last name begins with "l".

2 ● **Type l* in the Find What text box.**

● **Click** Find Next **eight times to move from one located record to the next.**

Your screen should be similar to Figure 2.25

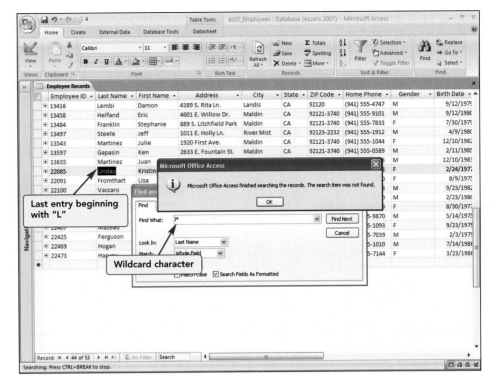

Figure 2.25

Using the wildcard located seven records whose last name starts with the letter l. The more specific you can make your criteria, the quicker you can locate the information you want to find. In this case, you want to find a specific last name, so you will enter the complete name in the Find What text box.

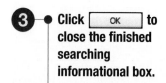

3 ● Click [OK] to close the finished searching informational box.

● Click on the entry in the Find What text box to select it and type **lettow**.

Additional Information

Because the Match Case option is not selected in the Find and Replace dialog box, you can enter the text to be located in uppercase, lowercase, or mixed-case letters—Access will ignore the case and look for the specified text.

● Click [Find Next].

Your screen should be similar to Figure 2.26

Having Trouble?

If the Find command did not locate this record, try it again. Make sure that you entered the name "lettow" (uppercase or lowercase) correctly and that Last Name is the selected field in the Look In box.

Figure 2.26

Access searches the table and moves to the first located occurrence of the entry you specified. The Last Name field is highlighted in record 14. You need to change the last name from Lettow to Richards.

4 ● **Click in the Last Name field of record 14.**

Additional Information
You do not need to close the Find and Replace dialog box before you make a change to the table. You will be using this dialog box again to perform more searches, so leave it open for now.

● **Double-click Lettow to select the entry.**

● **Type Richards.**

● **Press Enter.**

Your screen should be similar to Figure 2.27

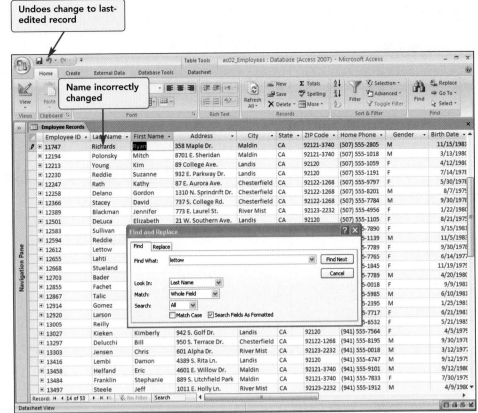

Figure 2.27

Now that the highlight is on the First Name field, you notice that this is the record for Ryan Lettow, not Melissa. You changed the wrong record. You will use the Undo command next to quickly fix this error.

Using Undo

Undo will cancel your last action as long as you have not made any further changes to the table. Even if you save the record or the table, you can undo changes to the last edited record by clicking 🔄 Undo. After you have changed another record or moved to another window, however, the earlier change cannot be undone. You will use Undo to return Ryan's record to the way it was before you made the change.

1 ● Click ↩ ▾ Undo.

Another Method
The keyboard shortcut is Ctrl
+ Z.

*Your screen should be
similar to Figure 2.28*

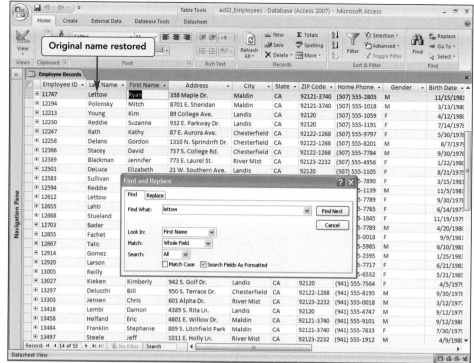

Figure 2.28

The original field value of Lettow is restored. Now, you want to continue
the search to locate the next record with the last name of Lettow.

2 ● Move back to the
Last Name field of
record 14.

● Click Find Next in the
Find and Replace
dialog box.

● When Access locates
the record for Melissa
Lettow (record 25),
change her last name
to **Richards** and the
Address to **5522 W.
Marin Lane**.

Having Trouble?
If necessary, move the Find
and Replace dialog box.

*Your screen should be
similar to Figure 2.29*

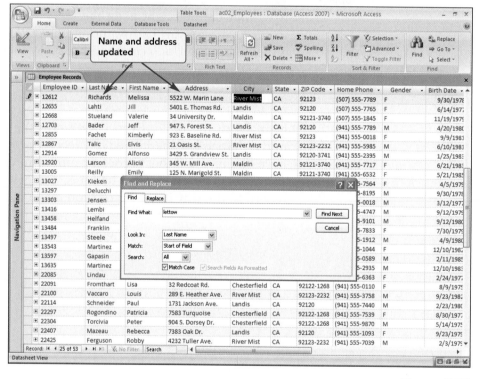

Figure 2.29

The Find method works well when you need to locate an individual field in order to view the data and/or modify it. However, when you need to make the same change to more than one record, the Replace command is the quicker method because it both finds and replaces the data.

Replacing Data

You have checked with the U.S. Postal Service and learned that all zip codes of 92120 have a four-digit extension of 3741. To locate all the records with this zip code, you could look at the ZIP Code field for each record to find the match and then edit the field to add the extension. If the table is small, this method would be acceptable. For large tables, however, this method could be quite time consuming and more prone to errors. A more efficient way is to search the table to find specific values in records and then replace the entry with another.

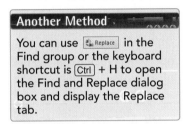

1 ● **Move to the ZIP Code field of record 1.**

● **Open the Replace tab.**

Another Method

You can use [⚙ Replace] in the Find group or the keyboard shortcut is [Ctrl] + H to open the Find and Replace dialog box and display the Replace tab.

Your screen should be similar to Figure 2.30

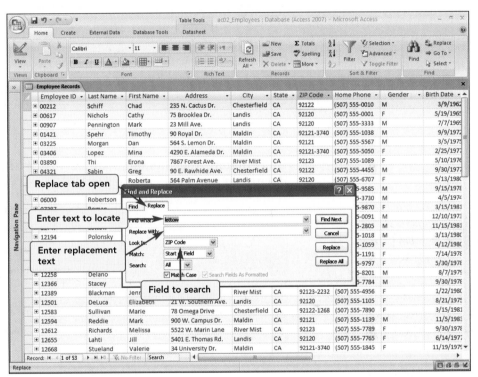

Figure 2.30

The options in the Replace tab are the same as those in the Find tab, with the addition of a Replace With text box, where you enter the replacement text exactly as you want it to appear in your table.

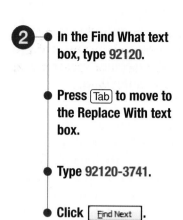

2
- In the Find What text box, type **92120**.

- Press Tab to move to the Replace With text box.

- Type **92120-3741**.

- Click **Find Next**.

Your screen should be similar to Figure 2.31

Having Trouble?
If necessary, move the dialog box so you can see the highlighted entry.

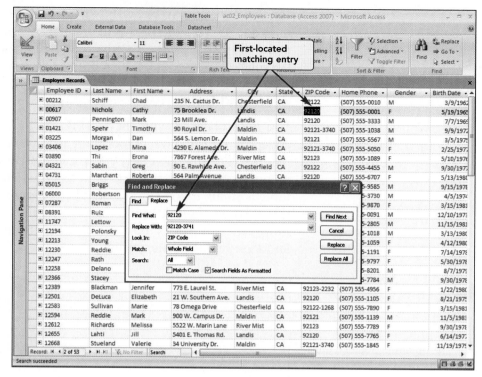

Figure 2.31

Immediately, the highlight moves to the first occurrence of text in the document that matches the Find What text and highlights it. You can now replace this text with the click of a button.

3
- Click **Replace**.

Your screen should be similar to Figure 2.32

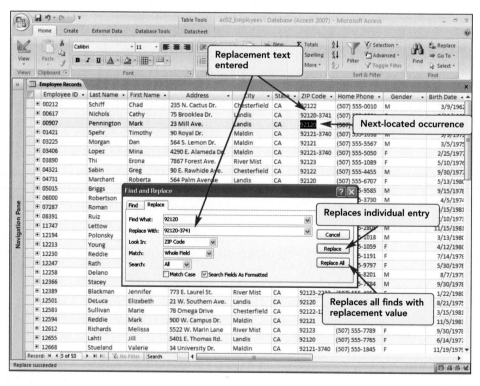

Figure 2.32

The original zip code entry is replaced with the new zip code. The program immediately continues searching and locates a second occurrence of the entry. You decide that the program is locating the values accurately and that it will be safe to replace all finds with the replacement value.

4 ● Click [Replace All].

● Click [Yes] in response to the advisory message.

● Close the Find and Replace dialog box.

Your screen should be similar to Figure 2.33

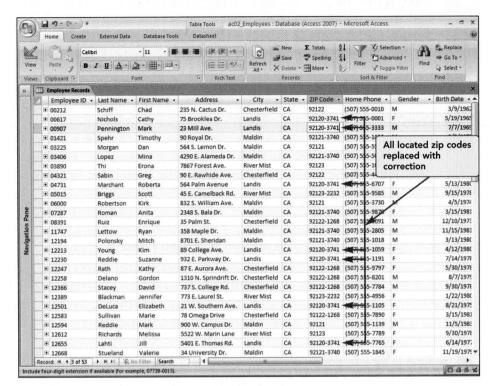

Figure 2.33

All matches are replaced with the replacement text. It is much faster to use Replace All than to confirm each match separately. However, exercise care when using Replace All, because the search text you specify might be part of another field and you may accidentally replace text you want to keep.

Sorting Records

As you may recall from Lab 1, the records are ordered according to the primary key field, Employee ID. The accounting manager, however, has asked you for an alphabetical list of all employees. To do this, you will sort the records in the table.

Concept 6

Sort

6 You can **sort** the data in a table to quickly rearrange the order of the records. Sorting data helps you find specific information more quickly without having to browse the data. You can sort data in **ascending sort order** (A to Z or 0 to 9) or **descending sort order** (Z to A or 9 to 0).

You can sort all records in a table by a single field, such as State, or you can select adjacent columns and sort by more than one field, such as State and then City. When sorting on multiple fields, you begin by selecting the columns to sort. Access sorts records starting with the column farthest left (the outermost field) and then moves to the right across the selected columns to sort the innermost fields. For example, if you want to sort by State, and then by City, the State field must be to the left of the City field. The State field is the outermost field and the city field is the innermost field.

Access saves the new sort order with your table data and reapplies it automatically each time you open the table. To return to the primary key sort order, you must remove the temporary sort.

Sorting on a Single Field

You will sort the records on a single field, Last Name. To perform a sort on a single field, you move to the field on which you will base the sort and click the button that corresponds to the type of sort you want to do. In this case, you will sort the Last Name field in ascending alphabetical order.

1 ● **Move to the Last Name field of any record.**

● **Click [↑] Ascending in the Sort & Filter group.**

Additional Information

Clicking [↓] Descending arranges the data in descending sort order.

Your screen should be similar to Figure 2.34

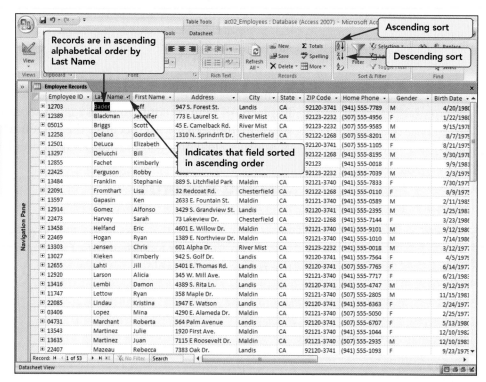

Figure 2.34

The employee records are displayed in alphabetical order by last name. The Last Name field header displays a [⌄] to show that the field is in ascending sorted order. Next, you want to check the rest of the table to see if there is anything else you need to do.

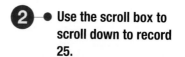

2 ● Use the scroll box to scroll down to record 25.

Additional Information

As you drag the scroll box, the record location is displayed in a Screen Tip (for example, "Record 25 of 53").

Your screen should be similar to Figure 2.35

Records with same last name not sorted by first name

Employee ID	Last Name	First Name	Address	City	State	ZIP Code	Home Phone	Gender	Birth Date
13543	Martinez	Julie	1920 First Ave.	Maldin	CA	92121-3740	(941) 555-1044	F	12/10/1982
13635	Martinez	Juan	7115 E Roosevelt Dr.	Maldin	CA	92121-3740	(507) 555-2935	M	12/10/1983
22407	Mazeau	Rebecca	7383 Oak Dr.	Landis	CA	92120-3741	(941) 555-1093	F	9/23/1979
03225	Morgan	Dan	564 S. Lemon Dr.	Maldin	CA	92121	(507) 555-5567	M	3/5/1975
00617	Nichols	Cathy	75 Brooklea Dr.	Landis	CA	92120-3741	(507) 555-0001	F	5/19/1965
00907	Pennington	Mark	23 Mill Ave.	Landis	CA	92120-3741	(507) 555-3333	M	7/7/1969
12194	Polonsky	Mitch	8701 E. Sheridan	Maldin	CA	92121-3740	(507) 555-1018	M	3/13/1980
12247	Rath	Kathy	87 E. Aurora Ave.	Chesterfield	CA	92122-1268	(507) 555-9797	F	5/30/1978
12230	Reddie	Suzanne	932 E. Parkway Dr.	Landis	CA	92120-3741	(507) 555-1191	F	7/14/1978
12594	Reddie	Mark	900 W. Campus Dr.	Maldin	CA	92121	(507) 555-1139	M	11/5/1983
13005	Reilly	Emily	125 N. Marigold St.	Maldin	CA	92121-3740	(941) 555-6532	F	5/21/1985
12612	Richards	Melissa	5522 W. Marin Lane	River Mist	CA	92123	(507) 555-7789	F	9/30/1978
06000	Robertson	Kirk	832 S. William Ave.	Maldin	CA	92121	(507) 555-3730	M	4/5/1974
22297	Rogondino	Patricia	7583 Turquoise	Chesterfield	CA	92122-1268	(941) 555-7539	F	8/30/1977
07287	Roman	Anita	2348 S. Bala Dr.	Maldin	CA	92121-3740	(507) 555-9870	F	3/15/1981
08391	Ruiz	Enrique	35 Palm St.	Chesterfield	CA	92122-1268	(507) 555-0091	M	12/10/1973
04321	Sabin	Greg	90 E. Rawhide Ave.	Chesterfield	CA	92122	(507) 555-4455	M	9/30/1977
00212	Schiff	Chad	235 N. Cactus Dr.	Chesterfield	CA	92122	(507) 555-0010	M	3/9/1962
22114	Schneider	Paul	1731 Jackson Ave.	Landis	CA	92120-3741	(941) 555-7440	M	2/23/1980
01421	Spehr	Timothy	90 Royal Dr.	Maldin	CA	92121-3740	(507) 555-1038	M	9/9/1972
12366	Stacey	David	737 S. College Rd.	Chesterfield	CA	92122-1268	(507) 555-7784	M	9/30/1978
13497	Steele	Jeff	1011 E. Holly Ln.	River Mist	CA	92123-2232	(941) 555-1912	M	4/9/1980
12668	Stueland	Valerie	34 University Dr.	Maldin	CA	92121-3740	(507) 555-1845	F	11/19/1979
12583	Sullivan	Marie	78 Omega Drive	Chesterfield	CA	92122-1268	(507) 555-7890	F	3/15/1981
12867	Talic	Elvis	21 Oasis St.	River Mist	CA	92123-2232	(941) 555-5985	M	6/10/1981
03890	Thi	Erona	7867 Forest Ave.	River Mist	CA	92123	(507) 555-1089	F	5/10/1976
22304	Torcivia	Peter	904 S. Dorsey Dr.	Chesterfield	CA	92122-1268	(941) 555-9870	M	5/14/1975

Record: 1 of 53

Figure 2.35

Now, you can see that the records for Julie and Juan Martinez are sorted by last name but not by first name. You want all records that have the same last name to be further sorted by first name. To do this, you need to sort using multiple sort fields.

Additional Information

If the columns to sort were not already adjacent, you would hide the columns that are in between. If the columns were not in the correct order, you would move the columns. You will learn how to do this in Lab 3.

Sorting on Multiple Fields

When sorting on multiple fields, the fields must be adjacent to each other in order to designate the inner and outer sort fields. The outer sort field (primary field in the sort) must be to the left of the inner sort field. The Last Name and First Name fields are already in the correct locations for the sort you want to perform. To specify the fields to sort on, both columns must be selected.

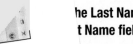
...he Last Name
...t Name field

● Click 2↓ Sort
  Ascending.

● Scroll down to record
  25 again.

*Your screen should be
similar to Figure 2.36*

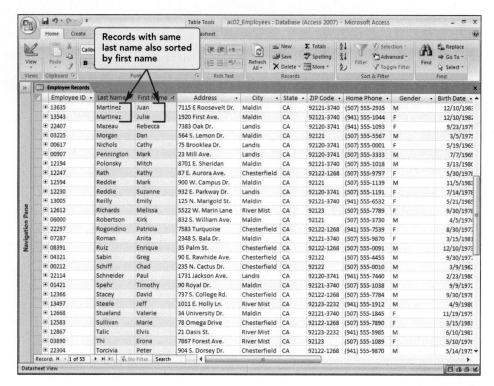

Figure 2.36

The record for Juan Martinez now appears before the record for Julie. As you can see, sorting is a fast, useful tool. The sort order remains in effect until you remove the sort or replace it with a new sort order. Although Access remembers your sort order even when you exit the program, it does not actually change the table records.

You can remove the sort at any time to restore the records to the primary key sort order. You decide to return to primary key sort order and resort the table alphabetically for the Accounting department later, after you have finished making changes to it.

2 ● Click 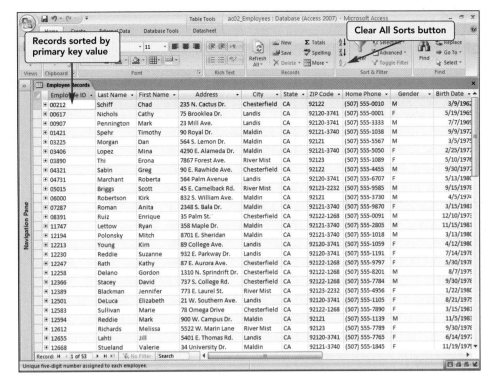 **Clear All Sorts.**

● **Click anywhere in the datasheet to clear the selection.**

Your screen should be similar to Figure 2.37

Figure 2.37

All the sorts are cleared and the data in the table is now in order by the primary key field, Employee ID.

Formatting the Datasheet

Finally, you want to **format** or enhance the appearance of the datasheet on the screen to make it more readable or attractive by applying different effects. Datasheet formats include settings that change the appearance of the cell, gridlines, background and gridline colors, and border and line styles. In addition, you can change the text color and add text effects such as bold and italics to the datasheet. Datasheet formats affect the entire datasheet appearance and cannot be applied to separate areas of the datasheet.

Changing Background and Gridline Color

The default datasheet format displays alternate rows in white and light gray backgrounds with a gridline color of blue. The text color is set to black. You want to see the effect of changing the color of the alternate rows and gridlines in the datasheet.

1 ● **Click ▣ Datasheet Formatting in the Font group of the Home tab.**

Your screen should be similar to Figure 2.38

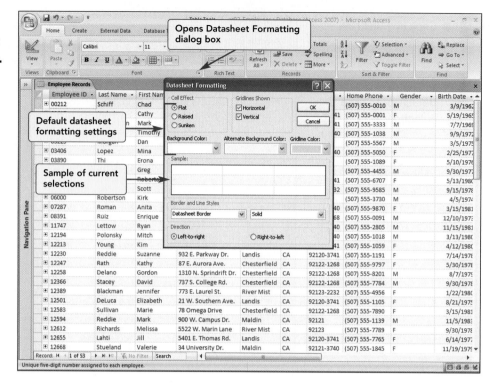

Figure 2.38

The default datasheet formatting settings are displayed in the dialog box and the Sample area shows how the settings will appear in the datasheet. You will leave the background color white and change the color of the alternate rows.

2 ● **Open the Alternate Background Color drop-down menu.**

Your screen should be similar to Figure 2.39

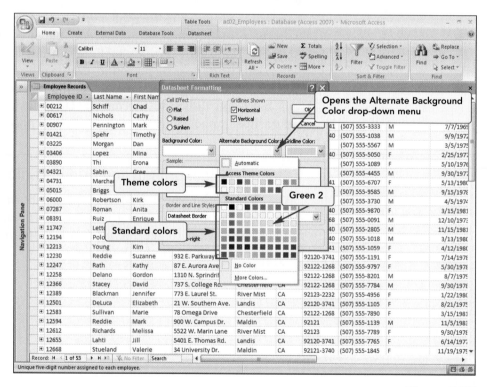

Figure 2.39

The color gallery displays the Access Theme Colors in the upper section and standard colors in the lower section. **Theme colors** are a combination of coordinating colors that are used in the default datasheet. Each color is assigned to a different area of the datasheet, such as label text or table background. Pointing to a color identifies where it is used in a ScreenTip. The colors in the Standard Colors gallery are not assigned to specific areas on the datasheet. Pointing to a Standard Color displays the name assigned to the color.

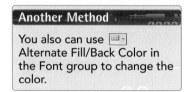

3 • **Point to several theme colors to see where they are used in the datasheet.**

• **Click on the Green 2 color in the Standard Colors area.**

Another Method

You also can use [ ] Alternate Fill/Back Color in the Font group to change the color.

Your screen should be similar to Figure 2.40

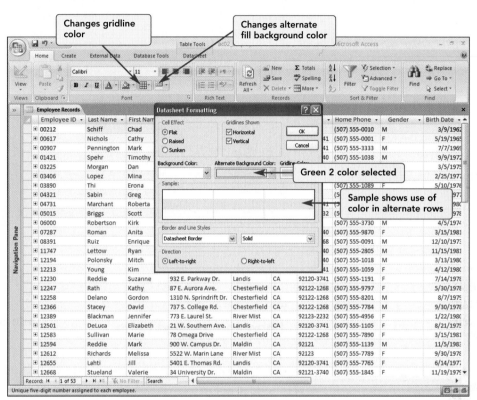

Figure 2.40

The sample area displays how the selection will appear in the datasheet. You like the green shading and want to change the gridline color to a darker shade of the same green.

4
- Open the Gridline Color drop-down menu.
- Select Green 5 from the Standard colors area.
- Click [OK].

Your screen should be similar to Figure 2.41

Another Method

You also can use 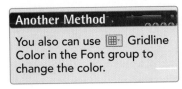 Gridline Color in the Font group to change the color.

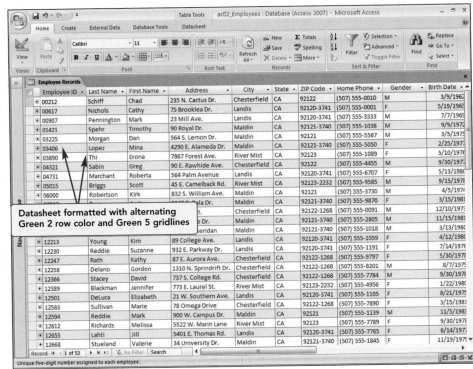

Datasheet formatted with alternating Green 2 row color and Green 5 gridlines

Figure 2.41

The selected alternating row and gridline color formatting has been applied to the datasheet.

Changing the Text Color

The datasheet background colors brighten the screen appearance, but you think the text is a little light, making it difficult to read. You will change the text color to a dark blue and bold.

1 ● Open the [A] Font Color drop-down menu in the Font group.

● Select Dark Blue from the Standard Colors section of the color gallery.

● Click [B] Bold in the Font group.

Your screen should be similar to Figure 2.42

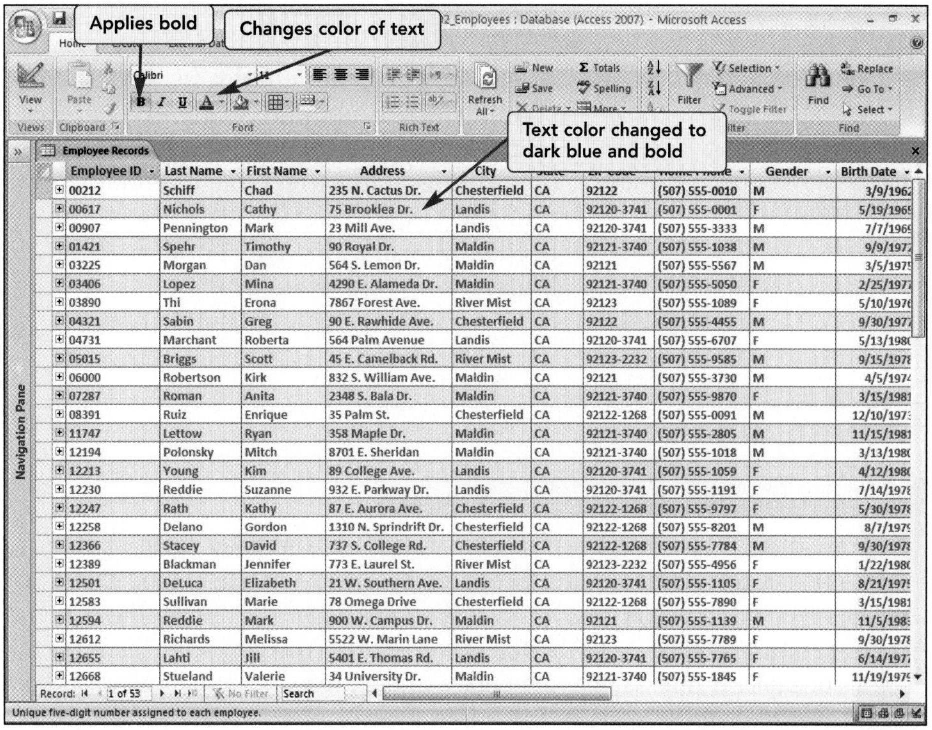

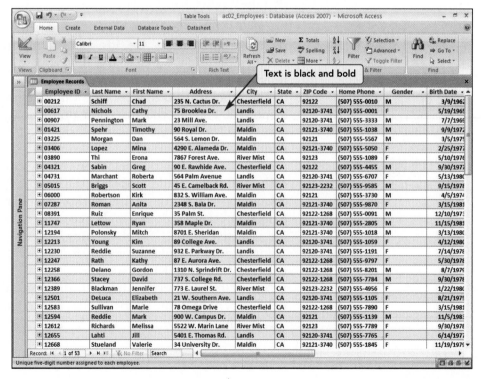

Figure 2.42

You do not like how the blue text color looks and want to change it back to the default color. You cannot use Undo to remove formatting, so you will need to select the text color again.

2 ● Open the [A] Font Color drop-down menu.

● Choose Automatic to restore the default font color.

Your screen should be similar to Figure 2.43

Figure 2.43

The black text color is restored. The text is still bolded and is easier to read.

Filtering a Table

Juan Martinez, an employee at the Landis location, is interested in forming a car pool. He recently approached you about finding other employees who also may want to carpool. You decide this would be a great opportunity to use the table of employee data to find this information. To find the employees, you could sort the table and then write down the needed information. This could be time-consuming, however, if you had hundreds of employees in the table. A faster way is to apply a filter to the table records to locate this information.

Concept 7

Filter

7 A **filter** is a restriction placed on records in the open table or form to quickly isolate and display a subset of records. A filter is created by specifying the criteria that you want records to meet in order to be displayed. A filter is ideal when you want to display the subset for only a brief time and then return immediately to the full set of records. You can print the filtered records as you would any form or table. A filter is only temporary, and all records are redisplayed when you remove the filter or close and reopen the table or form. The filter results cannot be saved. However, the last filter criteria you specify can be saved with the table, and the results quickly redisplayed.

Using Filter by Selection

Juan lives in Maldin and works at the Lifestyle Fitness Club located in Landis. You can locate other employees who live in Maldin quite easily by using the Filter by Selection feature. Filter by Selection displays only records containing a specific value. This method is effective when the table contains only one value that you want to use as the criterion for selecting and displaying records.

> **Additional Information**
>
> If the selected part of a value starts with the first character in the field, the subset displays all records with values that begin with the same selected characters.

The process used to select the value determines the results that will be displayed. Placing the insertion point in a field selects the entire field contents. The filtered subset will include all records containing an exact match. Selecting part of a value in a field (by highlighting it) displays all records containing the selection. For example, in a table for a book collection, you could position the mouse pointer anywhere in a field containing the name of the author Stephen King, choose the Filter by Selection command, and only records for books whose author matches the selected name, "Stephen King," would be displayed. Selecting just "King" would include all records for authors Stephen King, Martin Luther King, and Barbara Kingsolver.

You want to filter the table to display only those records with a City field entry of Maldin. To specify the city to locate, you select an example of the data in the table.

1 **Move to the City field of record 4.**

Click [Selection ▾] **in the Sort & Filter group of the Home tab.**

Your screen should be similar to Figure 2.44

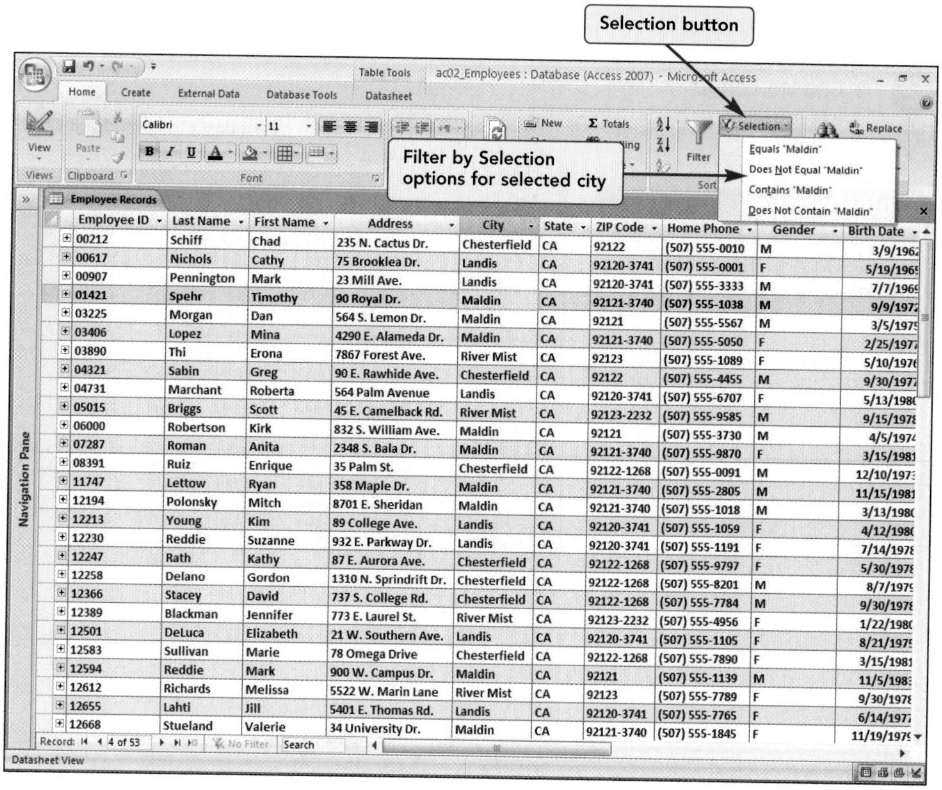

Figure 2.44

The drop-down list of commands contains the current selected value in the field. The commands that appear will vary depending on the data type of the selected value. Also, the commands will vary depending on how much of the value is selected. If the selection is a partial selection, the commands allow you to specify a filter using the beginning, middle, or end of a field value. In this case, the entire value is selected and the four commands allow you to specify whether you want the selection to equal, not equal, contain, or not contain the value.

2 ● Choose Equals
   "Maldin".

Another Method
You also can display the Filter by Selection commands using the selection's shortcut menu.

Your screen should be similar to Figure 2.45

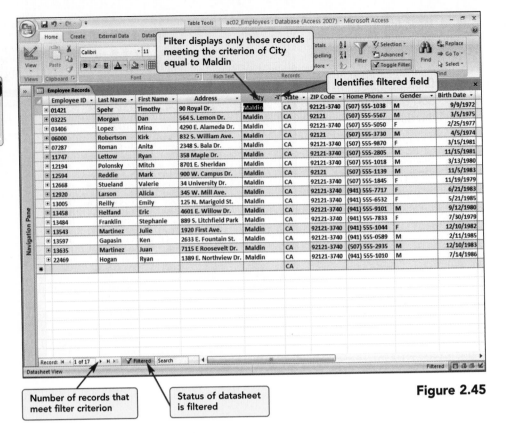

Figure 2.45

Additional Information
You can print a filtered datasheet just like any other table.

The table displays only those records that contain the selected city. All other records are temporarily hidden. The status bar displays the ⟨▼ Filtered⟩ button to show that the datasheet is filtered and the record number indicator shows that the total number of filtered records is 17. The City field name also displays a filter icon to identify the field on which the table was filtered.

After seeing how easy it was to locate this information, you want to locate employees who live in Chesterfield. This information may help in setting up the car pool, because the people traveling from the city of Maldin pass through Chesterfield on the way to the Landis location.

Removing and Deleting Filters

Before creating the new filter, you will remove the current filter and return the table to its full display.

1 ● Click 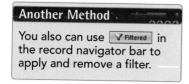 in the Sort & Filter group.

Another Method

You also can use ▼ Filtered in the record navigator bar to apply and remove a filter.

Your screen should be similar to Figure 2.46

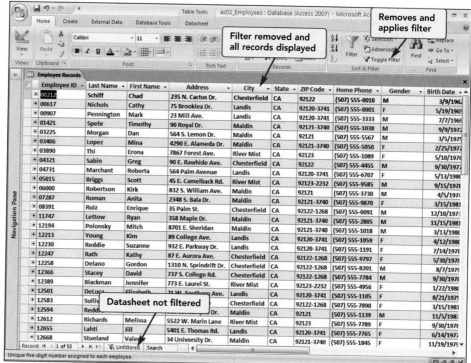

Figure 2.46

The filter is temporarily removed from the field and all the records are displayed again. The navigator bar displays ▼ Unfiltered . The filter is still available and can be reapplied quickly by clicking ▼ Toggle Filter or ▼ Unfiltered .

You will reapply the filter and then you will permanently remove these filter settings.

2 ● Click ▼ Toggle Filter to redisplay the filtered datasheet.

● Click ▼ Advanced ▼ in the Sort & filter group.

● Choose Clear All Filters.

The filter is removed and all the records are redisplayed. The ▼ Toggle Filter button is dimmed because the table does not include any filter settings.

Filtering Using Common Filters

To filter the employee data by two cities, Chesterfield and Maldin, you can select from a list of several popular filters. Using this list allows you to perform filters on multiple criteria within a single field.

1 ● Click on the ⏷ in the City column header to open the field's drop-down menu.

Another Method

You also can move to the field to filter on and click 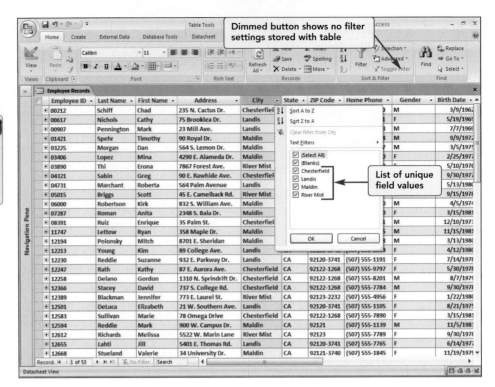 in the Sort & Filter group to display the Filter list.

Your screen should be similar to Figure 2.47

Figure 2.47

A list of all the unique values that are stored in the current field is displayed. Selecting a value from the list filters the table based on the selected value. Depending on the data type of the selected value, you may be able to filter for a range of values by clicking on a value and specifying the appropriate range. In this case, because the field is not filtered, all the values are selected. You will first clear the selection from all values, and then select the names of the two cities you want displayed in the filtered list.

2
- Click the Select All check box to clear the selection from all values.

- Click the Chesterfield and Maldin check boxes to select them.

- Click [OK].

Your screen should be similar to Figure 2.48

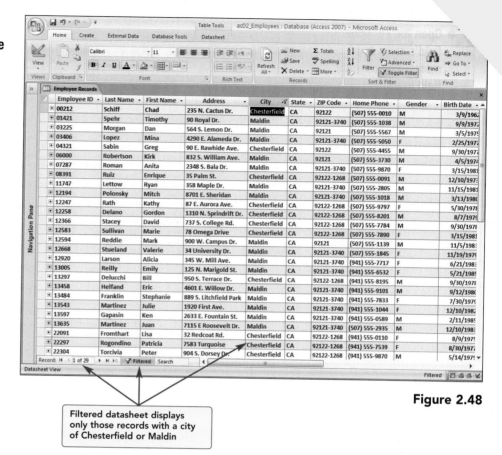

Filtered datasheet displays only those records with a city of Chesterfield or Maldin

Figure 2.48

The filtered datasheet displays the records for all 29 employees who live in the city of Chesterfield or Maldin.

Filtering on Multiple Fields

As you look at the filtered results, you decide to further refine the list by restricting the results to those records that have the same zip code as Juan's zip code of 92121. Although you can only specify one filter per field, you can specify a different filter for each field that is present in the view.

the ZIP Code
drop-down
to display the
ist.

● **Clear the checkmark
from the 92121-3740
value.**

● **Click** [OK].

*Your screen should be
similar to Figure 2.49*

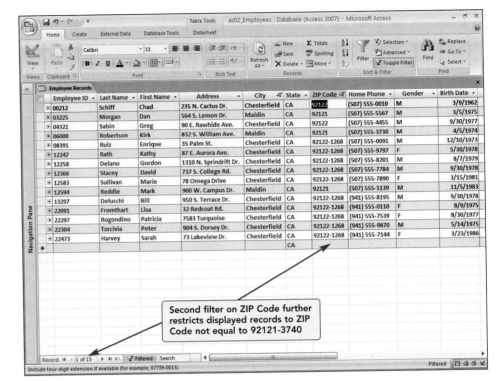

Second filter on ZIP Code further
restricts displayed records to ZIP
Code not equal to 92121-3740

Figure 2.49

Now there are only 15 records displayed in the filtered table. Applying the
second filter refined the results by removing all records from the filtered
list that had a zip code of 92121-3740.

Although you would like to provide a copy of this information to Juan,
you realize that it contains more information about each employee than
someone would need (or should even have access to) in order to form a
car pool. Also, because you are not finished adding records to the employee
database, these findings may not be complete.

You will redisplay all the records in the table, but you will not clear the
filter settings. If you do not clear the filters, the filter criteria you last
specified are stored with the table, and the results can be redisplayed
simply by applying the filter again.

2 ● **Click** [⛄ Toggle Filter] **to display the unfiltered datasheet.**

● **Close the table, saving your design changes.**

● **Redisplay the Navigation pane.**

The table is closed and the work area is empty. Next you will learn how to
create and use a form in Access.

Note: If you are ending your session now, close the database file and exit Access. When you
begin again, start Access and open the ac02_Employees database file.

Creating and Using Forms

One of your objectives is to make the database easy to use. You know from experience that long hours of viewing large tables can be tiring. Therefore, you want to create an onscreen form to make this table easier to view and use.

Concept 8
Form

8 A **form** is a database object used primarily to display records onscreen and to make it easier to enter new records and to make changes to existing records. Forms can control access to data, such as which fields or rows of data are displayed. That way, any unnecessary fields of data are not displayed, which makes it easier for people using the database. They enable people to use the data in the tables without having to sift through many lines of data to find the exact record.

Forms are based on an underlying table and can include design elements such as descriptive text, titles, labels, lines, boxes, and pictures. Forms also can use calculations to summarize data that is not listed on the actual table, such as a sales total. The layout and arrangement of information can be customized in a form. Using these features creates a visually attractive form that makes working with the database more enjoyable, more efficient, and less prone to data-entry errors.

You want the onscreen form to be similar to the paper form that is completed by each new employee when hired (shown below). The information from that form is used as the source of input for the new record that will be added to the table for the new employee.

EMPLOYEE DATA

Employee ID _____

First Name _____   Last Name _____
Street _____
City _____   State _____   Zip _____
Phone Number _____
Gender _____
Birth Date _____

MORE ABOUT

▶ To learn how to create a datasheet form, see "2 Creating and Formatting Database Elements" in the More About appendix.

There are several different methods you can use to create forms as described in the following table. The method you use depends on the type of form you want to create.

Method	Use to
Form Tool	Create a form containing all the fields in the table.
Split Form tool	Create a form that displays the form and datasheet in a single window
Blank Form tool	Build a form from scratch by adding the fields you select from the table
Datasheet tool	Create a form using all the fields in the table and display it in Datasheet view
Multiple Items tool	Create a form that displays multiple records but is more customizable than a datasheet
Form Wizard	Create a form using a wizard that guides you through the steps to create a complex form that displays selected fields, data groups, sorted records, and data from multiple tables

Using the Form Tool

Using the Form tool is the quickest method to create a simple form. You decide to see if the Form tool will create the form you need.

1 ● **If necessary, select the Employee Records table in the Navigation pane.**

● **Open the Create tab.**

● **Click** ▦ **in the Forms group.**

Your screen should be similar to Figure 2.50

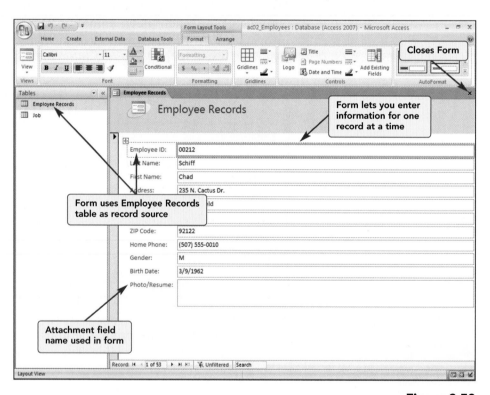

Figure 2.50

A form that allows you to enter data for one record at a time was quickly created. The fields from the Employee Records table were used to create the form because it was the selected object in the Navigation pane. The underlying table that is used to create a form is called the **record source.**

The fields are in the same order as in the datasheet. Notice the field name you specified for the Attachment field is used in the form, although it is not used in the table.

This form does not quite meet your needs and you decide to try another method to create the form.

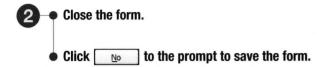

Close the form.

Click [No] to the prompt to save the form.

Using the Multiple Items Tool

Next, you will use the Multiple Items tool to create a form.

If necessary, open the Create tab.

Click [Multiple Items] in the Forms group.

Your screen should be similar to Figure 2.51

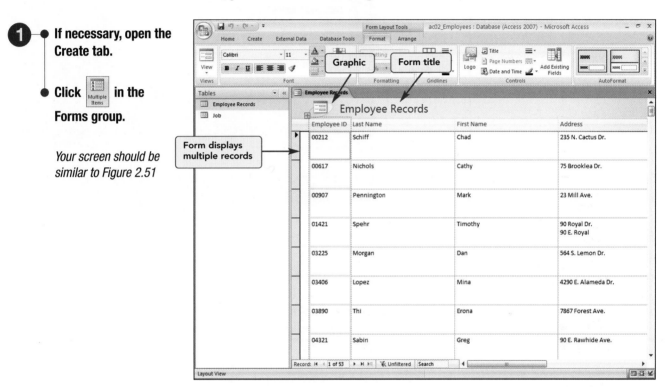

Figure 2.51

A form that displays multiple records at a time was quickly created. Although it looks similar to datasheet view, it is easier to read and includes a title and graphic. However, this form still does not work and you decide to use the Form Wizard to create a form that is closer to your needs.

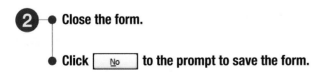

Close the form.

Click [No] to the prompt to save the form.

Using the Form Wizard

The Form Wizard will help you create a form that is closer to your needs by guiding you through a series of steps that allow you to specify different form features.

1 ● Click [More Forms ▾] in the Forms group of the Create tab.

● Choose Form Wizard.

Your screen should be similar to Figure 2.52

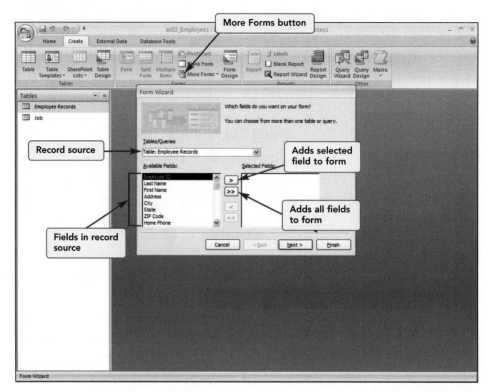

Figure 2.52

The Form Wizard dialog box displays the name of the current table, Employee Records, in the Tables/Queries list box. This is the table that will be used as the record source. If you wanted to use a different table as the record source, you could open the Tables/Queries drop-down list to select the appropriate table.

The fields from the selected table are displayed in the Available Fields list box. You use this box to select the fields you want included on the form, in the order that you want them to appear. This order is called the **tab order** because it is the order that the highlight will move through the fields on the form when you press the [Tab↹] key during data entry. You decide that you want the fields to be in the same order as they are on the paper form shown in the illustration on the previous page.

Select First Name.

Click `>` **Add Field.**

Another Method

You also can double-click on each field name in the Available Fields list box to move the field name to the Selected Fields list box.

Additional Information

The `>>` Add All Fields button adds all available fields to the Selected Fields list, in the same order that they appear in the Available Fields list.

Your screen should be similar to Figure 2.53

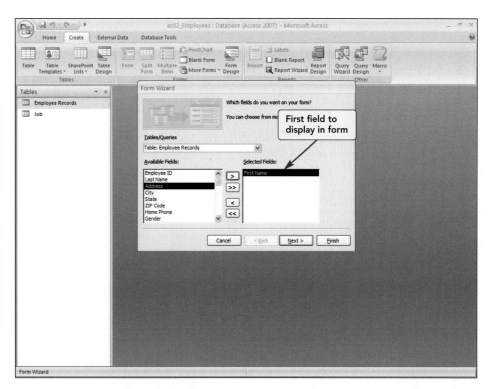

Figure 2.53

The First Name field is removed from the Available Fields list and added to the top of the Selected Fields list box. It will be the first field in the form.

In the same manner, add the following fields to the Selected Fields list in the order shown here:

Last Name

Address

City

State

ZIP Code

Home Phone

Gender

Birth Date

Employee ID

Photo/Resume

Your screen should be similar to Figure 2.54

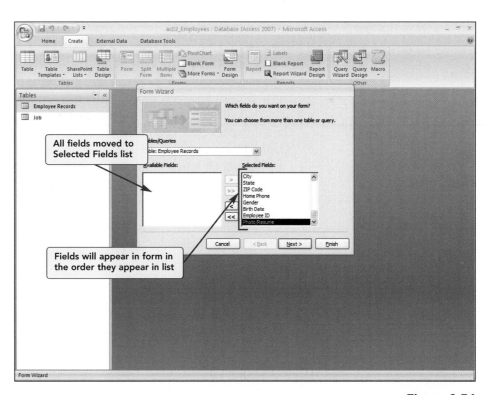

Figure 2.54

When finished, the Available Fields list box is empty and the Selected Fields list box lists the fields in the selected order.

You are now ready to move on to the next Form Wizard screen.

4 ● Click Next > .

Your screen should be
similar to Figure 2.55

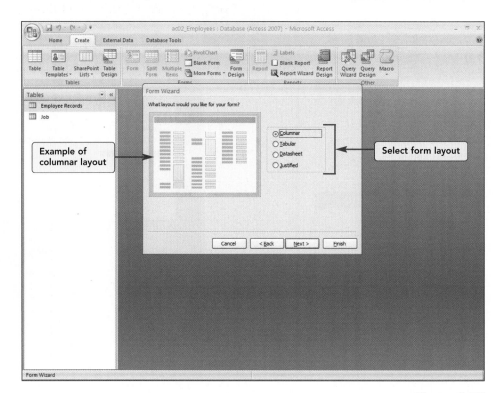

Figure 2.55

In this Form Wizard screen, you are asked to select the control layout for the form. **Layouts** control how the data is displayed in the form by aligning the items horizontally or vertically to give the form a uniform appearance.

The controls are contained in a control layout that was created automatically when the form was created. A control layout aligns controls horizontally and vertically to give the form a uniform appearance. There are two types of layouts: tabular and stacked. **Tabular layouts** arrange the data in rows and columns, with labels across the top. **Stacked layouts** arrange data vertically with a field label to the left of the field data. A form can have both types of layouts in different sections.

The four form layouts offered by the Form Wizard are variations of the two basic layouts as described in the following table.

Form	Layout Style	Description
Columnar		This is a stacked layout that presents data for the selected fields in columns. The field name labels are displayed down the left side of the column with the data for each field just to the right of the corresponding label. A single record is displayed in each Form window.
Tabular		This is the basic tabular layout that presents data with field name labels across the top of the page and the corresponding data in columns under each heading. Multiple records are displayed in the Form window, each on a single row. All fields are displayed across the top of the Form window.
Datasheet		This is a tabular layout that displays data in rows and columns similar to the Table Datasheet view. It displays multiple records, one per row, in the Form window. You may need to scroll the form horizontally to see all the fields.
Justified		This is a tabular layout that displays data in rows, with field name labels across the top of the row and the corresponding field data below it. A single record may appear in multiple rows in the Form window in order to fully display the field name label and data. A single record is displayed in each Form window.

Additional Information

Using [icon] in the Forms group creates a form using the stacked layout.

The columnar layout appears most similar to the paper form currently in use by the club, so you decide to use that layout for your form.

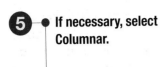

5 • If necessary, select Columnar.

• Click [Next >].

Your screen should be similar to Figure 2.56

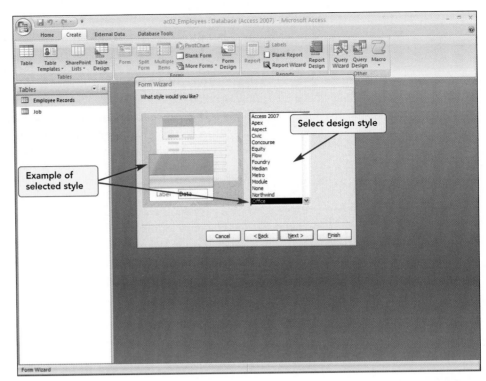

Figure 2.56

Next you select a design style for your form. Design styles consist of different combinations of colors, fonts, and graphic elements. A sample of each style as it is selected is displayed on the left side of the dialog box. None is the default selection. You will create the form using the Flow style.

6 • Select several design styles to view the example.

• Select the Flow design style.

• Click [Next >].

Your screen should be similar to Figure 2.57

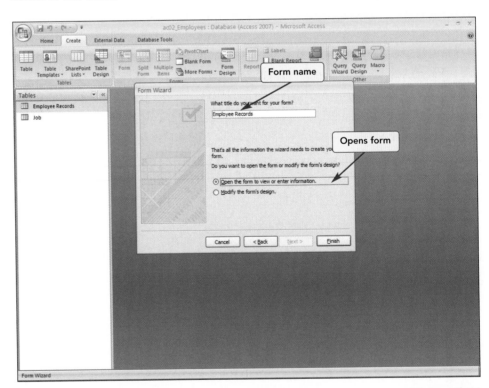

Figure 2.57

In the final Form Wizard dialog box, you can enter a form title to be used as the name of the form, and you can specify whether to open the form or to modify it. The Form Wizard uses the name of the table as the default form title. You will keep the proposed form title and the default of opening the form.

7 ● Click  .

Your screen should be similar to Figure 2.58

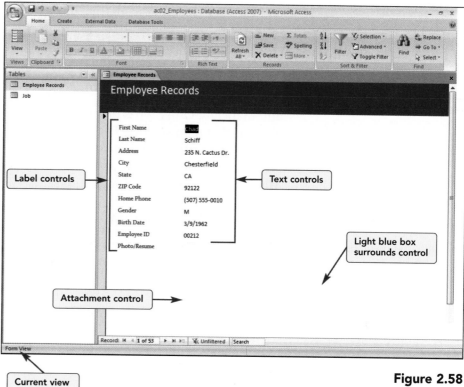

Figure 2.58

The completed form is displayed in the work area in Form view. The form title appears at the top of the form. The employee information for Chad Schiff, the first record in the table, is displayed in the form.

The form displays the selected fields in columnar layout using the Flow design style. A single column displays the field name labels down the left side of the column with the data for each field displayed just to the right of the corresponding label.

Each item in the form is a separate object contained in boxes, called controls.

Concept 9
Controls

9 Controls are objects that display information, perform actions, or enhance the design of a form or report. Access provides controls for many types of objects, including labels, text boxes, check boxes, list boxes, command buttons, lines, rectangles, option buttons, and more. The most common controls are **text controls** and **label controls**. Text controls display the information in the field from the record source. Label controls display descriptive labels.

There are two basic types of controls: bound and unbound. A **bound control** is linked to a field in an underlying table. An example of a bound control is a text control that is linked to the record source (usually a field from a table) and displays the field entry in the form or report. An **unbound control** is not connected to an underlying record source. Examples of unbound controls are labels such as the title of a form or elements that enhance the appearance of the form such as lines, boxes, and pictures.

Additional Information
You will learn about reports in Lab 3.

This form contains two types of controls: label controls that display the field names and text controls that display the field data. The text controls are bound controls. Changing information in the text controls will change the data for the record in the underlying table. Even though the label controls display the field names that are used in the underlying table, they are unbound controls. If you were to change the text in the form's label control, the field name in the table would not change. The columnar layout controls the layout and position of these controls.

Notice the Photo/Resume field control is an **attachment control** that is surrounded by a very light blue box. It is a bound control that allows you to add, edit, remove, and save attached files to the field directly from the form, just as you can in the datasheet. The attachment control displays image files automatically. Other types of attachments, such as Word documents, appear as icons that represent the file type and must be opened to view them.

The Photo/Resume field's control is empty because there are no attachments for this record. You would like to see the record for Roberta Marchant that contains attachments.

Navigating in Form View

You use the same navigation keys in Form view that you used in Datasheet view. You can move between fields in the form by using the Tab, Enter, and Shift + Tab keys. The → and ← keys are used to move character by character through the entry. You can use Page Up and Page Down, as well as the navigation buttons at the bottom of the form, to move between records.

You will try out several of these navigation keys as you try to locate the record for Roberta Marchant.

1 ● Press Tab **three times.**

● Press Page Down **three times.**

Your screen should be similar to Figure 2.59

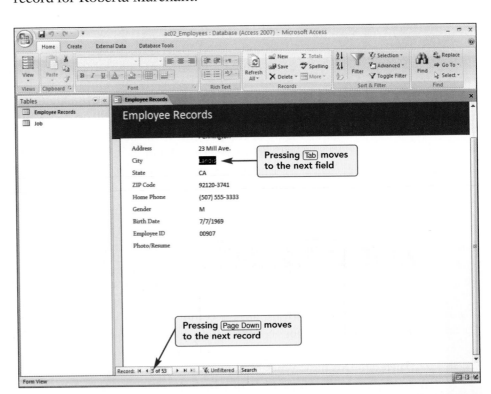

Figure 2.59

First you moved down three fields to the City field in the current record. Then you moved down three records to record four. The field that was selected in the previous record remains the selected field when you move between records. As you navigate the form, it automatically scrolls to display additional controls. To view controls that are no larger visible, simply use the vertical scroll bar.

Searching in Form View

A quicker way to locate a record is to use the Find command or the Search feature. The Find command works just as it does in Datasheet view. The Search feature simply locates information in a table by searching every field for a match to the text you enter in the Search box. It begins a search with the first field of the first record in the table. To try this out, you will search for the record for Roberta Marchant by entering the characters of her last name in the Search box.

1 ● **Click in the Search text box at the bottom of the work area.**

● **Type m.**

Your screen should be similar to Figure 2.60

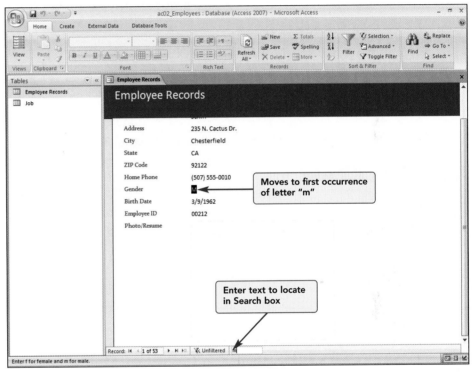

Figure 2.60

The first occurrence of the letter "m" in the table is located and highlighted. The more characters you type in the search text box, the more refined the search becomes. You will type more characters to continue looking for Roberta Marchant's record. As you type the characters, watch how the search advances through the table and highlights matching text.

2 • **Type arc in the Search box.**

Your screen should be similar to Figure 2.61

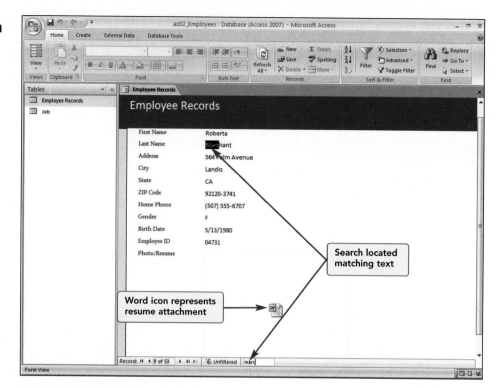

Figure 2.61

The Search feature located Roberta Marchant's record and displays it in the form. The Photo/Resume field displays a Word icon for the resume file. To move to the next attachment, you make the attachment control active to display the Mini Toolbar. It contains three buttons that are used to work with attachment controls. You can scroll through attached files using the ⊕ and ⊕ buttons or add or view attachments using 🔘 to open the Attachments dialog box.

Additional Information
The Mini Toolbar appears dimmed until you point to it.

3 ● Click on the Photo/Resume field to make it active.

● Point to the Mini Toolbar and click 🅰 to move to the next attachment.

Your screen should be similar to Figure 2.62

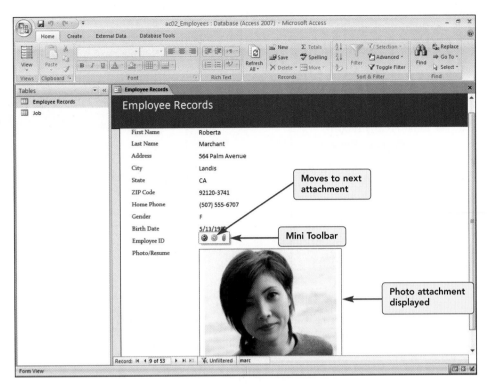

Figure 2.62

Now the photo is displayed in the Photo/Resume field control.

Sorting and Filtering Data in a Form

Just as in the table datasheet, you can sort and filter the data that is displayed in a form. You will use these features to sort the records in alphabetical order by last name and display only those records who live in River Mist.

1

● **Right-click on the Last Name field.**

● **Choose Sort A to Z.**

● **Move to any record that displays River Mist and right-click on the city field.**

● **Choose Equals "River Mist".**

● **Display the last record.**

Your screen should be similar to Figure 2.63

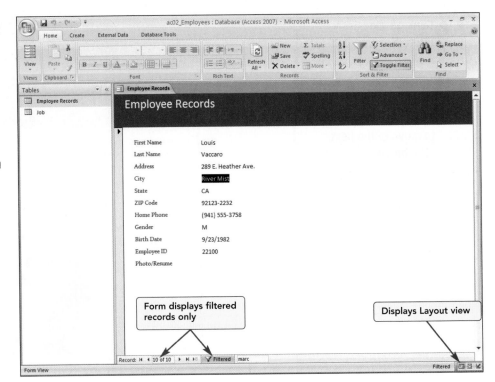

Figure 2.63

The record indicator tells you that there are only 10 records and the table is filtered. The records are also in sorted order by last name. The sort and filter settings apply only to the object in which they were specified, in this case the form.

Working with Controls

Although you are generally satisfied with the look of the form, there are a few changes that you want to make. The first change is to move the Employee ID field to the top of the form and size it to fit the data. Then you want to move the Photo/Resume control to the right of the other controls so that it is easier to see.

You can use Form Layout view or Form Design view to modify the design and layout of a form. As in Datasheet Design view, Form Design view displays the structure of the form, not the data in the form. It is used to make extensive changes to the form. Form Layout view displays the underlying data and allows you to make many basic modifications. You will use this view because you want to be able to see the data in the Employee ID field as you adjust the size of the field box.

1 ● Click 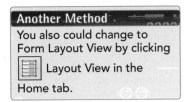 Layout View in the status bar.

● If necessary, close the Field List pane.

Another Method

You also could change to Form Layout View by clicking ▦ Layout View in the Home tab.

Your screen should be similar to Figure 2.64

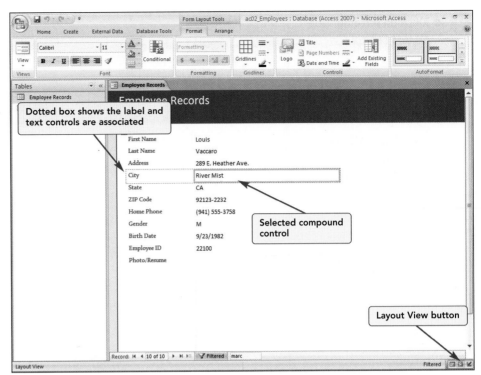

Figure 2.64

Additional Information

You will learn much more about selecting and modifying controls in Lab 3.

The Form Layout Tools Format and Arrange tabs are now available to help you modify the form design. Currently, the City text box control is surrounded with a solid orange box indicating the control is selected and is the control that will be affected by your actions. The dotted box around the label and text box controls shows they are associated. When the two parts of a control are associated, it is called a **compound control.**

First, you will select the Employee ID control to modify its size.

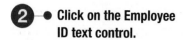

2 ● Click on the Employee ID text control.

Having Trouble?
The mouse pointer must be ◄► when selecting controls.

Your screen should be similar to Figure 2.65

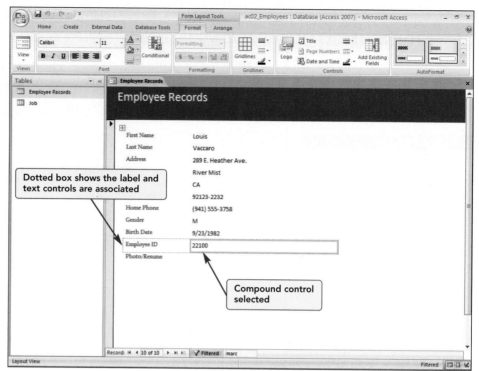

Dotted box shows the label and text controls are associated

Compound control selected

Figure 2.65

The text control of the Employee ID compound control is selected and surrounded in an orange box. Once controls are selected, they can be moved, sized, deleted, or modified. You will move the control to above the First Name control. When you point to the selected control and the mouse pointer appears as ◄►, you can move the control by dragging it. A solid orange line appears and shows you where the object will be placed when you stop dragging.

3 ● Point to the selected control and drag upward to move the control.

● When the solid orange line appears above the First Name control, release the mouse button to drop the control in the new location.

Your screen should be similar to Figure 2.66

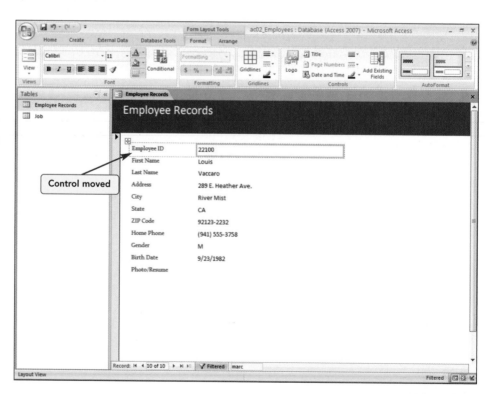

Control moved

Figure 2.66

Next, you want to reduce the size of the Employee ID text control to match the size of the entry. When you position the mouse pointer on the orange box surrounding the selected control, the pointer changes to ↔ and can be used to size the control. The direction of the arrow indicates in which direction dragging the mouse will alter the shape of the object. This action is similar to sizing a window.

4 ● **If necessary, click on the text box part of the Employee ID control to select it.**

Having Trouble?
The selected part of the control is contained in the orange box.

● **Point to the right edge of the selection box and, when the mouse pointer is ↔, drag to the left to decrease the size of the control as in Figure 2.67.**

Your screen should be similar to Figure 2.67

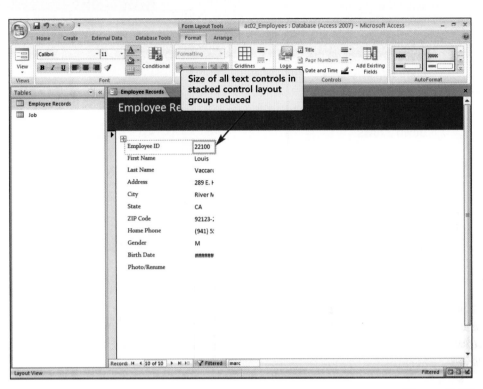

Figure 2.67

Unfortunately, the size of all the text box controls has been reduced. This is because in order for the stacked control layout to maintain the uniform appearance, it groups the controls so that they size as a unit. To size a control individually or move it outside the layout group, it must be removed from the group.

You want to move the Employee ID control outside the group so that it stands alone at the top of the form. Then you will size it to fit the contents. To make space at the top of the form, you will move all the controls in the group down first.

5 ● Increase the text control box to fully display the data as shown in Figure 2.68.

● Click the ⊕ layout selector box at the top-left corner of the layout to select all the controls.

● Drag the selection down 2 rows.

Having Trouble?
The control layout changes to dark blue as you move it to show the new position of the object.

● Scroll the window up to see the blank space above the control layout.

Your screen should be similar to Figure 2.68

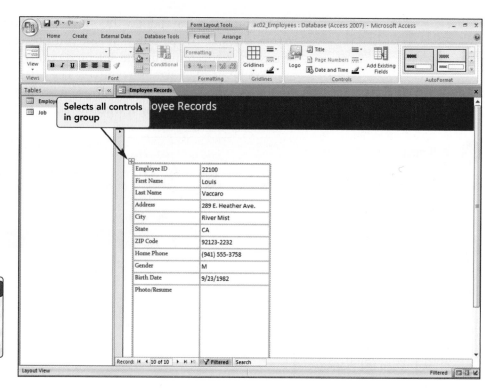

Figure 2.68

Next, you will remove the Employee ID control from the group and move and size it to fit the contents.

6 ● Select the Employee ID control.

● Click [Remove] in the Control Layout group of the Arrange tab.

Your screen should be similar to Figure 2.69

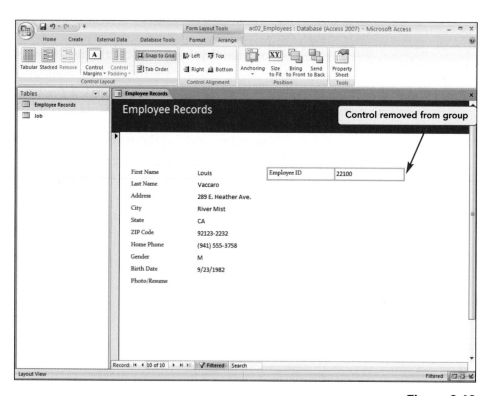

Figure 2.69

The Employee ID is now two separate objects that can be modified individually. Next, you will move the Employee ID control above the other controls.

7 ● Drag the Employee ID object to the position shown in Figure 2.70.

● Select the Employee ID text control and reduce its size as in Figure 2.70.

Your screen should be similar to Figure 2.70

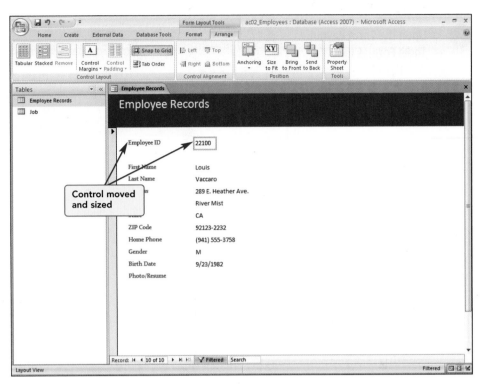

Figure 2.70

Now the Employee ID is clearly separate from the personal data on the form. Next, you will move the Photo/Resume control to the right of the other controls.

8 ● Remove the Photo/Resume control from the Layout control.

● Move the Photo/Resume control to the right of the other controls.

● Scroll the window up and reposition the controls as in Figure 2.71

Your screen should be similar to Figure 2.71

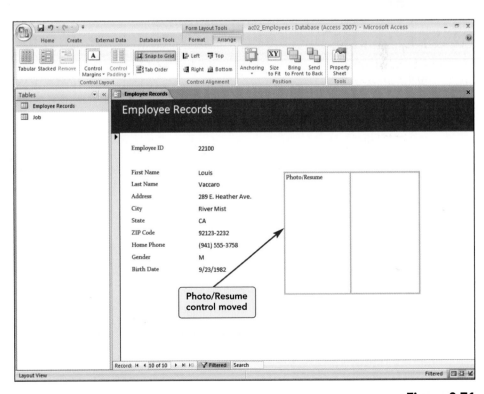

Figure 2.71

Changing the Form Design Style

Finally, you decide to change the form design style to another more colorful style.

1 ● **Open the Form Layout Tools Format tab.**

● **Click** ⊡ **More in the AutoFormat group.**

Your screen should be similar to Figure 2.72

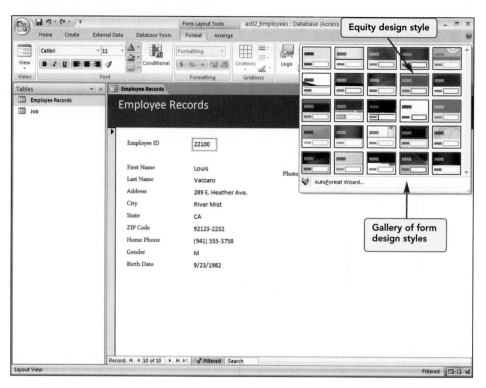

Figure 2.72

The gallery of the form design styles is displayed. You think the Equity design will be more interesting.

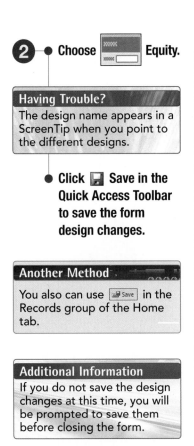

2 ● Choose [====] Equity.

Having Trouble?
The design name appears in a ScreenTip when you point to the different designs.

● Click 🖫 **Save** in the Quick Access Toolbar to save the form design changes.

Another Method
You also can use 🖫 Save in the Records group of the Home tab.

Additional Information
If you do not save the design changes at this time, you will be prompted to save them before closing the form.

Your screen should be similar to Figure 2.73

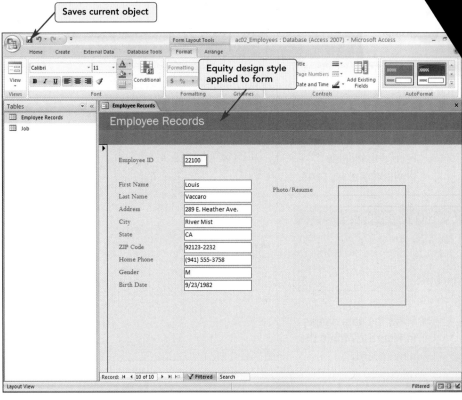

Figure 2.73

The selected design was applied to the form.

Adding Records Using a Form

Now, you need to add a new employee record to the database whose paper employee record form is shown here. You will add the record in Form view using the information on the paper form for the field entry data. You also will attach a picture to the Photo/Resume field.

Additional Information
You will learn more about working with form design and layout in later labs.

EMPLOYEE DATA		
Employee ID	12918	
First Name	Carlos	Last Name Ruiz
Street	10101 First St.	
City	Maldin	State CA Zip Code 92121-3740
Phone Number	(507) 555-5125	
Gender	M	
Birth Date	July 27, 1980	

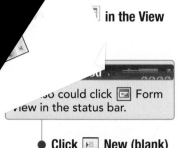

in the View

~~so could click~~ 📧 **Form**
~~View~~ in the status bar.

- Click ⊞ **New (blank) record** to display a new blank entry form.

- **Enter the data shown in Figure 2.74 into the new record.**

- **Double-click on the Attachment field control.**

- **Add the file** ac02_Carlos **from your data file location.**

  Your screen should be similar to Figure 2.74

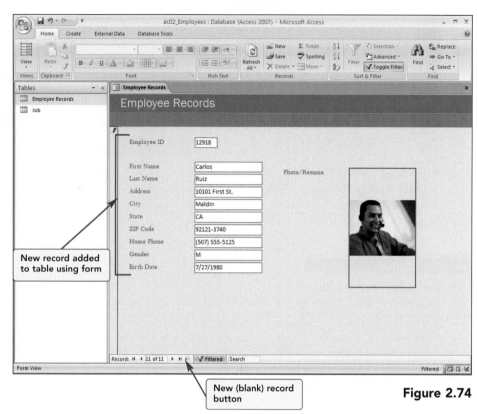

New record added to table using form

New (blank) record button

Figure 2.74

Using the form makes entering the new employee data much faster because the fields are in the same order as the information in the paper Employee Data form used by the personnel department.

Before you end this lab, you will add a record for yourself.

2 • Enter another record using your special Employee ID 99999 and your first and last names. The data in all other fields can be fictitious.

• Remove the filter.

The table now contains 55 records. Next, you need to add these two records to the Job table.

Organizing the Navigation Pane

Notice the name of the form does not appear in the Navigation pane. This is because initially the pane is set to display table objects only. To display other objects in the pane, you can change what objects are displayed in the pane and how they are grouped.

1 • Click

Tables

at the top of the Navigation pane to open the Tables drop-down menu.

Your screen should be similar to Figure 2.75

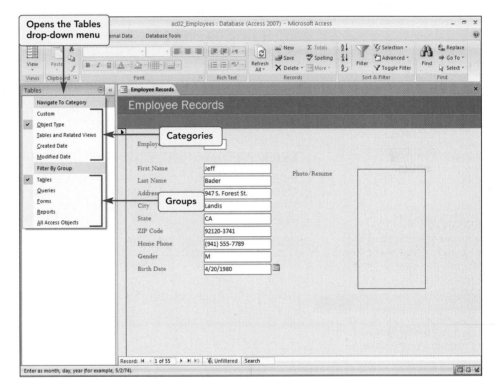

Figure 2.75

The upper section of the menu contains categories and the lower section contains groups. The groups change as you select different categories. Currently, Object Type is the selected category and Tables is the selected group. You want to keep the category selection as Object Type but want to change the group selection to display all object types in the pane at the same time.

2 ● From the Filter by Group section, choose All Access Objects.

● Double-click the Job table in the Navigation pane.

Another Method
You also can drag an object from the Navigation pane to the work area to open it.

● Add the two records in the following table.

Your screen should be similar to Figure 2.76

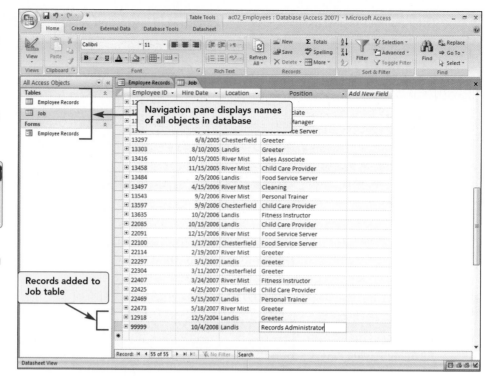

Figure 2.76

Employee ID	12918	99999
Hire Date	12/5/2004	Today's date
Location	Landis	Landis
Position	Greeter	Records Administrator

Additional Information
You will learn in later labs how to create a single form to update both tables.

Now both tables contain 55 records.

Previewing and Printing a Form

You want to preview and print only the form that displays your record.

1 ● **Click the Employee Records tab to display the form.**

● **Click** 🔘 **Office Button and choose Print/Print Preview.**

Your screen should be similar to Figure 2.77

Having Trouble?

Your form may display fewer records than in Figure 2.77.

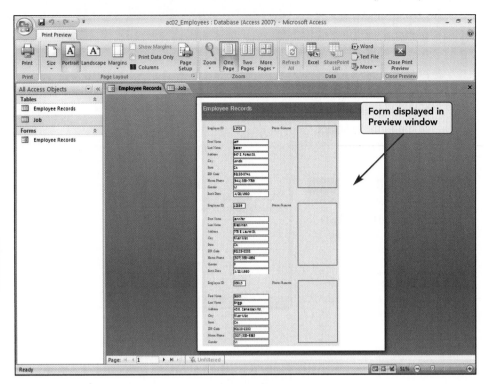

Figure 2.77

Print Preview displays the current object. In this case, because you were last in Form view, the form is displayed in the Preview window.

Printing a Selected Record

Access prints as many records as can be printed on a page using the Form layout. You want to print only the form displaying your record. To do this, you need to select your record first in Form view.

① • Click  .

• **Display your record in the form.**

• **Click the Record Selector bar (the blue bar along the left side of the form) to select the entire record.**

Another Method

You also can use 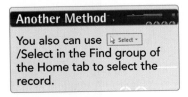 /Select in the Find group of the Home tab to select the record.

Your screen should be similar to Figure 2.78

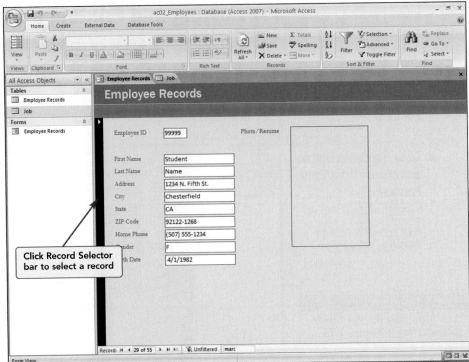

Click Record Selector bar to select a record

Figure 2.78

Now that the record is selected, you can print the record. The record will print using the current view, in this case, Form view.

② • **Click** 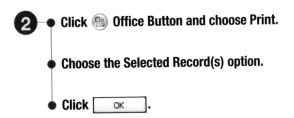 **Office Button and choose Print.**

• **Choose the Selected Record(s) option.**

• **Click** OK .

Identifying Object Dependencies

The form is the third database object that has been added to the file. Many objects that you create in a database are dependent upon other objects for their content. In this case, the form is dependent upon the Employee Records database table for its content. Sometimes it is helpful to be able to find out what objects an object is dependent on or that depend on it. To help in these situations, you can display the object dependencies.

1 ● **Select the Employee Records table object in the Navigation pane.**

● **Open the Database Tools tab.**

● **Click** [Object Dependencies] **in the Show/Hide group.**

● **If necessary, select "Objects that depend on me" from the Object Dependencies task pane.**

Your screen should be similar to Figure 2.79

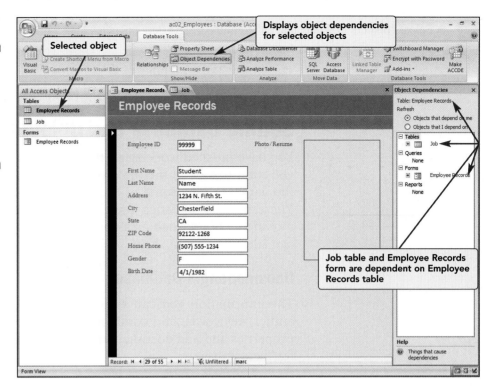

Figure 2.79

The Object Dependencies task pane identifies the two objects that are dependent on the table: the Job table and the Employee Records form. Next, you will see which objects depend on the Employee Records form.

2 ● **Select Employee Records in the Forms category of the Navigation pane.**

● **Click Refresh in the Object Dependencies task pane.**

Your screen should be similar to Figure 2.80

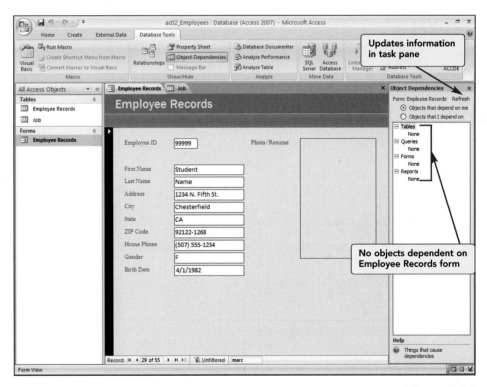

Figure 2.80

You can now see that the Employee Records object does not have any objects dependent on it.

3 Select "Objects that I depend on" from the Object Dependencies task pane.

The Object Dependencies task pane identifies the only object that the form depends on is the Employee Records table.

Setting Database and Object Properties

You have finished working on the database for now. Before exiting Access, you want to look at the file properties or settings that are associated with the database file. Some of these properties are automatically generated. These include statistics such as the date the file was created and last modified. Others such as a description of the file are properties that you can add.

Documenting a Database

The information you can associate with the file includes a title, subject, author, keywords, and comments about the file. You will look at the file properties and add documentation to identify you as the author and a title for the database.

1 ● **Close the Object Dependencies task pane.**

● **Click ▣ Office Button and choose Manage/Database Properties.**

● **Select each tab in the Properties dialog box and look at the recorded information.**

● **Display the Summary tab.**

● **Enter the following information in the Summary tab.**

| Title | Lifestyle Fitness Employee Database |
| Author | Your Name |

Having Trouble?
The Title and Author text boxes may be blank or may already show information. Clear the existing contents first if necessary.

Your screen should be similar to Figure 2.81

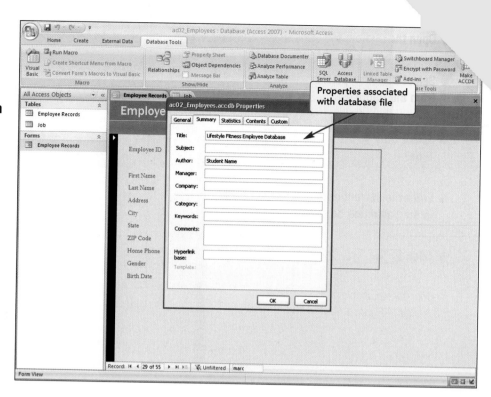

Figure 2.81

You also want to create a custom property to identify the completion date.

● e Custom tab.

● ate Completed
  e Name list.

● **Select Date as the Type.**

● **Enter the current date in the Value text box.**

● **Click** Add .

Your screen should be similar to Figure 2.82

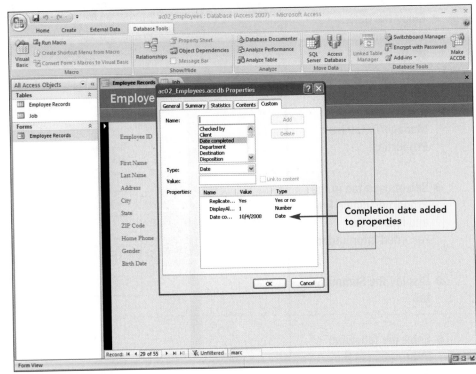

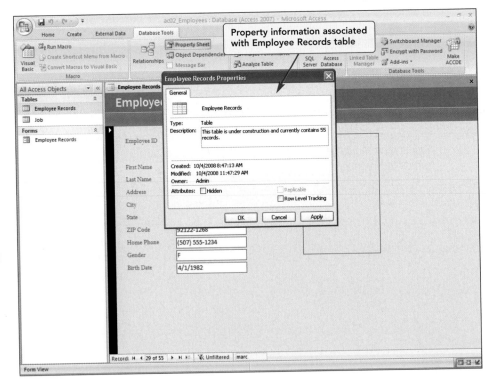

Figure 2.82

You have completed adding the properties to the file. You also can add limited documentation to each object in a database. You will add documentation to the Employee Records table object.

3 ● **Click** OK .

● **Select the Employee Records table object.**

● **Select**  Property Sheet **from the Show/Hide group.**

● **In the Description text box, type This table is under construction and currently contains 55 records.**

Your screen should be similar to Figure 2.83

Figure 2.83

MORE ABOUT

▶ For information about creating a report using the Database Documenter that details the properties of an entire database or any of its objects, see "6.2 Manage Databases" in the More About appendix.

You have added property information to both the database file and the Employee Records table.

4 ● Click [OK] to close the Properties dialog box.

● Close the form and table objects.

● Exit Access.

Focus on Careers

EXPLORE YOUR CAREER OPTIONS

Administrative Assistant

Administrative assistants are typically responsible for the efficient management of office operations. This position may involve conducting research, training new staff, scheduling meetings, and maintaining databases. As an administrative assistant, you could be responsible for updating an inventory or staffing database. The typical salary range of an administrative assistant is $24,000 to $35,000. Demand for experienced administrative assistants, especially in technology and health fields, is expected to increase through 2010.

Concept Summary

LAB 2
Modifying and Filtering a Table and Creating a Form

Format Property   (AC2.8)

The Format property is used to specify the way that numbers, dates, times, and text in a field are displayed and printed.

Default Value Property   (AC2.9)

The Default Value property is used to specify a value that is automatically entered in a field when a new record is created.

Validation Rule   (AC2.13)

Validation rules are used to control the data that can be entered in a field by defining the input values that are valid or allowed.

Expression   (AC2.14)

An expression is a formula consisting of a combination of symbols that will produce a single value.

Find and Replace   (AC2.24)

The Find and Replace feature helps you quickly find specific information and automatically replace it with new information.

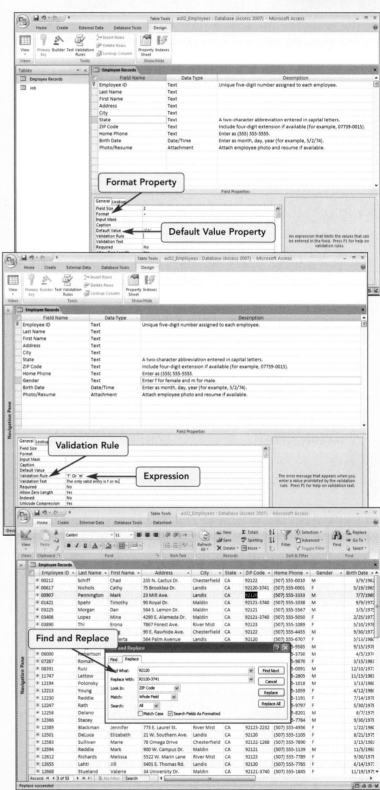

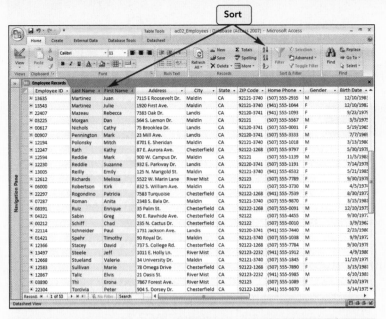

Sort (AC2.34)

You can sort the data in a table to quickly rearrange the order of the records.

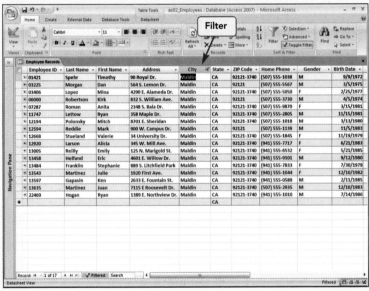

Filter (AC2.42)

A filter is a restriction placed on records in the open table or form to quickly isolate and display a subset of records.

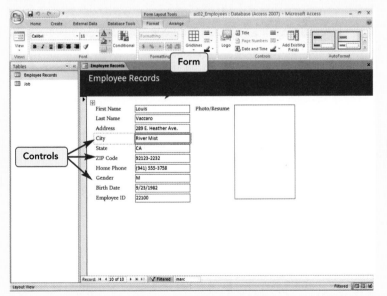

Form (AC2.49)

A form is a database object used primarily to display records onscreen to make it easier to enter new records and to make changes to existing records.

Controls (AC2.57)

Controls are objects that display information, perform actions, or enhance the design of a form or report.

key terms

ascending sort order AC2.34	**Find and Replace** AC2.24	**tabular layout** AC2.54
attachment control AC2.58	**form** AC2.49	**text control** AC2.57
bound control AC2.57	**format** AC2.37	**theme colors** AC2.39
character string AC2.10	**Format property** AC2.8	**unbound control** AC2.57
comparison operator AC2.14	**identifier** AC2.14	**Validation Rule property** AC2.13
compound control AC2.63	**label control** AC2.57	**Validation Text property** AC2.13
control AC2.57	**layout** AC2.54	**value** AC2.9
criteria AC2.25	**operator** AC2.14	**wildcards** AC2.25
Default Value property AC2.9	**record source** AC2.50	
descending sort order AC2.34	**sort** AC2.34	
expression AC2.14	**stacked layout** AC2.54	
filter AC2.42	**tab order** AC2.52	

MCAS Skills

The Microsoft Certified Applications Specialist (MCAS) certification program is designed to measure your proficiency in performing basic tasks using the Office 2007 applications. Getting certified demonstrates that you have the skills and provides a valuable industry credential for employment. See Reference 2: Microsoft Certified Applications Specialist (MCAS) for a complete list of the skills that were covered in Lab 2.

command summary

Command	Shortcut	Action
Office Button		
Manage/Database Properties		Allows changes to database properties
Quick Access Toolbar		
⟲ Undo	Ctrl + Z	Cancels last action
🖫 Save	Ctrl + S	Saves the current object
Home tab		
Views group		
Form View		Changes to Form view
Form Layout View		Changes to Form Layout view
Font group		
B Bold	Ctrl + B	Applies bold effect to all text in datasheet
A Font Color		Applies selected color to all text in datasheet
Gridlines		Changes gridline color of datasheet
Alternate Fill/Back Color		Changes background color of datasheet
Records group		
Save	Shift + Enter	Saves changes to object design
New	Ctrl + +	Adds new record
More /Hide Columns		Hides columns in Datasheet view
More /Unhide Columns		Redisplays hidden columns
Sort & Filter group		
Ascending		Changes sort order to ascending
Descending		Changes sort order to descending
Clear All Sorts		Clears all sorts and returns sort order to primary key order
Filter		Allows multiple filter criteria in a single field
Selection /Equals		Displays only those records containing selected value

Lab Review

command summary

Command	Shortcut	Action
Advanced ˅ /Clear all Filters		Removes all filters from table
Toggle Filter		Applies and removes filter from table
Find group		
Find	Ctrl + F	Locates specified data
Replace	Ctrl + H	Locates specified data and replaces it with specified replacement text
Go To ˅		Moves to First, Previous, Next, Last, or New record location
Select ˅ /Select		Selects current record
Select ˅ /Select All		Selects all records in database
Create tab		
Tables group		
(table icon)		Creates a new table in Datasheet view
Table Design		Creates a new table in Design view
Forms group		
Form		Creates a new form using all the fields from the underlying table
Blank Form		Displays a blank form to which you add the fields from the table that you want to appear on the form
More Forms ˅ /Form Wizard		Creates a new form by following the steps in the Form Wizard
Database Tools tab		
Show/Hide group		
Property Sheet		Specifies general properties associated with the database file
Object Dependencies		Shows the objects in the database that use the selected object

command summary

Command	Shortcut	Action
Table Tools Design tab		
Tools group		
⊨ Insert Rows		Inserts a new field in Table Design view
Table Tools Datasheet tab		
Fields & Columns group		
Lookup Column		Creates a lookup column
Form Layout Tools Format tab		
AutoFormat group		
⊤ More		Opens gallery of design styles
Form Layout Tools Arrange tab		
Control Layout group		
Remove		Removes selected control
Position group		
Bring to Front		Brings selected control to top of stack

Lab Exercises

matching

Match the numbered item with the correct lettered description.

1. *   _____   **a.** locates specified values in a field
2. filter   _____   **b.** an expression
3. tab order   _____   **c.** database object used primarily for onscreen display
4. character string   _____   **d.** order that the selection point moves in a form when Tab is used
5. find   _____   **e.** temporarily displays subset of records
6. >=   _____   **f.** operator
7. ascending sort   _____   **g.** a group of characters
8. ="Y" Or "N"   _____   **h.** rearranges records in A to Z or 0 to 9 order
9. record source   _____   **i.** wildcard character
10. form   _____   **j.** underlying table for a form

fill-in

Complete the following statements by filling in the blanks with the correct terms.

1. The upper section of the Navigation pane contains _____ and the lower section contains_____.

2. A(n) _____ is a symbol or word that indicates that an operation is to be performed.

3. _____ restrict the type of data that can be entered in a field.

4. _____ is displayed when an invalid entry is entered.

5. Format _____ is used to create custom formats that change the way numbers, dates, times, and text display and print.

6. The _____ property changes the way data appears in a field.

7. The most common controls are _____ controls and _____ controls.

8. A(n) _____ control is linked to the data in the resource table.

9. The _____ property is used to specify a value that is automatically entered in a field when a new record is created.

10. The two basic form layouts are _____ and _____.

Lab 2: Modifying and Filtering a Table
and Creating a Form

www.mhhe.com/oleary

true/false

Circle the correct answer to the following statements.

1.	The Default Value property determines the value automatically entered into a field of a new record.	True	False
2.	Forms are database objects used primarily for viewing data.	True	False
3.	Text controls display descriptive labels.	True	False
4.	Values are numbers, dates, or pictures.	True	False
5.	An expression is a sequence of characters (letters, numbers, or symbols) that must be handled as text, not as numeric data.	True	False
6.	Label controls are bound controls.	True	False
7.	A contrast operator is a symbol that allows you to make comparisons between two items.	True	False
8.	A validation rule is an expression that defines acceptable data entry values.	True	False
9.	Filter results can be saved with the database and quickly redisplayed.	True	False
10.	When the two parts of a control are associated, it is called a compound control.	True	False

multiple choice

Circle the letter of the correct response.

1. _____ control(s) how data is displayed in a form.
   a. Design styles
   b. Controls
   c. Layouts
   d. Tab order

2. A form is _____ an underlying table for its content.
   a. independent of
   b. reliant on
   c. contingent on
   d. dependent on

3. _____ layouts arrange data vertically with a field label to the left of the field data.
   a. Datasheet
   b. Justified
   c. Tabular
   d. Stacked

4. A _____ is a temporary restriction placed on a table to display a subset of records.
   a. wildcard
   b. control
   c. filter
   d. sort

5. The _____ is used to specify a value that is automatically entered in a field when a new record is created.
   a. Default Value property
   b. Sort property
   c. field value
   d. Format property

6. _____ is/are an explanatory message that appears if a user attempts to enter invalid information in a text field.
   a. Validation text
   b. Validation rule
   c. Expressions
   d. Validity checks

7. A(n) _____ control is linked to its underlying data source.
   a. bound
   b. label
   c. field
   d. unbound

8. A _____ is a feature that guides you step by step through a process.
   a. dialog box
   b. wizard
   c. task pane
   d. gallery

9. _____ properties change the way that data is displayed.
   a. Format
   b. Field
   c. Data
   d. Record

10. The _____ property is commonly used when most of the entries in a field will be the same for the entire table.
    a. AutoNumber
    b. Default Value
    c. Field Data
    d. Best Fit

Hands-On Exercises

step-by-step

Note: Before you begin, you may want to create a backup copy of each data file by copying and renaming it.

Second Time Around Inventory Database ★

1. You have already set up an inventory database for the Second Time Around consignment shop. It currently contains the item number, description, price, and consignor last name fields, and it has records for the inventory currently in stock. The owner of the shop is quite pleased with the database as it stands but has asked you to change the name of the existing price field to show that it is the original price and add a new field for the current selling price of the item. Also, she would like you to modify some existing records, create a form to ease data entry, and print a copy of the form. Your completed table and form are shown here.

   a. Open the database named ac02_Second Time Around and the table named Antiques Inventory.

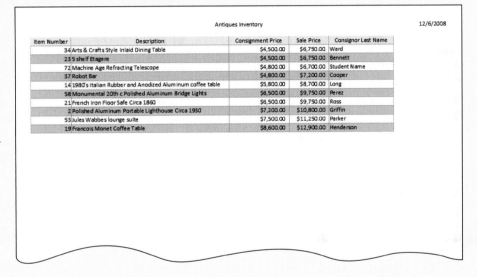

Antiques Inventory — 12/6/2008

Item Number	Description	Consignment Price	Sale Price	Consignor Last Name
34	Arts & Crafts Style Inlaid Dining Table	$4,500.00	$6,750.00	Ward
23	5 shelf Etagere	$4,500.00	$6,750.00	Bennett
72	Machine Age Refracting Telescope	$4,800.00	$6,700.00	Student Name
37	Robot Bar	$4,800.00	$7,200.00	Cooper
14	1980's Italian Rubber and Anodized Aluminum coffee table	$5,800.00	$8,700.00	Long
58	Monumental 20th c Polished Aluminum Bridge Lights	$6,500.00	$9,750.00	Perez
21	French Iron Floor Safe Circa 1860	$6,500.00	$9,750.00	Ross
2	Polished Aluminum Portable Lighthouse Circa 1930	$7,200.00	$10,800.00	Griffin
53	Jules Wabbes lounge suite	$7,500.00	$11,250.00	Parker
19	Francois Monet Coffee Table	$8,600.00	$12,900.00	Henderson

   b. Change the Price field name to **Consignment Price**. Change the Data Type for this field to Currency.

   c. Insert the following field above the Consignor Last Name field:

Field name:	Sale Price
Data type:	Currency

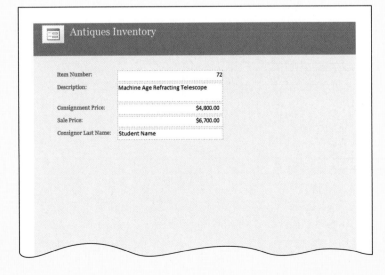

Antiques Inventory

Item Number:	72
Description:	Machine Age Refracting Telescope
Consignment Price:	$4,800.00
Sale Price:	$6,700.00
Consignor Last Name:	Student Name

   d. Make all fields except Sale Price required. (Hint: Set the Required property to Yes.) Reduce the field size of the Consignor Last Name field to **25**.

   e. Switch to Datasheet view and respond "yes" to all prompts and warnings when saving the design changes.

   f. Update the table by entering **0.00** in the Consignment Price field for all records that have a blank entry in this field. (Hint: Use copy and paste).

g. Enter appropriate values in the Sale Price field for each record. (Generally the sale price is 33 percent more than the consignment price.) Leave the Sale Price field blank for those items with $0.00 in the Consignment Price field.

h. Appropriately size all columns to fully display the data.

i. Find all occurrences of dates that include an apostrophe (1930's) and are preceded with the word circa. Manually delete the 's from each located item.

j. Filter the table to display all records with a consignment price greater than or equal to $4,500. Sort the filtered records in ascending sort order by consignment price.

k. Format the datasheet using alternate row fill colors. Close the table object.

l. Use the Form tool to create a simple form for the Antiques Inventory table.

m. Display the form in Layout view. Change the form design style to another style of your choice. Reduce the size of all the text controls (they will size together as a group).

n. Use the new form to enter the following records:

Record 1	Record 2
Machine Age Refracting Telescope	Mid Century School House Globe
$4,800	$1,100
$6,700	$3,150
[Your Last Name]	Lewis

o. Print the form for the record containing your name. Close the form, saving it as Inventory.

p. Open the table and rerun the filter to display your record in the results. Print the filtered datasheet in landscape orientation using the normal margin setting. Close the table.

q. Display all object types in the Navigation pane.

r. Add object documentation for the form. Add your name to the database properties and exit Access.

Enterprise Employment Client Database ★★

2. You work for a private employment agency as an administrative assistant. As part of your responsibilities, you maintain a client database that contains the job candidates' basic contact information: name, address, and phone number. The office manager has asked you to add to the database the date each candidate applied at your office, the date they were placed with an employer, and the employer's name. Also, because the database is getting rather large, you decide to create a form to make it easier to enter and update records. Your completed table and form are shown here.

a. Open the database named ac02_Enterprise Employment Agency and the table named Candidates.

b. Reduce the State field size to **2**. Change the State field Format property to display all entries in uppercase. Make the Default Value for the state field **FL**.

c. Change the Zip Code data type to Text with a field size of **10**.

d. Insert the following field after the Application # field.

Field name:	**Application Date**
Data type:	Date/Time
Format:	Short Date

e. Add the following two fields to the end of the table:

Field name:	**Hire Date**
Data type:	Date/Time
Format:	Short Date
Field name:	**Employed By**
Data type:	Text
Description:	**Enter the name of the employer**
Field size:	45

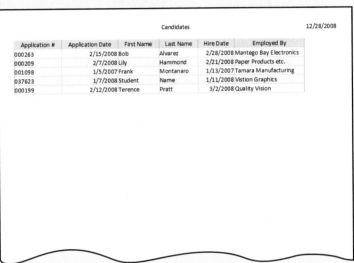

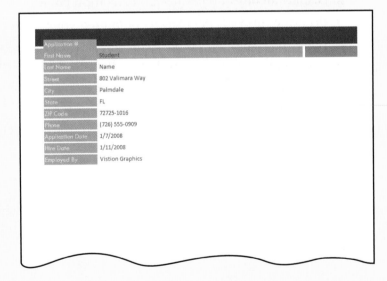

f. Switch to Datasheet view and save the table design changes.

g. All zip codes of 72725 need to be changed to **72725-1016**. Use Find and Replace to make this change in the database. Best fit the columns.

h. Use the Form Wizard to create a form for the Candidates table. Include all the table fields in their current order. Use the Columnar layout and a style of your choice. Title the form **Candidate Information**.

i. Use the new form to enter the following records:

Application #	001098	037623
First Name	Frank	Your first name
Last Name	Montanaro	Your last name
Address	124 Beach Front Way	802 Valimara Way
City	Lexington	Palmdale
State	FL	FL
ZIP Code	72724	72725-1016
Phone	(726) 555-7623	(726) 555-0909
Application Date	1/5/08	1/7/08
Hire Date	1/13/08	1/11/08
Employed By	Tamara Manufacturing	Vistion Graphics

j. Use the Search feature to locate the following records and update their data.

Locate	Application Date	Hire Date	Employed By
Lilly Hammond	2/7/08	2/21/08	Paper Products etc.
Terrence Pratt	2/12/08	3/2/08	Quality Vision
Bob Alvarez	2/15/08	2/28/08	Mantego Bay Electronics

k. Display all object types in the Navigation pane.

l. Print the form for the record containing your name.

m. Filter the Candidates table to display only those records displaying a hire date. Sort the records in ascending order by last name. Hide the Address through Phone columns.

n. Print the filtered datasheet using the Normal margin setting in landscape orientation.

o. Remove the filter and unhide the columns.

p. Add your name to the database properties. Close all objects and exit Access.

ARF Tracking Database ★★

3. You have created a database for tracking the animals that come into and go out of the Animal Rescue Foundation. Now you need to modify the database structure and customize field properties to control the data entered by the foundation's volunteers who are assigned this task. You also want to create a form to make it easier for the volunteers to enter the necessary information. The completed datasheet and form are shown here.

a. Open the file ac02_ARF Database and the table Rescues in Datasheet view.

b. Use Find to locate ID # R-904. Add the adoption date **6/13/2007**.

c. Use Search to locate the animal named Spreckels and change the age to B and enter **12/01/2007** as the Foster Date.

d. Add the following field before the Arrival Date field:

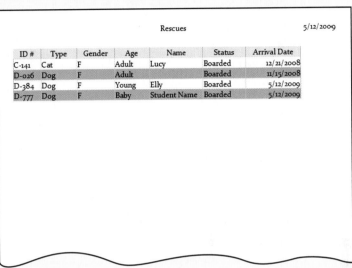

	Rescues						5/12/2009
ID #	Type	Gender	Age	Name	Status	Arrival Date
C-141	Cat	F	Adult	Lucy	Boarded	12/21/2008
D-026	Dog	F	Adult		Boarded	11/15/2008
D-384	Dog	F	Young	Elly	Boarded	5/12/2009
D-777	Dog	F	Baby	Student Name	Boarded	5/12/2009

Field name:	**Status**
Data type:	Lookup
Description:	**Select Boarded, Foster Care or Adopted**
Field size:	**15**

e. Make the following additional changes to the database structure:

- Restrict the entries in the Status field to list items only. Make Boarded the default value for Status.

- Add a validation rule and validation text to the Gender field to accept only M or F (male or female). Format the field to display the information in uppercase.

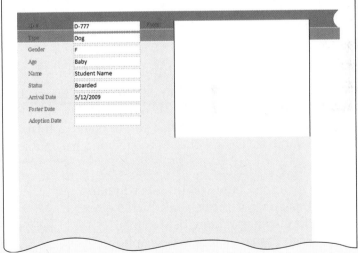

- Change the Age field to Lookup data type to accept only Baby, Young, or Adult. Increase the field size to **5**. Remove the validation rule and text and restrict the entries to items on the list only.

f. In Datasheet view, complete the data for the Status by entering F (if there is a Foster Date), A if there is an adoption date, or B. Best fit the columns.

g. Change the data in the Age column by selecting from the list for each record.

h. Best fit all columns.

i. Add formatting of your choice to the Datasheet. Change the font of the datasheet to Constantia, 12 point.

j. Use the Form Wizard to create a columnar form. Include all the fields in their current order and use a style of your choice. Title the form **Animals**.

k. Search in Form view to locate the animal named Titus and add the picture ac02_WhiteDog to the Attachment field.

l. Adjust the size of the attachment control in Form Layout view. Change the form design style to another and make any adjustments to controls that are needed.

m. Add two records using the new form. Use the current date as the arrival date and make the status Boarded. In the Name field of the second record you add, enter your name, so your name appears on the printed output.

n. Save the form and print the record with your name as the animal name.

o. Filter the Rescues datasheet to display only those animals with a status of Boarded. Sort the filtered datasheet by Type. Hide the Foster Date, Adoption Date, and Attachment columns. Print the Rescues datasheet in portrait orientation using the Wide margin setting.

p. Unhide all columns. Clear all sorts and remove the filter.

q. Display all object types in the Navigation pane.

r. Identify object dependencies.

s. Add your name to the database properties. Close all objects and exit Access.

Kodiak Construction Database ★★★

4. Although the database you designed for the expanding Kodiak Construction Company was well received, you have been asked to make several additions and improvements to the original design. In addition, they have asked you to create a form to make the process of entering new records in the database easier. The completed database table and form are shown here.

a. Open the file ac02_Kodiak Construction.

b. Open the Clients table and switch to Design view. Insert a new field before the Business Phone field named **Home Phone**. Include a description. Set the field size to **14**.

c. Enter the following Home Phone numbers into the table. Hide the fields between the Last Name and Home Phone fields. Use Find to locate the records. Unhide the columns when you are done.

			Jobs		11/6/2008
ID	Job	Priority	Client Last Name	Begin Date	
296	Amberly Oaks	1 (High)		4/28/2007	
884	Bella Greens	1 (High)		4/7/2006	
163	Frisco Lake View	1 (High)	King	11/4/2006	
489	Historia	1 (High)		12/10/2005	
587	Pinewood Glen	1 (High)		3/5/2006	
254	Shadow Hills	1 (High)		5/7/2006	
999	Student Name private res	1 (High)	Name	11/6/2008	
985	Willow Shoreline	1 (High)		3/21/2007	

Last Name	Home Phone
Lopez	303-555-3772
Miller	303-555-8831
Walker	303-555-6613
Young	303-555-0912

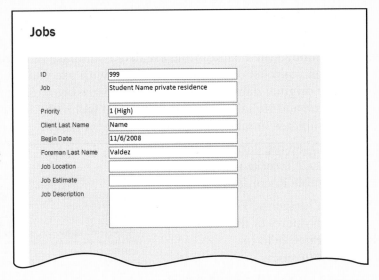

d. Change the City column to a Lookup Field data type. Include the following cities as the lookup list values: Aurora, Denver, Glendale, Lakewood, Littleton, Parker.

e. Open the City field drop-down list for each record and select a city.

f. Make the default value for the State field **CO**. Change the format to uppercase.

g. Next, you want to add a field for the job priority to the Jobs table. This field can only contain three possible values: High, Normal, or Low. Instead of typing this information in the field, you will make the field a Lookup field.

Open the Jobs table and insert the new field named **Priority** after the Job field. Select the Lookup Wizard from the Data Type list. Select the "I will type in the values that I want" option. In column 1, enter **High** in the first cell, **Normal** in the second cell, and **Low** in the third cell. Accept the field name. Set the field's size to **15** and the default value to Normal. Limit entries to values from the list.

h. Switch to Datasheet view, saving your design changes.

i. Open the Priority field drop-down list for each record and select a priority level.

j. Best fit the columns.

k. Add formatting of your choice to the Jobs datasheet. Change the font to Arial. Close the table.

l. Use the Form Wizard to create a form for the Jobs table. Include all of the fields from the Jobs table in order. Use the columnar form layout. Select a style of your choice and accept the default form name (**Jobs**).

m. In Form Layout view, search for the record for Kern Canyon Ranch. Change the foreman to **Valdez**.

n. Appropriately size the label and text controls (they will size together as a group).

o. Create similar forms for the Clients and Foremen tables. Size the controls appropriately.

p. Using the form, add a new record to the Client table using your first and last names as the client name. Save the changes and close the form.

q. Add a new record to the Jobs table with **999** as the ID and **[your last name] private residence** as the job; select your name as the Client Last Name, priority of High, the current date as the Begin Date, and a foreman of your choice.

r. Save the form object. Print your record in the form.

s. Open the Jobs table. Filter the records to display only those with a High priority. Sort the filtered records by Job in ascending sort order. Hide the Job Location, Job Estimate, and Job Description columns.

t. Print the filtered Jobs datasheet in landscape orientation.

u. Unhide all columns. Clear all sorts and remove the filter.

v. Display all object types in the Navigation pane.

w. Add your name to the database properties. Save and close the database.

EchoPlex Database ★★★

5. EchoPlex is an online record store that specializes in rare and collectible vinyl. You recently expanded the business and created a database to manage your inventory. The database initially began as a list of available titles, but with use you saw a need for more information. You changed the original database file design and have been using it for several weeks now, but it still needs some additional changes that you feel will make inventory control and data entry even easier. The completed database and form are shown here.

a. Open the database file ac02_EchoPlex and the table Records.

b. Change the Format property of the Sold Price field to Currency.

c. Use Search to find the record for Neil Young's *Harvest*. Enter the sold price of **155**.

d. Unhide the Comments field.

e. You want to add a new field to show the condition of each item. This field can only contain four possible values: Excellent, Good, Fair, or Poor. Insert a new field after Artist named **Condition**. Use a data type of Lookup and enter the following as the list values: **Excellent**, **Good**, **Fair**, and **Poor**. Accept the field name. Set the field's Default Value to **Good** and limit entries to list items.

f. Switch to Datasheet view and select a condition for each record.

g. Enter the following information as a new record:

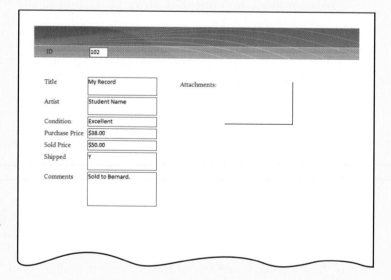

ID	**Title**	**Artist**	**Condition**	**Purchase Price**	**Sold Price**	**Shipped**
42	The Doors	The Doors	Excellent	$10.00	$0.00	N
41	Never Mind the Bollocks	The Sex Pistols	Excellent	$10.00	$0.00	N
56	Songs in the Key of Life	Stevie Wonder	Excellent	$12.00	$0.00	N
102	My Record	Student Name	Excellent	$38.00	$50.00	Y
6	What's Going On	Marvin Gaye	Excellent	$50.00	$86.00	Y
51	Bridge Over Troubled Water	Simon and Garfunkel	Excellent	$50.00	$0.00	N
10	The Beatles ("The White Album")	The Beatles	Excellent	$50.00	$0.00	N
15	Are You Experienced?	The Jimi Hendrix Experience	Excellent	$50.00	$0.00	N
81	Graceland	Paul Simon	Excellent	$87.00	$0.00	N

Records — 10/6/2008

Title:	School House Rocker
Artist:	Kate Lansbergen
Condition:	Fair
Purchase Price:	$45.00
Sold Price:	$47.00
Comments:	Traded to SearchLight Records for $47.00 in store credit.

h. Insert a new field after the Sold Price field named **Shipped**. Add **"Y or N"** as a validation rule. Add **Must be Y or N** as the Validation text.

i. Sort the list by Sold Price. For all of the entries with $0.00, enter **N** in the Shipped field. For entries with a Sold Price, enter **Y** in the Shipped field.

j. Find all instances of Beatles and replace with **The Beatles**.

k. Hide the Comments and Attachments fields.

l. Add formatting of your choice to the datasheet. Change the font of the datasheet to one of your choice.

m. Use the Form Wizard to create a form for the Records table. Include all of the fields from the Records table in order. Use the columnar form. Apply a style of your choice to the form and accept the default form name (**Records**).

n. Switch to Layout view. Select another design style. Move the grouped controls down on the form. Remove the ID field from the group. Move the ID field above the grouped controls. Size the ID field to fit the data. Adjust the size of the other form controls as needed (they will size together as a group). Move and size the Attachment label and text controls as needed.

o. Use the form to enter a new record with a title of your choice and your name as the artist. Include a condition of Excellent, a purchase price of $38, and a sold price of $50.

p. Preview and print the form for your record. Save and close the form.

q. Filter the records to display only those records with a condition of Excellent and a purchase price of $10 or more. Sort the records in ascending order by Purchase Price. Best fit the fields. Print the filtered datasheet in landscape orientation with Normal margins.

r. Display all object types in the Navigation pane.

s. Add your name to the database properties. Save the database and exit Access.

Adventure Travel Packages Form ★

1. You have heard from the employees of Adventure Travel Tours that the database table you created is a bit unwieldy for them to enter the necessary data, because it now contains so many fields that it requires scrolling across the screen to locate them. You decide to create a form that will make entering data not only easier, but more attractive as well. Open the ac02_ATT Database. Best fit the columns. Change the order of the Length and Description field columns in Design view. Apply formatting of your choice to the datasheet. Sort the table on Destination in ascending order. Use the Form Wizard to create a form called **Travel Packages** for the Packages table. Use the form to enter five new records with tour package information of your choice (use the newspaper travel section or the Web for ideas). Enter your name as the Contact in one of the new records. Print the form containing your name. Print the datasheet in landscape orientation.

EMP Account Tracking ★★

2. While creating the database table for EMP Enterprises, you learned that some employees have been receiving advances for anticipated expenses (such as for travel). You have also been informed that the CEO wants to start tracking the expenses by department. Open the database file **EMP Enterprise** (Lab 1, On Your Own 5). Add a new field named Advanced Amount with a currency data type to the Employee Expenses table. Also add a Yes/No field named Payment Made to record whether or not the expense has been paid, with a corresponding validation rule and message. In The Employee Info table, add a new field named Department to enter the department's charge code number. Update both tables to include appropriate values in the new fields in the existing records. Apply formatting of your choice to the Employee Expenses datasheet. Sort the Employee Expenses table on the Expense Amount field in Descending sort order. Close the table, saving the changes. Use the Form Wizard to create a form named **Expenses** for the Employee Expenses table. Include the form title Your Name Expenses. To test the form, enter a new expense record using the employee ID number for the record containing your name in the Employee Info table. Select your record in the form and print it.

Dental Patient Database Update ★★

3. The dentist office for which you created a patient database has expanded to include a second dentist and receptionist. The two dentists are Dr. Jones and Dr. Smith. You now need to modify the database to identify required fields and to add a new field that identifies which patient is assigned to which dentist. You also decide that creating a form for the database would make it easier for both you and the other receptionist to enter and locate patient information. Open the Dental Patients database (Lab 1, On Your Own 3) and the Personal Information table. Make the patient identification number, name, and phone number required fields. Add a Dentist Name Lookup list field, with the two dentists' names and an appropriate validation rule and message. Update the table to "assign" some of the patients to one of the dentists and some patients to the other dentist. Assign the record containing your name to Dr. Jones. Sort the table by dentist name to see the results of your new assignments. "Reassign" one of the displayed patients and then remove the sort. Filter the table to display only those patients for Dr. Jones. Apply formatting of your choice to the datasheet. Print the filtered datasheet and then remove the filter. Create a form called **Patient Data** for the table using the Form Wizard. Enter two new records, one for each of the dentists. Use the Search feature to locate the record that has your name as the patient, and then select and print the displayed record in the form.

Lewis & Lewis Employee Database ★★

4. You work in the Human Resource Management department at Lewis & Lewis, Inc. You recently created a simple database containing information on the employees Department and work telephone extension. Several of your co-employees also want to use the database. You decide to add a field for the employees job title and enhance the table. You also want to create a form that will make it easier for others to update the information in the database as well. Open the ac02_Lewis Personnel database and **Phone List** table and add the Job Title field after the Department field. Update the table to include information in the new field for the existing records. Add a new record that includes your name. Apply formatting of your choice to the datasheet. Sort the table by Department and Last Name. Use the Search feature to locate and delete the record for Anna Tai who has left the company. Print the datasheet in landscape ortientation, Remove the sort and

close the table, saving the changes. Create a form called **phone List** for the Phone List table using the Form Wizard. Enter five new records. Use the Replace command to locate and change the last name for Alexa Hirsch to Alexa Muirhead who has gotten married since you first created the database. Use the Search feature to locate the record form that has your name as the employee. Select and print the displayed record.

Timeless Treasures Inventory Database ★ ★ ★

5. You realize that you have left out some very important fields in the Inventory table you created in the Timeless Treasures database (On Your Own Exercise 4 of Lab 1)—fields that identify the sources where you can obtain the vintage watches your customers are looking for. Repeat your Web search for old watches and note the resources (for example, online shopping services, specialty stores, or individual collectors who are offering these items at online auctions) for the watches in your table. Add a Source Name field, a Source E-mail field and a Source Phone field to the table. Update the table to include this information in the existing records. Apply formatting of your choice to the datasheet. Sort the records according to the source name field and adjust the column widths to accommodate the new information. Print the datasheet. Remove the sort and close the table, saving the changes. Now, to make data entry easier, create a form named **Watches** using the Form Wizard. Use the form to locate the record with your name as the manufacturer, and then print it.

Querying Tables and Creating Reports

Objectives

After completing this lab, you will know how to:

1 Evaluate table design.

2 Establish relationships.

3 Enforce referential integrity.

4 Create and modify a simple query.

5 Query two tables.

6 Filter a query.

7 Find unmatched and duplicate records.

8 Create a Parameter query.

9 Create reports from tables and queries.

10 Display a Totals row.

11 Modify a report design.

12 Select, move, and size controls.

13 Change page margins.

14 Preview and print a report.

15 Compact and back up a database.

Case Study

Lifestyle Fitness Club

After modifying the structure of the table of Personal Data, you have continued to enter many more records. You also have created a second table in the database that contains employee information about location and job titles. Again, the owners are very impressed with the database. They are eager to see how the information in the database can be used.

As you have seen, compiling, storing, and updating information in a database is very useful. The real strength of a database program, however, is its ability to find the information you need quickly, and to manipulate and analyze it to answer specific questions. You will use the information in the tables to provide the answers to several inquiries about the club employees. As you learn about the analytical features, imagine trying to do the same task by hand. How long would it take? Would it be as accurate or as well presented? In addition, you will create several reports that present the information from the database attractively.

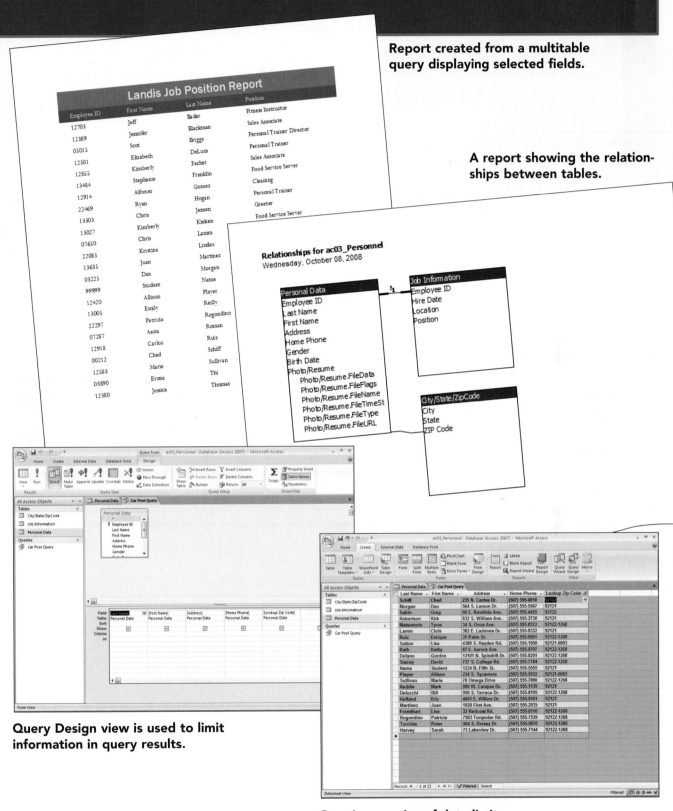

Report created from a multitable query displaying selected fields.

A report showing the relationships between tables.

Query Design view is used to limit information in query results.

Creating queries of data limits the information that is displayed in the results.

Refining the Database Design

You have continued to enter Personal Data into the Records table. The updated table has been saved for you as Personal Data in the ac03_Personnel database file.

Note: Before you begin, you may want to create a backup copy of the ac03_Personnel file by copying and renaming it.

1 • **Start Office Access 2007.**

• **Open the** ac03_Personnel **database file.**

• **If necessary, respond appropriately to the Security Warning.**

Your screen should be similar to Figure 3.1

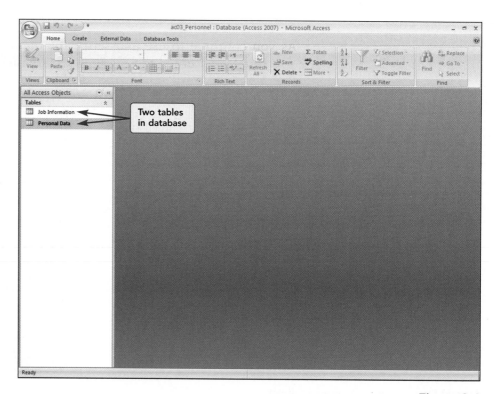

Figure 3.1

The Navigation pane displays the names of two tables in this database: Personal Data and Job Information.

2

- Open the Personal Data table.

- Add your information as record number 70 using your special ID number 99999 and your name. Enter Maldin as the city and 92121 as the zip code. Fill in the remaining fields as desired.

- Return to the first field of the first record.

- Hide the Navigation pane.

Your screen should be similar to Figure 3.2

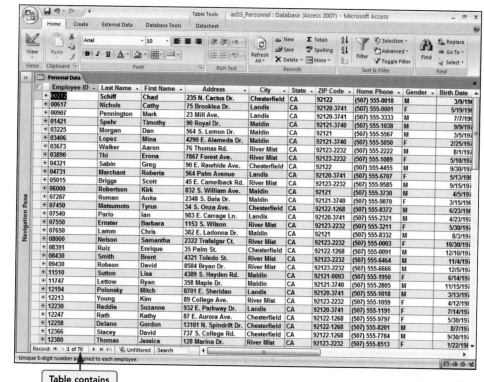

Table contains 70 records

Figure 3.2

Evaluating Table Design

As you continue to use and refine the database, you have noticed that you repeatedly enter the same city, state, and zip code information in the Personal Data table. You decide there may be a better way to organize the table information and will use the Table Analyzer tool to help evaluate the design of the Personal Data table.

1

- Open the Database Tools tab.

- Click [Analyze Table] in the Analyze group.

Your screen should be similar to Figure 3.3

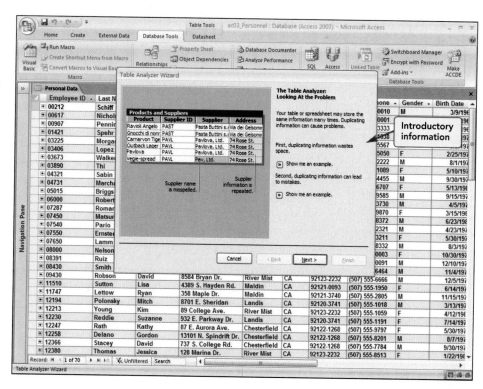

Introductory information

Figure 3.3

The first two windows of Table Analyzer Wizard are introductory pages that review the process that will be used. First it will analyze the information stored in the table by looking for duplicate information. Then, if duplicates are located, it will split the original table and create new tables to store the information a single time to solve the problem.

● Click Next > to see the next introductory page.

● Click Next > to move to the first step.

Your screen should be similar to Figure 3.4

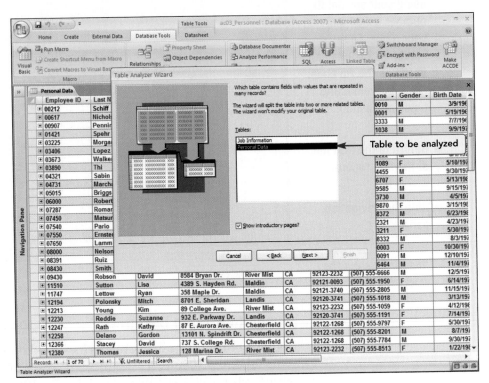

Figure 3.4

In the next two steps, you identify the table you want to evaluate and whether you want the wizard to decide what fields to place in the new table or to make that determination yourself.

3 ● Click [Next >] to accept analyzing the Personal Data table.

● Click [Next >] to accept letting the wizard decide.

Your screen should be similar to Figure 3.5

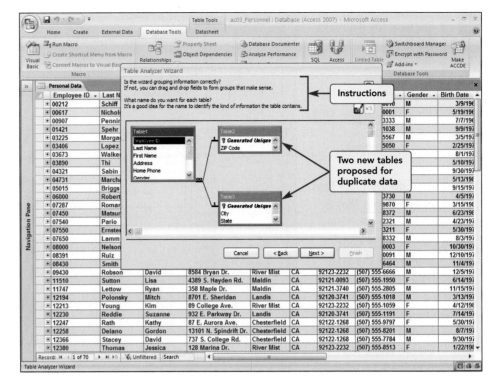

Figure 3.5

The wizard has identified duplicate data in the zip code, city, and state fields and proposes to move these fields into two additional tables: one for zip codes and the other for city and state where the information would be stored only once. The instructions at the top of the Table Analyzer Wizard box ask you to revise the grouping if needed and to create names for the tables. You decide that creating one new table containing the three fields will prevent the duplicate data and will revise the grouping by adding the ZIP Code field to Table3. You will then rename the new table and move to the next step.

4 ● **Increase the length of the Table1 list to display all the field names.**

Having Trouble?
Drag down the bottom border to size the object.

● **Drag the ZIP Code field in Table2 into Table3.**

● **Move the ZIP Code field below the State field.**

● **Move the Table2 object so that all fields in the list are displayed.**

● **Double-click on the Table3 title bar, enter City/State/ZipCode as the table name, and click** [OK] **.**

● **Click** [Next >] **to move to the next step.**

Your screen should be similar to Figure 3.6

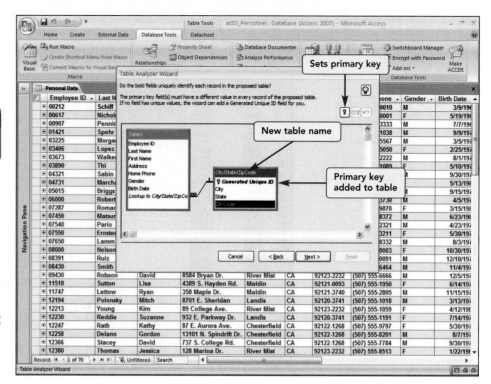

Figure 3.6

This step identifies the fields to use as a primary key in the new tables by bolding the field name. The wizard automatically added a Generated Unique ID field (AutoNumber) to the new table. You will define the zip code as the primary key field, which will also remove the Unique ID field.

5 ● If necessary, select the
ZIP Code field and
then click 📵.

● Click [Next >] to
move to the next step.

*Your screen should be
similar to Figure 3.7*

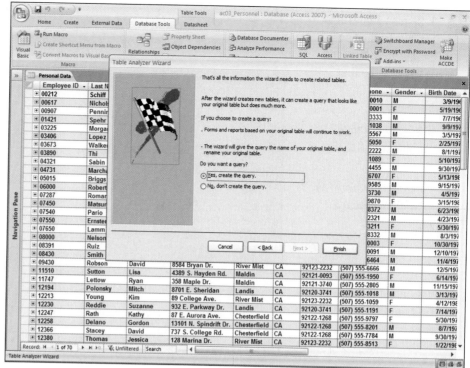

Figure 3.7

The final wizard step asks if you want to create a query. You will be
learning about queries shortly so you will not create a query at this time.

6 ● Choose No, don't
create the query.

● Click [Finish].

● If an informational
message appears,
click [OK] to
continue.

*Your screen should be
similar to Figure 3.8*

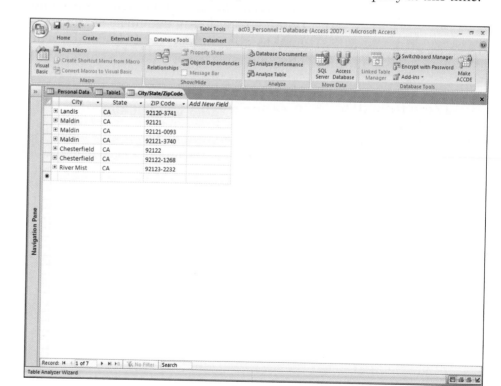

Figure 3.8

The two new tables are opened and the City/State/ZipCode table is
displayed. The ZIP Code field is the primary key field and has been
associated with the data in the new Table1.

7 • Display Table1 and
move to the Lookup to
City/State/ZipCode
field for the first
record.

• Best fit the field
column.

*Your screen should be
similar to Figure 3.9*

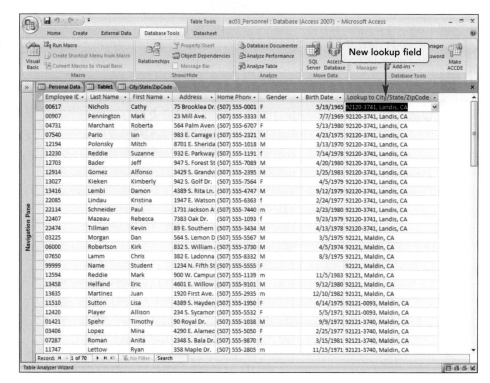

Figure 3.9

The Lookup field displays the zip code, city, and state information from
the associated table and the individual fields that stored this information
for each record have been deleted. You can now see how using a separate
table to store this data saves space by not duplicating the information and
also makes data entry more accurate. The zip code field appears first
because it is the primary key field.

Creating a Table List Lookup Field

Now your database contains two tables that hold duplicate data, Table1
and Personal Data, and you need to decide which table to keep. You notice
that Table1 did not maintain the association to the Job table and the field
and datasheet formatting. Rather than make these same changes again to
Table1, you decide to modify the Personal Data table by creating a lookup
field to the City/State/ZipCode table.

1 ● **Display the Personal Data table.**

● **Right-click on the Add New Field column and choose Lookup Column.**

● **Run the Lookup Wizard and specify the following settings:**

- **Look up the values in a table or query.**

- **Use the City/State/ZipCode table.**

- **Add all three columns to the selected fields list.**

- **Do not specify a sort order.**

- **Clear the checkmark from the Hide key column option to display all three columns.**

- **Store the ZIP Code value in the lookup column.**

- **Enter the field name Lookup Zip Code.**

● **Click** [Finish] **.**

● **Click in the Lookup field for the first record and display the drop-down list.**

Your screen should be similar to Figure 3.10

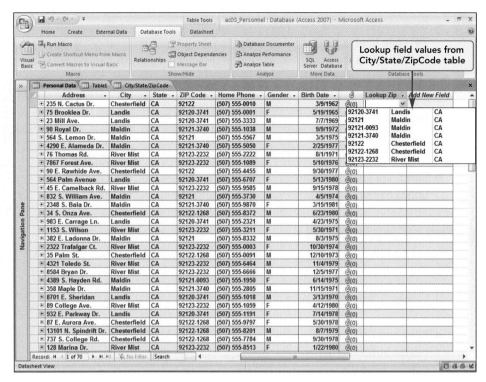

Figure 3.10

Now you need to add the data for this column. Instead of selecting each zip code, you will copy the data in the existing ZIP Code field column into the lookup column. Then, because you will no longer need them, you will delete the City, State, and ZIP Code fields. Finally, you will move the Lookup column after the Address column. You can move a column by selecting it and then dragging it to its new location.

2 • Copy the data in the ZIP Code field column to the Lookup Zip Code column.

• Delete the City, State, and ZIP Code columns.

• Select the Lookup Zip Code column.

Having Trouble?

Remember, to select an entire column, you click on its column heading when the mouse pointer is ↓.

• Click and hold the mouse button on the column heading.

Additional Information

When the mouse pointer is ▷, it indicates that you can drag to move the selection.

• Drag the Lookup column to the left until a thick line is displayed between the Address and Home Phone columns.

• Release the mouse button.

• Best fit the Lookup Zip Code column.

Your screen should be similar to Figure 3.11

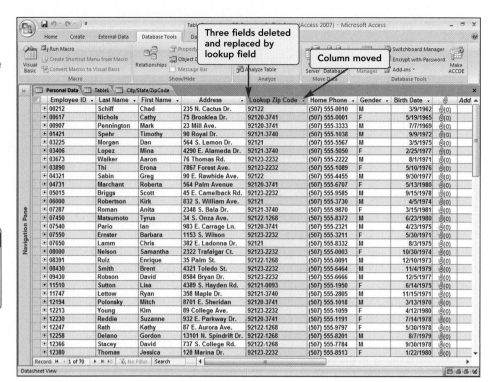

Figure 3.11

Deleting a Table

Now that the Personal Data table is modified, you will delete the duplicate Table1.

1 • **Close all tables, saving changes when prompted.**

• **Redisplay the Navigation pane.**

• **Select Table1 and click** ✕ Delete ▾ **in the Records group of the Home tab.**

• **Click** Yes **to confirm the deletion from all groups.**

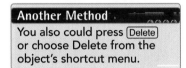

Another Method
You also could press [Delete] or choose Delete from the object's shortcut menu.

Your screen should be similar to Figure 3.12

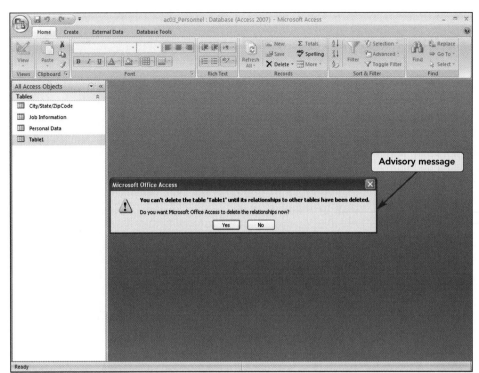

Figure 3.12

The advisory message warns that the table cannot be deleted until its relationships to other tables have been deleted.

Defining and Modifying Relationships

Rather than have the program remove the relationships for you, you will look at the relationships that have been created between all tables first.

1 • **Click** No .

• **Click** OK .

• **Click** Relationships **in the Show/Hide group of the Database Tools tab.**

• **Click** 🔠 All Relationships **in the Relationships group of the Relationship Tools Design tab.**

Your screen should be similar to Figure 3.13

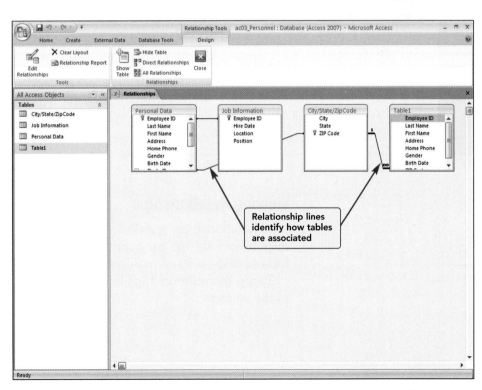

Figure 3.13

Defining and Modifying Relationships

Concept 1

Relationship

1   A **relationship** establishes the association between **common fields** in two tables. The related fields must be of the same data type and contain the same kind of information but can have different field names. The exception to this rule occurs when the primary key field in one of the tables is the AutoNumber type, which can be related to another AutoNumber field or to a Number field, as long as the Field Size property is the same for both. This is also the case when both fields are AutoNumber or Number—they always have to be the same field size in order to be related.

There are three types of relationships that can be established between tables: one-to-one, one-to-many, and many-to-many.

Relationship Type	Description
One-to-one 	An association between two tables in which each record in the first table contains a field value that corresponds to (matches) the field value of one record in the other table.
One-to-many 	An association between two tables in which the primary key field value in each record in the primary table (the "one" side of this relationship) corresponds to the value in the matching field or fields of many records in the related table.
Many-to-many 	An association between two tables in which one record in either table can relate to many records in the other table. In this type of relationship, a third table, called a **junction table**, is used to hold the primary key fields from the other two tables and serves as a bridge between them.

Once relationships are established, rules can be enforced, called the rules of **referential integrity**, to ensure that relationships between tables are valid and that related data is not accidentally changed or deleted. The rules ensure that a record in a primary table cannot be deleted if matching records exist in a related table, and a primary key value cannot be changed in the primary table if that record has related records.

Viewing Relationships

The Relationships window is used to create and edit relationships. It displays a field list for each table in the database and identifies how the tables are associated with relationship lines.

To see the relationships better, you will rearrange and size the field lists in the window.

1 ● **Click on the City/State/Zip Code field list title bar and drag the field list below the Job Information field list.**

● **Move the Table1 field list to the right of the City/State/ZipCode field list.**

● **Increase the length of the Personal Data field list so that all fields are displayed.**

● **Increase the length of the Table1 field list so that all fields are displayed.**

Your screen should be similar to Figure 3.14

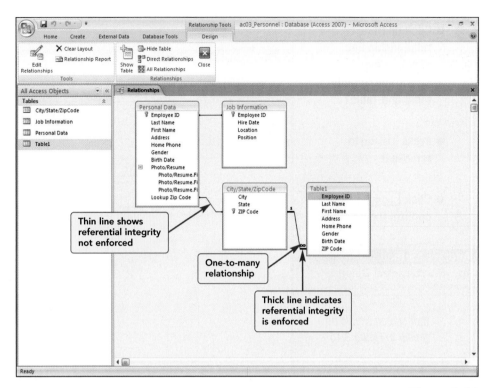

Figure 3.14

Now it is easier to follow the relationship lines. The Personal Data and the Job Information tables are related by the Employee ID fields and are connected by a thin relationship line. This relationship was established when you created the Job Information table by copying an existing field to a new table.

There is also a relationship between the Lookup Zip Code field and the ZIP Code field in the City/State/ZipCode table. A thin line between common fields shows the relationship does not support referential integrity.

The third relationship that exists is between the ZIP Code field in the City/State/ZipCode table and the ZIP Code field in Table1. This line is thicker at both ends, which indicates that referential integrity has been enforced. It also displays a 1 at one end of the line and an infinity symbol (∞) over the other end. This tells you the relationship is a one-to-many type relationship.

Deleting Relationships

The first relationship change you want to make is to remove the relationship between the City/State/ZipCode table and Table1 so that you can delete the table. To edit or delete a relationship, click on the relationship line to select it. It will appear thicker to show it is selected. Then it can be modified.

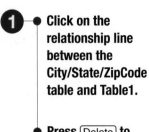

1 • Click on the relationship line between the City/State/ZipCode table and Table1.

• Press Delete to remove it.

• Click Yes to confirm the deletion.

Another Method
You also can select Delete from the shortcut menu.

Your screen should be similar to Figure 3.15

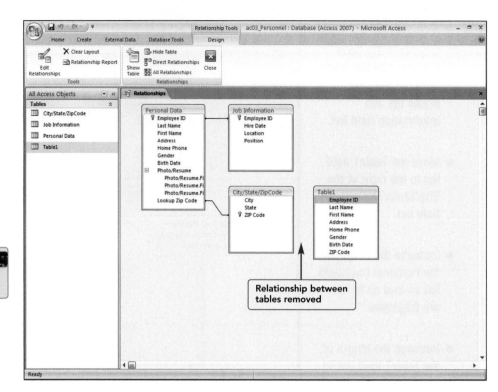

Figure 3.15

The relationship line has been removed between the tables. Now you can delete the table.

2 • Select Table1 in the Navigation pane and press Delete.

• Click Yes to confirm the deletion from all groups.

Your screen should be similar to Figure 3.16

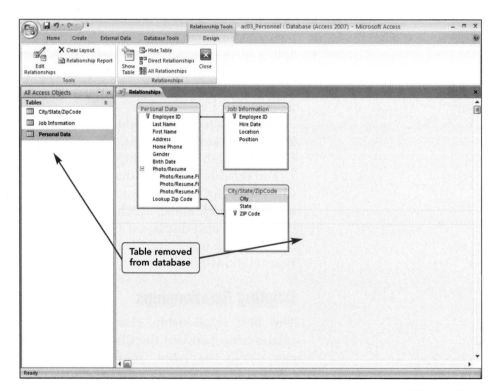

Figure 3.16

The Table1 field list is removed from the Relationships window and the table object is removed from the Navigation pane, showing the table has been deleted from the database.

Enforcing Referential Integrity

Next, you want to change the relationship between the Employee ID fields to support referential integrity.

1 ● **Right-click the relationship line between the Personal Data and the Job Information tables.**

● **Select Edit Relationship from the shortcut menu.**

 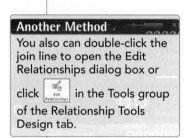
● **Select Enforce Referential Integrity.**

Your screen should be similar to Figure 3.17

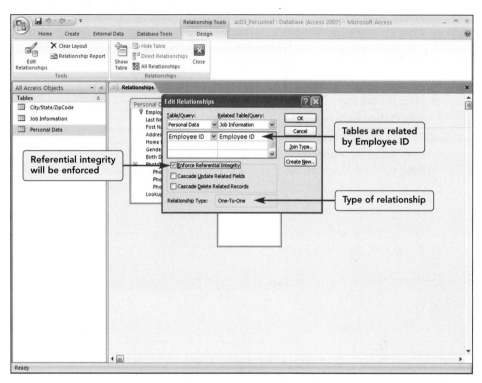

Figure 3.17

The Edit Relationships dialog box shows the tables and their current relationship. Selecting the Enforce Referential Integrity option also makes the Cascade Update and Cascade Delete options available. Selecting these options ensures that if you change a primary key or delete a record, all fields that reference the primary key of that record are likewise updated or deleted in both tables. This prevents inconsistent and orphaned records (records that do not have a matching primary key record in the associated table). You will select both these options. In addition, you can see the relationship type is one-to-one.

2 ● **Select Cascade Update Related Fields.**

● **Select Cascade Delete Related Records.**

● **Click OK .**

● **Click on the Job Information field list to remove the selection from the relationship line.**

Your screen should be similar to Figure 3.18

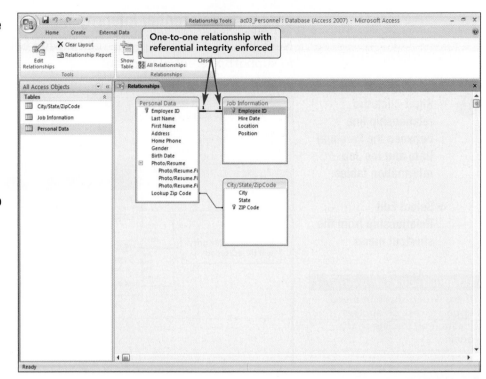

Figure 3.18

Once referential integrity is enforced, the relationship line changes and identifies the type of relationship. The relationship line appears thicker at each end indicating that referential integrity is enforced. Also, the type of relationship is identified. The number 1 next to each table above the relationship line shows a one-to-one relationship exists between these tables.

Creating a Relationship

Although the Lookup Zip Code relationship is already created, you will delete it and then create it again to learn how to create relationships. To do this, you drag the field that you want to relate from one table to the related field in the other table.

1 ● Select and delete the ZIP Code relationship.

● Drag the Lookup Zip Code field from the Personal Data table to the ZIP Code field in the City/State/ZipCode table.

● Click  .

Your screen should be similar to Figure 3.19

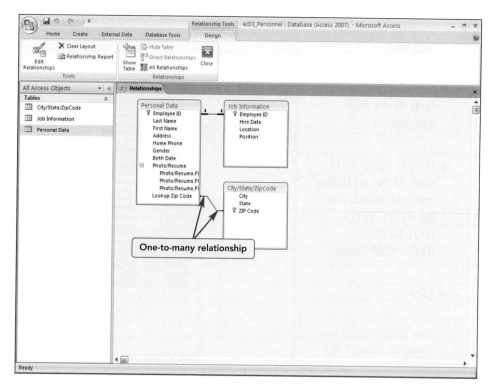

Figure 3.19

The related tables again have a relationship line connecting them. The relationship type is one-to-many because there are many records in the Personal Data table that use the same zip code value and only one record in the City/State/ZipCode table for each zip code. Referential integrity was not enforced because you will want to remove records in the Personal Data table that have matching data in the City/State/ZIPCode table.

The tables in your database are now all related. Once referential integrity has been enforced, a warning message is automatically displayed if one of the rules is broken, and you are not allowed to complete the action you are trying to do.

2 ● Click 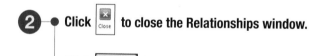 to close the Relationships window.

● Click ⬚ Yes ⬚ in response to the prompt to save the layout.

The relationships and layout are saved.

Creating a Filter

Now you are ready to start gathering some information from the database again. You have added many more records to the database tables and you decide to continue working on the list of employees to help Juan create a car pool. Because the table no longer contains a separate City field, you will need to create a new filter using the ZIP Code field.

1 • Open the Personal Data table.

• Open the Lookup Zip Code field's drop-down menu

• Choose Select all to clear all the selections and then select only the 92121, 92121-0093, 92122, and 92122-1268 values.

• Click [OK].

Your screen should be similar to Figure 3.20

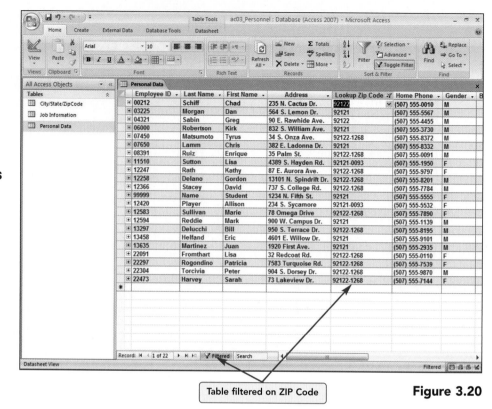

Table filtered on ZIP Code

Figure 3.20

Twenty-two records meet these criteria. However, the filtered datasheet still includes more information about each employee than Juan needs to contact people about car pooling.

Querying a Database

To obtain the exact information you need to give Juan for his car pool, you will use a query.

Concept 2

2 A **query** is a request for specific data contained in a database. Queries are used to view data in different ways, to analyze data, and even to change existing data. Because queries are based on tables, you also can use a query as the source for forms and reports. The five types of queries are described in the following table.

Query Type	Description
Select query	Retrieves the specific data you request from one or more tables, then displays the data in a query datasheet in the order you specify. This is the most common type of query.
Crosstab query	Summarizes large amounts of data in an easy-to-read, row-and-column format.
Parameter query	Displays a dialog box prompting you for information, such as the **criteria** for locating data. For example, a parameter query might request the beginning and ending dates, then display all records matching dates between the two specified values.
Action query	Used to make changes to many records in one operation. There are four types of action queries:

	Type	Description
	Make-table query	Creates a new table from selected data in one or more tables
	Update query	Makes update changes to records, when, for example, you need to raise salaries of all sales staff by 7 percent
	Append query	Adds records from one or more tables to the end of other tables
	Delete query	Deletes records from a table or tables

Query Type	Description
SQL query	Created using SQL (Structured Query Language), an advanced programming language used in Access.

You will create a simple select query to obtain the results for the car pool. Creating a query adds a query object to the database file. It is a named object, just like a form, that can be opened, viewed, and modified at any time.

Using the Query Wizard

Query Design view or the Query Wizard can be used to create a query. The process is much like creating a table or form. You will first use the Query Wizard to guide you through the steps.

1 • Click 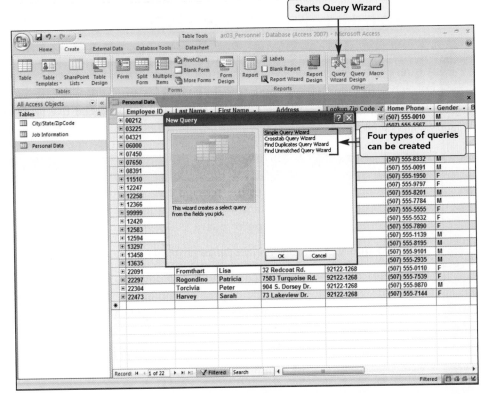 in the Other group of the Create tab.

• Click Yes in response to the prompt to save the table.

Your screen should be similar to Figure 3.21

Figure 3.21

From the New Query dialog box, you select the type of query you want to create using the wizard.

Query Wizard	Type of Query
Simple	Select query
Crosstab	Crosstab query
Find Duplicates	Locates all records that contain duplicate values in one or more fields in the specified tables
Find Unmatched	Locates records in one table that do not have records in another. For example, you could locate all employees in one table who have no hours worked in another table.

You will use the Simple Query Wizard to create a select query to see if it gives you the results you want.

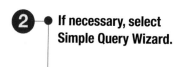

2 ● If necessary, select
   Simple Query Wizard.

● Click [OK].

*Your screen should be
similar to Figure 3.22*

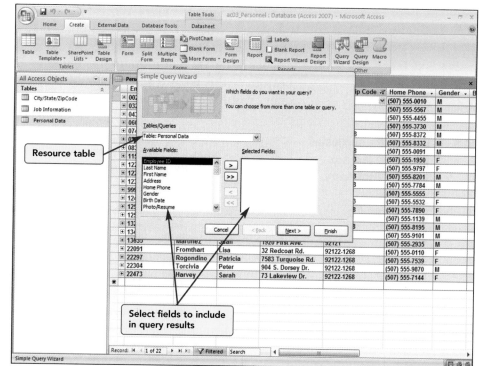

Figure 3.22

In the first Simple Query Wizard dialog box, you specify the resource table
that will be used to supply the data and the fields that you want displayed
in the query result, just as you did when creating a form. You will use the
Personal Data table as the resource table and select the fields you want
displayed in the query output.

3 ● If necessary, select the
   Personal Data table
   from the Table/Queries
   drop-down list.

● Add the Last Name,
   First Name, Address,
   Home Phone, and
   Lookup Zip Code fields
   to the Selected Fields
   list.

Additional Information
The quickest way to add a
field to the Selected Fields list
is to double-click its field name
in the Available Fields list.

● Click [Next >].

*Your screen should be
similar to Figure 3.23*

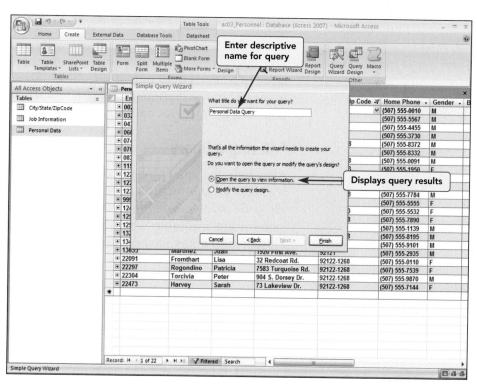

Figure 3.23

In the last Simple Query Wizard dialog box, you specify a name for your query and whether you want to open it to see the results or modify it in Design view. You also can have Access display Help messages while you are working on your query by clicking the corresponding box at the bottom of this wizard screen. You decide that you just want to display the query results, and you want to give the query a name that will identify it.

4 ● **Replace the suggested title in the text box with Car Pool Query.**

● **Click** ⬚ Finish ⬚ **.**

Your screen should be similar to Figure 3.24

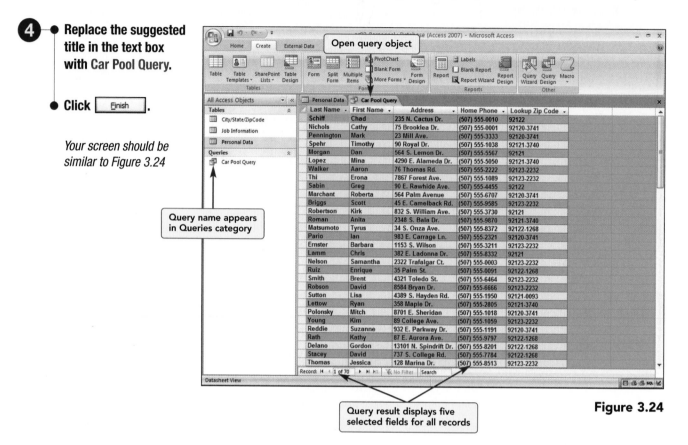

Figure 3.24

The query result displays the five specified fields for all records in the table in a new query datasheet object. The object's tab displays the query name. The Navigation pane also displays the name of the new query object in the Queries category.

Filtering a Query

Although the query result displays only the fields you want to see, it includes all the records in the table. To display only those records in the zip code areas needed for Juan, you can filter the query results. The filter criteria are available with the Personal Data table only and need to be recreated to apply to the query results.

1 ● **Filter the query to display only records with zip codes of 92121, 92121-0093, 92122, and 92122-1268.**

Your screen should be similar to Figure 3.25

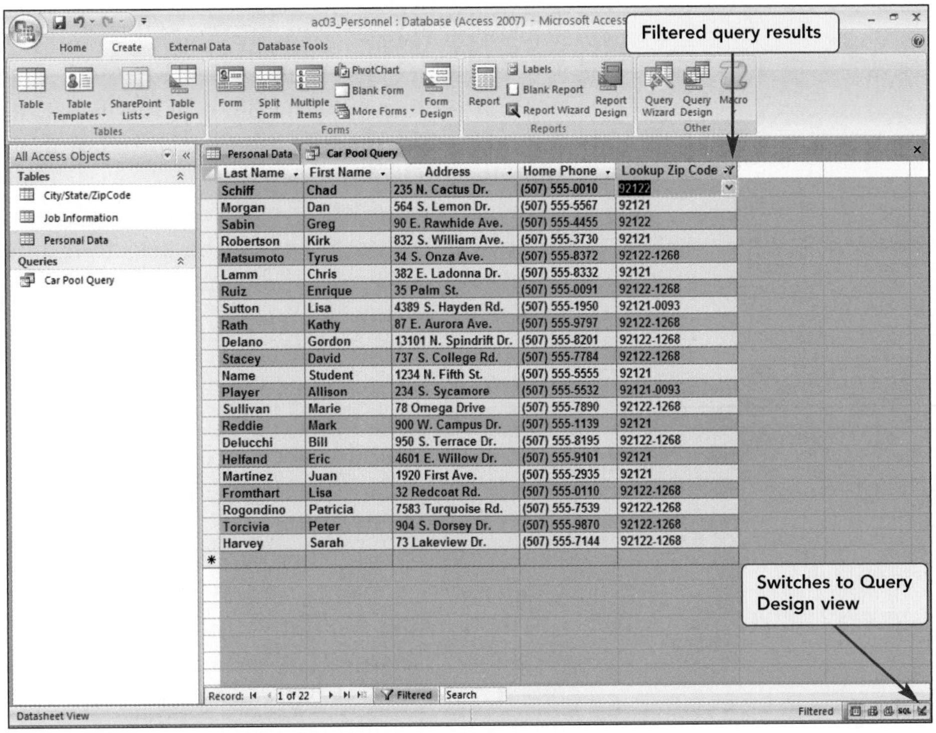

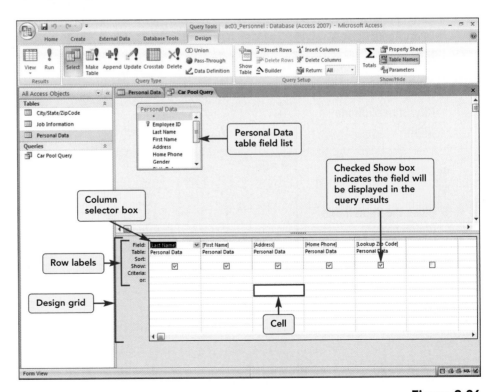

Figure 3.25

Now the Car Pool Query results display the same 22 records as the filtered Personal Data table. Although these results are closer to what you need, you are still not satisfied. You want the results to display the city as well as the zip code. Additionally, it does not tell you which employees work at the Landis location. To make these refinements to the query, you need to use Query Design view.

2 ● **Click** ⬛ **Design View in the status bar to switch to Query Design view.**

Your screen should be similar to Figure 3.26

Figure 3.26

Using Query Design View

Query Design view can be used to create a new query as well as modify the structure of an existing query. This view automatically displays the Query Tools Design tab, which contains commands that are used to create, modify, and run queries.

Query Design view is divided into two areas. The upper area displays a list box of all the fields in the selected table. This is called the **field list.** The lower portion of the window displays the **design grid** where you enter the settings that define the query. Each column in the grid holds the information about each field to be included in the query datasheet. The design grid automatically displays the fields that are specified when a query is created using a Query Wizard.

Above the field names is a narrow bar called the **column selector bar,** which is used to select an entire column. Each **row label** identifies the type of information that can be entered. The intersection of a column and row creates a cell where you enter expressions to obtain the query results you need.

The boxes in the Show row are called Show boxes. The **Show box** for a field lets you specify whether you want that field displayed in the query result. A checked box indicates that the field will be displayed; an unchecked box means that it will not.

Adding a Second Table to the Query

To display the city information for each employee in the query results, you need to add the City/State/ZipCode table to the query design. A query that uses information from two or more tables to get the results is called a **multitable query.**

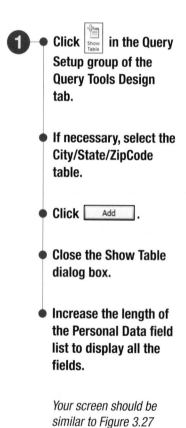

1 ● Click [Show Table] in the Query Setup group of the Query Tools Design tab.

● If necessary, select the City/State/ZipCode table.

● Click [Add].

● Close the Show Table dialog box.

● Increase the length of the Personal Data field list to display all the fields.

Your screen should be similar to Figure 3.27

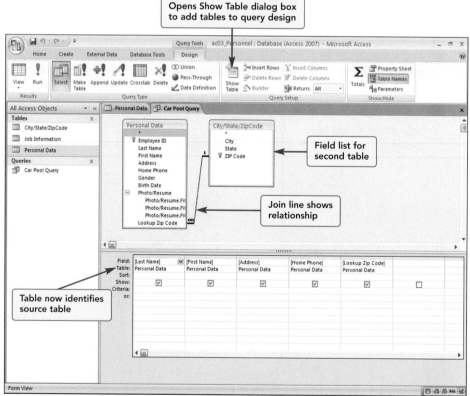

Figure 3.27

The field list for the second table has been added to the Query Design window. When multiple tables are added to a query, Access automatically creates joins between the tables.

Concept 3

Join

3 A **join** is an association that is created in a query between a field in one table or query and a field of the same data type in another table or query. The join is based on the relationships that have already been defined between tables. A **join line** between the field lists identifies the fields on which the relationship is based.

If a table did not already have a relationship defined, a join would be created between common fields in the tables if one of the common fields is a primary key. If the common fields have different names, however, Access does not automatically create the join. In those cases, you would create the join between the tables using the same procedure that is used to create table relationships.

The difference between a relationship line and a join line in a query is that the join line creates a temporary relationship that establishes rules that the data must match to be included in the query results. Joins also specify that each pair of rows that satisfy the join conditions will be combined in the results to form a single row.

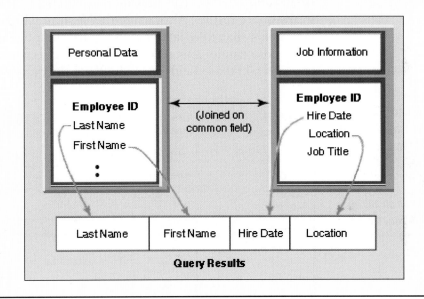

Having Trouble?
If the Table row is not displayed, click  in the Show/Hide group.

In this case, the join line correctly indicates that the two tables are related and that the ZIP Code is the common field.

Additionally a Table row has been added to the grid. It displays the name of the table from which each field is selected.

MORE ABOUT

▶ Sometimes you may want to add a second copy of the same table to a query. To learn how to do this, see "4 Creating and Modifying Queries" in the More About appendix.

Adding Fields

You want the query results to display the City information for each record. To do this, you need to add the City field from the City/State/ZipCode field list to the design grid. You can use the following methods to add fields to the design grid:

- Select the field name and drag it from the field list to the grid. To select several adjacent fields, press ⇧Shift while you click the field names. To select nonadjacent fields, press Ctrl while clicking the field names. To select all fields, double-click the field list title bar. You can then drag all the selected fields into the grid, and Access will place each field in a separate column.

- Double-click on the field name. The field is added to the next available column in the grid.

- Select the Field cell drop-down arrow in the grid, and then choose the field name.

In addition, if you select the asterisk in the field list and add it to the grid, Access displays the table or query name in the field row followed by a period and asterisk. This indicates that all fields in the table will be included in the query results. Also, using this feature will automatically include any new fields that may later be added to the table, and will exclude deleted fields. You cannot sort records or specify criteria for fields, however, unless you also add those fields individually to the design grid.

1 ● **Double-click City in the City/State/ZipCode field list to add it to the grid.**

Your screen should be similar to Figure 3.28

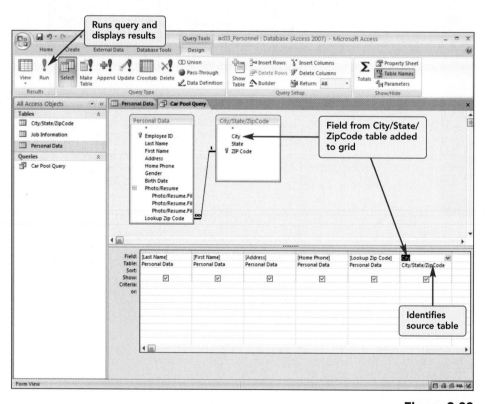

Figure 3.28

Notice the Table row displays the name of the table from which the City field was drawn. Sometimes when multiple tables are specified in a query, they have fields with the same names. For example, two tables may have fields named Address; however, the address in one table may be a personal address and the other table may be a business address. It is important to select the appropriate field from a table that contains the data you want to appear in the query. The Table row makes it clear from which table a field was drawn.

Now, you want to see the query results. To do this, you run the query.

2 ● Click 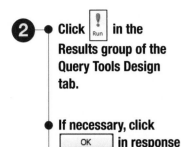 in the **Results group of the Query Tools Design tab.**

● **If necessary, click** OK **in response to the informational message.**

● **Click** ▼ Toggle Filter **in the Sort & Filter group to display the filtered list.**

Your screen should be similar to Figure 3.29

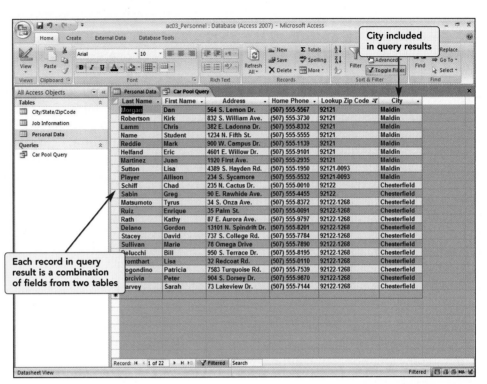

Figure 3.29

The city for each record is displayed in the results. Now, each record in the query result datasheet includes information from both tables. This is because of the type of join used in the query. There are three basic types of joins, as described in the table below.

Join Type	Description
Inner join	Tells a query that rows from one of the joined tables corresponds to rows in the other table on the basis of the data in the joined fields. Checks for matching values in the joined fields and when it finds matches, combines the records and displays them as one record in the query results.
Outer join	Tells a query that although some of the rows on both sides of the join correspond exactly, the query should include all rows from one table even if there is no match in the other table. Each matching record from two tables is combined into one record in the query results. One table contributes all of its records even if the values in its joined field do not match the field values in the other table. Outer joins can be left outer joins or right outer joins. In a query with a left outer join, all rows in the left table are included in the results and only those rows from the other table where the joining field contains values common to both tables are included. The reverse is true with a right outer join.
Unequal joins	Records to be included in the query results are based on the value in one join field being greater than, less than, not equal to, greater than or equal to, or less than or equal to the value in the other join field.

MORE ABOUT

▶ To learn how to create a left or right join, see "4 Creating and Modifying Queries" in the More About appendix.

In a query, the default join type is an inner join. In this case, it checked for matching values in the ZIP Code fields, combined matching records, and displayed them as one record in the query result.

Additionally, by applying the filter, only those records meeting the filter criteria are displayed.

Each time you run the query, you would need to reapply the filter. Rather than do this, you can specify the criteria in the query design and they would automatically be used each time the query is run.

Specifying Criteria

The Criteria row is used to enter the criteria expression (field value or values) and a comparison operator. A **criteria expression** is an expression that will select only records that meet certain limiting criteria. First, you will enter criteria in the City field to locate and display only those records where the city is Maldin. In the Criteria row of the City column, you will enter the criteria expression to select only those records. It is not necessary to enter = (equal to) in the criteria, because it is the assumed comparison operator.

Additional Information

Refer to Lab 2 for a review of expressions and operators.

1 ● Click 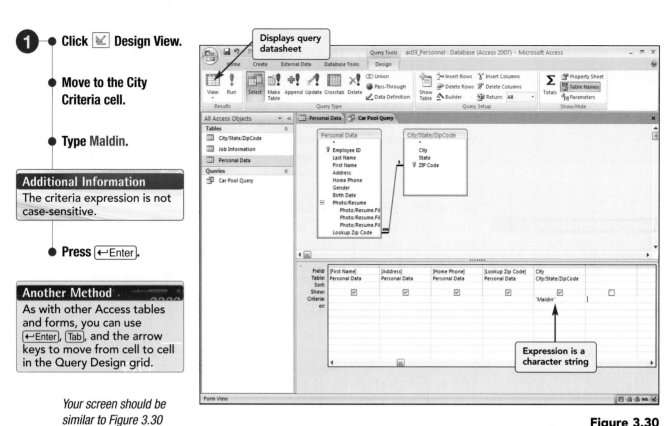 Design View.

● **Move to the City Criteria cell.**

● **Type Maldin.**

Additional Information
The criteria expression is not case-sensitive.

● **Press** ←Enter.

Another Method
As with other Access tables and forms, you can use ←Enter, Tab, and the arrow keys to move from cell to cell in the Query Design grid.

Your screen should be similar to Figure 3.30

Figure 3.30

The expression is enclosed in quotation marks because it is a character string. To display the query results, you will run the query. Another way to run a query is to change to Datasheet view.

2 ● Click 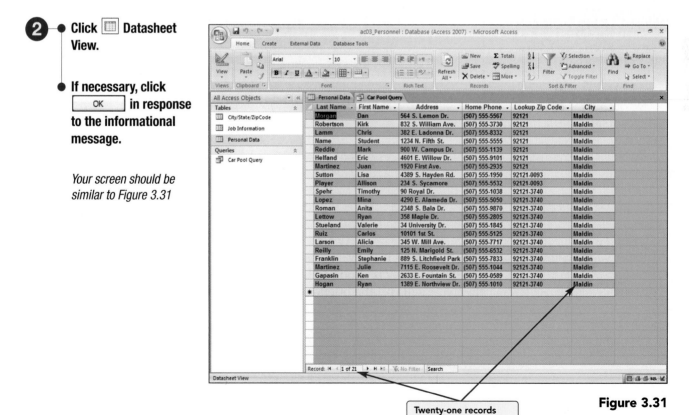 Datasheet View.

● **If necessary, click** OK **in response to the informational message.**

Your screen should be similar to Figure 3.31

Figure 3.31

Now the query datasheet displays 21 records meeting the city criterion. However, it does not include those who live in Chesterfield or exclude the people who live in the 92121-3740 zip code.

To include those who live in Chesterfield, you will add a second criterion to the City field. To instruct the query to locate records meeting multiple criteria, you use a **compound criterion.** The AND or OR criterion is used to specify multiple conditions that must be met for the records to display in the datasheet. The **AND operator** narrows the search, because a record must meet both conditions to be included. This condition is established by typing the word "and" in a field's Criteria cell as part of its criteria expression. The **OR operator** broadens the search, because any record meeting either condition is included in the output. This condition is established by typing the word "or" in a field's Criteria cell or by entering the first criteria expression in the first Criteria cell for the field, and the second expression in the Or criteria row cell for the same field.

Because you want to display the records for employees who live in either city, you will use the OR operator.

Additional Information

The Or criteria row must be used to enter "or" criteria for different fields.

3 ● **Switch to Design view.**

● **In the City Criteria cell, continue the criteria by typing or Chesterfield.**

● **Press ←Enter.**

Another Method

You also could type Chesterfield in the Or cell of the City column.

Your screen should be similar to Figure 3.32

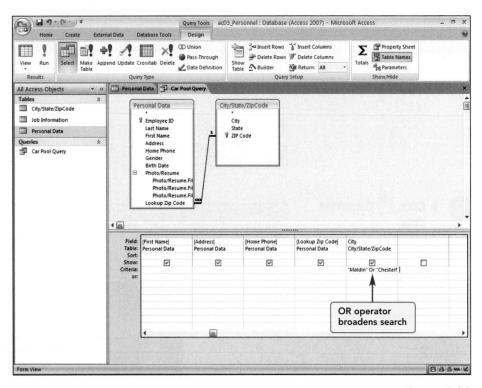

Figure 3.32

"Chesterfield" is now set as the Or condition. Next you will enter the criteria in the ZIP Code field to exclude the zip code of 92121-3740 and then you will run the query.

4 • **Enter <>92121-3740 in the LookUp Zip Code criteria cell.**

• **Run the query.**

• **If necessary, click** OK **in response to the informational message.**

Your screen should be similar to Figure 3.33

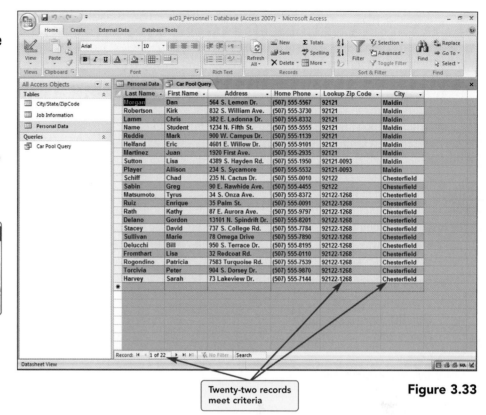

Twenty-two records meet criteria

Figure 3.33

The query located 22 records that met the specified criteria. These are the same results you obtained using a filter, except that only the fields you want displayed are included in the datasheet.

The final criterion you need to add to the query is to display only those employees who work at the Landis location. To do this, you need to add the Job Information table to the query design.

5 ● Switch to Design view.

● Click [Show Table] in the Query Setup group.

● Select the Job Information table.

● Click [Add].

● Close the Show Table dialog box.

● Move the City/State/ZipCode field list down as in Figure 3.34.

Your screen should be similar to Figure 3.34

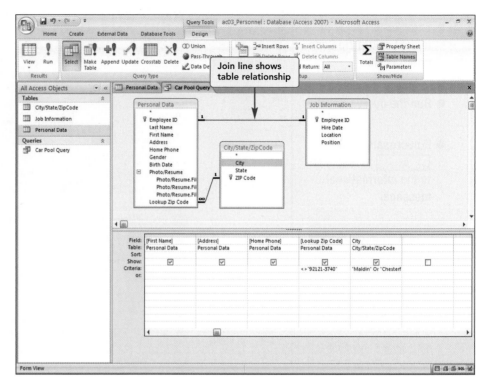

Figure 3.34

The field list for the third table was added to the Query Design window and the join line correctly links the Personal Data and Job Information field lists on the Employee ID fields.

6 ● Add the Location field to the design grid.

● Enter Landis in the Location Criteria cell.

Your screen should be similar to Figure 3.35

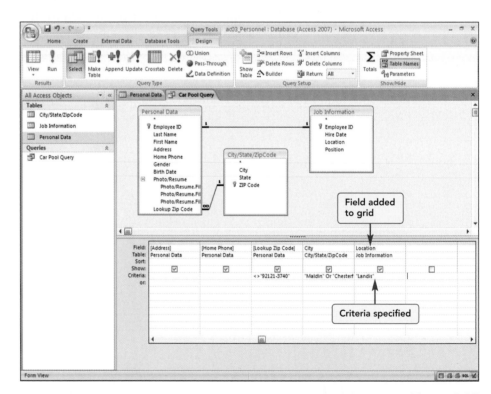

Figure 3.35

Hiding and Sorting Columns

Before running the query, you want to make a few additional changes to the query design. You do not want the ZIP Code field displayed in the results and would like the results to be sorted by last name and city.

1
- **Click the Show box of the Lookup Zip Code field to clear the checkmark.**

- **Click in the Sort row of the Last Name field.**

- **Open the Sort drop-down menu and choose Ascending.**

Having Trouble?
Scroll the grid to bring field columns into view.

Your screen should be similar to Figure 3.36

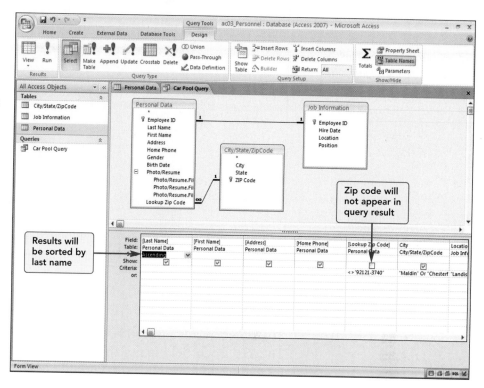

Figure 3.36

Now you can display the results.

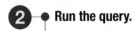 **Run the query.**

If necessary, click OK **in response to the informational message.**

Your screen should be similar to Figure 3.37

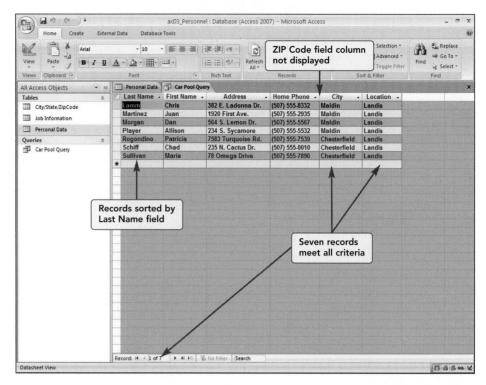

Figure 3.37

The query result now shows that seven employees meet all the criteria. The ZIP Code field is not displayed and last names are sorted by city in ascending alphabetical order.

Rearranging the Query Datasheet

The order of the fields in the query datasheet reflects the order in which they were placed in the Selected Fields list. You think the results will be easier to read if the Last Name field column followed the First Name column and the City column followed the Address column. You will then size the fields to fit the contents.

Moving a field column in the query datasheet is the same as in a table datasheet. Changing the column order in the query datasheet does not affect the field order in the resource table, which is controlled by the table design.

The two records in the Personal Data table that do not have matching records in the Job Information table are displayed in the query results. One record is the matching information for your own record that you added earlier to the Personal Data table. Now, you just need to add the information to the Job Information table for these two employees.

6 ● **Close the Query window.**

● **Add the following records to the Job Information table:**

Employee ID	Hire Date	Location	Position
03673	2/10/2001	River Mist	Greeter
99999	2/25/08	Landis	Human Resources Administrator

● **Best fit the Position field.**

Your screen should be similar to Figure 3.44

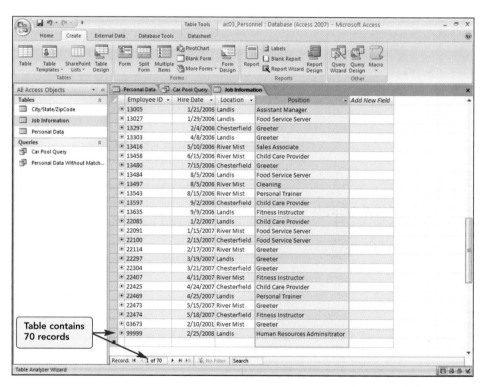

Figure 3.44

Both tables now contain 70 records. Notice that the Unmatched Records query was automatically saved and the object is listed in the Queries group of the Navigation pane. If you were to rerun this query, no results would be located because there are no longer any missing records.

Finally, you want to update all objects that use the Location table as the underlying record source to reflect the addition of the new records.

7 ● Display the Car Pool Query datasheet.

● Click [Refresh All] in the Records group of the Home tab.

Your screen should be similar to Figure 3.45

Query results now correctly include your record

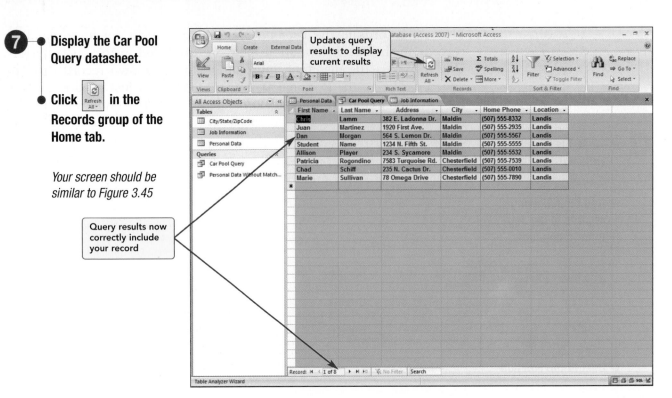

Figure 3.45

The query results list eight records that meet the criteria and now correctly include your record.

Finding Duplicate Records

Next, you want to check the Personal Data table for possible duplicate records. Even though this table uses the Employee ID as the primary key, it is possible to enter the same record with two different IDs. To check for duplication, you will use the Find Duplicates Query Wizard.

1 ● Click 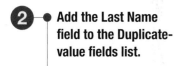 in the
Create tab.

● Click [Yes] to save
the Car Pool Query.

● Choose Find
Duplicates Query
Wizard.

● Click [OK].

● Select Table: Personal
Data.

● Click [Next >].

*Your screen should be
similar to Figure 3.46*

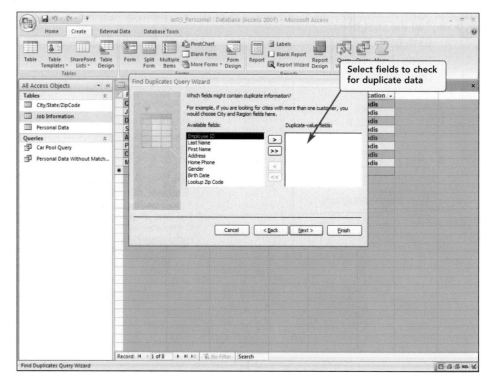

Figure 3.46

In this wizard dialog box, you identify the fields that may contain
duplicate data. In this case, you will check the Last Name fields for
duplicate values.

2 ● Add the Last Name
field to the Duplicate-
value fields list.

● Click [Next >].

*Your screen should be
similar to Figure 3.47*

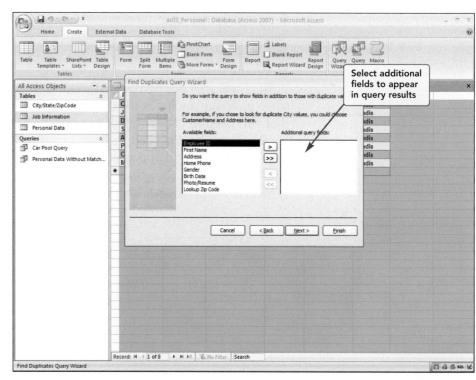

Figure 3.47

Next, you need to identify the additional fields you want to appear in the
query results.

3 ● Add the First Name, Birth Date, and Gender fields to the Additional Query Fields list.

● Click [Next >].

● Click [Finish].

Your screen should be similar to Figure 3.48

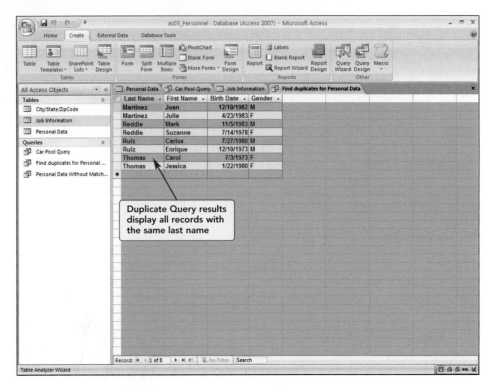

Duplicate Query results display all records with the same last name

Figure 3.48

All records with the same last name are listed. These all look like valid records, so you will not make any changes.

Creating a Parameter Query

Periodically the club director wants to know the employee number and names of the employees at each club and their job position. To find this information, you will create a simple query and sort the location field to group the records.

To create this query, you will modify the existing Car Pool Query design since it already includes the two tables, Personal Data and Job Information, that you need to use. You will remove the City/State/ZipCode table field list because you do not need any information from that table. Then you will clear the design grid and save the modified query using a new name.

1
- Display the Car Pool Query in Design view.

- Right-click on the title bar of the City/State/ZipCode table field list and choose Remove Table from the shortcut menu.

- Drag across the top of the six fields in the grid to select them and press ⟨Delete⟩.

- Click 🔵 Office Button and choose Save As/Save Object As.

- Enter Location Query as the new query name and click ⟨ OK ⟩.

Your screen should be similar to Figure 3.49

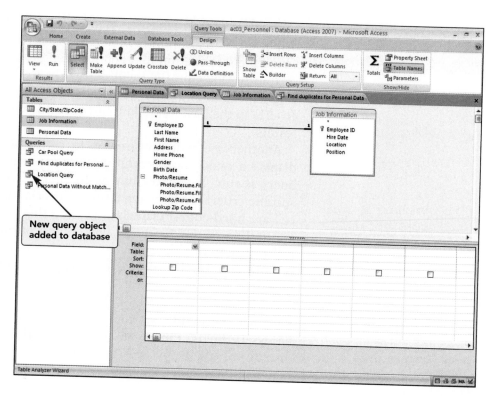

Figure 3.49

The query object is added to the Navigation pane and you are ready to define the query. You will add all the fields from the Personal Data table to the grid and the Location field from the Job Information table.

2
- Double-click * in the Personal Data field list.

- Double-click Location in the Job Information table.

- Sort the Location field in ascending sort order.

- Run the query.

- Hide the Navigation pane.

Your screen should be similar to Figure 3.50

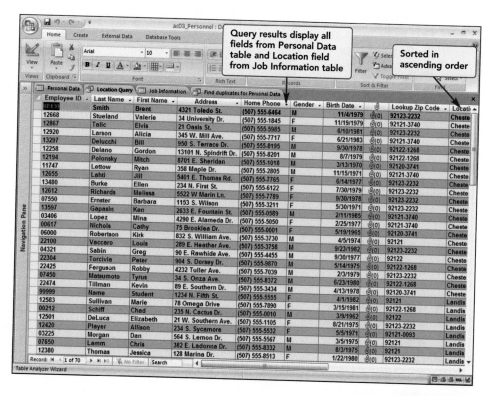

Figure 3.50

All the fields from the Personal Data table and the Location field are displayed. The location is in sorted order. However, because the director wants the information for each location on a separate page when printed, sorting the location field will not work. To display only the records for a single location at a time, you could filter the location field or change the criteria in the location field to provide this information and then print the results.

Another method, however, is to create a parameter query that will display a dialog box prompting you for location information when the query is run. This saves having to change to Design view and enter the specific criteria or applying a filter. Criteria that are entered in the criteria cell are **hard-coded criteria,** meaning they are used each time the query is run. In a parameter query, you enter a **parameter value** in the Criteria cell rather than a specific value. The parameter value tells the query to prompt you for the specific criteria you want to use when you run the query.

Additionally, the director does not need all the information from the Personal Data table, so you will change the design to include only the necessary fields. First, you will change the fields in the design grid to display only the Employee ID and the First and Last Name fields from the Personal Data table.

3 ● Display Design view.

● Select and delete the Personal Data column in the design grid.

● Select the Employee ID, Last Name, and First Name fields in the Personal Data table and drag them to before the Location field in the design grid.

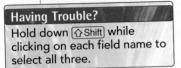

Having Trouble?
Hold down ⇧Shift while clicking on each field name to select all three.

● Remove the Sort from the Location field.

● Type [Enter Location] in the Location Criteria cell.

Your screen should be similar to Figure 3.51

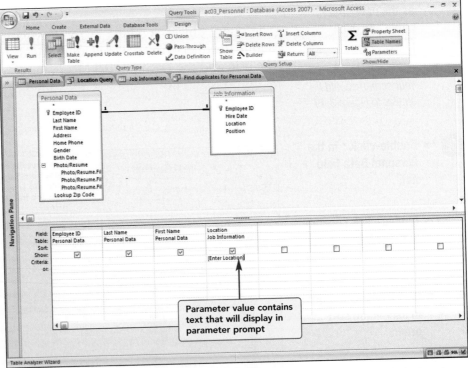

Parameter value contains text that will display in parameter prompt

Figure 3.51

The Location criterion you entered is the parameter value. Parameter values are enclosed in square brackets and contain the text you want to appear when the parameter prompt is displayed. The parameter value cannot be a field name, because Access will assume you want to use that particular field and will not prompt for input.

4 ● Run the query and type Landis in the Enter Parameter Value dialog box.

● Click [OK].

Your screen should be similar to Figure 3.52

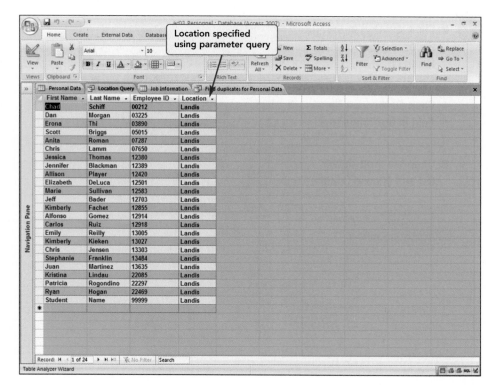

Figure 3.52

Only those records whose location is Landis are displayed. Additionally, only the fields you specified are included in the result. Now, each time you run the query, you simply need to specify the location in the parameter dialog box to obtain results for the different locations.

Displaying a Totals Row

As you look at the query results, you can see the record indicator tells you there are 24 records. The record indicator is a simple count of the total number of records in the table and only appears when you view the datasheet. You decide to display a Totals row in the datasheet that will display this information when you print the datasheet.

In addition to count totals, the Totals row can perform other types of calculations such as averages and sums on a column of data. Calculations that are performed on a range of data are called **aggregate functions.** Because aggregate functions perform calculations, the data type in a column must be a number, decimal, or currency data type. The Personal Data table does not use any of these data types. However, the Count function can be used on all data types.

Additional Information

Some functions can use a Date/Time data type also.

You will add a Totals row and then use the Count aggregate function to display the record count. The Totals row appears below the star (new record) row in the table and remains fixed on the window as you scroll the table. Clicking in a column of the Totals row selects the field to be calculated. Then, you open the drop-down list to select the function you want to use. For text data types, only the Count function is listed.

Additional Information

You will learn more about using the other aggregate functions in later labs.

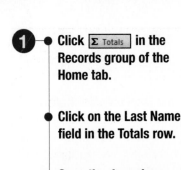

1 ● Click  in the Records group of the Home tab.

● Click on the Last Name field in the Totals row.

● Open the drop-down list and choose Count.

Your screen should be similar to Figure 3.53

Totals row displayed

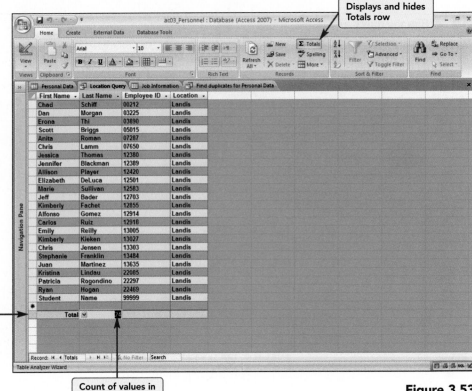

Count of values in Last Name field

Figure 3.53

Additional Information

If you select a function in the first column of the Totals row, the label is removed and the value displayed.

The Totals row displays 24 as the number of values in the column. The Totals label in the first column identifies the meaning of this value.

You can turn the display of the Totals row on and off any time by clicking ∑ Totals . When you redisplay the row, any functions that were selected are displayed again. A Totals row also can be displayed in a table datasheet.

You will print this query datasheet and then close all open objects.

2 ● Preview and then print the query datasheet.

● Close the query, saving changes when prompted.

● Close all remaining open objects, saving when prompted.

● Display the Navigation pane.

MORE ABOUT

► You also can save a filter as a query. To learn about this feature, see "4 Creating and Modifying Queries" in the More About appendix.

Note: If you are running short on time, this is an appropriate point to end your Access session. When you begin again, open the ac03_Personnel database.

Creating Reports

As you know, you can print the table and query datasheets to obtain a simple printout of the data. However, there are many times when you would like the output to look more professional. To do this, you can create custom reports of this information.

Concept 4

Report

4   A **report** is professional-appearing output generated from tables or queries that may include design elements, groups, and summary information. A report can be a simple listing of all the fields in a table, or it might be a list of selected fields based on a query. Reports generally include design elements such as formatted labels, report titles, and headings, as well as different design styles, layouts, and graphics that enhance the display of information. In addition, when creating a report, you can group data to achieve specific results. You can then display summary information such as totals by group to allow the reader to further analyze the data. Creating a report displays the information from your database in a more attractive and meaningful format.

The first step to creating a report is to decide what information you want to appear in the report. Then you need to determine the tables or queries (the report's record source) that can be used to provide this information. If all the fields you want to appear in the report are in a single table, then simply use that table. However, if the information you want to appear in the report is contained in more than one table, you first need to create a query that specifically fits the needs of the report.

There are several different methods you can use to create reports as described in the following table. The method you use depends on the type of report you need to create.

Report Tool	Creates a simple report containing all the fields in the table
Blank Report Tool	Builds a report from scratch in Report Layout view by adding the fields you select from the table
Report Design	Builds a report from scratch in Report Design view by adding the fields you select from the table
Report Wizard	Guides you through the steps to create a report

Using the Report Tool

Although you could give Juan a simple printout of the carpool query results, you decide to create a report of this information. Since the fastest way to create a report is to use the Report tool, you decide to try this method first. This tool uses the selected or displayed table or query object as the report source.

1 ● Select the Car Pool
   Query in the
   Navigation bar.

● Click 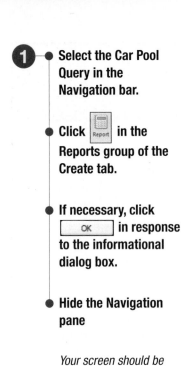 in the
   Reports group of the
   Create tab.

● If necessary, click
   OK in response
   to the informational
   dialog box.

● Hide the Navigation
   pane

   *Your screen should be
   similar to Figure 3.54*

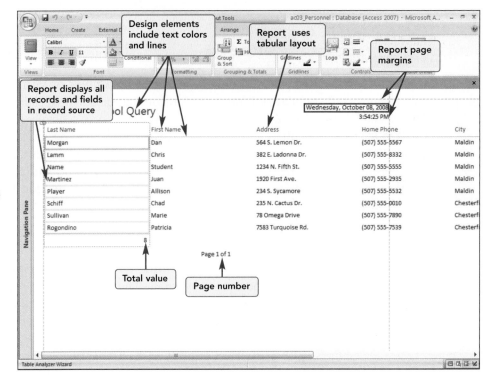

Figure 3.54

The Report tool creates a report that displays all fields and records from the record source in a predesigned report layout and style. It uses a tabular layout in which each field name appears at the top of the column and each record appears in a line, much like in Datasheet view. The fields are displayed in the order they appear in the table. It also displays the object name as the report title and the current date and time in the title area. The report design elements include blue font color for the report title and field names and a horizontal blue line below the field names. The title is also in a larger text size. The last row displays a total value of the number of records in the report. The dotted lines identify the report page margins and show that the Home Phone field data will be split between two pages.

Viewing the Report

The report is displayed in Layout view. As in Form Layout view, you could modify the report design if needed in this view. Instead, you will switch to Report view to see how the report will look when printed.

1 Click 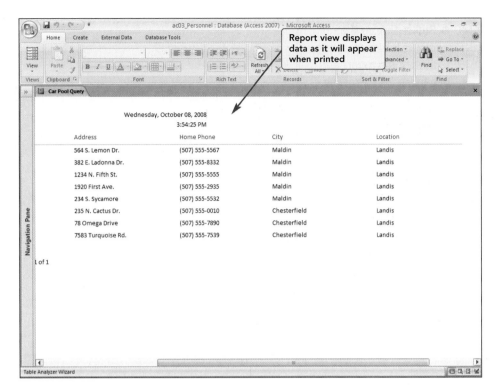 **Report View in the Views group of the Report Layout Tools Format tab.**

● **Scroll to the right to see the last field column.**

Your screen should be similar to Figure 3.55

Figure 3.55

Report view displays the data in the report as it will appear when printed. It does not show how the data will fit on a page. This view is useful if you want to copy data from the report and paste it into another document such as a Word file. It also can be used to temporarily change what data is displayed in the report, by applying a filter.

The last view you can use is Print Preview. This view will show you exactly how the report will look when printed and can be used to modify the page layout and print-related settings. Another way to display this view is from the object's shortcut menu.

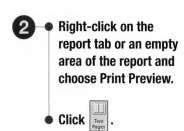

2 • **Right-click on the report tab or an empty area of the report and choose Print Preview.**

• **Click** 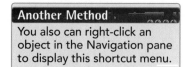 .

Another Method

You also can right-click an object in the Navigation pane to display this shortcut menu.

Your screen should be similar to Figure 3.56

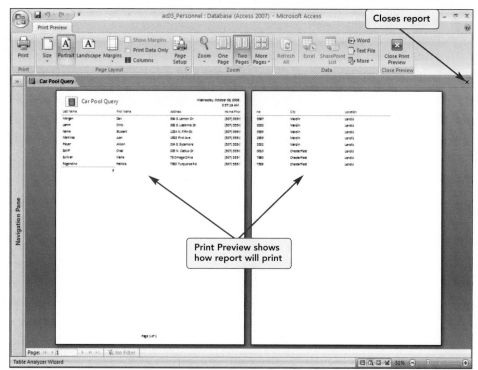

Figure 3.56

It is now easy to see exactly how the report will look when printed. After looking over the report, you decide that although the tabular layout is appropriate for your report, you do not want the report to include all the fields from the query. Rather than modify the report design by removing the unneeded fields, you will close this report without saving it and then use the Report Wizard to create a report that is more appropriate for your needs.

3 • **Close Print Preview.**

• **Click** 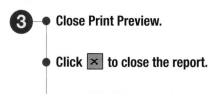 **to close the report.**

• **Click** [No] **in response to the dialog box to save the report.**

Using the Report Wizard

Using the Report Wizard, you can easily specify the fields you want to include in the report. The Report Wizard consists of a series of dialog boxes, much like those in the Form and Query Wizards. In the first dialog box, you specify the table or query to be used in the report and add the fields to be included. The Car Pool Query object is already correctly specified as the object that will be used to create the report.

1 • Click  in the Reports group of the Create tab.

• Add the First Name field to the Selected Fields list.

• Add all the remaining fields to the list. Remove the Location field.

• Click [Next >].

Your screen should be similar to Figure 3.57

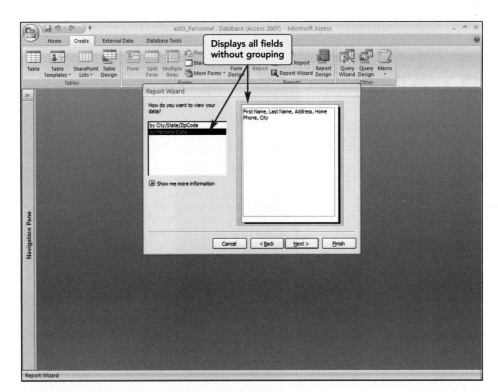

Figure 3.57

This dialog box asks you to decide how to display or group the data in the report based on the relationships between the tables. The selected option, by Personal Data, is appropriate for your needs and allows you to specify the fields you may want to group yourself. In the following dialog box, you will be asked if you want to add any grouping levels to the report. You do not want the report grouped by any category, so you do not need to do anything in this dialog box.

2 • Click [Next >] twice.

Your screen should be similar to Figure 3.58

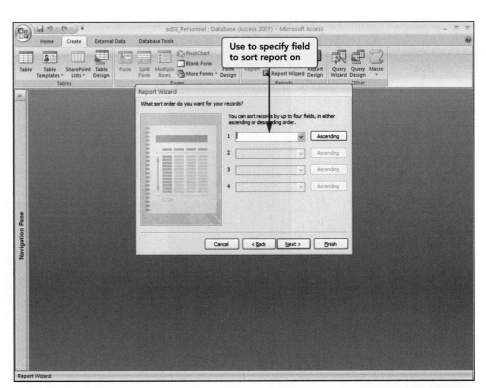

Figure 3.58

In this dialog box, you can specify a sort order for the records. Because the query already specifies the sort order, you do not need to specify this again.

3 ● **Click** Next > .

Your screen should be similar to Figure 3.59

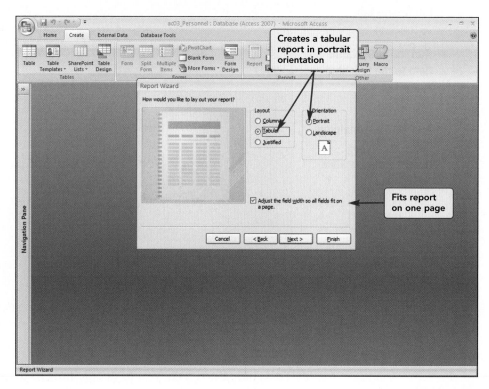

Figure 3.59

Additional Information
Reports use the same layouts as Forms.

This dialog box is used to change the report layout and orientation. The default report settings create a tabular layout using portrait orientation. In addition, the option to adjust the field width so that all fields fit on one page is selected. The default settings are acceptable.

4 ● **Click** Next > .

Your screen should be similar to Figure 3.60

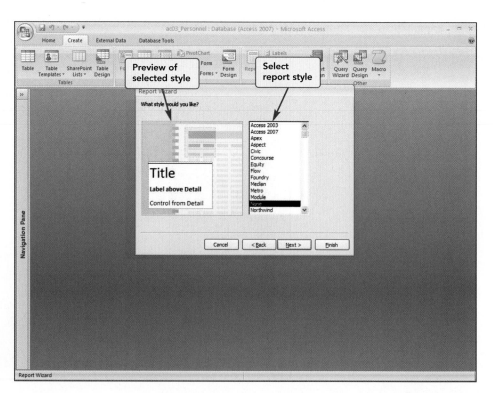

Figure 3.60

From this dialog box, you select a design style for the report. The preview area displays a sample of each style as it is selected.

5
- Select each style to preview the style options.
- Select Northwind.
- Click Next >.

Your screen should be similar to Figure 3.61

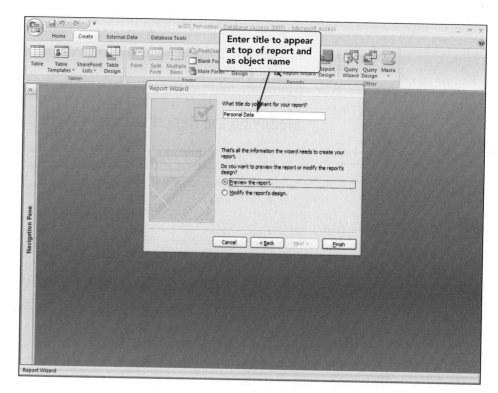

Enter title to appear at top of report and as object name

Figure 3.61

The last Report Wizard dialog box is used to add a title to the report and to specify how the report should be displayed after it is created. The only change you want to make is to replace the query name with a more descriptive report title.

6
- Enter Maldin to Landis Car Pool Report as the title.
- Click Finish.

Your screen should be similar to Figure 3.62

Report uses tabular layout and Northwind design style

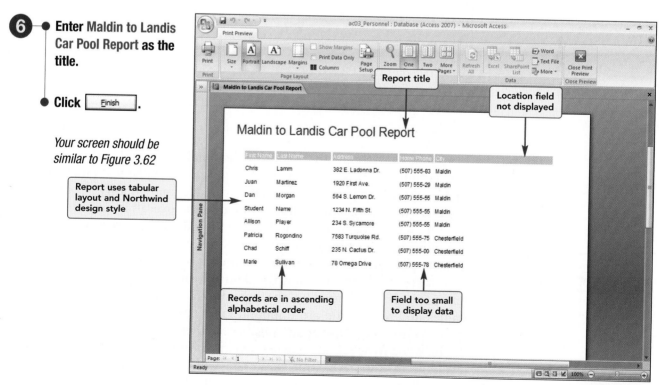

Report title

Location field not displayed

Records are in ascending alphabetical order

Field too small to display data

Figure 3.62

In a few moments, the completed report with the data from the resource query is displayed in Print Preview. The report appears in the tabular layout using the Northwind design style. The title reflects the title you specified. The records are in alphabetical order as specified by the query.

However, there are a few problems with the design. The most noticeable is that the City field is much larger than it needs to be and, consequently, the Home Phone field is truncated. Additionally, you want the City field to follow the Address field.

Modifying the Report in Layout View

To make these changes, you need to modify the report design. You can modify a report in either Design view or Layout view. To make these simple changes, you will use Layout view.

1 ● Click **⊞** Layout View in the status bar.

● If necessary, close the Field list pane.

Your screen should be similar to Figure 3.63

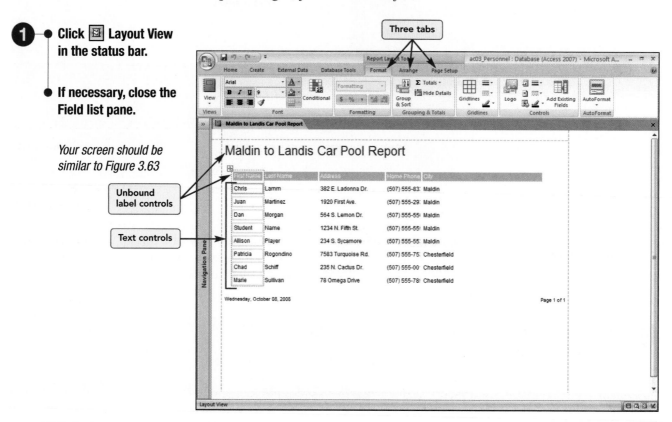

Figure 3.63

In Layout view, three tabs are available to help you modify the report. The Format tab contains commands that are used to make text enhancements such as fonts and colors, as well as to add and modify report design objects. The Arrange tab is used to modify the overall layout of the report or of individual elements. The Page Setup tab is used to control the page layout of the report for printing purposes.

Just as in forms, each item in the report is a separate control. The field names are label controls and the field information is a text control. The text controls are bound to the data in the underlying table. The field names and report title are unbound label controls. The columnar report layout controls the layout and position of these controls.

The same features you learned when working in Form Layout view are available in Report Layout view. You will begin by sizing the City and Home Phone fields. Then you will move the Home Phone field.

Having Trouble?
See Concept 8 in Lab 2 to review controls.

2 ● **Click on the City field.**

Additional Information

The dotted box around the label and text box controls shows they are a compound control.

● **Reduce the size of the field to fit the contents.**

● **Click on the Home Phone field and increase the size of the field to display the contents.**

● **Drag the Home Phone field object to the right of the City field.**

● **Adjust the size of the fields as in Figure 3.64.**

Your screen should be similar to Figure 3.64

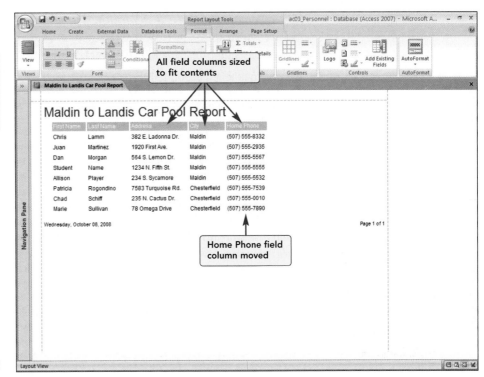

Figure 3.64

The last changes you want to make are to the appearance of the report. You decide to change the report design style to another more colorful style. This feature works similarly to the Form AutoFormat feature. The same selection of report design styles that were available in the wizard are displayed in the AutoFormat gallery.

3 ● **Click [AutoFormat] in the AutoFormat group of the Format tab.**

● **Choose Equity.**

Having Trouble?

The design name appears in a ScreenTip when you point to the different designs.

Your screen should be similar to Figure 3.65

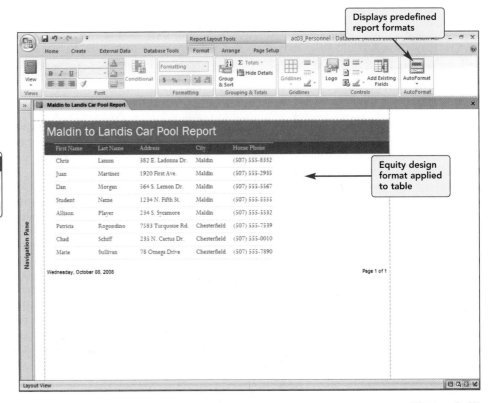

Figure 3.65

The selected design was applied to the report. You are finished making changes to the report and will close and save the report.

4 ● Close the report, saving the changes when prompted.

● Display the Navigation pane.

The name of the report you created appears in the Reports category of the Navigation pane.

Modifying a Report in Design View

After seeing how easy it was to create a report for the carpool information, you decide to create a custom report for the job position and location information requested by the club director.

1 ● Select the Location Query from the Queries category and click [🔍 Report Wizard] in the Create tab.

● Add all the fields to the report.

● Click [Finish].

● Enter River Mist as the location and click [OK].

Your screen should be similar to Figure 3.66

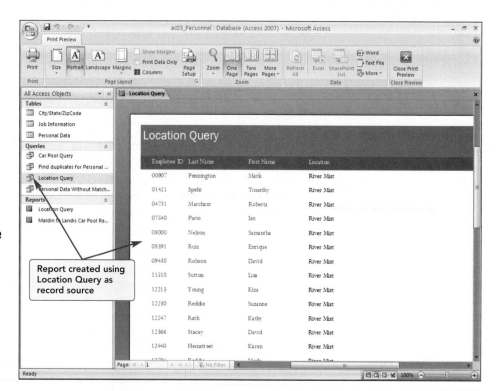

Figure 3.66

Rather than moving through each step of the wizard, if you know that you will be using the default or last-used settings, you can end the wizard at any point. The report displays the specified fields and uses the tabular layout and the Equity design style. This style was used because it was the last style used in the database.

As you look at the report, you realize you forgot to include the Position field. You will modify the query and then add this field in Design view to the report.

2

- **Open the Location Query and enter River Mist as the location.**

- **Change to Design view and add the Position field to the design grid.**

- **Click 📄 Save in the Quick Access Toolbar to save the query design changes.**

- **Display the Location Query report and click** [Close Print Preview] **.**

- **Hide the Navigation pane.**

- **If the Field List pane is not displayed, click** [Add Existing Fields] **in the Tools group of the Design tab.**

Another Method
You also can use the shortcut key [Alt] + [F8] to hide and display the Field List pane.

Your screen should be similar to Figure 3.67

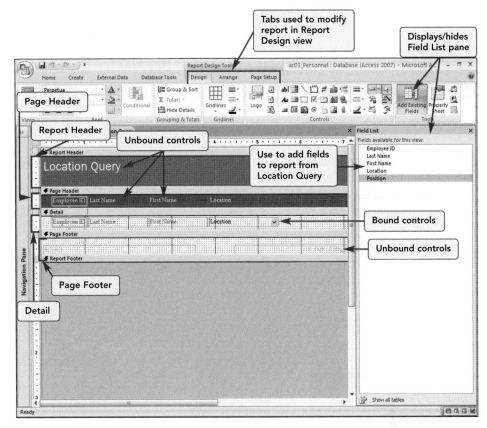

Figure 3.67

The report is displayed in Report Design view. It includes three tabs that help you modify the report. The Design tab contains commands that are used to make text enhancements such as fonts and colors, as well as to add and modify report design objects. The Arrange tab is used to modify the overall layout of the report or of individual elements. The Page Setup tab is used to control the page layout of the report for printing purposes.

Additionally, the Field List task pane displays the field names from the design grid of the Location Query and is used to add fields to the report.

The Report Design window is divided into five sections: Report Header, Page Header, Detail, Page Footer, and Report Footer. The contents of each section appear below the horizontal bar that contains the name of that section. The sections are described in the following table.

Section	Description
Report Header	Contains information to be printed once at the beginning of the report. The report title is displayed in this section.
Page Header	Contains information to be printed at the top of each page. The column headings are displayed in this section.
Detail	Contains the records of the table. The field column widths are the same as the column widths set in the table design.
Page Footer	Contains information to be printed at the bottom of each page such as the date and page number.
Report Footer	Contains information to be printed at the end of the report. The Report Footer section currently contains no data.

The field name controls in the Page Header section are unbound label controls whereas those in the Detail section are bound text controls. The control in the Report Header that displays the report title and those in the Page Footers that display the date and page numbers are unbound controls. Finally, there are other unbound controls that enhance the appearance of the report such as lines, boxes, and pictures.

First you will add the missing field to the report.

3 ● **Drag the Position field from the Field List to the right of the Location text control and when a vertical orange bar appears, release the mouse to drop it at that location.**

● **Close the Field List pane.**

Additional Information

You also can double-click on the field from the field list to move it into the report design.

Your screen should be similar to Figure 3.68

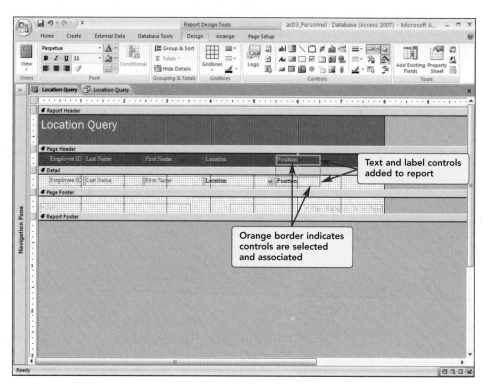

Figure 3.68

Position text and label controls have been added to the report. The Position label control was inserted in the Page Header section and the Position text control in the Detail section. This is because the controls were inserted into the tabular control layout and comply with the horizontal and vertical alignment settings of the layout.

Both controls are surrounded by an orange border indicating that they are selected and that they are **compound controls.** This means the controls are associated, and that the two controls will act as one when moved. Additionally, the text control is a bound control that is tied to the Position field data.

Now you want to move the Last Name controls to the right of the First Name controls. Controls can be moved to any location within the control layout by clicking on the control to select it and then dragging it to the new location. The mouse pointer changes to ⁺ₖ to indicate that a selected control can be moved.

Additional Information

If you want to move a control out of the control layout, it needs to be removed from the group as you did when designing the form.

Another Method

You also can move controls using [Ctrl] + the directional arrow keys.

4 • **Select the Last Name text control.**

• **Point to the control and when the mouse pointer changes to 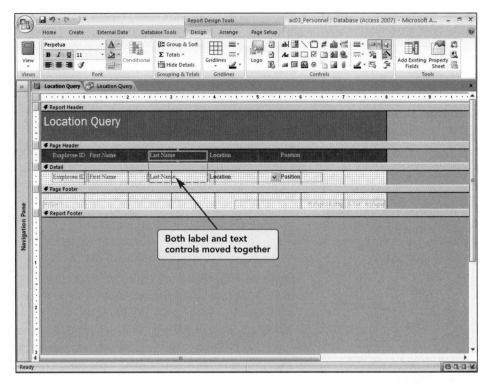, drag it to the right of the First Name text control.**

Your screen should be similar to Figure 3.69

Figure 3.69

Notice that the Last Name label control in the Page Header area also moved and was automatically placed and aligned above the Last Name text control. The controls in both the Page Header and Detail sections are horizontally and vertically aligned and spaced an equal distance apart.

Format Controls

Next, you decide to change the text of the report title and center it over the report. First you will enlarge the title control to extend the width of the report and then center the text within the control.

1

- Select the report title control.

- Drag the right edge of the control to the right margin (8" ruler position).

- Click ☰ Center in the Font group of the Report Design Tools Design tab.

- Click in the control to place the cursor in the text and select the text.

- Type Landis Job Position Report.

Having Trouble?

The title text is difficult to see because it is white on a white background when the text is selected.

- Click outside the report design area to clear the selection.

Your screen should be similar to Figure 3.70

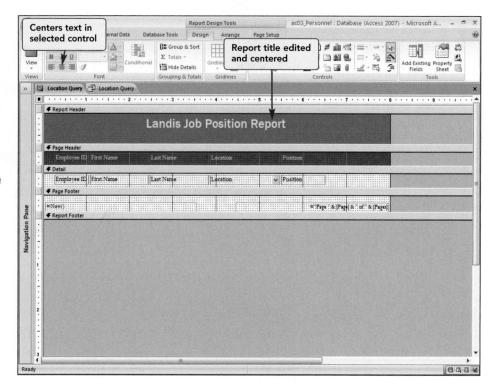

Figure 3.70

The revised title is centered over the report columns. Changing the title text does not change the name of the report object.

Now you want to see the effects of your changes. You will be prompted to enter the location. This time, you will enter Landis as the location because the report title now includes the location.

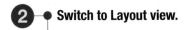

Switch to Layout view.

Enter the location of Landis.

Your screen should be similar to Figure 3.71

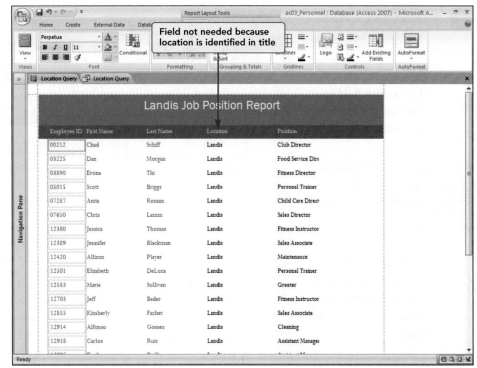

Figure not needed because location is identified in title

Landis Job Position Report

Employee ID	First Name	Last Name	Location	Position
00212	Chad	Schiff	Landis	Club Director
03225	Dan	Morgan	Landis	Food Service Dire
03890	Erona	Thi	Landis	Fitness Director
05015	Scott	Briggs	Landis	Personal Trainer
07287	Anita	Roman	Landis	Child Care Direc
07650	Chris	Lamm	Landis	Sales Director
12380	Jessica	Thomas	Landis	Fitness Instructor
12389	Jennifer	Blackman	Landis	Sales Associate
12420	Allison	Player	Landis	Maintenance
12501	Elizabeth	DeLuca	Landis	Personal Trainer
12583	Marie	Sullivan	Landis	Greeter
12703	Jeff	Bader	Landis	Fitness Instructor
12855	Kimberly	Fachet	Landis	Sales Associate
12914	Alfonso	Gomez	Landis	Cleaning
12918	Carlos	Ruiz	Landis	Assistant Manage

Figure 3.71

The report is really shaping up. However, there are still a few changes you need to make. You want to remove the Location field because the title now identifies the location. Then you will adjust the sizes of the fields to make the report fill more of the width of the page.

Deleting a Field

You will delete the field and resize the other fields in Layout view so you can see the field content and layout while sizing them.

1 • Select the Location field and press Delete.

• Increase the size of the Position field to fully display the field contents.

Having Trouble?
Scroll to the end of the report to make sure that the largest Position name is fully displayed.

• Increase the size of the Employee ID field to approximately the same size as the name fields.

Your screen should be similar to Figure 3.72

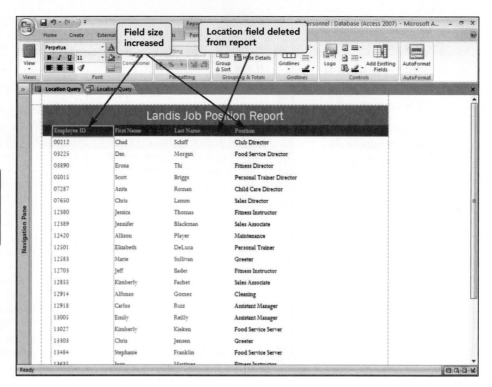

Figure 3.72

Now, each time you run the report, you simply need to change the location in the title to reflect the location you specify as the query parameter.

Sorting and Filtering Data in a Report

You also notice that the records in the report are in Employee ID order. This is because a sort order was not specified in the query or the report when they were created. Just as in a table datasheet, query, or form, you can sort and filter the data that is displayed in a report. You will use these features to sort the records in alphabetical order by last name and display only those records whose job is a fitness instructor.

1 ● **Right-click on the Last Name field of any record.**

● **Choose Sort A to Z.**

● **Right-click on the Position field of any record that displays Fitness Instructor.**

● **Choose Equals "Fitness Instructor".**

Your screen should be similar to Figure 3.73

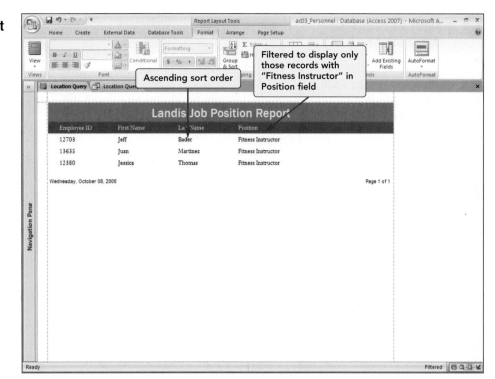

Figure 3.73

Only the three records meeting the filter requirements are displayed in the report. They are in alphabetical order by last name. You will remove the filter but maintain the sorted record order.

2 ● **Right-click on the Position field of any record.**

● **Choose Clear filter from Position.**

Additional Information

You also can click 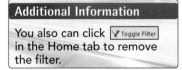 in the Home tab to remove the filter.

All the records are redisplayed again.

Preparing Reports for Printing

You can print the report from any view or even when the report is closed. However, unless you are sure the page settings are correct, it is a good idea to open the report and check its layout in Layout view or Print Preview first. In Layout view, you can easily make any adjustments to the report if you find the changes you make to the page layout affect how the report will print.

Modifying the Page Setup

As you look at the layout of the report on the page, you see the columns are not centered on the page. This is because the first column starts at the default left margin setting of 0.25 inch. You decide to increase the size of the margins, which will push the columns to the right and better center them on the page.

1 ● **Open the Page Setup tab.**

● **Click** [Margins] **in the Page Layout group.**

● **Choose Wide.**

Your screen should be similar to Figure 3.74

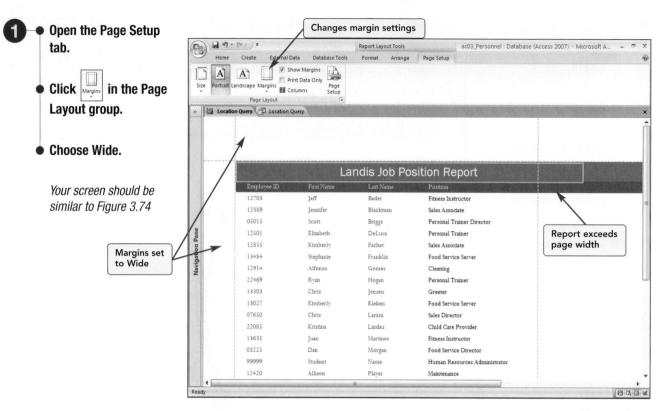

Figure 3.74

The Wide margin option increases the left and right margins to 0.75 inch. The columns now begin at the left margin and the report appears more balanced on the page; however, now the report width exceeds a single page. This is because some of the controls in the report exceed the new page margins. Additionally, the title is no longer centered because the control is wider than the new page width. These problems can be quickly fixed by reducing the size of the controls that are causing the problem. You decide to increase the margins to 1 inch and then make the adjustments to the controls to fit the new page width. To do this, you will set a custom left and right margin.

2 ● Click 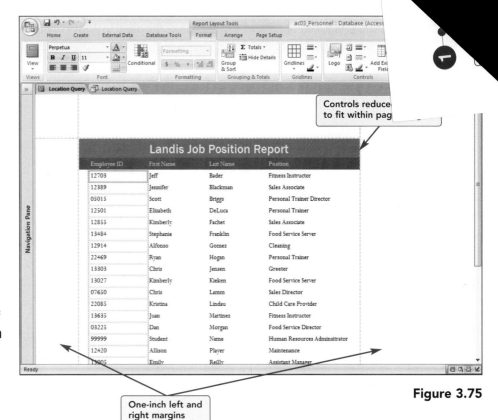 in the Page Layout group.

● Enter **1** in the Left and Right Margin text boxes.

● Click [OK].

● Click on the title control and size the control to fit the new page width.

● Scroll to the bottom of the report and click on the page number control in the footer.

● Reduce the control size (from the right edge) until it is inside the right margin line.

● If the report still exceeds the margins, click on the Position column and reduce the size of the column.

● Scroll to the top of the report.

Your screen should be similar to Figure 3.75

Controls reduced to fit within page

Landis Job Position Report

Employee ID	First Name	Last Name	Position
12703	Jeff	Bader	Fitness Instructor
12389	Jennifer	Blackman	Sales Associate
05015	Scott	Briggs	Personal Trainer Director
12501	Elizabeth	DeLuca	Personal Trainer
12855	Kimberly	Fachet	Sales Associate
13484	Stephanie	Franklin	Food Service Server
12914	Alfonso	Gomez	Cleaning
22469	Ryan	Hogan	Personal Trainer
13303	Chris	Jensen	Greeter
13027	Kimberly	Kieken	Food Service Server
07650	Chris	Lamm	Sales Director
22085	Kristina	Lindau	Child Care Provider
13635	Juan	Martinez	Fitness Instructor
03225	Dan	Morgan	Food Service Director
99999	Student	Name	Human Resources Adminsitrator
12420	Allison	Player	Maintenance
13905	Emily	Reilly	Assistant Manager

One-inch left and right margins

Figure 3.75

Now the columns are spaced attractively across the page. The page layout settings you specify are saved with the report, so unless you make changes to the report design, you only need to set them once.

Previewing and Printing Reports

Although you believe the report is ready to print, you will preview it first and then print it.

Click  Print Preview in the status bar to change the view to Print Preview.

● Click 🖶 .

● Specify your printer settings and then print the report.

● Close the report, saving the changes.

● Close the query.

● Open the Navigation pane and rename the Location Query report Job Position Report.

Your printed report should look like the one shown in the Case Study at the beginning of the lab.

Printing a Relationships Report

Before exiting Access, you want to print a report that shows the relationships between the tables in your database.

1 ● Open the Database Tools tab.

● Click 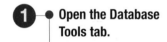 .

● If necessary, click ▦ All Relationships to show all table relationships.

● Click 🗐 Relationship Report in the Tools group of the Relationship Tools Design tab.

● Click Margins and select Last Custom Setting from the drop-down menu.

● Print the report.

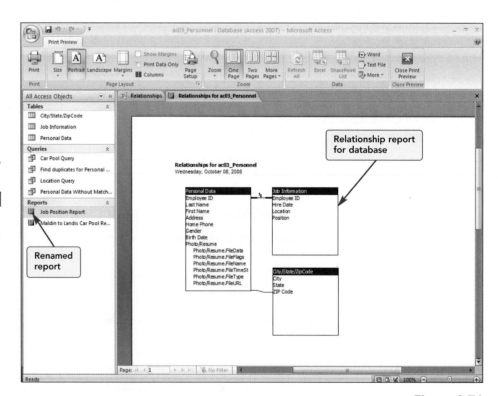

Figure 3.76

Your screen should be similar to Figure 3.76

A preview of how the report will look when printed is displayed on the screen. The database name and creation date are automatically used as the report header. You can print this report as well as save it for future reference.

2 ● Close the relationship report without saving it.

● Close the Relationships window.

Additional Information
A file is fragmented when it becomes too large for your computer to store in a single location on your hard disk. When this happens, the file is split up and stored in pieces in different locations on the disk, making access slower.

Compacting and Backing Up the Database

As you modify a database, the changes are saved to your disk. When you delete data or objects, the database file can become fragmented and use disk space inefficiently. To make the database perform optimally, you should **compact** the database on a regular basis. Compacting makes a copy of the file and rearranges the way that the file is stored on your disk.

1 ● Click 🗔 Office Button and choose Manage/Compact and Repair Database.

Although it appears that nothing has happened, the database file has been compacted and repaired as needed. It is also a good idea to back up your databases periodically. This will ensure that you have a copy of each database in case of a power outage or other system failure while you are working on a file, or in case you need to access a previous version of a database that you have changed.

2 ● Click 🗔 Office Button and choose Manage/Back Up Database.

Your screen should be similar to Figure 3.77

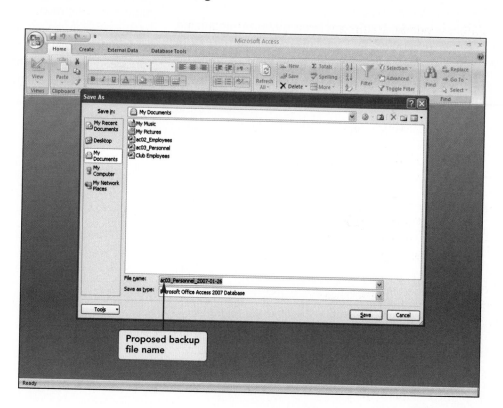

Proposed backup file name

Figure 3.77

The Save As dialog box displays your database name (which in this case is ac03_Personnel) with the current date appended to it. This is a good way to keep track of when you performed the backup on the database, so you will not change this file name.

3 • **If necessary, change the Save In location to your data file location.**

• **Click** [Save].

• **Close the database and exit Access.**

The backup database file has been saved to your data file location. If you need to restore a backed up database, you just change the name of the backup file (so it does not conflict with another file of the same name that you may have created since the backup) and then open it in Access.

Focus on Careers

EXPLORE YOUR CAREER OPTIONS

Database Administrator

Database administrators are responsible for organizing and maintaining an organization's information resources. This position generally involves training new users to use the database, testing new objects, and backing up the data. As a database administrator, your position also would include safeguarding the system from threats. The typical salary range of a database administrator is $40,000 to $65,000. A bachelor's degree in computer science is typically preferred in addition to practical experience. Demand for skilled database administrators is expected to make it one of the fastest-growing occupations.

Concept Summary

Querying Tables and Creating Reports

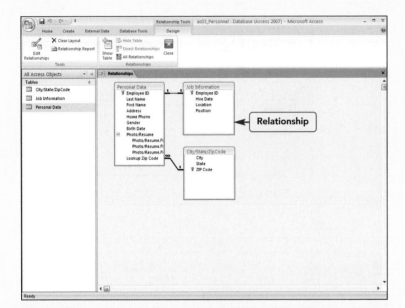

Relationship (AC3.14)

A relationship establishes the association between common fields in two tables.

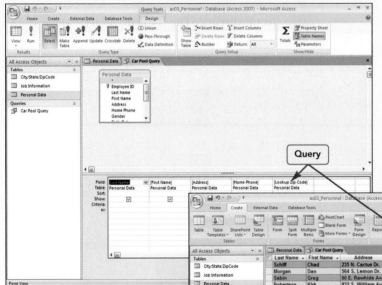

Query (AC3.21)

A query is a request for specific data contained in a database. Queries are used to view data in different ways, to analyze data, and even to change existing data.

Concept Summary

Join (AC3.27)

A join is an association between a field in one table or query and a field of the same data type in another table or query.

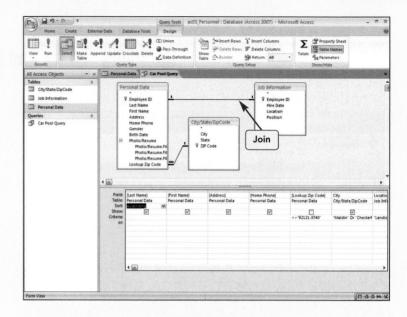

Report (AC3.49)

A report is professional-appearing output generated from tables or queries that may include design elements, groups, and summary information.

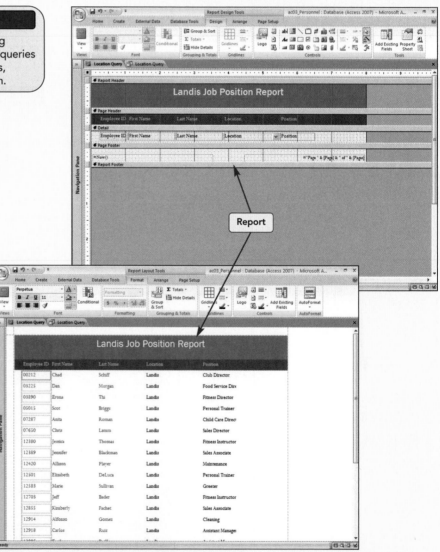

Lab Review

Querying Tables and Creating Reports

key terms

Action query   AC3.21

aggregate functions   AC3.47

AND operator   AC3.32

column selector bar   AC3.26

common field   AC3.14

compact   AC3.69

compound control   AC3.60

compound criterion   AC3.32

criteria   AC3.21

criteria expression   AC3.30

Crosstab query   AC3.21

design grid   AC3.26

field list   AC3.26

hard-coded criteria   AC3.46

inner join   AC3.30

join   AC3.27

join line   AC3.18

junction table   AC3.14

many-to-many   AC3.14

multitable query   AC3.26

one-to-many   AC3.14

one-to-one   AC3.14

OR operator   AC3.32

outer join   AC3.30

Parameter query   AC3.21

parameter value   AC3.46

query   AC3.21

referential integrity   AC3.14

relationship   AC3.14

report   AC3.49

row label   AC3.26

Select query   AC3.21

Show box   AC3.26

SQL query   AC3.21

unequal join   AC3.30

MCAS skills

The Microsoft Certified Applications Specialist (MCAS) certification program is designed to measure your proficiency in performing basic tasks using the Office 2007 applications. Getting certified demonstrates that you have the skills and provides a valuable industry credential for employment. See Reference 2: Microsoft Certified Applications Specialist (MCAS) for a complete list of the skills that were covered in Lab 3.

Lab Review

command summary

Command	Shortcut	Action
🔘 Office Button		
Save As		Saves database object with a new file name
Manage/Back Up Database		Backs up database
Manage/Compact and Repair		Compacts and repairs database file
Home tab		
Views group		
🖼 Report View	🖼	Displays report in Report view
🖼 Report Layout View	🖼	Displays report in Layout view
Records group		
Refresh All ▾		Updates selected object
Σ Totals		Displays/hides Totals row
Create tab		
Reports group		
Report		Creates a report using all fields in current table
Blank Report		Creates a report using Report Design view
Report Wizard		Creates a report using the Report Wizard
Other group		
Query Wizard		Creates a query using the Query Wizard
Query Design		Creates a query using Query Design view
Database Tools tab		
Show/Hide group		
Object Dependencies		Evaluates table design and suggests modifications
Relationships		Defines how the data in tables is related

command summary

Command	Shortcut	Action
Analyze group		
Analyze Table		Evaluates table design
Query Tools Design tab		
Results group		
! Run		Displays query results in Query Datasheet view
Query Setup group		
Show Table		Displays/hides Show Table dialog box
Show/Hide group		
XYZ Table Names		Displays/hides the Tables row
Report Layout Tools Format tab		
Font group		
≡ Center		Centers text in selected control
Controls group		
Add Existing Fields		Displays/hides Add Existing Fields task pane
AutoFormat group		
AutoFormat		Applies selected predesigned styles to report
Report Layout Tools Page Setup tab		
Page Layout group		
Margins		Sets margins of printed report
Page Setup		Sets features related to the page layout of printed report

command summary

Command	Shortcut	Action
Report Design Tools Design tab		
Font group		
≡ Center		Centers text in selected control
⊞		Sizes text in selected control
Tools group		
Add Existing Fields		Displays/hides the Fields List task pane
Relationship Tools Design tab		
Tools group		
Relationship Report		Creates a report of the displayed relationships
Print Preview tab		
Page Layout group		
Margins		Adjusts margins in printed output

Lab Exercises

matching

Match the numbered item with the correct lettered description.

1. one-to-many _____ **a.** intersection of a column and row

2. compact _____ **b.** calculations that are performed on a range of data

3. multitable query _____ **c.** runs a query and displays a query datasheet

4. aggregate functions _____ **d.** a type of table relationship

5. query _____ **e.** makes a copy of the file and rearranges the way that the file is stored on your disk

6. cell _____ **f.** an association between fields in related tables

7. [! Run] _____ **g.** used to ask questions about database tables

8. referential integrity _____ **h.** query that uses data from more than one table

9. criteria _____ **i.** set of limiting conditions

10. parameter value _____ **j.** prompts you for the specific criteria you want to use when you run the query

fill-in

Complete the following statements by filling in the blanks with the correct terms.

1. Enforcing _____ ensures that relationships between tables are valid and that related data is not accidentally changed or deleted.

2. The _____ operator narrows the search for records that meet both conditions.

3. A(n) _____ control is used to enter multiple criteria.

4. A(n) _____ is a request for specific data contained in a database.

5. A(n) _____ is used to display the results of a query.

6. A(n) _____ is an association that tells Access how data between tables is related.

7. The _____ is where you enter the settings that define the query.

8. In a report, a(n) _____ is not connected to a field.

9. _____ are the set of limiting conditions used in filters and queries.

10. To be joined, the tables must have at least one _____ field.

Lab Exercises

true/false

Circle the correct answer to the following statements.

1. Values that tell Access how to filter the criteria in a query are called filter expressions. True False
2. Queries are used to view data in different ways, to analyze data, and to change existing data. True False
3. Reports can be generated from tables only. True False
4. Fields in different tables must have the same name to create a relationship. True False
5. A compound control consists of two controls that are associated. True False
6. A join line shows how different tables are related. True False
7. Related fields are fields that have the same data type and the same kind of information, but different field names. True False
8. A compound criterion is created using the AND operator. True False
9. A Select query is the most common type of query. True False
10. Hard-coded criteria are used each time the query is run. True False

multiple choice

Circle the letter of the correct response.

1. A join line creates a _____ relationship that establishes rules that the data must match to be included in the query results.
   a. permanent
   b. partial
   c. temporary
   d. complete

2. The query _____ is where you enter the settings that define the query.
   a. field list
   b. Show box
   c. design grid
   d. objects

3. The _____ operator is assumed when you enter criteria in multiple fields.
   a. OR
   b. AND
   c. BETWEEN
   d. EQUAL TO

4. A report title is a(n) _____ control because it is not connected to a field.
   a. bound
   b. associated
   c. unbound
   d. text

5. A(n) _____ query prompts you for the specific criteria you want to use when you run the query.
   a. Parameter
   b. SQL
   c. Update
   d. Append

6. _____ view is used to create and modify the structure of a query.
   a. Design
   b. Update
   c. Layout
   d. Datasheet

7. When a file is _____, it uses disk space inefficiently.
   a. broken
   b. fragmented
   c. compacted
   d. repaired

8. _____ view can be used to view the data in a report and modify the report design and layout.
   a. Layout
   b. Design
   c. Print Preview
   d. Datasheet

9. The operator that broadens the filter, because any record meeting either condition is included in the output, is _____.
   a. AND
   b. OR
   c. MOST
   d. ALL

10. Bound and unbound are types of _____.
   a. buttons
   b. forms
   c. properties
   d. controls

Hands-On Exercises

step-by-step

Scensations Spa Database ★

1. The Scensations Salon and Day Spa offers hair and spa treatments exclusively for women. The owner of the spa is offering a new spa package that would include various anti-aging skin treatments and massages. She wants to send an announcement about this package to her clients who are over the age of 40. You will get this information for her from the client information that is stored in an Access 2007 database file. Your printed report will be similar to that shown here.

   a. Open the database file named ac03_Scensations Spa and the table named Clients.

   b. Find and delete any duplicate records using the Last Name field as the field to check for duplicate data.

   c. Use the Table Analyzer Wizard to create a second table containing the City, State, and Zip Code information. Name the new table **City/State/Zip**. Make the Zip Code field the primary key in this table.

   d. Delete the Clients table. Rename Table1 **Clients**. Move the Lookup field after the Address field. Best fit all the fields in the table.

   e. Query the Clients table to display the First Name, Last Name, Address, and City/State/Zip fields for those records with a birth date before 1/1/69.

   f. Display a Totals row showing a count of the Last Name field. Save the query as **40+ Clients**. Print the query results.

	40+ Clients		Wednesday, October 08, 2008 9:34:05 AM
First Name	Last Name	Address	Lookup to City/Sate/Zip
Mary	Smith	560 E. West	89430, Smith Valley , NV
Patricia	Johnson	24486 S. 11th	89430, Smith Valley , NV
Linda	Williams	495 W. Cherry	89430, Smith Valley , NV
Barbara	Jones	738 N. Eighth	89430, Smith Valley , NV
Elizabeth	Brown	1008 E. Adams	89430, Smith Valley , NV
Jennifer	Davis	984 N. 7th	89430, Smith Valley , NV
Maria	Miller	448 E. Williams	89430, Smith Valley , NV
Margaret	Moore	246 N. 1st	89430, Smith Valley , NV
Dorothy	Taylor	1238 E. Fifth	89430, Smith Valley , NV
Lisa	Anderson	7428 S. Hill	89447, Yerington , NV
Nancy	Thomas	6190 E. Main	89447, Yerington , NV
Karen	Jackson	4952 S. Ridge	89706, Mound House , NV
Betty	White	3714 E. Washington	89706, Mound House , NV
Helen	Harris	246 N. 6th	89706, Mound House , NV
Heather	Morris	385 E. 5th	89403, Dayton , NV
Teresa	Rogers	55 N. 2nd	89403, Dayton , NV
Doris	Reed	10494 N. Forest	89403, Dayton , NV
Gloria	Cook	224 E. Laurel	89403, Dayton , NV
Evelyn	Morgan	6190 N. Ninth	89403, Dayton , NV
Mildred	Bailey	31482 E. Smith	89403, Dayton , NV
Katherine	Rivera	123 N. Willow	89403, Dayton , NV
Christina	Ramirez	492 N. First	89403, Dayton , NV
Beverly	Brooks	13992 S. River	89403, Dayton , NV
Andrea	Henderson	8666 N. 9th	89403, Dayton , NV
Kathryn	Coleman	784 E. Fourteenth	89403, Dayton , NV
Anne	Powell	112 E. Forest	89408, Fernley , NV
Tina	Simmons	27984 W. 14th	89408, Fernley , NV
Phyllis	Foster	27984 W. Dogwood	89408, Fernley , NV
Norma	Gonzales	9904 E. Elm	89408, Fernley , NV
Diana	Alexander	246 E. 9th	89408, Fernley , NV

Page 1 of 2

g. Use the Report tool to create a report based on the 40+ Clients query.

h. Change the report margins to Normal. Adjust the controls to fit the report on a single page width-wise.

i. Add a new record to the Clients table that includes your name in the first and last name fields and a birth date of 2/11/68.

j. Refresh the query and report to update them.

k. Save the report as **40+ ClientsReport**. Print the report.

l. Compact and repair the database. Back up the database.

m. Close the database, saving as needed, and exit Access.

EchoPlex Reports ★

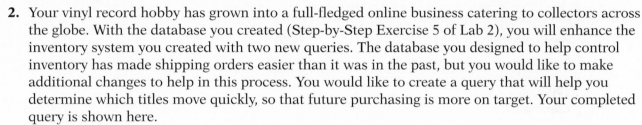

2. Your vinyl record hobby has grown into a full-fledged online business catering to collectors across the globe. With the database you created (Step-by-Step Exercise 5 of Lab 2), you will enhance the inventory system you created with two new queries. The database you designed to help control inventory has made shipping orders easier than it was in the past, but you would like to make additional changes to help in this process. You would like to create a query that will help you determine which titles move quickly, so that future purchasing is more on target. Your completed query is shown here.

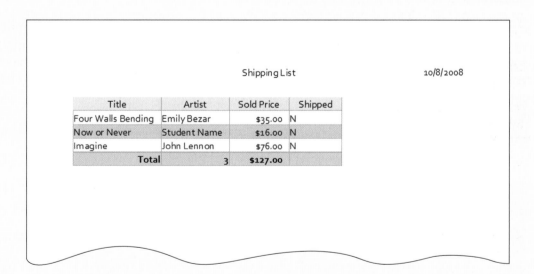

Title	Artist	Sold Price	Shipped
Four Walls Bending	Emily Bezar	$35.00	N
Now or Never	Student Name	$16.00	N
Imagine	John Lennon	$76.00	N
Total		3	$127.00

Shipping List   10/8/2008

a. Open the database file named ac02_EchoPlex that you modified in Step-by-Step Exercise 5 of Lab 2. Open the Records table.

b. Make **N** the default value for the Shipped field and change the Format property to display uppercase. Save the changes to the table.

c. You have sold Fleetwood Mac's *Rumours* for $16.00. Change the record accordingly. Enter **Y** in the Shipped field. You also have sold John Lennon's *Imagine* for $76.00. Adjust the record and leave N in the Shipped field.

d. Using the Records form, add the following new records to the table:

ID		
Title	Four Walls Bending	Now or Never
Artist	Emily Bezar	[Your Name]
Condition	Good	Poor
Purchase Price	$15.00	$4.00
Sold Price	$35.00	$16.00
Shipped	N	N
Comments		
Attachments		

e. Create a query that displays inventory that has a sold price but has not been shipped yet. Include the Title, Sold Price, and Shipped fields. Name the query **Shipping List**. Add the Artist field after the Title field to the query. Best fit the query datasheet columns. Display a Total row with a count in the Artist field column and a Sum in the Sold Price column. Print the query results.

f. Close all objects. Compact and repair the database. Exit Access.

Downtown Internet Café Inventory ★★

3. The Inventory database you created for the Downtown Internet Café (Lab 1, Step-by-Step Exercise 4) has been in use several weeks now and is working well. During this time, you have modified the table design and added more information to the table. Evan, the owner, has asked you to submit a daily report on all low-quantity items so he can place the necessary orders. You will use the database to monitor inventory levels and respond to Evan's request. First you decide to run a query to find the low-stock items, and then you can generate the requested report from the query. Your completed report should look similar to the report below.

a. Open the database file named ac03_Café Inventory. Open the Stock table to view its content. Replace the contact name for Cuppa Jo with your name in the Suppliers table.

b. Use the Query Wizard to create a query based on the Stock table. Include all fields, except Item, in their current order. Name the query **Low Stock**.

c. In Query Design view, enter the criteria to display only those records with an In Stock value less than 30, and run the query.

d. Upon reviewing the datasheet, you realize that it needs to include the contact name, phone, and e-mail addresses for Evan to use when he places orders. Add these fields to the query design.

e. Use the Report Wizard to create a report based on the Low Stock query. Include all the fields in the order listed. Select Supplier as the only sort field. Select the Tabular layout and a design style of your choice. Name the report **Stock Report**.

f. In Report Layout view, change the report design to Opulent. Adjust the column widths as needed to appropriately display the data. Center the data in the Special Order column. Change the left- and right-page margin setting to Normal and resize or move any controls that cause the report to overlap to a second page.

g. Preview and print the report. Close the Report window, saving the changes.

h. Compact and repair the database.

i. Back up the database. Exit Access.

Kodiak Construction Reports ★★

4. The database you created for Kodiak Construction (Step-by-Step Exercise 4 of Lab 2) has been very well received. Now that the database has been in use for a few months, several new requests have been made. You will create a query and a report to fulfill these requests. Your completed report should look similar to the report below.

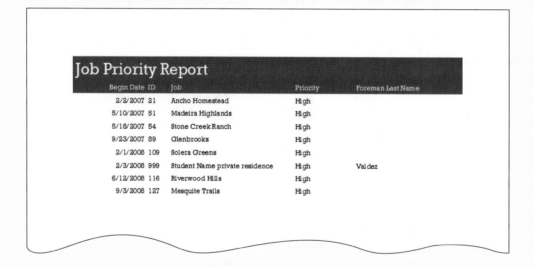

a. Open the database file named ac02_Kodiak Construction that you modified in Step-by-Step Exercise 4 of Lab 2.

b. Create a Parameter query named **Priority** that displays all fields from the Jobs table that have a high priority.

c. Create a report using the Priority query for those jobs with a high priority. Include the ID, Job, Priority, Begin Date, and Foreman Last Name fields. Sort the report by Begin Date. Use the tabular layout in portrait orientation and the Foundry style. Name the report **Job Priority Report**.

d. Change the page margins to Wide. Adjust the size of the report controls in Layout view to appropriately display the data.

e. Preview and print the report.

f. Clear all filters from the table. Close all objects.

g. Display the database relationships. Enforce referential integrity for all relationships. Create and print a relationships report.

h. Compact and repair the database. Save the changes and exit Access.

ARF Reports ★★★

5. The Animal Rescue Foundation volunteers are successfully using the database you created to enter information for all the rescued animals. Meanwhile, you created another table containing information about the foster homes (including names, addresses, and phone numbers). The Animal Rescue Foundation management has now asked you for a report, shown below, of all animals placed in foster homes in the past year (2008) and the names and addresses of those providing foster care, so the appropriate thank you notes can be sent. Your completed report will be similar to the report shown here.

2008 Foster Parents Report

Foster First Name	Foster Last Name	Foster Street	Foster City	Foster State	Foster Zip	Type
Gloria	Atherton	808 McDonald Rd.	Mesa	AZ	85205-0346	Dog
Bonnie	Brookfield	7 N. Williams Ave.	Tempe	AZ	86301-1268	Dog
Bonnie	Brookfield	7 N. Williams Ave.	Tempe	AZ	86301-1268	Cat
Fran	Calco	799 Summer St.	Tempe	AZ	86301-1268	Cat
Betty	Cavender	453 Orange St.	Tempe	AZ	85201-1268	Cat
Theresa	Fox	959 Price Rd.	Tempe	AZ	85201-1268	Cat
Theresa	Fox	959 Price Rd.	Tempe	AZ	85201-1268	Dog
Judith	Gold	663 Alameda Dr.	Scottsdale	AZ	85201-6760	Dog
Judith	Gold	663 Alameda Dr.	Scottsdale	AZ	85201-6760	Cat
Lucy	Granger	61 Lincoln Blvd.	Mesa	AZ	85205-0346	Pig
Bradley	Hawkins	789 University Ave.	Tempe	AZ	85201-1268	Dog
Mark	Lemon	900 Thomas Rd.	Phoenix	AZ	82891-9999	Dog
Susan	Malik	22 Sunrise Dr.	Mesa	AZ	85205-0346	Cat
Calvin	Summerset	912 N. Central Ave.	Phoenix	AZ	82891-9999	Goat
Calvin	Summerset	912 N. Central Ave.	Phoenix	AZ	82891-9999	Monkey
Ned	Young	387 Rawhide Rd.	Chandler	AZ	83174-2311	Cat

a. Open the database file named ac03_ARF3. Open both tables to review their content.

b. Find and delete any duplicate records in the Fosters table using the Last Name field as the field to check for duplicate data. Delete the duplicate records that have the highest Foster ID number.

c. Add your name as a new foster parent with the ID number 999.

d. To generate the requested information, you need to add a new field to the Rescues table that identifies the foster person that was assigned to the animal. Instead of checking the Fosters table to find the number and then entering the number in the Rescues table, you will make the new field a Lookup field that will display values from the Fosters table.

In Design view, add the **Foster ID#** field after the ID# field of the Rescues table. Select Lookup Wizard from the Data Type list. Select the following options from the LookUp Wizard:

- Look up values in a table.
- Use the Fosters table
- Display the Foster ID, Foster Last Name, and Foster First Name fields.
- Sort by the last and first names.
- Clear the Hide Key column option.
- Select Foster ID as the value to store.
- Use the Foster ID field name.

e. Switch to Datasheet view. Now you need to enter the Foster ID for all animals that were sent to a foster home. Query the datasheet to display only those records with a 2008 foster date or F in the Status column. Display the Foster ID, Status, and Foster Date columns only. From the Foster ID drop-down list, select a foster name for each record. Select your name as the foster parent for the last animal.

f. Next you will modify the query to display the information you need in the report. Add the Fosters tables to the query grid. Delete the Foster ID field from the grid. Add the following fields from the tables specified in the order listed below.

Rescues table

- Type

Fosters table

- Foster First Name
- Foster Last Name
- Foster Street
- Foster City
- Foster State
- Foster Zip

g. Sort the Foster Last Name column in ascending order. Hide the Status field. Run the query and review the resulting datasheet. Save the query as **2008 Foster Parents**.

h. Use the Report Wizard to create a report based on the 2008 Foster Parents query you just saved. Include the following fields in the order listed below:

- Foster First Name
- Foster Last Name
- Foster Street
- Foster City
- Foster State
- Foster Zip
- Type

i. View the data by Rescues, use the tabular layout, landscape orientation, and the Apex style. Name the report **2008 Foster Parents Report**.

j. Center the Report Header control at the top of the page. Change the design style to another of your choice. Change the page margin setting to Wide. Size the controls as needed to enhance the report appearance and fit the entire report on a single page.

k. Preview and then print the report. Close the report window, saving the changes you made.

l. Compact and repair the database.

m. Back up the database and exit Access.

Lab Exercises

Timeless Treasures Report ★

1. The owners of Timeless Treasures have decided to expand their offerings to include vintage clocks as well as watches. Open the database file Timeless Treasures that you worked on in Lab 2, On your Own exercise 5. Revisit the Web to obtain information on vintage clocks. Create a second table in the database with the same fields as the Watches table to use for maintaining the clock inventory. Name this table **Clocks**. Enter 10 records in the new table. Create an inventory report called **Timeless Treasures Watches Inventory** that displays the identification number, description, price and quantity on hand fields of information. Use a design style and layout of your choice. Modify the report design as needed to improve its appearance. Create the same report for the Clocks table and name it **Timeless Treasures Clocks Inventory**. Preview and print both reports. Compact and back up the database.

P&P W2 Forms ★

2. As an administrative assistant at Parker & Pisaño, Inc., you are responsible for sending out W2 forms to all of the employees. Create a database named P&P Employees and a table named **Employees** that includes fields for the employee ID number, first and last names and home contact information (Street, City, State, Zip Code and Phone). Enter 15 records in the table. Include your name as the employee name in one of the records. Then use this table to create a query that includes only the employee first and last name and home address fields of information. Sort the query by last name. Save the query as **Employee Addresses**. Create a report named **Employee Addresses** using the query as the record source. Use a design style and layout of your choice. Modify the report design as needed to improve its appearance. Compact and back up the database.

Learnsoft Developers ★★

3. Learnsoft Inc. develops computer-based curriculum for grades K-8. The company uses a database to track which software titles that have been worked on by the project managers. The program manager for the Learnsoft company wants a report of this information so he can use it for the employee reviews the following week. Open the database file ac03_Learnsoft and the table named Software. Add a new field named Project Manager before the Release Date field to include the name of the project manager for each title. Make this field a Lookup list field that will lookup the names of the five project managers. (Use names of your choice, but include your name as one of the project managers.) Complete the data for this field by selecting a project manager for each record. Assign your name as project manager to one of

the records with a release date in 2010. Create a report named **Project Manager Report** that shows the titles, subject and project manager names for the years 2009 through 2010. Use a design style and layout of your choice. Modify the report design as needed to improve its appearance. Compact and back up the database.

ARF Adoptions Report ★★★

4. The Animal Rescue Foundation would like you to create a report showing foster information. Open the database file ac03_ARF3 and the Rescues table. Add a new field before the Foster Date field named Foster Parent. Make it a Lookup field to the Foster ID field in the Fosters table. Edit the relationship to enforce referential integrity. Open the Fosters table and change the name for Foster ID F-001 to your name. For each record in the Rescues table that has a Foster Date entry, specify a Foster Parent by selecting a Foster ID. Make sure to include your Foster ID in at least one record. Add the Foster Parent field to above the Foster Date field in the ARF Animals form. Create a query that displays all fields from the Rescues table except the Photo Attachment field and the Foster First Name and Foster Last Name fields from the Fosters table. Sort the query by Foster Parent. Display the Foster First Name and Foster Last Name fields after the Foster Parent field. Name the query **Animal-Foster Query**. Create a report based on the Animal-Foster query that shows the Foster Date, Foster First Name, Foster Last Name, Type, Gender, Age and Name. Use a design style and layout of your choice. Modify the report design as needed to improve its appearance. Name the report **Foster Report**. Preview and print the report.

EMP Expense Account Report ★★

5. One of the department managers at EMP Enterprises has requested a report showing who in her department has submitted an expense reimbursement request but has not yet been paid. You decide this would be a good report to generate for all departments. In the EMP Enterprises database, open the Employee Expenses table you updated in On Your Own Exercise 2 of Lab 2. Create a one-to-many relationship between the Employee Info table and the Employee Expenses table based on the Employee ID fields. Enforce referential integrity and select the Cascade Update option. Create a query that displays all fields from both tables, sorted by Department. View the query results. Modify the query to not show the Employee ID field and to display only those employees who have not been paid. Apply an ascending sort to the Submission Date field. Save the query as **Pending Payment**. Use the Report Wizard to create a report named **Open Expense Requests** based on the Pending Payment query. Use a design style and layout of your choice. Modify the report design as needed to improve its appearance. Preview and print the report. Compact and back up the database.

Working Together 1: Exporting Data

Lifestyle Fitness Club

Periodically, the club director wants to know the names of the employees at each club and their job position. You created a parameter query to obtain this information and then a custom report to display it professionally. Now you want to provide this information to the director.

You will learn about exporting Access data to Excel and Word using the Export Wizard. Then you will learn how to copy and paste objects and selections between Access and Word to create a memo to the director.

Your memo containing a copy of the query results and the report generated by Access will look like the one shown here.

Note: This tutorial assumes that you already know how to use Office Word 2007 and that you have completed Lab 3 of Access 2007.

Lifestyle Fitness Club

Memo

To:	Club Director
From:	Student Name
Date:	October 8, 2008
Re:	Job Positions

You recently asked me for a list of employees at each Club location and their job positions. I was easily able to gather this information using Access 2007. This memo contains the information for the Landis location. Below this paragraph is the output from the query I used to gather this information.

Location Query

Employee ID	First Name	Last Name	Location	Position
00212	Chad	Schiff	Landis	Club Director
03225	Dan	Morgan	Landis	Food Service Director
03890	Erona	Thi	Landis	Fitness Director
05015	Scot	Briggs	Landis	Personal Trainer Director
07287	Anita	Roman	Landis	Child Care Director
07650	Chris	Lamm	Landis	Sales Director
12380	Jessica	Thomas	Landis	Fitness Instructor
12389	Jennifer	Blackman	Landis	Sales Associate
12420	Allison	Player	Landis	Maintenance
12501	Elizabeth	DeLuca	Landis	Personal Trainer
12583	Marie	Sullivan	Landis	Greeter
12703	Jeff	Bader	Landis	Fitness Instructor
12855	Kimberly	Fachet	Landis	Sales Associate
12914	Alfonso	Gomez	Landis	Cleaning
12918	Carlos	Ruiz	Landis	Assistant Manager
13005	Emily	Reilly	Landis	Assistant Manager
13027	Kimberly	Kieken	Landis	Food Service Server
13303	Chris	Jensen	Landis	Greeter
13484	Stephanie	Franklin	Landis	Food Service Server
13635	Juan	Martinez	Landis	Fitness Instructor

Location Query

Employee ID	First Name	Last Name	Location	Position
22085	Kristina	Lindau	Landis	Child Care Provider
22297	Patricia	Rogondino	Landis	Greeter
22469	Ryan	Hogan	Landis	Personal Trainer
99999	Student	Name	Landis	Human Resources Administrator

Below this paragraph is a report that was generated from the Landis Location query. It displays the same information in a professional style report.

Job Position Report

Employee ID	First Name	Position	Last Name
00212	Chad	Club Director	Schiff
03225	Dan	Food Service Director	Morgan
03890	Erona	Fitness Director	Thi
05015	Scot	Personal Trainer Director	Briggs
07287	Anita	Child Care Director	Roman
07650	Chris	Sales Director	Lamm
12380	Jessica	Fitness Instructor	Thomas
12389	Jennifer	Sales Associate	Blackman
12420	Allison	Maintenance	Player
12501	Elizabeth	Personal Trainer	DeLuca
12583	Marie	Greeter	Sullivan
12703	Jeff	Fitness Instructor	Bader
12855	Kimberly	Sales Associate	Fachet
12914	Alfonso	Cleaning	Gomez
12918	Carlos	Assistant Manager	Ruiz
13005	Emily	Assistant Manager	Reilly
13027	Kimberly	Food Service Server	Kieken
13303	Chris	Greeter	Jensen
13484	Stephanie	Food Service Server	Franklin
13635	Juan	Fitness Instructor	Martinez
22085	Kristina	Child Care Provider	Lindau
22297	Patricia	Greeter	Rogondino
22469	Ryan	Personal Trainer	Hogan
99999	Student	Human Resources Administrator	Name

I have also found that I can easily provide the same information to you in and Excel workbook. This is convenient if you want to analyze the information. Please let me know which of the above two formats you would like me to use to provide the information for the other locations in and if you would also like it as an Excel workbook.

MORE ABOUT

 To learn how to save database objects as other file types, see "5 Presenting and Sharing Data" in the More About appendix.

Exporting Data

There are often circumstances when you will want to provide data from an Access database to someone else to use. The process of copying this information to a file outside the database is called **exporting.** There are a variety of methods you can use, depending upon the type of output needed. The most common export types are described below:

Export to	Description
Excel	Creates a copy of the selected data, table, query, or form object and stores the copy in an Excel worksheet.
Word	Creates a copy of the selected data, table, query, form, or report, including formatting, in a new Word (*.rtf) file.
Access database	Creates a copy of the table definition and data or just the table definition in another Access database.
Text file	Creates a copy of the selected data, table, query, form, or report, approximating formatting if possible, in a new text file (*.txt) document.
SharePoint site	Creates a copy of a table or query and stores it on a SharePoint site as a list.

MORE ABOUT

To learn about exporting to another Access database, see "2.2 Create Tables" in the More About appendix.

The director does not have Access 2007 installed on his computer, so you need to export the data in either Word 2007 or Excel 2007 format. You will try both methods to see what the output in each application looks like.

The Export Wizard is used for all types of exports. In addition, in some cases, you can copy and paste an object in another application. The file that you export from is the **source file** and the file that is created is the **destination file.**

Additional Information

Only one object can be exported at a time.

Additional Information

If you want to export a selection, you need to open the object and select the records you want to export.

Exporting to Excel 2007

When exporting to Excel, the database file you want to copy from must be open in Access. Then you select the object you want to export. The Export Wizard can copy selected data, a table, a query, or a form object, but it cannot export a report to Excel. Because you cannot export a report, you will export the Job Positions query instead.

1
- Start Access 2007 and open the database file acwt1_Personnel **from your data file location.**

- **If necessary, respond appropriately to the Security Warning.**

- **Select the Location Query in the Navigation pane.**

- **Click** ![Excel] **in the Export group of the External Data tab.**

Your screen should be similar to Figure 1

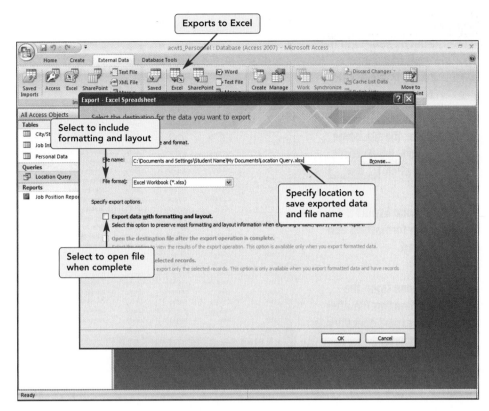

Figure 1

In the first Export - Excel Spreadsheet wizard dialog box, you specify the name of the destination file and the file format. The default file format of an Excel 2007 workbook file is acceptable; however, you need to change the file location and name. In addition, you want to include the formatting from the query object and want to see the new Excel workbook file after it is created. Because the query is a parameter query, you also will be asked to enter the location you want to copy to the destination.

2

- Click 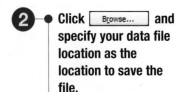 Browse... and specify your data file location as the location to save the file.

- Enter the file name Landis Job Positions and click  Save .

- Choose Export data with formatting and layout.

- Choose Open the destination file after the export operation is complete.

- Click OK .

- Enter **Landis** in the Parameter Value dialog box.

- Click OK .

- If necessary, maximize the Excel application window.

Your screen should be similar to Figure 2

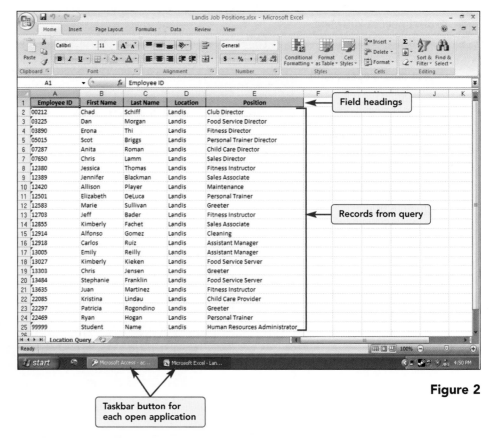

Figure 2

Now there are two applications open, Excel and Access, and application buttons for both open windows are displayed in the taskbar. The Excel 2007 application window is displayed and the exported data has been copied into a worksheet of the new workbook file. The field headings appear formatted in the first row of the worksheet and each following row is a record from the query datasheet. Notice that the Microsoft Access button in the taskbar is flashing. This is to tell you that the wizard is not yet done.

3 ● **Click on the Microsoft Access button in the taskbar to switch to the Access application window.**

Your screen should be similar to Figure 3

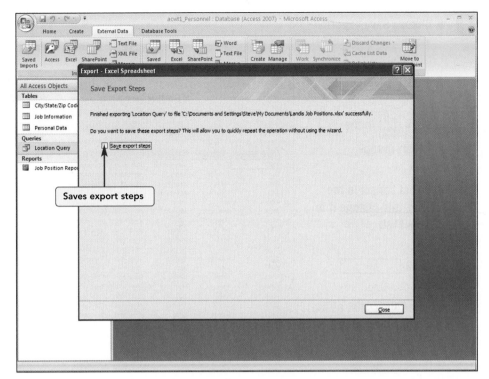

Figure 3

The final step tells you the export has been completed successfully and asks if you want to save the export steps. Saving the steps is useful if you think you will be running the same export operation on a routine basis. Since you need to repeat this operation for each location, you will save the steps using the suggested name. The wizard also can add a reminder for you in Outlook to run the export if you need to generate the results on a routine basis. You will not include this feature at this time.

Next, you will rerun the export operation to export the River Mist location data by selecting the name of the saved export steps from a list of saved exports. You also will need to edit the file name to reflect the location data and to save the exported data to a new file.

4 • Choose Save export steps.

• Click [Save Export].

• Click 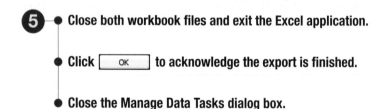 in the Export group.

• Select Landis in the path and change it to River Mist.

• Click [Run].

• Enter River Mist as the location parameter.

• Click [OK].

Your screen should be similar to Figure 4

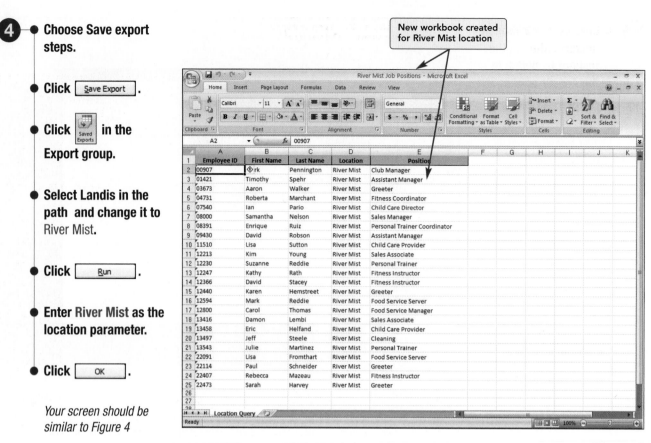

Figure 4

A separate workbook file was created and contains the data for the River Mist location. Now, all the Excel features can be used to analyze the data in the worksheets. After exporting each location to a workbook, you could combine the workbooks by copying the worksheet data from each worksheet into one workbook file.

5 • Close both workbook files and exit the Excel application.

• Click [OK] to acknowledge the export is finished.

• Close the Manage Data Tasks dialog box.

Exporting to Word 2007

Next, you will try exporting the Job Position Report to a Word document. When you use the Export Wizard to do this, a copy of the object's data is inserted into a Microsoft Word Rich Text Format file (.rtf).

1 • Select the Job Position Report in the Navigation pane.

• Click  in the Export group.

• If necessary, change the file location to your data file location.

Having Trouble?
The report will be saved using the default file name of Job Position Report.

• Choose Open the destination files after the export operation is complete.

• Click **OK**.

• Enter Landis in the Enter Parameter Value dialog box.

• Click **OK**.

Your screen should be similar to Figure 5

Having Trouble?
If WordPad is the open application, this is because your system has associated .rtf file types with this application. You could close WordPad and open the document in Word 2007.

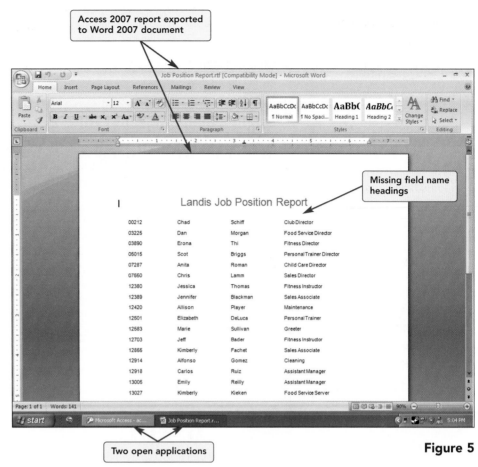

Access 2007 report exported to Word 2007 document

Missing field name headings

Two open applications

Figure 5

Now there are two applications open, Word 2007 and Access 2007, and application buttons for both open windows are displayed in the taskbar. The Word 2007 application window is displayed and the exported data has been copied into a document file and saved as Job Positions Report. The report resembles the Access report as closely as possible. The problem with the exported report is that the field name headings are missing.

Again, the Microsoft Access button in the taskbar is flashing. This time you will not save the steps.

② ● Switch to the Access application window.

● Click [Close] to close the Export Wizard.

Copying a Query Object to Word 2007

Finally, you decide to try copying an Access object to an existing Word document without using the Export Wizard. To do this, you use Copy and Paste or drag and drop between the Access and Word applications to copy a database object.

You have already started a memo to the club director about the Job Position query and report you created.

① ● Switch to the Word application window and close the Job Position Report document.

● Open the document acwt1_Job Positions.

● In the memo header, replace Student Name with your name.

Your screen should be similar to Figure 6

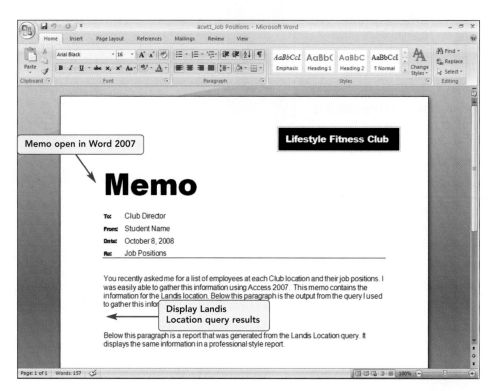

Figure 6

This document contains the text of the memo to the director. Below the first paragraph, you want to copy the output from the Landis Location query results using drag and drop. To do this, both applications must be open and visible, which you will do by tiling the application windows.

2 Right-click on a blank area of the taskbar to open the shortcut menu.

Having Trouble?
If your taskbar is hidden, point to the thin line at the bottom of the screen to redisplay it.

● Choose Tile Windows Vertically.

● Click in the Word application window.

Your screen should be similar to Figure 7

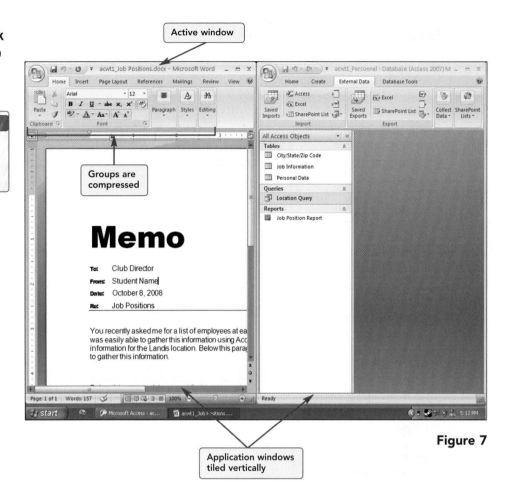

Figure 7

You can now see the contents of both the Access and Word applications. The Word document contains the insertion point and the window title bar text is not dimmed, which indicates that it is the **active window,** or the window in which you can work. Simply clicking on the other document makes it active. Because the windows are side by side and there is less horizontal space in each window, the Ribbon groups are compressed. To access commands in these groups, simply click on the group button and the commands appear in a drop-down list.

You will copy the query results to below the first paragraph of the memo.

3 ● Select the Location Query in the Access Navigation pane.

● Drag the selected object to the blank line below the first paragraph of the memo.

Having Trouble?

An insertion point appears and the mouse pointer is ⊡ when you can release the mouse.

● Enter **Landis** as the Location parameter and click [OK].

● Click in the Word document to deselect the table.

● Scroll the document to see the table.

Your screen should be similar to Figure 8

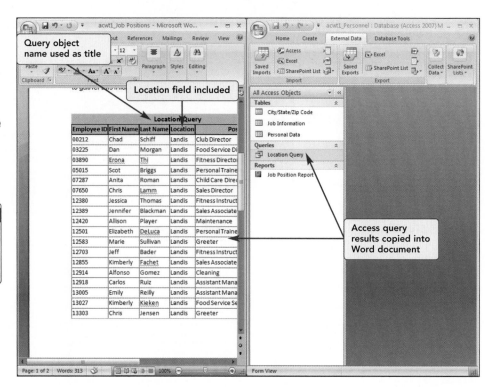

Figure 8

The query results have been copied into the Word document as a table that can be edited and manipulated within Word. The formatting associated with the copied object also is included. However, the title is the same as the query name and the Location field is displayed. To change this, you could edit the title and then delete the table column using Word 2007.

Copying a Report

Instead, you want to copy the report into the memo to see how it will look. To copy report data, you run the report in Access and then use copy and paste to copy the contents to a Word document.

1 ● Open the Job Position Report in Access using Landis as the location.

● Hide the Navigation pane.

● Select the report title and drag downward along the left edge of the rows to select the entire report, excluding the footer information.

● Open the Home tab and click 🗐 Copy in the Clipboard group.

Your screen should be similar to Figure 9

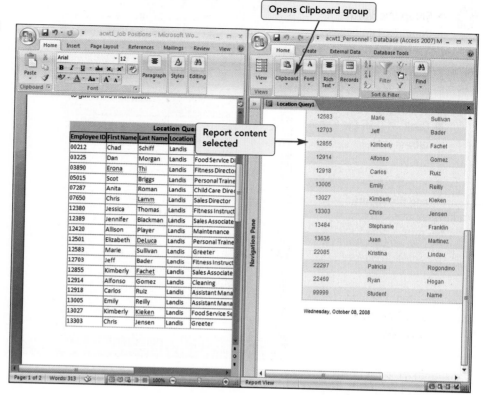

Opens Clipboard group

Report content selected

Figure 9

Next, you need to select the location in the memo where you want the copied data inserted.

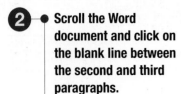

2 • Scroll the Word document and click on the blank line between the second and third paragraphs.

• Click 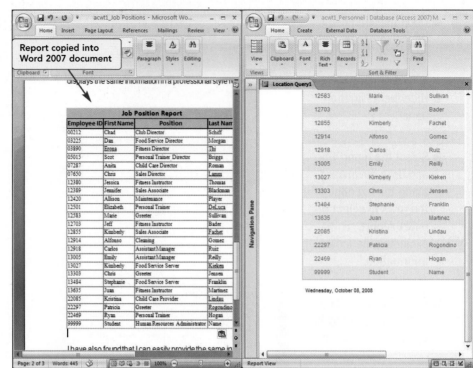Paste in the Home tab.

• Scroll the document to see the report.

Your screen should be similar to Figure 10

Figure 10

The copied report is similar to the copied query, except the correct title was included and the Location row is not included as specified by the report settings.

3 • Close the report in Access.

• Click No to not save the copied data that was placed on the Clipboard.

• Display the Navigation pane.

• Undo the tiled windows.

Having Trouble?
Choose Undo Tile from the taskbar shortcut menu.

• Exit Access.

• Delete the blank line above both tables in the memo.

• Save the memo as Job Positions.

• Preview, and then print the memo.

• Exit Word.

Your printed memo should look similar to the one shown in the Case Study at the beginning of this lab.

Lab Review

WORKING TOGETHER 1
Exporting Data

key terms

active window ACWT1.9
destination file ACWT1.2

export ACWT1.2
source file ACWT1.2

MCAS skills

The Microsoft Certified Applications Specialist (MCAS) certification program is designed to measure your proficiency in performing basic tasks using the Office 2007 applications. Getting certified demonstrates that you have the skills and provides a valuable industry credential for employment. See Reference 2: Microsoft Certified Applications Specialist (MCAS) for a complete list of the skills that were covered in this lab.

command summary

Command	Shortcut	Action
Home tab		
Clipboard group		
▣ Copy	Ctrl + C	Copies selection to Clipboard
External Data tab		
Saved Exports		View and run saved exports
Excel		Exports selected object to an Excel workbook
Word		Exports selected object to a Rich Text Format file

Hands-On Exercises

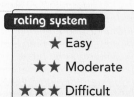
Spa Marketing Memo ★

1. The Scensations Salon and Spa database has been used extensively. The owner asked you for a list of clients who are over the age of 40 to get an idea of how much interest there would be in an anti-aging spa package she is considering offering. You already filtered the Clients table to locate this information and now want to include the results in a memo to Latisha. The first page of the memo is shown here.

a. Open the ac03_Scensations Spa database file and the Clients table that you modified in Step-by-Step Exercise 1 of Lab 3. Display the results of the 40+ Clients query.

b. Start Word 2007 and enter the following text in a new document.

> **To: Latisha Pine**
>
> **From: [Your Name]**
>
> **Date: [current date]**
>
> **Here is the information you requested on the clients who are over the age of 40:**

c. Select the query results and copy them into the Word document.

d. Save the memo as 40+ Spa Clients. Print the memo.

e. Close the document and exit Word.

f. Close the table and database.

To: Latisha Pine
From: Student Name
Date: Current Date

Here is the information you requested on the clients who are over the age of 40:

40+ Clients			
First Name	**Last Name**	**Address**	**Lookup to City/Sate/Zip**
Mary	Smith	560 E. West	89430, Smith Valley , NV
Patricia	Johnson	24486 S. 11th	89430, Smith Valley , NV
Linda	Williams	495 W. Cherry	89430, Smith Valley , NV
Barbara	Jones	738 N. Eighth	89430, Smith Valley , NV
Elizabeth	Brown	1008 E. Adams	89430, Smith Valley , NV
Jennifer	Davis	984 N. 7th	89430, Smith Valley , NV
Maria	Miller	448 E. Williams	89430, Smith Valley , NV
Margaret	Moore	246 N. 1st	89430, Smith Valley , NV
Dorothy	Taylor	1238 E. Fifth	89430, Smith Valley , NV
Lisa	Anderson	7428 S. Hill	89447, Yerington , NV
Nancy	Thomas	6190 E. Main	89447, Yerington , NV
Karen	Jackson	4952 S. Ridge	89706, Mound House , NV
Betty	White	3714 E. Washington	89706, Mound House , NV
Helen	Harris	246 N. 6th	89706, Mound House , NV
Heather	Morris	385 E. 5th	89403, Dayton , NV
Teresa	Rogers	55 N. 2nd	89403, Dayton , NV
Doris	Reed	10494 N. Forest	89403, Dayton , NV
Gloria	Cook	224 E. Laurel	89403, Dayton , NV
Evelyn	Morgan	6190 N. Ninth	89403, Dayton , NV
Mildred	Bailey	31482 E. Smith	89403, Dayton , NV
Katherine	Rivera	123 N. Willow	89403, Dayton , NV
Christina	Ramirez	492 N. First	89403, Dayton , NV
Beverly	Brooks	13992 S. River	89403, Dayton , NV
Andrea	Henderson	8666 N. 9th	89403, Dayton , NV
Kathryn	Coleman	784 E. Fourteenth	89403, Dayton , NV
Anne	Powell	112 E. Forest	89408, Fernley , NV
Tina	Simmons	27984 W. 14th	89408, Fernley , NV
Phyllis	Foster	27984 W. Dogwood	89408, Fernley , NV
Norma	Gonzales	9904 E. Elm	89408, Fernley , NV
Diana	Alexander	246 E. 9th	89408, Fernley , NV
Annie	Russell	123 E. 3rd	89408, Fernley , NV
Emily	Diaz	330 N. 3rd	89408, Fernley , NV

Low Stock Analysis ★★

2. Evan, the owner of the Downtown Internet Café, continues to be impressed with the cafe's inventory database (Step-by-Step Exercise 3 of Lab 3). He has asked you for a list of all special-order items and how many of these items are currently in stock. He wants this information as an Excel 2007 worksheet so that he can further analyze the data. You will provide this information by exporting the data from Access 2007 to Excel 2007. Your completed worksheet of this data should be similar to that shown here.

a. Open the ac03_Cafe Inventory database that you modified in Step-by-Step Exercise 3 of Lab 3.

b. Create a new query named Special Orders that will display items with Y in the Special Order? field, and include the Description, In Stock, Special Order?, and Supplier fields (in that order). Run the query. Save the query.

Description	In Stock	Special Order?	Supplier
Powdered cream	31	Y	ABC Restaurant Supply
T-Shirts	10	Y	By Design
Decaf Viennese	33	Y	Pure Processing
Decaf Sumatra	35	Y	Pure Processing
Business cards	43	Y	Pro Printing
Coffee mints	30	Y	Sweet Stuff
French Roast	47	Y	Café Ole
Guatamala coffee	45	Y	Cuppa Jo
Java coffee	46	Y	Cuppa Jo
Arabian coffee	47	Y	Cuppa Jo
Espresso	11	Y	Cuppa Jo
Darjeeling Tea	13	Y	Tea and Toast, Inc.

c. Export the data to Excel using the file name Special Orders.

d. Save the export steps.

e. Change the In-Stock in the query for T-Shirts to **10** and Coffee mints to **30**. Rerun the export using the saved steps, replacing the Special Orders file.

f. Print the worksheet. Exit Excel.

g. Save the query. Close the table and database.

Lab Exercises

Top Priority Jobs Memo ★★

3. The Job Audit report you created for Kodiak Construction needs to be sent to the company president. (See Step-by-Step Exercise 4 of Lab 3.) You want to include a brief note with the report and decide to export the report to a memo you create using Word. Your completed memo should be similar to that shown here.

a. Open the ac02_Kodiak Construction database and the Priority query showing the high-priority jobs that you modified in Step-by-Step Exercise 4 of Lab 3. Modify the query to show only the ID, Job, Begin Date, and Foreman Last Name fields and beginning dates of 2008 only.

To: Kevin Lindquist, President

From: Student Name

Date: Current Date

Here is the information you requested on high priority jobs that were started in 2008.

ID	Job	Begin Date	Foreman Last Name
109	Solera Greens	2/1/2008	
116	Riverwood Hills	6/12/2008	
127	Mesquite Trails	9/3/2008	
999	Student Name private residence	2/3/2008	Valdez

b. Export the Priority query results to a Word document.

c. Enter the following text above the table in the document.

   To: Kevin Lindquist, President

   From: [Your Name]

   Date: [current date]

   Here is the information you requested on high priority jobs that were started in 2008.

d. Apply formatting of your choice to the table. Size and center the table appropriately.

e. Save the memo as Kodiak Top Priority. Print the document.

f. Save the query changes. Close the table and database.

Access 2007
Command Summary

Command	Shortcut	Action
🔘 **Office Button**		**Opens File menu**
New		Opens a new blank database
Open	Ctrl + O	Opens an existing database
Save	Ctrl + S	Saves database object ·
Save As	F12	Saves database object with a new file name
Print/Print	Ctrl + P	Specifies print settings and prints current database object
Print/Print Preview		Displays file as it will appear when printed
Manage/Compact and Repair		Compacts and repairs database file
Manage/Back Up Database		Backs up database
Manage/Database Properties		Allows changes to database properties
Close Database		Closes open window
⬚ Access Options		Specifies program settings
✕ Exit Access		Closes Access 2007 application
Quick Access Toolbar		
↩ Undo	Ctrl + Z	Cancels last action
🖫 Save	Ctrl + S	Saves the current object
Home tab		
Views group		
◩ Design View	◩	Displays object in Design view
▥ Datasheet View	▥	Displays object in Datasheet view
▤ Form View	▤	Changes to Form view
▦ Form Layout View	▦	Changes to Form Layout view
▦ Report View	▦	Displays report in Report view
▦ Report Layout View	▦	Displays report in Layout view
Clipboard group		
✂ Cut	Ctrl + X	Removes selected item and copies it to the Clipboard
⧉ Copy	Ctrl + C	Duplicates selected item and copies to the Clipboard
📋 Paste	Ctrl + V	Inserts copy of item from Clipboard

Command	Shortcut	Action
Font group		
B Bold	Ctrl + B	Applies bold effect to all text in datasheet
A · Font Color		Applies selected color to all text in datasheet
Gridlines		Changes gridline color of datasheet
Alternate Fill/Back Color		Changes background color of datasheet
Records group		
Refresh All ·		Updates display of data
New	Ctrl + +	Adds new record
Save	⇧ Shift + ←Enter	Saves changes to records
✕ Delete ·	Delete	Deletes current record
Σ Totals		Displays/hides Totals row
More · /Hide Columns		Hides columns in Datasheet
More · /Unhide Columns		Redisplays hidden columns
More · /Column Width		Adjusts width of selected column
Sort & Filter group		
Ascending		Changes sort order to ascending
Descending		Changes sort order to descending
Clear All Sorts		Clears all sorts and returns sort order to primary key order
Filter		Allows multiple filter criteria in a single field
Selection · /Equals		Displays only those records containing selected value
Advanced · /Clear all Filters		Removes all filters from table
▼ Toggle Filter		Applies and removes filter from table
Find group		
Find	Ctrl + F	Locates specified data
Replace	Ctrl + H	Locates specified data and replaces it with specified replacement text
⇒ Go To ·		Moves to First, Previous, Next, Last, or New record location
Select · /Select		Selects current record
Select · /Select All		Selects all records in database
Create tab		
Tables group		
Table		Creates a new table in Datasheet view
Table Design		Creates a new table in Design view

Command	Shortcut	Action
Forms group		
Form		Creates a new form using all the fields from the underlying table
Blank Form		Displays a blank form to which you add the fields from the table that you want to appear on the form
More Forms /Form Wizard		Creates a new form by following the steps in the Form Wizard
Reports group		
Report		Creates a report using all fields in current table
Blank Report		Creates a report using Report Design view
Report Wizard		Creates a report using the Report Wizard
Other group		
Query Wizard		Creates a query using the Query Wizard
Query Design		Creates a query using Query Design view

External Data tab

Command	Shortcut	Action
Export group		
Saved Exports		View and run saved exports
Excel		Exports selected object to an Excel workbook
Word		Exports selected object to a Rich Text Format file

Database Tools tab

Command	Shortcut	Action
Show/Hide group		
Relationships		Define how the data in tables is related
Property Sheet		Specifies general properties associated with the database file
Object Dependencies		Shows the objects in the database that use the selected object
Analyze group		
Database Documenter		Creates a report showing object properties and settings
Analyze Table		Evaluates table design

Table Tools Datasheet tab

Command	Shortcut	Action
Views group		
Design View		Displays table in Design view
Datasheet View		Displays table in Datasheet view

Command	Shortcut	Action
Fields & Columns group		
New Field		Inserts a new field
Delete		Removes selected field column
Rename		Renames selected field
Lookup Column		Creates a lookup column
Data Type & Formatting group		
Data Type: Text		Changes the data type for current field

Table Tools Design tab

Command	Shortcut	Action
Views group		
Design View		Displays table in Design view
Datasheet View		Displays table in Datasheet view
Tools group		
Primary Key		Makes current field a primary key field
Insert Rows		Inserts a new field in Table Design view
Delete Rows		Deletes selected field row

Form Layout Tools Format tab

Command	Shortcut	Action
Views group		
Form view		Displays form in Form view
Form Layout view		Displays form in Layout view
AutoFormat group		
More		Displays gallery of form design styles

Form Layout Tools Arrange tab

Command	Shortcut	Action
Control layout group		
Remove		Removes selected control
Position group		
Bring to Front		Brings selected control to top of stack

Query Tools Design tab

Command	Shortcut	Action
Results group		
Run		Displays query results in Query Datasheet view
Query Setup group		
Show Table		Displays/hides Show Table dialog box
Show/Hide group		
Table Names		Displays/hides the Tables row

Command	Shortcut	Action
Report Layout Tools Format tab		
Views group		
Report View		Displays report in Report view
Report Layout View		Displays report in Report Layout view
Report Design View		Displays report in Report Design view
Font group		
Center		Centers text in selected control
Controls group		
Add Existing Fields		Displays/hides Add Existing Fields task pane
AutoFormat group		
AutoFormat		Applies selected predesigned styles to report
Report Layout Tools Page Setup tab		
Page Layout group		
Margins		Sets margins of printed report
Page Setup		Sets features related to the page layout of printed report
Report Design Tools Design tab		
Font group		
Center		Centers text in selected control
20 Size		Sizes text in selected control
Tools group		
Add Existing Fields		Displays/hides the Fields List task pane
Relationship Tools Design tab		
Tools group		
Relationship Report		Creates a report of the displayed relationships
Print Preview Tab		
Print group		
Print		Prints displayed object
Page Layout group		
Portrait		Changes print orientation to portrait
Landscape		Changes print orientation to landscape
Margins		Sets margins of printed output

Command	Shortcut	Action
Zoom group		
One Page		Displays one entire page in Print Preview
Two Pages		Displays two entire pages in Print Preview
Close Preview group		
Close Print Preview		Closes Print Preview window

Glossary of Key Terms

Action query A query that is used to make changes to many records in a table at once.

active window The window you can work in when multiple application windows are displayed on the screen at the same time.

aggregate functions Calculations that are performed on a range of data.

Allow Zero Length property Specified if an entry containing no characters is valid.

AND operator Used in criteria expression to narrow a search by specifying that a record must meet both conditions to be included.

ascending sort order Data that is arranged in A to Z or 0 to 9 order.

attachment control A control for a field that has an attachment data type.

Attachment data type Data type that allows multiple files of different types to be attached to a field.

AutoNumber data type Data type that enters a unique sequential number for each record as it is added to a table.

Best Fit feature A feature that automatically adjusts column width to fit the longest entry.

bound control A control that is linked to a field in an underlying table.

Caption property A property that specifies the field label other than the field name.

cell The intersection of a row and column in a datasheet where field data is entered.

character string A group of text characters.

Clipboard A temporary storage area in memory where copied or cut data is stored.

column selector bar In Query Design view, the thin gray bar just above the field name in the grid.

column width The size of a field column in Datasheet view. It controls the amount of data you can see on the screen.

common field A field that is found in two or more tables. It must have the same data type and the same kind of information in each table but may have different field names.

compact To make a copy of the database file and rearrange how the file is stored on disk for optimal performance.

comparison operator A symbol used in expressions that allows you to make comparisons. The > (greater than) and < (less than) symbols are examples of comparison operators.

composite key A primary key that uses more than one field.

compound control Controls that are associated and act as one when manipulated.

compound criterion Used to instruct the query to locate records meeting multiple criteria. The AND and OR operators are used to create a compound criterion.

control An object in a form or report that displays information, performs actions, or enhances the design.

criteria Limiting conditions that are used when specifying the information you want to appear in the query results.

criteria expression An expression that will select only the records that meet certain limiting criteria.

Crosstab query A query that summarizes large amounts of data in an easy-to-read, row-and-column format.

Currency data type Data type that allows entry of digits only and formats them to display decimal places and a currency symbol.

current field The field that is selected and will be affected by any changes you make.

current record The record containing the insertion point and that will be affected by the next action.

data type Attribute for a field that determines what type of data it can contain.

database An organized collection of related information.

Datasheet view View used to display table data or query results in a row and column format.

Date/Time data type Data type that accepts date and time entries only.

Default Value property A property used to specify a value that is automatically entered in a field when a new record is created.

descending sort order Data that is arranged in Z to A or 9 to 0 order.

design grid The lower part of the Query Design window, which displays settings that are used to define the query.

Design view View that is used to create or modify the structure of a table, form, query, or report.

destination The location where cut or copied data is inserted.

destination file The document in which a linked object is inserted.

drawing object A simple graphic consisting of shapes such as lines and boxes that can be created using a drawing program such as Paint.

export The process of copying data, tables, queries, forms, or report objects to a file outside the database.

expression A combination of operators, identifiers, and values that produce a result.

field A single category of data in a table, the values of which appear in a column of a datasheet.

field list In Query Design view, a list box that lists all the fields in the record source table. In Report Design view, a task pane that displays all the fields in the record source table.

field name A label used to identify the data stored in a field.

field property An attribute of a field that affects its appearance or behavior.

Field Size property Field property that limits a Text data type to a certain size or limits numeric data to values within a specific range.

field template A set of predefined fields from which you can select. Each field includes a field name, data type, and format settings that control the behavior and display of the field data.

filter A restriction placed on records in an open form or datasheet to temporarily isolate a subset of records.

Find and Replace A feature that helps you quickly find specific information and automatically replace it with new information.

foreign key A field that refers to the primary key field in another table.

form A database object used primarily to display records onscreen to make it easier to enter new records and make changes to existing records.

Form view View used to display records in a form.

format To enhance the appearance of the document to make it more readable or attractive.

Format property A property that specifies the way data is displayed.

graphic A nontext element or object, such as a drawing or picture, that can be added to a table.

hard-coded criteria Criteria that are entered in the criteria cell and are used each time the query is run.

header row The row at the top of a datasheet that displays the field names.

Hyperlink data type Data type that accepts hyperlink entries.

identifier A part of an expression that refers to the value of a field, a graphic object, or a property.

Indexed property Sets the field to an indexed field that controls the order of the records.

inner join Tells a query that rows from one of the joined tables correspond to rows in the other table on the basis of the data in the joined fields.

Input Mask property Restricts data that can be entered in a field to the entries you specify and controls the way the data is displayed.

join An association between fields of the same data type in multiple tables or queries.

join line In the Query Design window, the line that joins the common fields between one or more table field lists.

junction table When an association between two tables is created in which one record in either table can relate to many records in the other table, a third table, called a junction table, is used to hold the primary key fields from the other two tables and serves as a bridge between them.

label control   An unbound control that displays descriptive labels.

landscape orientation   Printing orientation that prints across the length of the page.

layout   Designs that control how data is displayed in a form or report.

Layout view   View used to display data while allowing modifications to the design and layout of the table, query, form, or report object.

lookup field   A field that lets you choose from a list of values you entered or that are from another table or query.

lookup list   The list of values from which you select when using a lookup field.

Lookup Wizard   Creates a lookup field.

many-to-many   A type of relationship in which there is an association between two tables where one record in either table can relate to many records in the other table.

margin   The blank space around the edge of a page.

Memo data type   Allows up to 1GB of characters or 2GB of storage in a field of which 65,535 characters can be displayed. Entries in this field can be formatted.

multitable query   A query that uses more than one table.

navigation buttons   Used to move through records in Datasheet and Form views. Also available in the Print Preview window.

Navigation pane   The pane to the left of the work area that is used to open and manage database objects.

normal form   A set of constraints or standards that must be satisfied to meet normalization.

normalization   A design technique that identifies and eliminates redundancy by applying a set of rules to your tables to confirm that they are structured properly.

Number data type   Data type that allows storage of digits only in a field.

object   A table, form, or report that can be selected and manipulated as a unit.

OLE Object data type   Use in fields to store an object such as a graphic (picture), sound, document, or graph.

one-to-many   A type of relationship in which there is an association between two tables where each record in the first table contains a field value that corresponds to the field value of many records in the other table.

one-to-one   A type of relationship in which there is an association between two tables where each record in the first table contains a field value that corresponds to the field value of one record in the other table.

operator   A symbol or word used to specify the type of calculation to perform in an expression.

OR operator   Used in a criteria expression to broaden a search by specifying that a record may include either condition in the output.

orientation   The direction the paper prints, either landscape or portrait.

outer join   Specifies that although some of the rows on both sides of the join correspond exactly, the query should include all rows from one table even if there is no match in the other table.

Parameter query   A query that displays a dialog box prompting you for the criteria information you want the query to use.

parameter value   In a Parameter query, the value that is entered in the criteria cell rather than a specific value. The parameter value tells the query to prompt you for the specific criteria you want to use when you run the query.

picture   An illustration such as a scanned photograph.

portrait orientation   Printing orientation that prints the report across the width of a page.

primary key   One or more fields in a table that uniquely identify a record.

Print Preview   View that displays a datasheet, form, or report as it will appear when printed.

query   Used to view data in different ways, to analyze data, and to change data.

record   A row of a table, consisting of a group of related fields.

record number indicator   A small box that displays the current record number in the lower-left corner of most views. The record number indicator is surrounded by the navigation buttons.

record source   The table or query that is the underlying source of data for a form or report.

referential integrity   Rules that ensure that relationships between tables are valid and that related data is not accidentally changed or deleted.

relational database   A database in which a relationship is created by having a common field in the tables. The common field lets you extract and combine data from multiple tables.

relationship   A relationship establishes the association between common fields in two tables.

report   Professional-appearing output generated from tables or queries that may include design elements, groups, and summary information.

Report view   View that displays the data in a report.

required property   Specifies whether a value must be entered in a field.

row label   In the design grid of Query Design view, identifies the type of information that can be entered in the row.

Select All button   The square to the left of each row in Datasheet view that is used to select an entire record.

Select query   A type of query that retrieves the specific data you request from one or more tables, then displays the data in a datasheet.

serial value   Sequential numbers assigned to each day beginning with January 1, 1900, whose serial number is 1 through December 31, 9999, whose serial number is 2958465.

Show box   A box in the Show row of the design grid that, when checked, indicates that the field will be displayed in the query result.

sort   To temporarily reorder table records in the datasheet.

source   The data that is copied or cut; the underlying table that provides the values in a lookup list.

source file   The document in which a linked object was created.

SQL query   A query that is created using SQL (Structured Query Language).

stacked layout   A layout that arranges data vertically with a field label to the left of the field data.

subdatasheet   A data table nested in another data table that contains data related or joined to the table where it resides.

tab order   The order in which Access moves through a form or table when the ⟨Tab⇆⟩ key is pressed.

table   Consists of vertical columns and horizontal rows of information about a particular category of things.

tabular layout   A layout that arranges data in rows and columns with labels across the top.

template   A ready-to-use database file that includes the data structure for a selected type of database.

text control   A control that is linked to a field in the record source and displays the information contained in that field.

Text data type   Data type that allows up to 255 characters (combinations of letters and numbers not used in calculations) to be entered in a field.

theme colors   Combinations of coordinating colors that are used in the default datasheet.

unbound control   A control that is not connected to a field in an underlying table.

unequal join   Records to be included in the query results are based on the value in one join field being greater than, less than, not equal to, greater than or equal to, or less than or equal to the value in the other join field.

Validation Rule property   An expression that defines the acceptable values in a validity check.

Validation Text property   Text that is displayed when a validation rule is violated.

value   A part of an expression that is a number, date, or character string.

value list   A lookup field that uses fixed values as the source for values in the list.

view   One of several windows or formats that Access provides for working with and looking at data.

wildcards   Symbols that are used to represent characters when specifying criteria.

wizard   A feature that guides you through the steps to create different database objects based upon your selections.

Yes/No data type   Data type that accepts only Yes/No, True/False, or On/Off entries.

Appendix

1 STRUCTURING A DATABASE

1.3 ADD, SET, CHANGE, OR REMOVE PRIMARY KEYS

DEFINE AND MODIFY MULTIFIELD PRIMARY KEYS

Most tables have at least one field that is selected as the primary key. Some tables may use two or more fields that, together, provide the primary key of a table. When a primary key uses more than one field, it is called a composite key. The fields do not need to be the same data type.

To define multiple fields as primary keys in a table, follow these steps:

- Open the table in Design view.
- Select (highlight) the two or more fields you want to be primary keys.
- Click [Primary Key].

Now the data in both fields will operate as primary key fields. Multifield primary keys can be removed by selecting the primary key field and clicking [Primary Key] to turn off this setting.

2 CREATING AND FORMATTING DATABASE ELEMENTS

2.2 CREATE TABLES

CREATE TABLES BY COPYING THE STRUCTURE OF OTHER TABLES

You can copy the structure of a table to another database file as a shortcut to creating a new table. Exporting the definition creates a blank copy of the table in the destination database. Follow these steps to export a table's definitions to another database:

- Open the database file that contains the table whose structure you want to copy.
- Click [More ▾] in the Export group of the External Data tab.
- Choose Access Database.
- In the File name box, specify the name of the destination database and then click [OK].
- In the Export dialog box, change the name of the new object if you do not want to overwrite an existing object with the same name in the destination database.
- Select Table definition only.
- Click [OK] to finish the operation.
- Choose the Save export steps option if you want to save the steps and click [Close]; otherwise, simply click [Close].

2.4. CREATE FIELDS AND MODIFY FIELD PROPERTIES

CREATE COMMONLY USED FIELDS

The steps to create Memo and Yes/No fields is the same, the only difference being the data type that you select. The resulting format and properties associated with each data type, of course, are different. See Concept 3 in Lab 1 to review data types. The following steps are used to create Memo and Yes/No data types.

- Open the table in which you want to create a new field in Design view.
- Click in a blank Field Name row and enter a new field name.
- Open the Data Type drop-down list and choose the Memo or Yes/No data type.

MODIFY FIELD PROPERTIES: SET MEMO FIELDS AS APPEND ONLY

When creating a Memo data type field, you can set the field to Append only. When this feature is on, users can add data to the Memo field, but they cannot change or remove existing data. Follow these steps to enable append only in a memo field.

- Open the table in which you want to change the properties of a Memo field in Design view.
- Click in the memo field's Field Name row.
- Click in the Append Only property box.
- Click ![icon] Design View to open the drop-down list of options and choose Yes.

By default, when you try to position the mouse pointer in a Memo field with this property enabled, Access hides the text.

2.5 CREATE FORMS

CREATE DATASHEET FORMS

The Datasheet tool is used to create a form using all the fields in the table.

- Open the table in which you want to create a form.
- Open the Create tab.
- Click ![More Forms] .
- Choose Datasheet.

The newly created form is displayed in Datasheet view. It can be modified just like any other form by adding controls and other design elements.

3 ENTERING AND MODIFYING DATA

3.4 ATTACH DOCUMENTS TO AND DETACH FROM RECORDS

EXPORT ATTACHMENTS

Files that have been added to an attachment field can be saved to other locations on your computer. To do this, follow these steps:

- Open the table in Datasheet view and double-click on the Attachment field cell for the record containing the attachment you want to export.
- Select the file you want to export from the Attachments dialog box.
- Choose Save As.
- In the Save Attachments dialog box, specify the name and location where you want a copy of the attached file saved.
- Click ![Save] and then ![OK] .

A copy of the file is saved to the specified location.

> **Additional Information**
> If you want to save all the attachments, choose Save All.

4 CREATING AND MODIFYING QUERIES

4.1 CREATE QUERIES

CREATE QUERIES BASED ON MORE THAN ONE TABLE

When two tables have fields with the same name, it is important to select the field from the table list that contains the data you want displayed in the query output. To identify which table to draw a field from, follow these steps:

- Create a query that contains multiple tables that use the same field name in at least one field.
- In Query Design view, add the field that has the same name from each table to the grid.
- Run the query to see the content from both fields.
- Remove the field from the grid whose content you do not want displayed.

SAVE FILTERS AS QUERIES

You can save a filter as a query so that the results are always available or to provide a head start in creating a query. To do this, follow these steps:

- Open the table you want to filter and specify the filter criteria.
- Click [Advanced ▾] in the Sort & Filter group and choose Filter by Form.
- Click [Advanced ▾] and choose Save as Query.
- Enter a name for the query in the Save As Query dialog box.

4.2 MODIFY QUERIES

ADD TABLES TO AND REMOVE TABLES FROM QUERIES

There are times that you may want to add a second copy of a table to a query to produce the results you need. To do this, follow these steps:

- Create a query that contains the table you want to use as the source.
- In Query Design view, open the Show Tables dialog box and select the same table from the list.

The duplicate table is identified with a number following the table name so that you can easily identify from which table you are specifying fields in the design grid.

CREATE JOINS

As you learned in Lab 3, an inner join is created by default. (See Concept 3 in Lab 3 to review this feature.) You also can create a left or right outer join. Left outer joins include all of the records from the first (left) of two tables, even if there are no matching values for records in the second (right) table. Right outer joins include all of the records from the second (right) of two tables, even if there are no matching values for records in the first (left) table. To change the join to a left or right outer join, follow these steps:

- Open the database file that contains the tables you want to join.
- Click [Relationships] in the Show/Hide group of the Database Tools tab.
- Click [All Relationships] in the Relationships group of the Relationship Tools Design tab.

- If necessary, first create a relationship between the tables.
- Right-click the relationship line and choose Join Type.
- Select option 2 from the Join Properties dialog box to create an inner join or option 3 to create an outer join.
- Click [OK] twice.

5 PRESENTING AND SHARING DATA

5.5 SAVE DATABASE OBJECTS AS OTHER FILE TYPES

In addition to the Access 2007 object types, database objects can be saved in other file formats that make it easy to share and print the file and hard to modify. Two common types of files that do this are the Portable Document Format (PDF) file format and the XML Paper Specification (XPS) file types. Both these file formats preserve the original document formatting and make it ease to view the file online and print it. They also make it difficult to change the data in the file.

To save a table (or other Access object) as either a PDF or XPS file, you must have first installed the free add-in to save or export this type of file. Then, to view a PDF file, you must have a PDF reader installed on your computer. One reader is the Acrobat Reader, available from Adobe Systems. To view a file in XPS format, you need a viewer. You or the recipient of your file can download a free viewer from Downloads on Microsoft Office Online.

Follow these steps to learn how to save a database object as a PDF or XPS file type:

- Open the table or report that you want to save as PDF or XPS.
- Click 🔘 Office Button, select Save As, and then choose PDF or XPS.
- Enter a file name and location to save the file.
- Open the Save as type list and choose XPS Document or PDF.
- Next to Optimize for, do one of the following, depending on whether file size or print quality is more important to you:
  - If the report requires high print quality, click Standard (publishing on-line and printing).
  - If the print quality is less important than file size, click Minimum size (publishing online).
- Choose Options to specify various options for the file.
- Click [OK].
- In the Publish as PDF or XPS dialog box, choose Publish.

6 MANAGING AND MAINTAINING DATABASES

6.1 PERFORM ROUTINE DATABASE OPERATIONS

SAVE DATABASES AS A PREVIOUS VERSION

If you have an Office Access 2007 (.accdb) database that you want to save in an earlier Access file format (.mdb), you can do so as long as your .accdb database does not contain any multivalued lookup fields, offline data, or attachments. This is because older versions of Access do not support these new features. If you try to convert an .accdb database containing any of these elements to an .mdb file format, Access displays an error message.

Follow these steps to save an Access 2007 database file as a previous version:

- Open the database file you want to save as a previous version. Do not have any objects open.
- Click ⊞ Office Button, select Save As, and from the Save the database in another format section of the menu, choose the appropriate Access file format for your needs.
- In the Save As dialog box, enter a file name for the copy of the database in the File name box and then click [Save].

Access creates the copy of the database and then opens the copy. Access automatically closes the original database.

6.2 MANAGE DATABASES

CONFIGURE DATABASE OPTIONS: ENABLE ERROR CHECKING

Access can display error indicators in controls in forms and reports that experience one or more types of errors. The indicators appear as triangles in the upper-left or upper-right corner of the control, depending on how you set the default text direction. The default indicator color is green, but you can change that to suit your needs. Error checking is on by default, and clearing this check box disables all types of error checking.

To enable error checking if it is off, follow these steps:

- Click ⊞ Office Button and click [Access Options].
- Open the Object Designer area and choose Enable error checking from the Error Checking section of the dialog box.
- Click [OK].

CONFIGURE DATABASE OPTIONS 2: SHOW/HIDE THE NAVIGATION PANE

The Navigation pane is on by default and displayed automatically when you open a database file. If you do not want the pane to appear when you open a specific database file, you can turn off this feature.

To turn on or off the display of the Navigation pane, follow these steps:

- Click ⊞ Office Button and click [Access Options].
- Open the Current database area and choose Display Navigation Pane in the Navigation section to select or deselect this option.
- Click [OK].

PRINT DATABASE INFORMATION USING THE DATABASE DOCUMENTER

Access 2007 includes a feature that will quickly create a report showing all the properties and details of the different objects in a database. This report is created using the Database Documenter tool.

To create a database report using the Database Documenter, follow these steps:

- Open the database file on which you want to create a report.
- On the Database Tools tab, click [Database Documenter] in the Analyze group.
- From the Documenter dialog box, select the tab that corresponds to the type of object on which you want to create a report.
- Select the objects that you want to document and then click [OK].

The database report is created, opened, and displayed in Print Preview by default.

Data File List

Supplied/Used	Created/Saved As
Lab 1	
ac01_Roberta.jpg (graphic) ac01_Resume (Word document)	Club Employees: Employee Records (table) Job (table)
Step-by-Step	
1.	Oak Ridge School: Students (table)
2. ac01_Guitar.jpg (graphic)	EchoPlex: Records
3.	County Library: Catalog (table)
4. ac01_Flavoring.jpg (graphic)	Cafe Inventory: Stock (table)
5. ac0_Valdez.jpg (graphic)	Kodiak Construction: Jobs, Clients, Foremen (tables)
On Your Own	
1.	Valley View News: Advertisers (table)
2.	Music Collection: CD Catalog (table)
3.	Dental Patients: Personal Information (table)
4.	Timeless Treasures: Watches (table)
5.	EMP Enterprises: Employee Expenses, Employee Info (table)
Lab 2	
ac02_Employees ac02_Employees: Records (form) ac02_Carlos.jpg (graphic)	
Step-by-Step	
1. ac02_Second Time Around	ac02_ Second Time Around: Inventory (form)
2. ac02_Enterprise Employment Agency	ac02_Enterprise Employment Agency: Candidate Information (form)
3. ac02_ARF Database ac02_WhiteDog.jpg (graphic)	ac02_ARF Database: Animals (form)
4. ac02_Kodiak Construction	ac02_Kodiak Construction: Jobs (form)
5. ac02_EchoPlex	ac02_EchoPlex: Records (form)

Supplied/Used	Created/Saved As
On Your Own	
1. ac02_ATT Database	ac02_ATT Database: Travel Packages (form)
2. EMP Enterprises (from Lab 1)	EMP Enterprises: Expenses (form)
3. Dental Patients (from Lab 1)	Dental Patients: Patient Data (form)
4. ac02_Lewis Personnel	ac02_Lewis Personnel: Phone List (form)
5. Timeless Treasures (from Lab 1)	Timeless Treasures: Watches (form)
Lab 3	
ac03_Personnel	ac03_Personnel: City/State/Zip Code (table) Car Pool Query (query) Location Query (query) Find duplicates for Personal Data (query) Personal Data without Matching Job Information (query) Maldin to Landis Car Pool Report (report) Job Position Report (report) ac03_Personnel/current date
Step-by-Step	
1. ac03_ Scensations Spa	ac03_ Scensations Spa: City/State/Zip 40+ Clients (query) 40+ Clients Report (report)
2. ac02_EchoPlex (from Lab 2)	ac02_EchoPlex: Shipping List (query)
3. ac03_Cafe Inventory	ac03_Cafe Inventory: Low Stock (query) Stock Report (report)
4. ac02_ Kodiak Construction (from Lab 2)	ac02_ Kodiak Construction: Priority (query) Job Priority Report (report)
5. ac03_ARF3	ac03_ARF3: 2008 Foster Parents (query) 2008 Foster Parents Report (report)
On Your Own	
1. Timeless Treasures (from Lab 2)	Timeless Treasures: Clocks (table) Timeless Treasures Watches Inventory (report) Timeless Treasures Watches Inventory (report)
2.	P&P Employees: Employees (table) Employee Addresses (report)
3. ac03_LearnSoft	ac03_Learnsoft: Project Manager Report
4. ac03_ARF3	ac03_ARF3: Animal-Foster Query (query) Foster Report (report)
5. EMP Enterprises (from Lab 2)	EMP Enterprises: Pending Payment (query) Open Expense Requests (report)

Supplied/Used	Created/Saved As
Working Together 1	
acwt1_Personnel	Landis Job Positions (Excel)
	River Mist Job Positions (Excel)
	Job Position Report (Word document)
acwt1_Job Positions (Word document)	Job Positions (Word document)
Step-by-Step	
1. ac03_ Scensations Spa (from Lab 3)	40+ Spa Clients (Word document)
2. ac03_Cafe Inventory (from Lab 3)	ac03_Cafe Inventory: Special Orders (query)
	Special Orders (Excel worksheet)
3. ac02_Kodiak Construction (from Lab 3)	ac02_Kodiak Construction: Top Priority (query)
	Kodiak Top Priority (Word document)

Microsoft Certified Applications Specialist (MCAS)

Microsoft Office Access 2007

The Microsoft Certified Applications Specialist (MCAS) certification program is designed to measure your proficiency in performing basic tasks using the Office 2007 applications. Getting certified demonstrates that you have the skills and provides a valuable industry credential for employment.

After completing the labs in the Microsoft Office Access 2007 Brief edition, you have learned the following MCAS skills:

Skill	Lab
1. Structuring a Database	
1.1 Define data needs and types	Lab 1
1.2 Define and print table relationships	Lab 3
1.3 Add, set, change, or remove primary keys	Lab 1, More About
1.4 Split databases	
2. Creating and Formatting Database Elements	
2.1 Create databases	Lab 1
2.2 Create tables	Lab 1, More About
2.3 Modify tables	Labs 1, 2, 3
2.4 Create fields and modify field properties	Labs 1, 2, 3, More About
2.5 Create forms	Lab 2, More About
2.6 Create reports	Lab 3
2.7 Modify the design of reports and forms	Labs 2, 3
3. Entering and Modifying Data	
3.1 Enter, edit, and delete records	Lab 1
3.2 Navigate among records	Labs 1, 2
3.3 Find and replace data	Lab 2
3.4 Attach documents to and detach from records	Lab 1, WT1, More About
3.5 Import data	
4. Creating and modifying queries	
4.1 Create queries	Lab 3, More About
4.2 Modify queries	Lab 3, More About

Skill	Lab
5. Presenting and Sharing Data	
5.1 Sort data	Labs 2, 3
5.2 Filter data	Labs 2, 3
5.3 Create and modify charts	
5.4 Export data	WT1
5.5 Save database objects as other file types	More About
5.6 Print database objects	Labs 1, 2, 3
6. Managing and Maintaining Databases	
6.1 Perform routine database operations	Labs 1, 2, 3, More About
6.2 Manage Databases	Lab 2, More About

Reference 2: Microsoft Certified Applications
Specialist (MCAS)

www.mhhe.com/oleary

Index

E

Edit
  entries, AC1.15–AC1.17
  field name, AC1.28
Edit Relationships dialog box, AC3.17
Enter
  data, AC1.13–AC1.14
  field description, AC1.30
Evaluating table design, AC3.5–AC3.10
Excel 2007, I.4–I.6
Exiting Access, AC1.78
Exiting an application, I.30
Expand indicators, AC1.76
Exporting data, ACWT1.2–ACWT1.12
  copy query object to Word 2007, ACWT1.8–ACWT1.10
  copy report to Word 2007, ACWT1.10–ACWT1.12
  Excel 2007, to, ACWT1.2–ACWT1.6
  overview, ACWT1.2
  Word 2007, to, ACWT1.6–ACWT1.7
Expression, AC2.14

F

Features
  Access. *See* Access 2007 features
  common. *See* Common Office 2007 interface features
Field
  add, to query, AC3.28–AC3.29
  add existing, AC1.59–AC1.60
  commonly used, ACA.1
  define, AC1.12–AC1.13
  defined, AC1.4
  delete, AC1.31–AC1.32
  delete, in report, AC3.63–AC3.64
  insert, AC1.66–AC1.67, AC2.11–AC2.12
  move between, AC1.45–AC1.47
  show/hide, AC2.17–AC2.19
  zoom, AC1.47–AC1.49
Field description, AC1.30
Field list, AC3.26
Field List pane, AC1.60
Field name
  edit, AC1.28
  naming conventions, AC1.14
Field property
  defined, AC1.24
  modify, AC1.25–AC1.26
  names and functions, AC1.24
Field Size property, AC1.24
Field size restriction, AC1.37
Field template, AC1.20–AC1.22
Field Templates pane, AC1.21
File, attach, AC1.40–AC1.45
File and object documentation, AC2.76–AC2.79
File menu, I.11–I.15
File name, AC1.9
File New Database dialog box, AC1.9
File properties, AC2.76–AC2.79
Filter. *See also* Filtering
  create, AC3.19–AC3.20
  defined, AC2.42
  delete, AC2.44–AC2.45
  query, as, ACA.3
  save as query, ACA.3

Filtering. *See also* Filter
  common filters, AC2.45–AC2.47
  filter by selection, AC2.42–AC2.44
  form, AC2.61–AC2.62
  multiple fields, AC2.47–AC2.48
  query, AC3.24
  removing/deleting filters, AC2.44–AC2.45
  report, AC3.64–AC3.65
Find and replace, AC2.24–AC2.33
Find Duplicates Query Wizard, AC3.42
Find Unmatched Query Wizard, AC3.38
Finding data, AC2.24–AC2.31
Foreign key, AC1.59
Form, AC1.10
  adding records, AC2.69–AC2.71
  controls, AC2.57–AC2.58, AC2.62–AC2.67
  defined, AC2.49
  design style, AC2.56, AC2.67–AC2.69
  filtering, AC2.61–AC2.62
  Form tool, AC2.50–AC2.51
  Form Wizard, AC2.52–AC2.58
  layout, AC2.54, AC2.55
  Multiple Items tool, AC2.51
  navigating, AC2.58–AC2.59
  searching, AC2.59–AC2.61
  sorting, AC2.61–AC2.62
Form Design view, AC2.62
Form design style, AC2.56, AC2.67–AC2.69
Form Layout view, AC2.62
Form tool, AC2.50–AC2.51
Form view, AC1.12, AC2.58–AC2.61
Form Wizard, AC2.50, AC2.52–AC2.58
Format, AC2.37
Format property, AC1.24, AC2.8
Formatting the datasheet
  change background/gridline color, AC2.37–AC2.40
  change text color, AC2.40–AC2.41
Fragmented file, AC3.69

G

Gallery, I.18–I.19
Getting Started with Microsoft Office Access pages, AC1.5
Graphic, AC1.40
Gridline color, AC2.37–AC2.40
Group, I.11

H

Hands-on instructions, ACO.7
Hard-coded criteria, AC3.46
Header row, AC1.12
Help, I.23–I.30
Hide. *See* Show/hide
Hyperlink data type, AC1.18

I

Identifier, AC2.14
In-Ribbon gallery, I.18
Indexed property, AC1.24
Inner join, AC3.30
Input Mask property, AC1.24
Insert field, AC1.66–AC1.67, AC2.11–AC2.12.
  See also Add